Worldview and Mind

The Eric Voegelin Institute Series in Political Philosophy

Beginning the Quest: Law and Politics in the Early Work of Eric Voegelin
by Barry Cooper

How World Politics Is Made: François Mitterand and the Reunification of Germany
by Tilo Schabert

Rethinking Rights: Historical, Political, and Philosophical Perspectives
edited by Bruce P. Frohnen and Kenneth L. Grasso

The Philosopher and the Storyteller: Eric Voegelin and Twentieth-Century Literature
by Charles R. Embry

The Constitutionalism of American States
edited by George E. Connor and Christopher W. Hammons

Voegelin Recollected: Conversations on a Life
edited by Barry Cooper and Jodi Bruhn

The American Way of Peace: An Interpretation
by Jan Prybyla

Faith and Political Philosophy: The Correspondence between Leo Strauss and Eric Voegelin, 1934–1964
edited by Peter Emberley and Barry Cooper

New Political Religions, or an Analysis of Modern Terrorism
by Barry Cooper

Art and Intellect in the Philosophy of Étienne Gilson
by Francesca Aran Murphy

Robert B. Heilman and Eric Voegelin: A Friendship in Letters, 1944–1984
edited by Charles R. Embry

Voegelin, Schelling, and the Philosophy of Historical Existence
by Jerry Day

Transcendence and History: The Search for Ultimacy from Ancient Societies to Postmodernity
by Glenn Hughes

Eros, Wisdom, and Silence: Plato's Erotic Dialogues
by James M. Rhodes

The Narrow Path of Freedom, and Other Essays
by Eugene Davidson

Hans Jonas: The Integrity of Thinking
by David J. Levy

A Government of Laws: Political Theory, Religion and the American Founding,
by Ellis Sandoz

Augustine and Politics as Longing in the World
by John von Heyking

Lonergan and the Philosophy of Historical Existence
by Thomas J. McPartland

Books in the Eric Voegelin Institute Series in Political Philosophy: Studies in Religion and Politics

Etty Hillesum and the Flow of Presence: A Voegelinian Analysis
by Meins G. S. Coetsier

Christian Metaphysics and Neoplatonism
by Albert Camus; translated with an introduction by Ronald D. Srigley

Voegelin and the Problem of Christian Political Order
by Jeffrey C. Herndon

Republicanism, Religion, and the Soul of America
by Ellis Sandoz

Michael Oakeshott on Religion, Aesthetics, and Politics
by Elizabeth Campbell Corey

Jesus and the Gospel Movement: Not Afraid to Be Partners
by William Thompson-Uberuaga

The Religious Foundations of Francis Bacon's Thought
by Stephen A. McKnight

Worldview and Mind

Religious Thought and Psychological Development

Eugene Webb

University of Missouri Press
Columbia and London

University of Missouri Press, Columbia, Missouri 65201
Printed and bound in the United States of America

5 4 3 2 1 13 12 11 10 09

Library of Congress Cataloging-in-Publication Data

Webb, Eugene, 1938–
Worldview and mind : religious thought and psychological development / Eugene Webb.
p. cm.
Includes bibliographical references and index.
Summary: "Looking at a broad spectrum of religions, Webb examines the relation between religion and modernity and explores what psychological analysis reveals about the relationship between stages of psychological development and ways of being religious that range from closed-minded to open-minded tolerance"—Provided by publisher.
ISBN 978-0-8262-1833-9 (alk. paper)
1. Psychology and religion. 2. Psychology, Religious. 3. Psychology and philosophy. 4. Philosophy and religion. I. Title.
BF51.W425 2008
200.1'9—DC22 2008037412

∞™ This paper meets the requirements of the American National Standard for Permanence of Paperfor Printed Library Materials, Z39.48, 1984.

Designer and Typesetter: Kristie Lee
Printer and Binder: Thomson-Shore, Inc.
Typefaces: Minion and Chevalier

Publication of this book has been assisted by a contribution from the Eric Voegelin Institute, which gratefully acknowledges the generous support provided for the series by the Earhart Foundation and the Sidney Richards Moore Memorial Fund.

For Marilyn,
and For
Aya,

who we hope will grow up to live lovingly
in the possible world this book is an attempt to
articulate and evoke

Contents

Acknowledgments

I owe a great debt of gratitude to a number of colleagues at various universities who have read the manuscript for this book, in part or in whole, in the various stages of its development and who made very helpful suggestions and also gave me much appreciated encouragement: Rodney Kilcup, Glenn Hughes Jr., Martin Jaffee, James Wellman, Douglas Collins, and Steven Shankman. It was also a special pleasure to read through the entire manuscript over a period of months with two friends in Seattle who asked helpful questions and made greatly appreciated suggestions of their own, the Reverend David Marshall and Greg Finger. I would also like to express my gratitude to Archbishop Chrysostomos of Etna for his comments and encouragement, although I would not want anyone to hold him (or indeed any of the others mentioned above) responsible for any of the views expressed here.

Finally, I wish to express my gratitude to my wife, Marilyn, to whom along with our granddaughter this book is dedicated. Without Marilyn's constant support and encouragement over more than four decades, I could never have accomplished this project or even much else of what I have in my career. I am grateful to have this opportunity to speak my thanks to her aloud in public, as it were.

Worldview and Mind

Introduction

The Power of Worldviews

No human being lives without a worldview, but comparatively few ever give much thought to what worldviews are, how they come into being, how they change, and how they are held. These are questions that come to our minds only when the worldviews we hold cease to be obvious to us. Viewing the matter in a broad historical perspective, it seems safe to say that most people at most times have been blessed with circumstances that have helped them take their worldviews sufficiently for granted that they never needed to wonder much about other possible ways of interpreting their world and their place in it, let alone reflect on questions about the phenomenon of worldview as such.

We do not, however, live in a time that favors the enjoyment of such confidence. Almost every person alive today is aware that there are people who hold visions of life different from his or her own, and almost everyone suffers at least some degree of anxiety about the lack of certainty this implies. Sociologists have coined the term *anomie* to refer to the feeling of disorientation and emptiness people experience when their worldviews are shaken, and they have observed that it can be a powerful force. Peter Berger, for example, has said that "anomy is unbearable to the point where the individual may seek death in preference to it," since there is "a human craving for meaning that appears to have the force of an instinct," and "the danger of meaninglessness . . . is the nightmare *par excellence,* in which the individual is submerged in a world of disorder, senselessness and madness."[1]

1. Berger, *The Sacred Canopy: Elements of a Sociological Theory of Religion,* 22.

Of course, anomie does not often become so acute. Most people manage to find ways of bolstering their sense of *nomos*, a term sociologists sometimes use for the sense of coherent wholeness of worldview that stands as the opposite of anomie. But the uncomfortable fact is that to be human is to live never in a perfect state either of confidence in nomos or of anomie, but rather somewhere between the two, with some feeling that things add up, but also with some fear that they might not do so perfectly or perhaps not even very well. And the ways people try to deal with challenges to their sense of a secure worldview may have important implications—not only for the success with which they will stave off anomie but also for the beneficial or destructive consequences their efforts will have for other people who inhabit the same *real* world, if not the same nomos or phenomenological "world."

The simplest way, after all, to avoid anomie is to eliminate challenges to the taken-for-grantedness of one's own vision of the world. But the very existence of other people with different fundamental beliefs can be the most disturbing of such challenges, and the only way to avoid it altogether is either to withdraw to some place of relative isolation (as hermits, Amish, and others have sometimes done) or to purge the world, or at least one's near vicinity, of other voices. In a world as structurally pluralistic as ours has become, both through modern media of communication and through the mixing of populations with diverse cultural heritages, this makes for dangerous possibilities of conflict.

The anxiety of uncertainty seems to be one motive behind the current resurgence of xenophobic ethnicity and religious militancy around the world. The end of the Soviet empire had among other effects the crumbling of walls that served in part to insulate many populations from the shock of too strong a dose of pluralism. As Mark Jurgensmeyer says in *The New Cold War? Religious Nationalism Confronts the Secular State,* "The new world order that is replacing the bipolar powers of the old Cold War is characterized not only by the rise of new economic forces, a crumbling of old empires, and the discrediting of communism, but also by the resurgence of parochial identities based on ethnic and religious allegiances." He also suggests that "proponents of the new [ethnic and religious] nationalisms hold the potential of making common cause against the secular West, in what might evolve into a new Cold War. Like the old Cold War, the confrontation between these new forms of culture-based politics and the secular state is global in its scope, binary in its opposition, occasionally violent, and essentially a difference of ideologies; and, like the old Cold War, each side tends to stereotype the other."[2] Of course, it is not only the secular West that an anxious people may seek to drive away. The Jewish settlers in Hebron and their Palestinian rivals, for example, are neither of them especially "secular" or "Western" in the usual senses of those words. This does not detract from Jurgensmeyer's point, however, which is that cultural ideology can be a potent source of conflict.

Samuel P. Huntington proposed a similar thesis in 1996 in *The Clash of Civilizations and the Remaking of World Order*, arguing that what had been global political alignments defined by political ideology and superpower relations are giving way to new alignments based on cultural affiliation that may be much more challenging to deal with. He says, for example, that although a Western democrat could carry on an intellectual debate with a Soviet Marxist, it would be impossible for him to do so with a Russian Orthodox nationalist—or, he might say today, a radical Islamist. Huntington's principal theme is the idea of civilizational "fault lines," points where different civilizations encounter each other and compete. He refers especially to the former Yugoslavia, where Western Christian (principally Roman Catholic), Byzantine Christian (Eastern Orthodox), and Muslim populations were in open conflict when he wrote his book. Another is the clash between Israelis, Palestinians, and the Arab states. His main point is that cultural, and especially religious, worldviews, their defense and their preservation, are much more important to many people throughout the world than the secularly oriented, pragmatic Western intellectual is normally inclined to believe and that this factor must be taken into account if we are to understand the challenges that he predicted would face the world in the twenty-first century. Events since that time have underscored his point even if, as I will later suggest, there are other ways of understanding the strains in the world today and other types of fault lines besides those of clashing civilizations.

One of the other major points of Huntington's analysis is that "people use politics not just to advance their interests, but also to define their identity," because "cultural identity is what is most meaningful to most people." Religion and cultural worldview are powerful instruments of identity, and when a people is faced with threats to them, the drive to defend and reinforce identity can produce a combustible polarization of their perceived "world" into a dramatic face-off of "us" versus "them." As Huntington rather starkly puts it, "We know who we are only when we know who we are not and often only when

2. Jurgensmeyer, *New Cold War?* 1–2.

we know whom we are against."[3] One of the purposes of the present book is to explore the roots of such polarization in psychological impulses and mechanisms, but another purpose is to try to understand what psychological and spiritual counterforces may also be present that can provide hope for the development of personhood beyond such blind, reactive defenses.

At the end of his book, Huntington leaves the reader with a series of questions: "Is there a general, secular trend, transcending individual civilizations, toward higher levels of Civilization? If there is such a trend, is it a product of the processes of modernization that increase the control of humans over their environment and hence generate higher and higher levels of technological sophistication and material well-being? In the contemporary era, is a higher level of modernity thus a prerequisite to a higher level of Civilization? Or does the level of Civilization primarily vary within the history of individual civilizations?"[4] These are questions that open out, as we shall see, onto still others about the range of possible meanings of words such as *modern* or *modernity, traditional,* and even *postmodern.* More important, to consider such questions is to consider not periods or even cultural trends but, rather, types of mental organization, and exploring them in turn points toward the possibility of different patterns of organization within both traditional and modern minds.

These authors are right to draw attention to the important role of religion in maintaining for most people a sense of the meaningful coherence of life. Religion has been at the heart of every traditional society, and as sociologists from Emil Durkheim and Max Weber to the present have said, it is unlikely that any society anywhere could have taken shape without the role religion has always played in that process.

This is true for several reasons. One is that for a worldview to achieve stability, it must be internalized—that is, incorporated into consciousness in such a way that it is deeply ingrained to the point that it becomes virtually automatic. As Clifford Geertz has said, this kind of secure belief is something that normally "comes from the social and psychological workings of religious symbols." The socially mediated interaction with sacred symbols in society, especially in the form of ritual, is the major mechanism, as Geertz puts it, by means of which people "come not only to encounter a worldview but actually to adopt it, to internalize it as part of their personality."[5]

3. Huntington, *Clash of Civilizations,* 20–21.
4. Ibid., 320.
5. Geertz, *Islam Observed: Religious Developments in Morocco and Indonesia,* 99, 100.

Another reason is that religion is the principal social vehicle of the sense of the sacred, that powerful feeling of awe and fascination that phenomenologists of religion such as Rudolf Otto and Mircea Eliade have described as closely linked to the sense of standing in the presence of the mysteriously other and the really real. Eliade speaks of the sacred as equivalent to "reality," because it is saturated with "being," that is, with enduringness and force. "Religious man's desire to live in the sacred," he says, "is in fact equivalent to his desire to take up his abode in objective reality," to put an end to the "tension and anxiety" of relativity. Peter Berger, pursuing this line of thought, has suggested, "It appears likely that only by way of the sacred was it possible for man to conceive of a cosmos in the first place."[6] Religion, then, is the principal device by which a phenomenological "world," a world that looks coherent and feels real to those who imaginatively dwell in it, is socially constructed.

That a worldview must be *socially* constructed is an important point. No one comes to adult consciousness without first having passed through a cultural gestation, and no one begins to think by constructing a worldview on his or her own. Every human being is endowed with one from the start by the mere fact of having been born into a milieu where language is spoken and stories are told. Some eventually think of new questions and work out conceptions of their own or at least variations on what they have inherited, but it is inherently difficult, and for most people virtually impossible, to construct and actually believe in a worldview all by oneself.

This is probably one reason, besides altruism, that the founders of new religions seek followers; it is easier to believe one's own new vision of life if there are others who share it. It is also why those who feel the force of questions that challenge conventional views, but who are not themselves able to develop satisfying answers to them, seek leaders to follow and fellow believers to worship with. As sociologists have often said, charisma is not an inherent quality of certain individuals but a reciprocal relationship between its bearers and those who perceive and defer to it.

It is also a reason that adherents of different religious or secular worldviews seek unanimity around them and sometimes seek to eliminate or at least silence competing views—which, of course, brings us back to the dangers of conflict and polarized worldviews that Huntington and Jurgensmeyer warn us about. Both emphasize the possibility of global conflict arising out of the

6. Eliade, *The Sacred and the Profane: The Nature of Religion*, 12, 27–28; Berger, *Sacred Canopy*, 27.

competition of religions and civilizations—a danger that took a terrifyingly concrete form on September 11, 2001, with the suicide attack of al Qaeda terrorists on the World Trade Center in New York and the Pentagon in Washington, D.C. What that began and what continues from it do not seem to fit very well the model of either a new cold war, as Jurgensmeyer imagined in 1993, or the sort of conventional military war the American administration of the early 2000s tried to cast it as. Other versions of the same danger almost certainly lie ahead, though in unpredictable, unconventional forms and possibly from very different sources.

To call this a clash of civilizations, however, may not be the best approach to understanding it, either. There is certainly a sense in which conflicts arising from some group's religion, sense of ethnicity, or historical resentments involve a civilizational heritage. But to conceive the sort of conflict that is now erupting as an expression of one unitary "civilization" against another seems just one more way of trying to imagine it in the mold of conventional military warfare. I would like to suggest that the real problem is of quite a different order: the great upheaval in worldview going on throughout the world today, within each civilizational heritage, is the transition from a traditional worldview, and the traditional mind that supports it and depends on it, to something new—usually called "modernity"—with all the demands it makes for a reorganization of minds.

Not long ago it was widely supposed that an inevitable implication of this process would be the fading away of religion while a scientific, secular worldview replaced religious worldviews of any kind. When Peter Berger published *The Sacred Canopy: Elements of a Sociological Theory of Religion* in 1967, he took this tendency for granted. Defining the term *secularization* there as "the process by which sectors of society and culture are removed from the domination of religious institutions and symbols," he said that it "affects the totality of cultural life and of ideation, and may be observed in the decline of religious contents in the arts, in philosophy, in literature, and, most important of all, in the rise of science as an autonomous, thoroughly secular perspective on the world." He also predicted that the secularization process would produce not only a new worldview with a new content but also a new kind of mind. "Moreover," he said, "the process of secularization has a subjective side as well. As there is a secularization of society and culture, so is there a secularization of consciousness."[7]

7. Berger, *Sacred Canopy,* 107–8.

Three decades later, however, Berger acknowledged that his secularization hypothesis had been proved false in the actual course of events, with religion of all sorts becoming an ever stronger force in many parts of the world, including the eminently modern North America. In 1997 Berger even edited a collection of essays titled *The Desecularization of the World: Resurgent Religion and World Politics,* with an introduction in which he said that "the assumption that we live in a secularized world is false. The world today . . . is as furiously religious as it ever was, and in some places more so than ever. This means that a whole body of literature by historians and social scientists loosely labeled 'secularization theory' is essentially mistaken." He also said that even if modernization can have some secularizing effects, "secularization on the societal level is not necessarily linked to secularization on the level of individual consciousness." "To say the least," he concluded, "the relation between religion and modernity is rather complicated."[8]

The main purpose of the present book will be to bring to light and explore that relation in all its complexity, which I think is profoundly underestimated by many who write on the topic, especially critics less sympathetic than Berger, of whom there are legion, from Sigmund Freud to Daniel Dennett. I will be discussing the ideas of both of these particular critics of religion later, especially in Chapters 6 through 9, so there is no need to go into them here except to indicate that I think that although many of their criticisms of the types of religion and religiousness they focus on are well founded, the conception of religion among both the critics who think religion can and should be argued away and the secularization theorists who thought it would fade away all by itself tends to be rather one-dimensional, overlooking the great inner diversity of religious worldviews and ways of being religious. Such critics tend to reduce religion as a whole to something that is easily dismissed, but I hope to show that religious traditions, when looked at more closely, can be found to have greater complexity and also greater spiritual depth than their critics usually seem to be aware of and thus have a greater potential for development along lines their critics might even favor.

Religious traditions are not solid blocks or even single streams but consist of many strands and elements that make up an unstable, dynamic mix that is constantly in flux and can develop in various, sometimes contradictory directions. Most observers recognize that there can be diversity *among* religions,

8. Berger, *Desecularization of the World,* 2, 3.

but few seem to give much thought to the diversity *within* them, yet it is this inner diversity that makes for the possibility of change and development that under some circumstances might promise a solution to the problems and dangers the critics of religion point to. Within religious traditions there is the frequently realized possibility of developing toward what might be called a monological mode of faith, a way of believing that tries to fend off uncertainty and anomie by shutting out or silencing all competing voices. But I will try to show that there are also possibilities of religions developing toward an open, dialogical mode of faith in which a diversity of voices and perspectives can be not only tolerated but even religiously embraced.

Whether and how such developments take place must depend not only on elements of tradition that might be interpreted as encouraging it but also on the circumstances of the religious groups and individuals who try to carry the traditions forward and on the types of personal development that take place within them under those circumstances. The conditions of life in the modern world exert pressure on persons everywhere, among the members of both what we think of as "modern" societies and, through "globalization," what are sometimes referred to as "traditional" societies—although the distinction between them is becoming less and less clear, and even to try clearly to distinguish them might tempt one to the same mistake about societies and cultures that is so often made about religions, that is, to think of them as uniform cultural blocs. It was to underscore this issue that Robert Kegan, whose thought will be the principal focus of Chapter 3, titled his 1994 book *In over Our Heads: The Mental Demands of Modern Life;* his point is that different types of social and psychological environments are pulling against each other within our own society, to the point that individuals can often feel overwhelmed by their conflicting demands.

For good or ill, welcome or unwelcome, the pressure of these circumstances undermines, as I said at the beginning, the sort of easy confidence that might under earlier circumstances have helped people take their worldviews sufficiently for granted that they would rarely need to think about other possible ways of interpreting their world and their selves in relation to it. This tends to force the growth of critical reflection and with it the sense of individual consciousness. In 2002, in a volume of essays on globalization that he coedited with Samuel Huntington, Peter Berger wrote, "If there is one theme that all [types of globalization] have in common, it is individuation: all sectors of the emerging global culture enhance the independence of the individual over against tradition and collectivity. Individuation must be seen as a social and psychological process, manifested empirically in the behavior and consciousness of people regardless of the ideas they may hold about this."[9] That process can be both liberating and acutely uncomfortable.

Whatever the nature of the worldviews they cherish and wherever they may live, virtually all people living today feel the pressure exerted by modern conditions on both their worldviews and their minds. This is why my own focus will be on worldviews and on psychological factors that can contribute to their development and character. The first part of this study will examine some psychological approaches that seem especially helpful for understanding the subjective factors that contribute to shaping worldviews. These fall into two patterns: psychologies of the unconscious that try to bring to light the forces that shape consciousness without our being aware of their workings and psychologies of conscious functioning, primarily in the tradition of Jean Piaget, that focus on the ways consciousness can develop as it addresses itself to various sorts of stimuli and challenges.

As will be discussed in Chapter 1, Karl Jaspers, the originator of the idea of a psychology of worldviews, distinguished worldview as such into a subjective and an objective pole, with the subjective pole (psychological dispositions and basic patterns of thinking and imagining) playing a much larger role than he believed was generally realized in shaping the "what" (the objective pole) of what people think. Jaspers did not believe, however, that what is thought was necessarily reducible to the simple product of unconscious forces in the mind. Rather, he believed that the major challenge for all human beings is to develop a differentiated consciousness that will make careful, conscious thinking possible, which is why he has since become known primarily as a philosopher. The ultimate purpose of the present book is also to point toward the possibilities of developing a critical, philosophically reflective consciousness within traditions of religious thinking.

With Chapter 2, in the discussion of Jean Piaget, we will begin the exploration of the type of psychological thinking that puts its emphasis not on the way minds may be driven by unconscious forces but on the possibility of their developing a capacity to operate intentionally and reflectively. Piaget's tradition, as we will see, is as much philosophical in its way as it is psychological,

9. Berger and Huntington, *Many Globalizations: Cultural Diversity in the Contemporary World,* 9. Berger also says in the next sentence that "individuation as an empirical phenomenon must be distinguished from 'individualism' as an ideology (though, of course, the two are frequently linked)"—a point whose significance will be developed in Chapter 8, "Religion and Personhood."

since it focuses on the way the development of a capacity for conscious operations enables people to construct the phenomenological world they live in and the selves they take shape as in doing so. We will also see how that same stream of thinking has fed into modern theological thought, especially through the integration of theology and cognitional theory by the influential Jesuit thinker Bernard Lonergan, whose thought is rooted as much in his early reading of Piaget as it is in the philosophical and theological traditions he also drew on and gave new shape to.

As the founder of modern developmental psychology, Piaget has had many heirs. The most important of them for the analysis of religious thought and its possibilities that I will be undertaking is Robert Kegan, whose ideas about stages of development from infancy to adulthood and also about what he calls the "orders of consciousness" that can develop within adulthood will be discussed both in Chapter 3 and in Chapter 8, on religion and personhood. Some other important Piagetian thinkers who have actually focused more directly than Kegan on specifically religious issues are James W. Fowler, whose study of stages of faith will also be discussed in Chapter 3, and Lawrence Kohlberg, whose efforts to explain moral development led him eventually to something like theological speculation on the ultimate goal of such development, as will be discussed in the first section of Chapter 6.

Lest the emphasis of these thinkers on the possibilities of conscious thinking and positive psychological development seem to neglect the dark side of human psychology, two chapters will take up two different approaches to psychology that emphasize the sort of unconscious forces that subvert reason and tend to generate the kind of polarized worldviews that engender and perpetuate conflict. In Chapter 4 we will look at Ernest Becker and a group of experimentalists working within the framework of his thought, which emphasizes the way anxiety over one's own possible death can shape our thinking and behavior before we are even aware of it. In Chapter 5 we will consider René Girard's idea that a virtually automatic tendency to imitate on a preconscious level the feelings, desires, and attitudes of others can drive us both to divinize and to demonize them. We will also see how many scientists working in various fields, some inspired by Girard and others completely independently, have been showing the ways this kind of preconscious "mimesis," as Girardians call it, has evolved as a hardwired feature of humanity and manifests itself in all areas of psychic life.

Of course, there have also been many other psychologists of the unconscious, most notably Sigmund Freud, whose critique of religion I will take up in Chapter 8, but my principal reason for focusing on the thought of Becker and Girard, besides what I think is the intrinsic interest and originality of their ideas and the fact that, unlike many others, each has a well-developed basis in experimental studies, is that they simultaneously appreciate the positive potential of religion and are able to be critical of it without reductionism. I recognize that there are also many other thinkers and schools of psychological thought in addition to these, many of great interest in themselves, but it is the ones I have chosen to focus on that I think have most to offer for understanding the special strains, and possible growing pains, that religious thought is experiencing at the present time, especially on the level of larger social movements.

The remainder of the book will relate these patterns of psychological thinking and the philosophical issues connected with them to the principal religious worldviews that are currently playing salient roles in the larger world of affairs in the twenty-first century. This will not, therefore, be an attempt at a comprehensive survey of world religions any more than the preceding part was an attempt at a comprehensive survey of modern systems of psychological thought. Rather, I will focus on those aspects of religious traditions that especially pertain to the exploration of certain central questions of concern in the world today.

One of these is the question of what subjective factors sometimes render religions conflictual and even aggressive and injurious not only to nonmembers but also to their own adherents by stifling their development toward full personhood. Another is the question of what conditions might foster less dangerous, and even perhaps helpful and reconciling, forms of religiousness. These questions are in part psychological, since they pertain to what sorts of unconscious forces drive us and what sorts of psychological development might win us at least a partial freedom from those forces. Developmental issues and philosophical issues related to what human thinking can become at its most developed are directly pertinent to these questions, since differences over cognitive claims and over identity or selfhood are at the root of almost all religious conflict. But there is more to religious thinking than can be encompassed by psychology alone, and so the remainder of the book will also give attention to questions of how religious traditions themselves think about development: What sorts of personhood, both individual and in community, do they seem to aim at? How do religions foster or possibly inhibit psychological, intellectual, and spiritual development? How do these forms of development relate to one another? How do the possible ways religious thinkers conceive of transcendence and ultimacy pertain to all of these questions?

In exploring these issues I will not be attempting to offer a portrait in depth of each of the principal world religions, and I will not try to give even the ones I do talk about equal attention. My purpose, like that which Karl Jaspers stated in the preface to his *Psychology of Worldviews,* is "not simply to present a gallery of worldviews, like pictures at an exhibition, but to illuminate the space in which existential decisions are made."[10] I will, however, try to go into enough depth on the points pertinent to my questions to make clear what some of the major problems and possibilities in the various traditions are. One of my points, the special focus of Chapter 7, will be that despite superficial appearances, there is great diversity not just among religious traditions but also within them, so much diversity, in fact, that it can seem rather arbitrary to lump them together into the kinds of unit we commonly speak of when we talk, for example, about a "Hinduism," an "Islam," or a "Christianity"—as though each of these distinct traditions, to name only these three, constitutes something with enough common characteristics to amount to a single religious stream.

The problem with this sort of attempt to see a tradition as unitary shows up most obviously in the case of Hinduism, a tradition I actually will not be discussing much but can serve to illustrate the point. Far from being one religion, *Hinduism* is simply a term coined by Europeans in the nineteenth century (the earliest recorded instance in the *Oxford English Dictionary* is from 1829) to categorize together the vast variety of different religious traditions in different languages, cultures, and ethnicities that happened to flourish in the Indian subcontinent from ancient times until then. There are certain practices common to most of the Indian religious traditions (such as distinction of social castes) and certain ancient texts many of them refer to (the Vedas and Upanishads), but to call them a single religion has about as much justification as for someone from India to coin a term such as *West Asianism,* for example, to designate a supposed religious tradition lumping together Judaism, Christianity, and Islam on the grounds that they are principally found at the western end of the Eurasian continent, share a tendency to represent the divine by the image of a single deity, and tell some partially overlapping stories about ancient Middle Eastern ancestors.

I will not be giving much attention to the religious traditions grouped under that broad classification called Hinduism for the simple reason that the indigenous religious traditions of the Indian subcontinent, however much conflict they have given rise to in India in the past century, are not currently

10. Jaspers, *Psychologie der Weltanschauungen,* xi.

a major factor in the tensions gripping the world as a whole. Judaism, Christianity, and Islam, on the other hand, clearly are. But these traditions, too, involve considerable inner diversity. To illustrate what I mean, let me just mention the problem of conceiving of Christianity as a unitary phenomenon. Most discussion of the issues involved in the encounter of Christian traditions and modernity, from the attacks of the Enlightenment *philosophes* in the eighteenth century to theological programs of demythologizing in the twentieth, have focused on the clash between modern scientific views of the world and a Christian worldview that is usually taken to have been fairly uniform. In Chapter 7 I will show how in the Christian tradition, as in Islam, there have been quite different worldviews present simultaneously, competing with each other sometimes tacitly and sometimes overtly over the centuries and persisting today. This dynamic diversity within religious traditions offers both problems and opportunities for the development of less dangerous worldviews.

Besides clarifying and exploring the implications of the inner diversity of worldviews within the religious traditions most involved in the conflicts of the present century, I will be concerned to show that the objective characteristics of worldviews are in reality only the tip of an iceberg, because they are also the expressions of subjective psychological structures, in the sense of habitual patterns of mental organization and operation. Chapters 8 and 9 will turn from the objective pole of worldviews, from the "what" of belief, to the subjective pole, the "how." Chapter 8, "Religion and Personhood," will take up a number of questions pertaining to the ways religious thinking can relate to psychological development—among them, to list just a few, how Freud's idea of "God" as a projection might relate to theological traditions about the relativity of all images and concepts used to think about radical transcendence, whether religion must be intellectually repressive and what it might mean to speak of rational inquiry as having a spiritual dimension, and the question of what it might mean to speak of a radically self-transcending "self." Chapter 9, "Dialogical Faith," will explore these issues further by first taking up the changing history of the idea of what it means "to believe" and the question of what "faith" has meant in relation to both "belief" (in the modern sense of that word) and religious love, then discussing the ways religious thinkers have thought about the relation between love and knowledge and the need for religious thinking to take place in a dialogical community if it is to be authentic and spiritually as well as intellectually open. The conclusion will consider the bearing of all of these questions as well as the historical circumstances of religious traditions today on what kinds of future development may be possible in religion.

There are many critics of religion who fear its dangerous potential and who therefore wish it would simply go away. I share much of these critics' concern, but I also believe there is a positive potential in religions that can develop with the right encouragement, just as there is in human beings. Religions are not born and do not live as monolithic blocks, but develop over time. That development can involve change in the ideas religious people hold about the world, its source, its possibilities, and its ultimate purpose. But religious development may also involve an inner process in which some people within a religious tradition develop the ability to step back from the ideas they hold and from patterns of thinking so intimate to them that they might be said more to be held by them than to hold them. In such stepping back they can discover both new ways of thinking and new ways of relating, with a more differentiated consciousness, to what they think. In the process, they may also become new persons. This is where the psychology underlying worldviews becomes important, and it is therefore to that that we shall now turn.

1

The Idea of a Psychology of Worldviews

It was Karl Jaspers who first conceived the idea of a psychology of worldviews. Although he is now remembered as an existential philosopher, he began his academic career in the field of psychiatry but moved into philosophy as the natural outgrowth of the ideas he explored in *Psychologie der Weltanschauungen* (Psychology of Worldviews), published in 1919. In the foreword for the fourth edition of that book in 1954 he said that its idea came to him when he noticed that scientific disputes did not seem to be determined simply by empirical or logical considerations. This led him to suspect that there were deeper factors, working below the level of consciousness, that helped to shape thought and conviction. Although many further conceptions of what those deeper factors might be have been developed in various schools of thought since Jaspers's pioneering work, his ideas on the subject still offer useful insights, many of which have found echoes among later thinkers, from developmental psychologists such as Jean Piaget and Robert Kegan to such figures as Ernest Becker and René Girard.

One of these ideas is his emphasis on psychological development and the construction of worldviews as a continuous, lifelong process stimulated by the experience of disturbance. This happens as a result both of the way one's action and thought can clash with reality and of involvement in what he called "boundary situations" *(Grenzsituationen)*, examples of which include struggle, death, accident, guilt, and encounter with mystery, experiences that give rise to ideas of possible transcendence. Fundamental to all boundary situations, he said, is the paradoxical character of human existence and the experience of tension *(Spannung)* it can entail. The fundamental paradox of human existence, or "antinomy," as Jaspers called it, is that to be human is to be neither simply an object in the world nor simply a subject contemplating worldly existence from some standpoint beyond it but rather something of both—as Ernest Becker would dramatically put it a half century later, to be "half animal and half symbolic . . . out of nature and hopelessly in it . . . up in the stars and yet housed in a heart-pumping, breath-gasping body that once belonged to a fish and still carries the gill marks to prove it." Becker, whose thought will be examined more closely in Chapter 5, zeroed in as nobody has before or since on the link between this "antinomic" experience of life and the anxiety it can generate, especially as it bears on one's possible death, the ultimate boundary situation.

Jaspers's own reflections on the implications of existing between a subjective and an objective pole of consciousness reach beyond the boundary situation alone, however, and point in directions that others have taken up and explored further. Eric Voegelin, for example, who studied with Jaspers and who told me he was especially influenced by this particular book early in his career, came to define the human mode of existence as *metaxy,* or "in-between," existence, taking the term from the Greek word for "the between," as used by Plato. It was probably Jaspers who prepared Voegelin to find it there. Describing the universal human experience of living in the "between," Jaspers said that "the actual—thinking, feeling, acting—human being stands simultaneously between two worlds: before him the realm of objectivity, behind him the powers and tendencies of the subject. His situation is determined from both sides, before him the object, behind him the subject, both limitless, both inexhaustible and impenetrable. On both sides lie decisive antinomies."[1] To be human is to exist between these, and it is also to feel torn by their dissociation, to long to hold fast to one or the other pole but to find both perpetually out of reach. Utopianisms seek to transcend this existential dilemma, but its reality is inexorable.

The most fundamental requirement of a systematic psychology of worldviews, said Jaspers, is that it be able to encompass all the manifold relations between subject and object, in all their indefiniteness and fluidity. The truly

1. Becker, *The Denial of Death,* 26; Webb, *Eric Voegelin: Philosopher of History,* 20, 23–24; Jaspers, *Psychologie der Weltanschauungen,* 233.

ultimate point of view would see the subject-object relation in movement, and the best systematic ordering of worldviews would depict them as a developmental sequence *(Entwicklungsreihe)*.[2] This points toward the sort of philosophy of history that Eric Voegelin's thought exemplified, since worldviews take shape historically in communities and their limits of development are largely set by the prevailing levels of psychological and spiritual development among those who engage actively in intellectual and spiritual exploration. But it points equally toward the work of developmental psychologists such as Jean Piaget, Lawrence Kohlberg, and Robert Kegan.

For Jaspers, it meant that one could talk about a psychology of worldviews only in periods that included some degree of individuation *(Individualisierung)*. Where a worldview is shared obviously by all, he said, there can be only a "social psychology" of worldviews. The key element in individuation is the development of what he called "differentiation of consciousness," a term he used to refer to a multifaceted process that could involve in varying degrees (1) becoming conscious of oneself and one's experience; (2) the development of a capacity for rational analysis; (3) separation *(Trennung)* into opposites where previously there was unity (as, for example, in the realization that consciousness has subjective and objective poles); (4) bringing to formulated consciousness what one previously knew only implicitly; and (5) the expansion of the material of experience into what follows from it, its consequences or implications.[3]

What "differentiation of consciousness" is, to put it in simple terms, is a kind of inward stepping back from something that was implicitly present *in* consciousness but not exactly present *to* it, something one was too close to or even subjectively embedded in, one might say, for it to be noticed. We are constantly engaged in interpreting our experience of concrete involvement in a world that we first become aware of through sensory experience, but we usually do not reflect on the fact that simple sensory experience by itself would be just a "buzzing, blooming confusion," in William James's famous phrase, if it were not put together into perceptual packages that can give it some sort of apparent unity and coherence. One walks into a room, for example, and sees "tables," "chairs," "windows," "carpets," and so on; one does not usually advert to the process by which particular patterns of color, shape, and texture are organized by the perceiving mind into these interpretive clusters, nor does one

2. Jaspers, *Psychologie der Weltanschauungen*, 20, 28.
3. Ibid., 39–40.

normally realize that a considerable cultural background has previously gone into the development of the ideas that constitute them for us.

I was once on the dissertation committee of a doctoral candidate studying the problems of adaptation faced by Laotian refugees brought to the United States in the 1970s from a remote mountainous region in which there were virtually none of the ordinary things that make up the modern American world. Her dissertation cited studies of the experience of these Laotians that described how when they were first brought to Seattle and saw its tall buildings from the airplane windows, they perceived them as mountains, since the only experience they had had in the world they came from of anything so high was of the mountains their villages nestled among. It took sometimes painful effort for them to learn to interpret the objects in their new world the way their American hosts taught them to. It can take similar somewhat disconcerting and dislocating effort for a philosopher to step back from the processes of interpreting and knowing in order to develop a cognitional theory, as in the case of Bernard Lonergan, or for a psychologist such as Jean Piaget to work out the relations among preoperational, concrete operational, and formal operational thinking not only in childhood development but also in that of the investigating scientist and in the development of science as such.

This sort of stepping back will be a central theme of much of this book, since it is at the heart of any psychological or philosophical reflection on subjectivity and also of any religious reflection on spirituality. There are three distinct but related types of differentiation of consciousness with which we will be concerned: philosophical, psychological, and spiritual. The philosophical differentiation of consciousness is the development of critical awareness of the mental operations involved in interpreting and knowing so that one can perform those operations consciously and carefully. Philosophy might be defined as what develops when one steps back from one's initial naive experience of "perceiving" what one takes to be reality and begins to ask questions about whether that really is what it appears to be, how interpretation is involved in knowing, what knowing itself might be, and how one can determine the difference between real and only apparent knowing.

Psychological differentiation of consciousness has two aspects. On the one hand, it is the process by which a person begins to win some freedom from unconscious mechanisms of the sort that Sigmund Freud began the study of, and on the other hand, it also takes place as the process in which the developing person begins from infancy, as we will see in our discussion of Jean Piaget, to develop conscious operative capacities and to use those to construct a phenomenological "world" and a worldview. This duality at the heart of psychological differentiation was nicely expressed by Freud in his famous injunction: "Wo Es war, soll Ich werden." This is translated in the Standard Edition of Freud's Works as "Where id was, there shall ego be," but it can be translated more literally, and I think with a greater sense of Freud's actual intent, as "Where 'it' was, there should be 'I.'"[4] Where there had been a virtual mechanism driven by blind forces, there should come into being a conscious thinker making decisions on the basis of careful deliberation. One way of understanding psychological differentiation, therefore, is to see it as the movement from "it" to "I," a movement that begins in blind mechanism and moves toward fully conscious, rational thought.

Another way, which does not contradict this but supplements it with a Piagetian developmental perspective, is to see psychological differentiation as a gradual process of awakening of the "I" as it expands within conscious operations. As we will see in detail in Chapter 3, Robert Kegan discusses psychological development as proceeding through a regular sequence of differentiations of consciousness in which a person who was previously "embedded" in some features of subjectivity (such as impulses, desires, feelings, or conventions) gradually begins to differentiate from those so that what was experienced as simply one with his or her subjective being becomes an object for contemplation and regulation. A child of six or seven, for example, who previously was governed by impulses that he or she simply identified with begins to develop the ability to step back from the impulse of the moment and to think about "motives" as a matter of enduring needs and dispositions that may be satisfied more effectively through the control of impulse rather than by simply flowing with its surge.

Spiritual differentiation of consciousness is less easily definable than philosophical or psychological and inherently more controversial, since different religious traditions may be expected to approach it in different even if possibly somewhat overlapping ways, so I will not attempt to define it as neatly as

4. Freud, *Gesammelte Werke,* 15:86; *The Standard Edition of the Complete Psychological Works of Sigmund Freud,* 22:80. A still more literal translation would be "Where 'it' was, should 'I' become," which would have the advantage of emphasizing that what Freud is talking about is a process of becoming more conscious and intentional in one's psychic life, but this would sound unidiomatic in English. Bruno Bettelheim discusses the problems of the English translation of Freud extensively in *Freud and Man's Soul.* On "Es" and "Ich," see especially 49–64. Bettelheim's main point is that the English translators were trying to make many of Freud's terms sound more scientific by translating his everyday German expressions not with equally ordinary-sounding English but with Latin and Greek.

the others, but it is an inescapable element of any religious tradition that gives attention to spirituality in any form. It has to be distinguished from theology, as that term is usually used in Western traditions, which is what develops when a religious person steps back from direct immersion in religious experience and tries to find language to articulate that experience, understand it, and relate it to other ways of understanding what it means to be a human being in an interpreted world. Spiritual differentiation of consciousness, on the other hand, lies on the side of the experience that theology reflects on.

When Eric Voegelin took Jaspers's idea of differentiation of consciousness and used it to discuss the distinctive intellectual and spiritual developments in ancient Greece and Israel, he spoke of them as "noetic" and "pneumatic" differentiations of consciousness, respectively—his terms for what I am calling "philosophical" and "spiritual." Essentially, what Voegelin meant by pneumatic differentiation (from the Greek *pneumatikos,* or "spiritual") was the experiential realization of existential tension (another term he found in Jaspers) as a pull toward a pole of transcendent perfection; historically, it meant for Voegelin the realization among both the ancient Israelites and the early Christians of an absolute distinction between the finite realm and a radically transcendent source and goal of being.[5] This is a definition that can work fairly well for Western religious traditions, including Islam in its Sufi form. As regards Indian traditions, Voegelin himself spoke of how it was reading the Upanishads in his youth that first stimulated him to think about such issues. It is also compatible with the more challenging, nontheistic thinking of Buddhism, since terms like *tension, transcendence,* and *perfection* need not necessarily entail the imagery and terminology of divinity. So perhaps it can suffice for the time being as a working definition of spiritual differentiation. Theology, on the other hand, as a reflection on and articulation of spiritual experience, must lie at the intersection of the philosophical and spiritual differentiations.

Any such differentiations of consciousness, when they occur, will bring with them a corresponding alteration of worldview, said Jaspers. Similarly, as soon as one formulates a worldview, one becomes altered inwardly by that very fact. "Whatever I am, I cannot remain simply that if I also develop self-awareness with regard to it, if I come to know it."[6]

5. I will not go further into the thought of Eric Voegelin in the main text of this book, since I have already written extensively about him in two earlier books, *Eric Voegelin: Philosopher of History* and *Philosophers of Consciousness: Polanyi, Lonergan, Voegelin, Ricoeur, Girard, Kierkegaard,* but its pertinence to this topic is extensive, as I will occasionally indicate in notes.

6. Jaspers, *Psychologie der Weltanschauungen,* 40.

In his approach to the psychological study of worldviews, Jaspers looked first for their relatively most differentiated forms. He divided the field of worldview *(Weltanshauung)* as such into subjective and objective aspects or poles: dispositions *(Einstellungen)* on the subjective side and particular world pictures *(Weltbilder)* on the objective. He described dispositions as general ways of relating to the objective pole of consciousness; they could be considered something like Kant's transcendental forms, he suggested, insofar as they involve a tendency of the subject to apply a particular grid of interpretation to experience.

These dispositions fall into three basic patterns, according to Jaspers's analysis: object-oriented dispositions, self-reflective dispositions, and enthusiastic dispositions. The object-oriented dispositions could lean toward the active (he mentions Marx as an example) or the contemplative (Plato, Eckhart, Spinoza, Kant, Schopenhauer, Hegel), as could the self-reflective ones. He thought of the enthusiastic disposition as trying to reach beyond the subject-object division. It was caught up in striving and movement not toward a grasp of some object, but "upward" or "beyond." The enthusiastic disposition, he said, is essentially love, enthusiasm for life itself, transcending all particular drives.[7] Enthusiasm, Jaspers believed, is not only the predominant element in mystical experience (it is worth remembering that the word enthusiasm originally meant "filled with the divine" or "possessed by a god") but also present in all the other dispositions as the principle of vitality in each—which means, he said, that the vital principle of psychic life as such is love.[8] Enthusiasmus in Jaspers's thought is clearly somewhat like what élan vital was in that of Henri Bergson or "existential tension" in that of Eric Voegelin. Behind all three, of course, lay Plato's concept of Eros, to which Jaspers himself explicitly referred as a parallel and which might most precisely, if a little clumsily, be rendered into English as something like "existential appetite" or "longing for fullness of life" or even "love of being."

Each of the dispositions, he said, tends toward some particular pattern of objective worldview (that is, *Weltbild*):[9] the "sensory-spatial," the "intellectual-cultural," and the "metaphysical," which, in Jaspers's scheme, includes both

7. Ibid., 123.

8. "Wie in allen Einstellungen der Enthusiasmus das eigentlich Lebendige ist, ebenso gilt allgemein, dass Leben Liebe ist" (ibid.).

9. Since English does not distinguish in Jaspers's manner between *Weltanschauung* and *Weltbild,* I should explain that in my own use of the term *worldview,* I mean by it, as I think English usage does generally, the "object" of thought that Jaspers refers to as *Weltbild.*

the "mythic-demonic" and the "philosophical," which in turn includes within itself the effort to use reason in the construction of worldviews, negative theology (the attempt to stretch thinking beyond all images and conceptualization), and the mythic-speculative worldview, which, he believed, satisfies the enduring human need to objectify whatever one thinks about and can never be entirely transcended by the efforts of negative theology. There is no need, however, to go into further detail about Jaspers's analysis of dispositions and their corresponding worldviews; the psychology of dispositions as such is not a focus of the thinkers whose thought we will be exploring in this book.

What Jaspers's approach calls to attention that is important for the present purpose is that every way of conceiving of the world is related to some more fundamental but less easily noticeable factor in subjectivity. There have been many further suggestions regarding what these subjective factors may be, from death anxiety, Freudian biological drives, and Girardian mimetic impulses to Piaget's operations and psychological structures, and all of them are valuable as at least partial explanations of why and how we come to think as we do under various circumstances. The next five chapters, beginning with the thought of Piaget and thinkers working out of his tradition, will explore some of those factors that I think are especially helpful for understanding the various forms that religious thinking can take in its manifold evolutions.

Jean Piaget and Bernard Lonergan

Existential Eros: The Energy of Development

One thing that all schools of psychological thought agree on is that psychic life requires an energy of movement. The type of psychological development that can lead beyond the half-blind, virtually automatic twitches of death anxiety and unconscious mimesis we will see Ernest Becker and René Girard talking about requires a motivating force of its own if it is to take place. Fortunately, there is good evidence that there is also a force of conscious development at least as strong as those of death anxiety, mimesis, and the sort of biological need drives that Sigmund Freud focused on. We saw in the last chapter how Karl Jaspers spoke of *Enthusiasmus,* which he associated with the Eros of Plato, as the vital principle of all the dispositions in the subjective pole of worldviews. Ernest Becker, too, speaks of an "Eros" of development. Becker was not uniquely focused on death anxiety, despite the impression one might get from his dramatic descriptions of the omnipresence of this force in our lives. Following his principal mentor in psychology, Otto Rank, he explicitly stated in the preface to *The Denial of Death* that in addition there is also "Eros, the urge to unification of experience, to form, to greater meaningfulness," and at the end of that book he wrote with regard to this same force, "Life seeks to expand in an unknown direction for unknown reasons. Not even psychology should meddle with this sacrosanct vitality, concluded Rank."[1] But psychology, when it does not become a reductionistic psychologism, may have a great deal to contribute to our understanding of what that expansion must involve. Jaspers considered the principal types of development in the psychology of worldviews to be differentiation of consciousness and the individuation that it makes possible. Both of these he saw as involving a change in the relations between the subjective and objective poles of consciousness—between the powers and tendencies of the subject "behind" us and the realm of objectivity, including particular objective worldviews *(Weltbilder),* "before" us.

How do those relations change and why? Jaspers did not himself go into detail about this in 1919. It remained for developmental psychology to study the particulars of these changing relations, beginning in the 1920s with Jean Piaget's *Le langage et la pensée chez l'enfant* (The language and thought of the child [1923]) and *Le jugement et la raisonnement chez l'enfant* (Judgment and reasoning in the child [1924]). Piaget, whose studies of what he called "genetic epistemology" and "psychogenesis" essentially created the field of developmental psychology, shared with Jaspers a background in Kantian philosophy with its way of distinguishing between subjectivity (as operative capacities and tendencies) at the one pole of consciousness and the objects on which they operate at the other. Interested, first, in explaining how adult consciousness became organized and how it operates, Piaget studied the way operative capacities developed in children and the effects these then had on their subjective mental organization, or what he called "psychological structures," and on what these in turn enabled them to do in the way of interpreting or "constructing" the worlds of their experience.

This supposes an internal engine of development, an appetite to develop operative powers and actually to perform the operations that constitute a more developed subjectivity. I will use the term *existential eros* or *existential appetite* for this inward dynamism of operations. Commonly, when one hears the word *eros,* one thinks of it as an appetite to "have" or possess something (when, that is, one does not simply identify it with sexual appetite, as so commonly happens), and in Christian religious thought in particular it has been common to treat eros (conceived as an egoistic, possessive motive) and agape (as a self-transcending, generous one) as opposites and even as conflicting.[2]

1. Becker, *The Denial of Death,* x, 284.
2. For a classic study of this theme in Christian theology, see Anders Nygren, *Agape and Eros.*

But it is helpful to distinguish between an eros that reaches for objects (whether external objects or internal ones, such as a pleasant sensation, an item of knowledge, or an image of egoistic triumph) and an eros that is an appetite to perform the operations of actively experiencing, interpreting, weighing and considering, judging, or deciding that constitutes the subjective actuality of conscious life. Something known, for example, is an object of knowledge, but the process of knowing is not itself an object but rather an activity bearing on objects. It is *by* and *in* such activity that we may be said to exist subjectively. In our bodily existence we are real objects in the world even when subjectively we may be not there at all, as when in deep sleep or a coma—but as subjects we are actual only to the extent that we perform the operations that constitute our subjective life.

This conception of what it means to exist as a subject has been a theme of existential philosophy since Kierkegaard, whose persona, Johannes Climacus, distinguishes in the *Concluding Unscientific Postscript* between what he considers existence in the proper and full sense and existence in a loose sense of the word. It is significant that he links the true conception of existence with passion:

> It is impossible to exist without passion, unless we understand the word "exist" in the loose sense of a so-called existence. . . . I have often reflected how one might bring a man into a state of passion. I have thought in this connection that if I could get him seated on a horse and the horse made to take fright and gallop wildly, or better still, for the sake of bringing the passion out, if I could take a man who wanted to arrive at a certain place as quickly as possible, and hence already had some passion, and could set him astride a horse that can scarcely walk. . . . Or if a driver were otherwise not especially inclined toward passion, if someone hitched a team of horses to a wagon for him, one of them a Pegasus and the other a worn-out jade, and told him to drive—I think one might succeed. And it is just this that it means to exist, if one is to become conscious of it. Eternity is the winged horse, infinitely fast, and time is a worn-out jade; the existing individual is the driver. That is to say, he is such a driver when his mode of existence is not an existence loosely so called; for then he is no driver, but a drunken peasant who lies asleep in the wagon and lets the horses take care of themselves. To be sure, he also drives and is a driver; and so there are perhaps many who—also exist.[3]

3. Kierkegaard, *Concluding Unscientific Postscript*, 276.

Many other thinkers have also discussed this idea of an appetite, or eros, for subjective existence. Paul Ricoeur, for example, drawing like Jaspers on the imagery of Plato's "Between" *(metaxy)*, spoke of human existence as rooted in an experience of "tendency and tension" and described it as an eros in tension between and participating in Pascal's two infinities of God and nothing—symbols that Ricoeur explicated in terms of the difference between consciously intentional and involuntary human acts. These are poles of human possibility, and we live always between them, with neither ever so fully actualized that a human being becomes either a mere neurological mechanism (that is, simply objective) or a completely conscious and intentional agent (fully subjective). To become the latter may be what we aim at and hope for, but we never experience it as our full actuality. "Thus the Self," Ricoeur said, "the Self as a person, is given first in an intention. . . . [T]he person is primarily the ideal of the person."[4] A fully actual person is something we are always either on the way to becoming or in retreat from.

In his Aquinas lecture of 1968, "The Subject," philosopher and theologian Bernard Lonergan analyzed a range of possibilities of subjective existence, corresponding both to the levels of operation—experiencing, interpreting, critical reflection and judgment, deliberation and decision—that come into play in the subject's life and to the ways in which one can relate to those in terms of recognizing and affirming them, ignoring, or denying them. With regard to our levels of operation, he said that "we are subjects, as it were, by degrees":

> At a lowest level, when unconscious in dreamless sleep or in a coma, we are merely potentially subjects. Next, we have a minimal degree of consciousness and subjectivity when we are the helpless subjects of our dreams. Thirdly, we become experiential subjects when we awake, when we become the subjects of lucid perception, imaginative projects, emotional and conative impulses, and bodily action. Fourthly, the intelligent subject sublates the experiential, i.e., it retains, preserves, goes beyond, completes it, when we inquire about our experience, investigate, grow in understanding, express our intentions and discoveries. Fifthly the rational subject sublates the intelligent and experiential subject, when we question our own understanding, check our formulations and expressions, ask whether we have got things right, marshal the evidence *pro* and *con*, judge this to be so and that not to be so. Sixthly, finally, rational consciousness

4. Ricoeur, *Fallible Man*, 13, 110. See also *Freedom and Nature: The Voluntary and Involuntary.* Ricoeur wrote his own first two books on the thought of Jaspers: *Karl Jaspers et la philosophie de l'existence* (with Mikel Dufrenne) (1947) and *Gabriel Marcel et Karl Jaspers* (1948).

> is sublated by rational self-consciousness, when we deliberate, evaluate, decide, act. Then there emerges human consciousness at its fullest. Then the existential subject exists and his character, his personal essence, is at stake.

The metaphor of "levels of consciousness," Lonergan said, refers to this cumulative sublation of operations, which means that the lower operations are "retained, preserved, yet transcended and completed by a higher."[5]

What characterizes the "existential subject" as existential, for Lonergan, is that at the highest level of development not only are all the operations of cognition and decision active and integrated, but the subject is also aware, at least implicitly, that their exercise constitutes a choice of how to be, of the quality of existence: "Though concerned with results, he or she more basically is concerned with himself or herself as becoming good or evil and so is to be named, not a practical subject, but an existential subject."[6]

This choice is only possible, however, when the subject is aware of itself as such, that is, when it is aware not only of the objects it senses, understands, or knows but also of performing the operations by which it does so. The "neglected subject" does not know itself, because although it performs the operations that constitute it, it is not aware of doing so. The "truncated subject" not only is unaware of performing these operations but resists recognizing them as well. The "alienated subject" carries this self-ignorance even to the point of refusal: "If . . . he renounces authentic living and drifts into the now seductive and now harsh rhythms of his psyche and of nature, then man is alienated from himself."[7]

The movement in the opposite direction, toward full subjective awareness and active life, is an existential decision, the choice of a mode and quality of existence: "The transition from the neglected and truncated subject is not . . . just a matter of finding out and assenting to a number of true propositions. More basically, it is a matter of conversion, of a personal philosophical experience, of moving out of a world of sense and of arriving, dazed and disorientated for a while, into a universe of being."[8]

When Lonergan discussed the psychic energy of the operations that constitute subjectivity, he spoke of them as moved by "active potencies . . . revealed

5. Lonergan, *Second Collection,* 80.
6. Ibid., 84.
7. Ibid., 73, 86.
8. Ibid., 79.

in questions for intelligence, questions for reflection, questions for deliberation." These can be best understood, I think, as dynamic anticipations of what it would be like actually to perform the operations of understanding, critically reflective judgment, and ethical decision and in that performance to attain their objects. They are, that is, expressions of what I referred to earlier as existential eros. In *Insight: A Study of Human Understanding,* Lonergan himself spoke of them as moved by an "Eros of [the] mind" that expresses itself in the form of appetites for operation that he called "transcendental notions." Defining these in *Method in Theology* he said, "The transcendental notions are the dynamism of conscious intentionality. They promote the subject from lower to higher levels of consciousness, from the experiential to the intellectual, from the intellectual to the rational, from the rational to the existential." They "promote the subject to full consciousness and direct him to his goals" and "provide the criteria that reveal whether the goals are being reached."[9] The drive to understand (that is, the "transcendental notion of the intelligible"), for example, is satisfied when the act of understanding is successfully performed, whereas incompleteness of understanding leaves a residue of tension impelling one to further questions. Similarly, the transcendental notions of the true and the good find satisfaction only when the conditions for reasonable assent or deliberated choice are fulfilled. All of these expressions of existential appetite move the subject in a process that is his or her coming to be, on the successive levels of conscious operation, as an actual rather than merely a potential subject. But their enactment is not automatic. They can be resisted, and whether we resist them or give ourselves to them is the fundamental existential decision of our lives.

Differentiation and Integration of Psychological Structures

To discuss these mental operations (attention to experiential data, interpretation, critical reflection and judgment, deliberation and decision) in terms of cognitional theory and philosophy of existence is to focus on an upper level of development presupposing processes that emerge only very gradually in human life and build on developments taking place in early childhood. This is what makes the contributions of Jean Piaget so valuable; he mapped out

9. Lonergan, *Method in Theology,* 120; Lonergan, *Insight,* 474; Lonergan, *Method in Theology,* 34–35.

systematically the formative stages of the course of development that can culminate, at its highest levels, in the philosophical processes analyzed by Lonergan—and he did so in a way that is fully compatible with and complementary to the critical realist cognitional theory Lonergan advocated.

A comparison between Piaget and Lonergan is especially germane to the present study, since not only was Lonergan influenced by Piaget—David Tracy speaks of Lonergan's "highly personal use of the genetic child psychology theory of Jean Piaget" and says Lonergan began speaking of "differentiation of consciousness" after reading him[10]—but their respective lines of inquiry also converged in significant ways. There is direct continuity between the developmental processes Piaget studied and the issues of cognitional theory that Lonergan analyzed and applied to theology—which should not be surprising, of course, since as I mentioned above it was with an eye to understanding fully developed adult consciousness that Piaget first began to study the early childhood beginnings of mental operation that can eventually develop toward that.

Lonergan worked more directly, and to greater effect, than probably any other modern theologian to correlate the method of theology with scientific method. His cognitional theory, which he considered the foundation of theology and philosophy as well as all other intellectual disciplines, he referred to as "generalized scientific method" or "transcendental method."[11] This consists of the operations mentioned above and the "heightening of consciousness that brings to light our conscious and intentional operations and thereby leads to the answers to three basic questions. What am I doing when I am knowing? Why is doing that knowing? What do I know when I do it?"[12] Lonergan said that the answer to the first is a cognitional theory, to the second is an epistemology, and to the third is a metaphysics. Or, to state it in a slightly different, more general phrasing pertinent to the present purpose, the answer to the last question (What do I know?) would be in its most basic form "a worldview"; a "metaphysics," as Lonergan used that term, would be

10. Tracy, *The Achievement of Bernard Lonergan,* 15, 153n48.

11. Perhaps I should explain here, since the word *transcendental* can carry so many different connotations for different readers (sometimes involving presuppositions about other realms of being), that in Lonergan's use (as in that of earlier thinkers such as Aquinas and Kant), the term means simply "having universal applicability." So his "transcendental method" refers to systematic methodological procedures applicable in any domain of inquiry, and his "transcendental notion of the intelligible" refers to the broadest possible conception of what might be capable of being understood and what it might mean to do the act of understanding.

12. Lonergan, *Method in Theology,* 25.

an explicitly theoretical reflection on the structural features of the world as known in the worldview—although inquirers operate on many levels of development, of course, and most hold worldviews that are pretheoretical.

Jean Piaget was actively interested in all three of these basic questions. He usually referred to his own field of study as "genetic epistemology," and he conceived it as the study of the way cognitive operations develop and lead to changes both in one's subjective mental organization and in one's picture of the world. "The fundamental hypothesis of genetic epistemology," he said in the lectures he gave at Columbia University under that title in 1968, "is that there is a parallelism between the progress made in the logical and rational organization of knowledge and the corresponding formative psychological processes." Another way to put this would be to say that, according to Piaget, there are both subjective and objective structures that develop in parallel and correlate with each other—the same principle that Lonergan referred to as "the isomorphism that obtains between the structure of knowing and the structure of the known."[13]

A "structure" in psychological terminology is an enduring organization, pattern, or aggregate of elements. It contrasts with a "function," which is transitory. As Piaget conceived them, operative capacities are structures in this sense; they are self-regulating, dynamic systems that structure subjectivity and perdure in it. Subjective structures develop as a repertoire of abilities to perform inward and outward actions. Each develops through differentiations of operations and of their objects, and each moves toward an integration that has both subjective and objective aspects. As Piaget put it in *Logic and Psychology*, "Since operations do not exist in isolation they are connected in the form of *structured wholes*. Thus, the construction of a class implies a classificatory system."[14]

In his last book, *Psychogenesis and the History of Science*, written in collaboration with physicist Rolando Garcia, Piaget tried to correlate the historical development of science with his theory of the way consciousness develops in individuals. Both science and individual psychology start with an undifferentiated field of experience, and each develops by differentiating both subjective and objective aspects of that field, then by integrating and grouping them, then by reflecting on them and forming groups of groups. For example, an infant learns to move legs, feet, hands, and fingers independently, then

13. Piaget, *Genetic Epistemology*, 13; Lonergan, *Insight*, 399.
14. Piaget, *Logic and Psychology*, 8; emphasis in the original.

combines these capacities into the integrated activities of walking or grasping and moving some object. Eventually, it becomes able to form a conception of movement as such. This grouping of groups produces abstract categories that can themselves be operated on. The child learns to crawl back and forth, discovering that there are various ways of arriving at the same place, and thereby constructs a notion of space. It rotates objects and looks at their various surfaces, which can become the foundation for developing a science of geometry. The child may discover, as François Viète did for Western mathematics in the sixteenth century, that numerical quantities can be grouped into abstract categories and then develop an algebra (a science of the general relations of mathematical operations) in which letters stand not for particular numbers but for number in general as the intentional object of a "second intention," that is, a concept that directly intends another concept and not an entity.[15] Eventually, the child or adult may even realize that in doing all this it is performing mental operations and may thus become able to reflect on them as such and on the fact that all actual knowledge of the world is constructed by means of them.

This realization, however, is always a late development, because of what Piaget called "the law of conscious awareness": "We are not immediately aware of the operations of our minds; these function by themselves so long as they are not hindered by external obstacles. Conscious awareness is therefore centripetal and not centrifugal, that is, it emanates from the external results of operations before going back to their intimate mechanism." In accord with this law, "the Greeks handled operations before becoming aware of their importance and subjective reality, thus enabling them to 'achieve' the product of these operations in the form of entities projected into the external world and dissociated from the subject's activity." That is why, he said, Euclid neglected the importance of spatial operations of displacement in our grasp of geometric figures, why Pythagoras interpreted numbers as substantially real without suspecting that he constructed them, and why Aristotle projected his hierarchy of logical categories into the physical universe. "It was not until the advent of eighteenth century mathematics that this initial realism was shaken by the awareness of the subject's constructive activity," said Piaget.[16]

Such initial naive realism tends to equate knowing with perception or sensation and therefore to think of it as essentially passive on the part of the

15. Piaget and Garcia, *Psychogenesis,* 146–48.
16. Piaget, *Psychology and Epistemology,* 104.

subject. This is why scientists have sometimes tended to favor a positivist or empiricist conception of knowledge. As Piaget and Garcia said in *Psychogenesis and the History of Science,* "Scientists are only partly conscious of what they do," with the result that "many physicists, orthodox positivists, have made their discoveries by using procedures that run counter to basic positivist tenets." Piaget and Garcia disagreed fundamentally with the positivist conception of science: "Something observable, no matter how elementary, presupposes much more than a perceptual reading, since perception as such is itself subordinated to action schemes. . . . [A]n observable is from the beginning a product of the union between a content given by the object and a form required by the subject as an instrument necessary in any reading of facts. Now, if this is true of simple registering of facts, it is obvious that the part played by the subject's constructions becomes increasingly important as one goes on to the different levels of interpretation."[17]

The levels of interpretation are made possible by levels of mental activity, which develop in stages. As Piaget mapped them, there are four main stages in our basic psychological development. First is the sensorimotor stage, which begins in infancy and lasts about two years. At the beginning of this period objects are not thought of as permanent, because in the absence of a notion of

17. Piaget and Garcia, *Psychogenesis,* 24, 17–18. Cf. Lonergan's *reductio ad absurdum* of naive realism in *Method in Theology:* "We have considered, first, experiencing the operations and, secondly, understanding their unity and relatedness. There arises the question for reflection. Do these operations occur? Do they occur in the described pattern? Is not that pattern just hypothetical, sooner or later due for revision and, when revised, sooner or later due for still further revision? First, the operations exist and occur. Despite the doubts and denials of positivists and behaviorists, no one, unless some of his organs are deficient, is going to say that never in his life did he have the experience of seeing or of hearing, of touching or smelling or tasting, of imagining or perceiving, of feeling or moving; or that if he appeared to have such experience, still it was mere appearance, since all his life long he has gone about like a somnambulist without any awareness of his own activities. Again, how rare is the man that will preface his lectures by repeating his conviction that never did he have even a fleeting experience of intellectual curiosity, of inquiry, of striving and coming to understand, of expressing what he has grasped by understanding. Rare too is the man that begins his contributions to periodical literature by reminding his potential readers that never in his life did he experience anything that might be called critical reflection, that he never paused about the truth or falsity of any statement, that if ever he seemed to exercise his rationality by passing judgment strictly in accord with the available evidence, then that must be counted mere appearance for he is totally unaware of any such event or even any such tendency. Few finally are those that place at the beginning of their books the warning that they have no notion of what might be meant by responsibility, that never in their lives did they have the experience of acting responsibly, and that least of all in composing the books they are offering the public. In brief, conscious and intentional operations exist and anyone that cares to deny their existence is merely disqualifying himself as a non-responsible, non-reasonable, non-intelligent somnambulist" (16–17).

space, there is literally no *place* for them to reside when they are not perceived. A notion of space is developed by way of sensorimotor actions (moving, returning, change of direction, and so on) until it attains an equilibrium by becoming organized as a group of such displacements. The permanent object is an invariant whose notion is constructed by means of such a group. It is with these rudimentary activities that we begin to construct our worldviews, starting with space as the world we can crawl around in, then proceeding in later stages to objects, first in their relation to us and then in relation to each other.

Piaget's second stage, which lasts from about two to seven years of age, is preoperational thought. This is prepared by a crucial development between approximately ages eighteen months and two years, in which the child develops a capacity for deferred imitation "and that kind of internalized imitation which gives rise to mental imagery." Piaget called the latter "the symbolic function," which makes possible "the internalization of actions into thoughts."[18] The child's thinking at this point is "figurative," as he termed it.

Thinking as such can have two aspects: the figurative and the operative. "The figurative aspect," Piaget said, "is an imitation of states taken as momentary and static. In the cognitive area the figurative functions are, above all, perception, imitation, and mental imagery, which is actually interiorized imitation." The operative aspect of thought, on the other hand, "deals not with states but with transformations from one state to another. For instance, it includes actions themselves, which transform objects or states, and it also includes the intellectual operations, which are essentially systems of transformation," capable of being carried out interiorly through mental representation.[19] During the first two stages of development the figurative is the only type of thinking that has yet developed, and it always remains an aspect of the thinking of even the most developed mind.

This accords well, by the way, with the findings of some of the experimental mimetic theorists who will be discussed in Chapter 5 regarding the innate and fundamental character of imitation in human development.[20] What both lines of research suggest is that as consciousness develops, it begins with activities, including imitation, in which subjectivity is so immersed that there is

18. Piaget, *Logic and Psychology,* 10, 11.

19. Piaget, *Genetic Epistemology,* 14.

20. As will be explained in Chapter 5, Andrew Meltzoff, of the Institute for Learning and Brain Science at the University of Washington, began his research by showing that the mimetic drive functions even in neonates, well before Piaget thought was possible.

little or no capacity for regulation of the activity. That is, the infant, though conscious *in* the activity, is not conscious *of* it. And since development is gradual and may remain only partial, there is plenty of room in ordinary human life for the psychological patterns analyzed by mimetic psychologists and other versions of psychology of the unconscious—Freudian, Jungian, Beckerian, and so on.[21] But in proportion as operations become differentiated and the subject becomes conscious of them, preconscious psychological processes can be expected to become less dominant. We may become gradually less, to use Jean-Michel Oughourlian's image, the "puppets of desire" and more our own masters.[22] We may become, by degrees, agents whose thought and action are more to be understood by a psychology of consciousness such as Piaget's or Robert Kegan's than by psychologies of the unconscious.

In an actual adult case, a given individual, in his or her various activities and states of mind, may be anywhere on a continuum of differentiation of consciousness, but if anyone ever becomes more conscious and capable of intentional self-regulation rather than automatism, it is because the initial movements in that direction took place in childhood in the form of capacities for conscious operation. According to Piaget's observations, the first psychological operations in the proper sense appear at around seven or eight years of age, and verbal or propositional operations at ages eleven or twelve. What he meant by "operations" is "actions which are internalizable, reversible, and coordinated into systems characterized by laws which apply to the system as a whole."[23] This is why he could say that they do not appear in children younger than seven. A younger child "manipulates" objects, but usually has no notion of "transforming" them systematically or of reversing such transformations.

To understand more concretely what all this means, it may help to consider the way Piaget thought the notion of "conservation" develops. By "conservation," he meant the preservation of something invariant beneath changing ap-

21. It is perhaps worth mentioning that as remote as Piaget may seem from psychologies of the unconscious, in his early career he studied in Zurich with Carl Jung and Eugen Bleuler, both of whom were early members of Freud's Vienna Psychoanalytic Society.

22. Oughourlian, *The Puppet of Desire: The Psychology of Hysteria, Possession, and Hypnosis.* Oughourlian will be discussed at greater length in Chapter 5.

23. Piaget, *Logic and Psychology,* 8. I should note that Piaget's definition of *operation* as a technical term in his system of thought gives it a very specific focus. When talking about Piaget's thought, I will use the term in his sense, but in much of what follows (especially when speaking of Lonergan's four levels of operation), I will use it in a broader sense to include the mental activity of focused attention, which Piaget would not consider properly an "operation" in his own technical sense.

pearances. This is a notion that he believed does not appear until age seven or so, because it depends on the ability to use operations to produce reversible transformations. Instead of conservation, a younger child has only a notion of "form constancy": "'Form constancy,' which is precisely one of the essential geometric characteristics of a solid object, is only acquired (during the first year of existence) thanks to the manipulation of objects. When a baby aged six to eight months, for example, is presented with a bottle upside down, he will try to suck it at the wrong end before granting this object a permanent form, and it is only after learning to turn it around in the visual field that he achieves this perceptive constancy." The child turning its bottle in this way does not "transform" it but only "manipulates" it. Later, when it learns that it can form a group of objects—say, pebbles—by adding one to another, and learns also that it can reverse this process by taking one pebble after another away, it is engaged in an "operation," because something is transformed (their number) and the transformation is reversible. "Operations of intelligence," as Piaget defined them, "are nothing more than such actions interiorized and comparable among themselves in a reversible manner"; a play of perceptions, on the other hand, "is essentially an irreversible mechanism determined by the one-way development of internal or external events."[24] When a younger child, whose thinking is still organized around a play of perceptions, sees, for example, a liquid poured from a short, squat beaker into a tall, thin one, it will think the quantity of liquid has changed as a result. At around age seven, the child will realize that because the operation of pouring could be reversed (the tall, thin beaker of liquid could be poured back into the short, squat one), the quantity of liquid underlying the change in appearances remains the same.

The exact timetable, of course, is not essential, and later investigators have revised some of Piaget's timings; what is essential is the sequence in which these possibilities of operation and mental organization must develop. First must come manipulations and form constancy, then operations and conservation. And when operations develop, they must begin on an elementary level before more abstract and reflective operations become possible.

It is in the period from seven to eleven years of age that Piaget's third stage develops, what he called the stage of "concrete operations," by which he meant that operations are carried out only on concrete objects. There may already be the beginning of an interest in classes and relations, but the operations

24. Piaget, *Psychology and Epistemology,* 107, 108.

involved in determining them are not yet dissociated from the data to which they apply, or to put it another way, form has not yet been abstracted from subject matter.[25]

The fourth stage, which normally begins to appear sometime between eleven to twelve and fourteen to fifteen years of age, is "formal" or "hypothetical deductive operations." The transition to this stage is marked by the ability to construct abstract propositional representations of alternative possibilities and deduce their implications. With this the realm of the possible becomes not just particular representations of concrete situations but the full range of alternative realities that constitute the framework of general structural limits within which the actual must necessarily occur.

This development brings the ability to reason by hypothesis. The child's logic is now concerned with propositions as well as objects, which makes it possible to construct operations about implication, disjunction, and incompatibility. Along with this comes the ability to construct "operational schemata" not directly related to the logic of propositions, such as proportions. Proportional operations do not appear in the adolescent's thought as unrelated discrete operations; in accordance with the principle stated earlier, they form a system, or "structured whole," "a set of virtual transformations, consisting of all the operations which it would be possible to carry out starting from a few actually performed operations."[26] For example, halves are a form of proportion; when one understands the principle of halving, one grasps all relations in which one number is half of another. One grasps implicitly that as 2 is to 4, so 3 is to 6, 16 to 32, 128 to 256, ad infinitum, without having to do the concrete calculation in each instance to check the principle.

In the process of thinking, Piaget said, the subject is affected by such structures without being conscious of them; one finds oneself carrying out operations determined by the laws of the whole operational field. Here one's world expands to something much greater than one can consciously grasp; one might spend all one's life gradually working out and realizing the implications of the implicit systematic order of the structural wholes formed by the operative capacities one develops (as Euclid did with his geometric intelligence and Mozart with his musical intelligence).

I realize that some readers may be feeling at this point that all of this sounds a little too abstract to grasp securely. At the risk of oversimplifying,

25. Piaget, *Logic and Psychology*, 17.
26. Ibid., 41.

perhaps it may help to think of Piaget's schema of psychological development in the following more easily imaginable way. In the sensorimotor stage, the child begins to crawl around and discover objects by bumping into them. In the preoperational stage, the child moves the objects and begins to imagine them going through such movements. In the concrete operational stage, the child shifts from moving and imagining objects to thinking about ways they might be broken down into their parts and recombined and transformed. In the formal operational stage, the child not only thinks about objects but also thinks about thinking and in doing so discovers ways of thinking in more efficient, powerful, and generalized ways—progressing from concrete arithmetic operations, for example, to the formal operations on operations of an algebra or calculus. As the child progresses through this sequence of stages, the activities and objects that constituted the earlier stages are carried forward and continued in the activities and objects of the subsequent stages. The objects that were simply encountered in the sensorimotor stage and were only manipulated in the preoperational stage become material for transformation in the concrete operational, and those in turn become the specifiable contents of the abstract classes and systems of relation that are developed in the formal operational. This is what it means to say that the entire sequence is "hierarchically integrated." It is also the reason the sequence of stages is invariant: the new activities and objects of the later stages can develop only by integrating what was developed in the earlier ones.

The same is true for Lonergan's philosophical analysis of cognitive operations (which we will return to in more detail in Chapter 6). Attention to experience, interpretation, critical reflection, and evaluative deliberation are also hierarchically integrated in exactly the same sense. It would be a serious misunderstanding to think of them as discrete operations that could be carried out simply by themselves, as though understanding could be divorced from experience or truth from understanding. One cannot begin to be an interpreter without first attending to some kind of experiential data, whether sensory or imaginative; one cannot reflect critically on the adequacy of an interpretation without first understanding what one is trying to verify; one cannot adequately evaluate possible courses of action without first assessing how they relate to the reality of the situation one has come to understand through the necessary sequence of attention, interpretation, critical reflection, and judgment. To put this so simply is, of course, to elide a great deal of what will have vast implications for much of our later discussion of religious thinking, but that will be made up for as we return again and again to Lonergan's contributions in the chapters that follow. For now, this brief survey will at least suffice to introduce Lonergan and to indicate the basic features of the thought of Piaget that were important both for him and for later psychological thinkers in his tradition, especially Robert Kegan. Perhaps it will be helpful to end with a concise digest of Piaget's ideas as summarized by another important figure in his tradition, Lawrence Kohlberg:

> 1. Stages imply qualitative differences in children's modes of thinking or of solving the same problem.
>
> 2. These different modes of thought form an invariant sequence, order, or succession in individual development. While cultural factors may speed up, slow down, or stop development, they do not change its sequence.
>
> 3. Each of these different and sequential modes of thought forms a "structural whole." A given stage response on a task does not just represent a specific response determined by knowledge and familiarity with that task or tasks similar to it; rather, it represents an underlying thought organization.
>
> 4. Cognitive stages are hierarchical integrations. Stages form an order of increasingly differentiated and integrated *structures* to fulfill a common function.[27]

Of course, these observations do not apply only to children. In Kohlberg's own investigations of specifically moral development, he found himself obliged by his observations to push some of his own stages further and further into adulthood, and Robert Kegan, as we shall see in the next chapter, began by studying child development but has turned in his more recent work increasingly to the analysis not of maturational stages but of what he calls "orders of consciousness," which develop in already mature adults, if circumstances call for them and they meet with a response.

27. Kohlberg, *Essays on Moral Development,* 1:57–58; emphasis in the original.

From Psychological Stages to Orders of Consciousness

Robert Kegan: An Existential Developmentalism

Robert Kegan draws on the psychological tradition of Jean Piaget to study the changing relation between the subjective and objective poles of consciousness at the different stages of psychological development. Kegan considers the dynamic reciprocal relation between the subjective and objective poles of consciousness to be the key to understanding in its full dimensions the movement from one level of development to another. He suggests that "the underlying motion of evolution, setting terms on what the organism constitutes as self and other, may both give rise to the stage-like regularities in the domains they explore and describe the process of movement from one stage to the next."[1]

This is certainly a cognitive process, as Piaget argued, but Kegan thinks it is also much more: "I suggest that human development involves a succession of renegotiated balances, or 'biologics,' which come to organize the experience of the individual in qualitatively different ways. In this sense, evolutionary activity is intrinsically cognitive, but it is no less affective; we *are* this activity and we experience it." It is this intrinsic phenomenological duality of cognition and affect that led Kegan to try to integrate the cognitive-developmental psychol-

1. Kegan, *The Evolving Self: Problem and Process in Human Development,* 74.

ogy of Piaget (and of his own mentor, Lawrence Kohlberg) with existential psychology. Piaget, he says, tended to look at meaning making descriptively, "from the outside," as a "naturally epistemological" process of constructing logical, systematically predictive theories to balance and rebalance subject and object, self and other. Existential psychology, on the other hand, looks at meaning making "from the inside," as an ontologically constitutive process in which "what is at stake in preserving any given balance is the ultimate question of whether the 'self' shall continue to *be*, a naturally *onto*logical matter."[2] The emergence of a Piagetian cognitive operation constitutes a new structure in the subjective pole of consciousness that naturally gives rise to ("constructs") a new structure in the objective pole, a new phenomenological "world." Looked at from the existential point of view, what happens in this process is a reconfiguration of "self" in relation to "other." When the change is radical—and movement from one stage to another can be experienced as quite radical—it can even feel like a death: the self one had been dissolves under the pressure of assimilation and accommodation, and a new self begins to form—or at least one hopes a renewal is taking place to balance what is being lost. But while a person is going through such a change, this may feel quite uncertain, threatening one with the loss of both world and self. The transition can be experienced, that is, as not only a cognitive but also an existential crisis.

One might, in fact, describe Kegan's approach as a neo-Piagetian existential psychology—hence, the centrality of "meaning making" for him. He says at the beginning of *The Evolving Self*, "This book is an organized way of wondering what happens if the evolution of the activity of meaning is taken as the fundamental motion in personality." And he conceives this evolution in distinctly existential terms: "Thus it is not that a person makes meaning as much as that the activity of being a person is the activity of meaning-making." Meaning making is an activity, in the first instance, of interpretation of experience: it assimilates experiential data and combines and recombines them in an effort to construct a worldview, a comprehensive picture of objective reality that will adequately accommodate them. But at certain points the process can also involve a restructuring of subjectivity itself, says Kegan. This involves a movement from "what Piaget calls 'decentration,' the loss of an old center, and what we might call 'recentration,' the recovery of a new center." It is this latter process that constitutes psychological growth, the basic element of which is a differentiation within consciousness: "Growth always involves a process

2. Ibid., 81, 12; emphases in the original.

of differentiation, of emergence from embeddedness, thus creating out of the former subject a new object to be taken by the new subjectivity."[3]

What does this mean concretely? Kegan offers some examples. One has to do with how a developing child may relate to its perceptions. He tells the story of two brothers looking down from the Empire State Building: "As their father reported it to me, both took one look down at the sidewalk and exclaimed simultaneously: 'Look at the people. They're tiny ants' (the younger boy); 'Look at the people. They look like tiny ants' (the older boy)." The younger boy was still at the preoperational stage, at which one looks at the world *through* one's perceptions but cannot reflect *on* them, so that if there is a change in what one sees, it can only seem a change in the object. As Kegan puts it, "For the 'preoperational' child, it is never just one's perceptions that change; rather, the world itself, as a consequence, changes." The older boy's "They look like tiny ants," on the other hand, "is as much about him looking at his perception as it is about the people."[4]

To put it another way, the preoperational younger brother was "embedded" in his perceptions. At an earlier time, as a newborn, he was embedded in something still more basic: his reflexes, or what Piaget called the "sensorimotor." In the sensorimotor stage a child has at most a very hazy sense of a world that could be called objective, and much of its cognitive activity is occupied with sorting out where he or she ends and the rest of the world begins. "The events of the first eighteen months," says Kegan, "culminate with the creation of the object and make evolutionary activity henceforth an activity of equilibration, of preserving or renegotiating the balance between what is taken as subject or self and what is taken as object or other." Typically by around age two, "the sensorimotoric has 'moved over' from subject to object, and the new subject, the 'perceptions,' has come into being. This is how our four-year-old got to be who he is—a meaning-maker embedded in his perceptions." The same process of mental evolution also creates "'the impulse,' the construction of feelings arising in *me,* which are mine as distinct from the world's"; the child at this age is embedded in perception with regard to cognition and in impulse with regard to action.[5]

The existential dimension is easy to understand when development is formulated in terms of embedding and differentiation. What we are "embedded"

3. Ibid., 15, 11, 31.
4. Ibid., 29.
5. Ibid., 81, 32, 32n.

in is irreducibly subjective to us, so that we experience it as simply what we *are*. The child embedded in perception and impulse can experience the thwarting of its impulses as though this were a threat to its very being. To move from this state to one that can reflect on perceptions and impulses not only means that something has "moved over" from the subjective pole to the objective but also means that a new experience of selfhood, of what it means and feels like to *be*, has taken shape. This can be wrenching. Kegan even suggests that the experience, "the phenomenological experience of evolving—of defending, surrendering, and reconstituting a center," is the intrinsic source of our emotions, and he also suggests that psychological pain, and perhaps even some physical pain, is the result of resistance to this movement.[6]

Embedding and differentiation are also points of connection between Kegan's Piagetian-existential psychology and Freudian object-relations theory, which focuses on the affective aspect of the same process of changing relations between subject and object that Piaget analyzed primarily in its cognitive aspects. Although this was not a theme he developed very far, Piaget himself once said, "There are not two developments, one cognitive and the other affective, two separate psychic functions, nor are there two kinds of objects: all objects are simultaneously cognitive and affective." Kegan comments, "This is because all objects are themselves the elaboration of an activity which is simultaneously cognitive and affective."[7]

There are important differences, however, between the Freudian psychoanalytic approach to object relations and the neo-Piagetian approach that Kegan favors. They will be worth some attention, since they make clearer exactly what Kegan's own position involves. One difference is that psychoanalysis emphasizes early childhood as determinative of the affective patterns of one's entire life and interprets it as fundamentally narcissistic, whereas Piaget considered each stage to have its own evolutionary dynamism in the present and said that Freud's "primary narcissism of nursing is really a narcissism without Narcissus"—since at that point in the child's life there is no more sense of self than there is of an other.[8] Another difference is that psychoanalysis interprets the fundamental psychological motive of the child as a wish to restore the condition of complete satisfaction it enjoyed in its mother's womb; it looks

6. Ibid., 81–82, 265.

7. Piaget, "Relations between Affectivity and the Mental Development of the Child," 39, quoted in ibid., 83.

8. Piaget, "Affectivity and Mental Development," 35, quoted in Kegan, *Evolving Self*, 79.

backward even as it reaches out to form object relations. These are therefore essentially a detour for it, a roundabout route toward the uterine home that is always the true goal of its longing. For Piaget, on the other hand, object relations are created for their own intrinsic value; the child's goal is equilibration in the present, not a return to the past, and the specific equilibration it seeks is adequacy of its cognitions to the new complexity of the objective world it is discovering. Both Freud and Piaget thought it was the infant's inability to satisfy itself that prompted its development, but Piaget believed, like Aristotle, that the exercise of our capacities is itself pleasurable, and he also believed, like Lonergan, that we therefore have an inherent dynamism toward the operations of interpreting, judging, and evaluating.

It is perhaps worth mentioning, especially since Piaget's thought was rooted in his earlier study of both philosophy and biology, that studies in the biology of the nervous system support this picture of an organism whose intrinsic mental dynamism impels it toward imaginative and cognitive activity. Research on neurons by Dr. Rodolfo Llinas shows they are constantly active, reaching for work to do, not just passive until triggered by environmental stimuli.[9] The brain itself generates an active internal state that is modified by sensory input but also continues to operate even in the absence of it, constantly producing a mental environment. When one is asleep, says Dr. Llinas, this activity is what we call dreaming; when one is awake but it is still strong, this is daydreaming; when one is aware of the outside world at the same time, it is called thinking. Also like Piaget, Llinas suggests that the brain is a "cognitive prediction machine"; it is there to make mental maps of the world sufficiently accurate to enable humans to predict what lies ahead in both space and time.

Developmental Stages: From Infancy to Adulthood

To return, however, to the course of human development as Kegan analyzes it, in *The Evolving Self* Kegan uses a scheme of six stages, or "selves": the incorporative, the impulsive, the imperial, the interpersonal, the institutional, and the interindividual. (His later book *In over Our Heads* offers a somewhat different five-level scheme, as we will see shortly.) As stages, he designates these six as 0 through 5. The numbered stages (1 through 5) each involve a balance be-

9. Philip J. Hilts, "Listening to the Conversation of Neurons," *New York Times*, May 27, 1997.

tween what is subjective and what is objective in the structure of consciousness at that point. The unnumbered "incorporative" stage (0) does not yet involve such a balance, because as its name indicates, everything in its phenomenological "world" is incorporated into its subjectivity. This is the condition of the newborn until about eighteen months—embedded in reflexes, sensing, and moving. (To relate this to Piaget, this corresponds to what he called the "sensorimotor stage" of development.) As was mentioned above, when these contents the child was embedded in move over to the side of the object, a new self, the impulsive (stage 1), takes shape in which the subjective principle is the child's perceptions and impulses, as distinct from the objects they bear on or reach toward (corresponding to what Piaget called the "preoperational" stage).

Kegan's stage 1 child, because it is embedded in its perceptions, is unable to hold two perceptions in mind together, which Kegan says is what gives that child's world its "Piagetian concreteness." Nor can it hold simultaneously two different feelings about a single thing, which is why it is impulsive; what it wants, it simply wants—and right now! This makes it as yet incapable of forming a notion of enduring dispositions over time.

Movement to the next stage (beginning at around age five to seven and solidifying by around age ten or so) takes place through objectification of the impulse as something that can be reflected on and controlled for the sake of longer-term goals defined by the enduring dispositions that now come to constitute its new subjective principle. Kegan terms these "needs," perhaps because a child embedded in its appetites can experience them only as that; the idea of a "desire" would require further differentiation. The "self" of this stage he calls "imperial," because the child, embedded in its "needs," organizes its forces for their fulfillment and pursues them with a determination that subordinates everything else. The imperial self conceives of others as either useful or the opposite. It does not feel guilt but rather feels anxiety over how others will react. Guilt would require something not yet possible at this stage, "the internalization of the other's voice in one's very construction of self."[10]

At Kegan's stage 3 (the interpersonal), in adolescence, inward imitation of the feelings and attitudes of others becomes central.[11] As Kegan puts it, "In the interpersonal balance the feelings the self gives rise to are, a priori, shared;

10. Kegan, *Evolving Self*, 91.

11. It is worth noting a link at this point to the mimetic psychological theory of René Girard and Jean-Michel Oughourlian that will be discussed in Chapter 5. The internalization of the other's voice is a mimetic function (an inward imitation) that becomes a structural element in

somebody is in there from the beginning. The self becomes conversational. To say that the self is located in the interpersonal matrix is to say that it embodies a plurality of voices." No longer does the child have to anticipate anxiously how others might react, since it is "able to bring inside to itself the other half of a conversation stage 2 had always to be listening for in the external world."[12]

Stepping back from its "needs," the child is also able to experience ambivalence as it feels the simultaneous force of different desires. In fact, one might say that what makes the difference between what I experience as a "need" and what I experience as a "desire" is precisely the differentiation that takes place when the "need" I was embedded in becomes something I can step back from and think about. I may still feel the same appetite, but when it becomes something I can notice and recognize as a desire, then I am able to place it imaginatively alongside other desires I may have and ask myself which is more important to me.

At the interpersonal stage, however, this last capability is still rather limited, since the different desires one feels are embedded in interpersonal relationships, which become the psychological ground of the "realities" one shares with particular others. Here "reality" becomes the "world" shaped by one's interpersonal relations. Ambivalence now, as Kegan puts it, is a matter of being pulled "between what I want to do as a part of *this* shared reality and what I want to do as part of *that* shared reality."[13] There is still no sense of a self capable of standing back from both "shared realities," because here one is simply embedded in them.

For a person at the interpersonal stage, personal relations not only are important but feel like a primary existential need: "You are the other by whom I complete myself, the other whom I need to create the context out of which I

---

the subjectivity of the next stage, the interpersonal. It may not be only at this point that mimesis comes to play a role, moreover. A full synthesis of mimetic theory with Kegan's would probably find that mimesis plays a role at each stage. One of René Girard's favorite examples of our need to learn from others what to desire is an experiment in which children (at what would be Kegan's stage 1) were lined up on one side of a room with identical toys on the other side, one for each child. Instead of all going to get the one directly opposite, they hung back until one child made a move toward a particular toy; then they all wanted that one (Thomas F. Bertonneau, "The Logic of the Undecidable: An Interview with René Girard," 17–18). Mimesis could also be expected to play different roles at different levels of development. Just as in Kegan's early stages we see *through* or *by way of* our perceptions or our impulses or "needs" instead of being able to look *at* them, mimesis itself, in its various forms, would be entirely subjective and therefore invisible to us in the earlier stages but could gradually emerge as an object of consciousness for later stages.

12. Kegan, *Evolving Self*, 95–96, 97.

13. Ibid., 96; emphasis added.

define and know myself and the world." This puts a limit on the kind of personal relationship that is possible. "This balance is 'interpersonal,'" says Kegan, "but it is not 'intimate,' because what might appear to be intimacy here is the self's *source* rather than its aim. There is no self to share with another; instead the other is required to bring the self into being." What one has here instead of intimacy, even though it may be called by that name, is really psychological "fusion" with the other, and "fusion is not intimacy." Genuine intimacy, which leaves each partner free to be the person he or she may be beyond the relationship, requires a level of individuation only to be found at the later stages, after one is no longer simply embedded in the interpersonal. At this stage personal relations are more a matter of mutual dragooning to fill needs that are felt but not understood. "If one can feel manipulated by the imperial balance," says Kegan, "one can feel devoured by the interpersonal one."[14]

Kegan calls his fourth stage "the institutional" because it constitutes the subjective structure that leads to the construction in the objective realm of normative social systems, including the roles one plays in various relationships and the obligations and expectations that go with them. Other persons are not lost when one emerges from embeddedness in the interpersonal; rather, they come to be seen in a larger, more complex framework of relations. Here one no longer "is" one's relationships; one "has" relationships, and one can think about how the variety of relationships people share can be regulated for mutual benefit.

The life of the emotions, too, becomes more complex at this stage, "a matter of holding both sides of a feeling simultaneously, where stage 3 tends to experience its ambivalences one side at a time." Even more important, stage 4 is "regulative of its feelings," just as it is of relations in society. In turn, Kegan suggests, "social constructions are reflective of that deeper structure which constructs the self itself as a system."[15]

Stage 4 brings obvious benefits, but like each of the earlier stages, it also has limitations. A major strength is "the person's new capacity for independence, to own herself, rather than having all the pieces of herself owned by various shared contexts." This is because she is no longer simply embedded in her relationships with others. The limitation at stage 4, however, comes from being embedded in the institutions one constructs: "The [stage 4] 'self' is identified with the organization it is trying to run smoothly; it *is* this organization." The pressing question, therefore, is no longer, as at stage 3, "Do you still like me?"

14. Ibid., 100, 96–97; emphasis in the original.
15. Ibid., 101.

but "Does my government still stand?"[16] At some point, just as the self of stage 3 could come to feel burdened by the cost of maintaining such consuming relationships, a person at stage 4 may come to feel like a captive of his or her institutional arrangements and feel burdened by the cost of upholding them or of living up to the standards and roles they demand.

The capacity for inward imitation of the feelings and attitudes of others, which was learned in the previous interpersonal stage and also continues here, seems both to offer rewards and to impose costs: Kegan says that his stage 4 is inherently ideological; its truths are truths for a group, and its sense of the rightness of its roles and its performance in them depends on recognition from a class of others that share its commitments.[17] The mimetic element is the internalized eyes and voices of others whose approval or disapproval we feel within ourselves. While the institutional balance is stable and the objective arrangements that give social expression to it are working well, these internalized eyes and voices may feel approving and sustaining, but when things begin to go wrong under the system's administration or when one begins to wonder if there is more to life than the system makes room for, one can feel the sting of their disapproval and experience frustration (if the problem seems the recalcitrance of the social material), doubt (if one begins to wonder about the adequacy of the system), or self-hatred (if one blames oneself for its failure). Such disturbances can prepare one for the next transition.

Stage 5, which Kegan calls "interindividual," brings an inner separation of the self from its institutions, thus producing the "individual," which Kegan defines as "that self who can reflect upon, or take as object, the regulations and purposes of a psychic administration which formerly was the subject [not the object] of one's attentions." Now "there is a self who runs the organization, where before there was a self who *was* the organization."[18]

Kegan sees this development as a process of differentiation of consciousness pressing toward "the evolution of a reduced subject and a greater object for the subject to take, an evolution of lesser subjectivity and greater objectivity."[19] Subjectivity, that is, comes to comprise less and less in the way of specific contents as it becomes disembedded from psychic material that moves over to become new content in an expanded objective pole of consciousness. To put

16. Ibid., 101, 102.
17. Ibid., 102.
18. Ibid., 103.
19. Ibid., 294.

it in slightly different language, rather than being made up of psychic "material," the self comes increasingly to consist of intentional "agency." Perhaps one might also say that in this process the subjective pole of consciousness, the seat of our psychic and spiritual activity, becomes not only "reduced" in content, as Kegan puts it, but also intensified in luminosity and operative power as we become capable of more actively and consciously performing the acts that constitute us as experiencers, interpreters, knowers, deciders, and ultimately ethical agents.

To experience one's own emergence in this way, as what Kierkegaard called "an existing individual," brings with it the recognition that others are capable of that too, and to value it in oneself implies valuing it in them as well. Respect for the other as an individual is at the heart of the interindividual mode of relating to others. The interpersonal (stage 3) gravitated toward "a fused commingling" with the other; the type of communion that takes place in the interindividual stage, in contrast, is one that values and supports distinct identities.

What about intimacy at this stage? Kegan believes it is only at the level of the interindividual that intimacy in the proper sense really becomes possible. This is both because the (objective) individuality of the other is recognized and cherished and because the subjective structure of a person at this stage embraces intimacy within itself: "Ego stage 5 which recognizes a plurality of institutional selves within the (interindividual) self is thereby open to emotional conflict as an interior conversation. Ego stage 5's capacity for intimacy, then, springs from its capacity to be intimate with itself, to break open the institutionality of its former balance." Intimacy involves taking a real interest in how the other feels, thinks, and perceives the world. This begins with and is rooted in the ability to appreciate different views *within oneself*, and it leads toward the acceptance of universal ethical principles, because here "the community is for the first time a 'universal' one in that all persons, by virtue of their being persons, are eligible for membership."[20]

Orders of Consciousness in Adult Development

With stage 5 we come to the end of Kegan's stage theory as presented in *The Evolving Self*. His next book, *In over Our Heads: The Mental Demands of Modern Life*, presupposes the processes of development described above and continues the analysis of the implications of his "subject-object theory," but it

20. Ibid., 106, 104.

does so in terms of a new schema made up of what he no longer calls "stages" but now terms "orders of consciousness." There is a great deal of continuity between what he earlier called "stages" and these "orders of consciousness," but the change of terminology is nevertheless crucial, since it implies recognition that there can be a variety of alternative forms of mental organization in adult life, each with its own strengths for dealing with different situations.

Kegan also makes one major conceptual revision. In the earlier book, he spoke of the desire "to be a part of" and the desire to be independent or autonomous as the two greatest yearnings in human experience, and he said that they remain in lifelong tension. He did not cease to think these are truly fundamental motives, but whereas in *The Evolving Self* he associated particular stages with one or the other of the two poles of this tension,[21] he later rejected this in favor of the idea that both tendencies had roles to play in each stage. To be more precise, he distinguishes in the later book between a relational analysis (that is, separate versus connected) and a subject-object theory analysis (differentiated versus embedded), and he says that previously he "confused what relational theory calls 'separateness' with what subject-object theory calls 'autonomy,'" that is, with differentiatedness.[22]

These pairs (separation and connectedness, differentiation and embeddedness) may look similar, but they are not at all the same. A person may be relatively more autonomous (differentiated) while at the same time being either separate or connected, and one may be relatively more embedded and also be either of the others. Separate and connected are matters of style, says Kegan, whereas differentiated and embedded are really matters of structure. He says he confused style and structure throughout *The Evolving Self.* Now he thinks "each order of consciousness can favor either of these two fundamental longings." Differentiation of consciousness does not imply social separation. Rather, it is a question of whether one "makes up" one's relationships or "gets made up" by them. Nor does increasing differentiation and autonomy necessarily mean increasing aloneness; it can mean employing self-regulation (the root meaning of "autonomy") for the sake of better preserving and protecting one's connections with others along lines one consciously and deliberately decides upon.[23]

21. See Kegan's diagram in ibid., 109.
22. Kegan, *In over Our Heads,* 219.
23. Ibid., 221, 222.

Before turning to the orders of *In over Our Heads,* however, there is one last topic in *The Evolving Self* that should be mentioned, because it is highly pertinent, as we will see in later chapters, to the subject of religion. It is an idea Kegan adapted from the object-relations theorist Donald W. Winnicott: "D. W. Winnicott was fond of saying that there is never 'just an infant.' He meant that intrinsic to the picture of infancy is a caretaker who, from the point of view of the infant, is something more than an 'other person' who relates to and assists the growth of the infant. She provides the very context in which development takes place, and from the point of view of the newborn she is a part of the self." Winnicott called this the "holding environment," and Kegan calls it the "culture of embeddedness." For Winnicott, it was a developmental factor that applied only to infancy, but Kegan generalizes it to all the stages of life: "In my view," he says, "it is an idea intrinsic to *evolution.* There is not one holding environment early in life, but a succession of holding environments, a life history of cultures of embeddedness. They are the psychosocial environments which hold us (with which we are fused) and which let go of us (from which we differentiate)."[24]

Each of us, at any point in development, is a combination of both differentiation and embeddedness. There is always something in which the person remains embedded, and this too is a component of the total personality. In fact, Kegan defines his idea of a "person" with reference to this intrinsic duality:

> What Winnicott says of the infant is true for all of us, even for you at this moment. There is never "just an individual"; the very word refers only to that side of the person that is individuated, the side of differentiation. There is always, as well, the side that is embedded; the *person* is more than an individual. "Individual" names a current state of evolution, a stage, a maintained balance of defended differentiation; "person" refers to the fundamental motion of evolution itself, and is as much about that side of the self embedded in the life-surround as that which is individuated from it. The person is an "individual" *and* an "embeddual."[25]

The importance of the culture of embeddedness is that, at least under the best circumstances, it (1) nurtures the developing person to the point that further development becomes possible, (2) encourages transition to the next stage, and then (3) encourages reintegration in a new form of what has been

24. Kegan, *Evolving Self,* 115, 116.
25. Ibid., 116; emphasis in the original.

transcended. Kegan terms these the functions of *confirmation, contradiction, and continuity.*[26] The circumstances, of course, may not always be the best; a culture of embeddedness may try not just to *hold* (in the nurturing sense) the developing person but to *hold on to* him or her. In the actual case, telling which is which may not be easy, especially for the people involved. This is probably why the separation of maturing children from their parents is often painful for both sides.

In the case of religious groups all sorts of examples might come to mind. To pick one that is probably sufficiently distant no longer to seem contentious, the inquisitors in fourteenth-century France who imprisoned most of the inhabitants of Montaillou over twelve years of age and then burned many of them at the stake were not, from their point of view, acting cruelly; they sincerely wished to "save" both them and others who might otherwise have become infected through them with the Catharist heresy.[27] It is likely that differences in psychological development of the sort Kegan analyzes also played some role in this history. The inquisitors clearly thought in the manner characteristic of Kegan's institutional self; they were committed to the institution of the church and its regulating role both in religious thought and in society. Some of the Cathars of Montaillou may have been people who were relatively more embedded in their impulses or desires—some, for example, seem to have found Catharism attractive because its dualism between flesh and spirit offered a legitimation for antinomian indulgence, which could persist until their sacramental purification just before death. Others seem to have been drawn to this alternative religious view out of a felt need to think some things through beyond the level of official dogma. People may deviate from an established group's positions for all sorts of reasons, some of which, at least, may have to do with a developmental urge to think for themselves—in fact, the word *heresy* derives from a Greek word meaning "to choose," that is, to choose one's own beliefs rather than accept those that have been established as standard for the group.

Some religious traditions evolve along lines that lead them to emphasize conformity to convention, others along lines that lead them to encourage the transcendence of at least some conventions (one might think of the role of many churches in the civil rights movement of the 1960s in the United States, for example). Just as a good family may offer confirmation, contradiction, and

26. Ibid., 258.
27. See Emmanuel Le Roy Ladurie, *Montaillou: The Promised Land of Error.*

continuity for its maturing children, so a religious community may seek to provide an atmosphere of reflection and worship that encourages evolving interpretations of its symbols as expressions of evolving religious minds. Kegan cites a passage from the theologian H. Richard Niebuhr to illustrate what he means by continuity: "The third function for the culture of embeddedness is that it remain in place during the period of transformation and re-equilibration so that what was a part of me and gradually becomes not-me can be successfully reintegrated as object or other of my new balance. . . . Growth involves as well the reconciliation, the recovery, the recognition of that which before was confused with the self. As H. Richard Niebuhr put it, 'We understand what we remember, remember what we forgot, and make familiar what before seemed alien.'"[28]

The orders of consciousness analyzed in *In over Our Heads* represent a further working out of the implications of the subject-object differentiations described in *The Evolving Self.* An "order of consciousness" is a total psychological structure constituted by such a differentiation. The first two of the orders correspond closely to stages 1 and 2 from the earlier book, the impulsive and the imperial, only here they are not even named, perhaps because the later book focuses on the last three almost exclusively. Here Kegan says he is interested primarily in adult development encompassing a variety of capacities of mind; the third, fourth, and fifth orders are adult systems of mental organization in which these capacities are the dynamic factor. It is these last three "orders" that I will focus on here.[29]

Kegan's third order of consciousness in *In over Our Heads* encompasses elements of both what was the "interpersonal" mode of relating to others in *The*

28. Kegan, *Evolving Self,* 129, quoting Niebuhr, *The Meaning of Revelation,* 81.

29. To complete the picture for those who would like the details, here is a brief summary of Kegan's first three orders: The first order of consciousness is that of a child who sees everything strictly in terms of his or her own immediate needs and feelings. It is embedded in perceptions and impulses, and its objects are movements and sensations. The underlying structural factor is the capacity to construct an immediate, atomistic datum, an independent element. The child can be aware, that is, of a particular movement or sensation, but it does not construct durable categories made up of relations between such items. The second order of consciousness is that of a maturing child who becomes capable of realizing there are other people with points of view and feelings of their own but who still understands these only in very concrete terms, that is, in terms of what the other must want and how that might agree or conflict with the child's own wants. The underlying structure here, says Kegan, is the "durable category," a pattern of mental organization that comprehends elemental properties and relates them to one another as a group. The "self" with its point of view and interests and the "other" with its own constitute "durable categories" of this sort. The same capacity that makes it possible for a child in a Piagetian experiment to understand that liquid poured from a short, fat

Evolving Self's stage 3 and what was the "institutional" mode in stage 4, but with the former tending to weigh more heavily. For the most part, this kind of development was all that was needed for almost anyone for a fully adequate adult life in a "traditional" society.

In over Our Heads employs as an overarching metaphor the image of culture as a "school" with a "curriculum." In a "traditional" curriculum the material to be learned takes a single standard shape suited to the capacities of the third order of consciousness. What the title phrase "in over our heads" refers to is the way we can feel when the curriculum of contemporary culture overwhelms us by making demands that are beyond our currently developed capacities for mental processing. The third order of consciousness is what gives us the capacity to form abstract concepts, formulate and test hypotheses, and function within a framework of roles and relationships—which Kegan says was all we needed until fairly recently. "The great religions of traditional cultures," he says, were "a paradigmatic example of one kind of effective culture-as-school."[30] The curriculum of a tradition is mastered by learning its contents—its roles, knowledge, skills, and ethos—and by holding on to them, in part with the aid of affective bonds and a network of personal loyalties. These form a system (a "world") in which third-order consciousness can dwell and feel at home. The underlying psychological structure of fourth-order consciousness, on the other hand, is the ability to step back from (to take as object) roles, relationships, and other contents of consciousness and use them as elements in the construction of complex systems.

What makes our own contemporary culture not only challenging but also sometimes overwhelming to us is that it involves both a "modern" curriculum demanding these new, more differentiated fourth-order capacities and also a "postmodern" one demanding those of a fifth order. When those who instruct us in our culture's curriculum are themselves unaware of the differences between these and of the need to advance sequentially from one order to the next, the individual is often beset with multiple conflicting demands that he

---

container into a tall, thin one will have the same quantity in the new container also enables the child to construct his or her point of view and grant to others their own distinct points of view. But in the second order of consciousness a child still cannot think from both his or her own point of view and that of the other person simultaneously. This requires what Kegan calls "cross-categorical" or "trans-categorical knowing," which instead of subsuming only elemental properties subsumes durable categories themselves as its members. This becomes the underlying structure or mental organization characteristic of the third order of consciousness.

30. Kegan, *In over Our Heads,* 44.

or she may not even be able to grasp, let alone cope with.[31] The demand for fourth-order thinking can produce confusion and frustration in people who might nevertheless function quite adequately within the framework of a traditional culture.

To illustrate this, Kegan offers a fictional example. Peter is a successful middle manager in a business whose boss decides to promote him to head of an independent unit. This gives him responsibilities that require him to make his own plans and decisions independently. Where before he had enjoyed working under his boss's supervision in a framework with a clearly defined set of procedures and expectations (in other words, a tradition), now he feels burdened and uncertain in the face of too many new possibilities and the need to choose for himself among them without the guidance of authority. His wife, Lynn, on the other hand, a teacher, is also given an administrative promotion that makes similar demands, but she thrives on them, because she has already developed a fourth-order mentality that enables her to examine critically the existing procedures and to develop and assess new ones.

An incident in Peter and Lynn's marriage also serves to illustrate on the personal level the difference between the orders of consciousness they represent. Kegan tells us a story about how they had planned a vacation together, just the two of them. This was important to both, since they felt they needed time away alone to nurture their relationship. But then Peter spontaneously invited his parents to join them. Lynn became annoyed and could not understand why Peter would do this. The reason was that while telling his parents about the trip Peter felt they seemed lonely, so he thought they might like to come, too. At that moment he simply forgot what he and Lynn were looking for from the vacation; instead, he found himself looking for a solution to an entirely different problem. His third-order consciousness was drawn by its greater interpersonal orientation into thinking about the feelings of the others who were right in front of him at that moment. Lynn, on the other hand, was concerned with something more systematic, the long-term needs of their marital relationship as an institution made up of fully individuated adults.

31. Kegan especially laments the way university faculty tend to demand fifth-order reflection on the part of students who mostly have not yet completed their transition from the third order to the fourth. This is something relatively few students manage to do even by the time they graduate from college; Kegan cites a longitudinal study he and some colleagues made of returning adult students in a graduate program that found 70 percent of them were not securely rooted in the fourth order when they entered the program—although it is encouraging, and perhaps an indication of the value of higher education, that 70 percent *had* reached the fourth order by the time they finished the program four years later (ibid., 293).

Kegan's fourth order of consciousness, embodied by Lynn both in her personal life and in her professional life, encompasses both of *The Evolving Self*'s institutional and interindividual balances. In addition, it also includes the ability to step back and take as objects not only abstractions, institutional systems, and personal relations but also subjectivity as such and self-consciousness. Kegan emphasizes "self-authorship" as its hallmark even more than institutional role regulation and multiple-role consciousness. Self-authorship is for Kegan the principal manifestation of the "modern" mentality, with Piaget's formal operational thinking as its structural foundation. It was less the taking on of a new role than it was the difficulty Peter had in taking up the authority to construct his own system of operation that made it difficult for him to manage the independent unit he was put in charge of at work, and it was precisely this capacity that enabled Lynn not only to do so but also at one point to stand up to her principal on behalf of the system she had made and to do this in the name of standards that transcended the organization itself.

How might Kegan's new framework of orders of consciousness relate to religion? It is easy to see how the third order of consciousness would be valuable from the point of view of a religion. For one thing, it represents a capacity for self-control and cooperation that religions generally try to elicit, either by positive exhortation or by warnings about possible punishment in the beyond. The third order's capacity for abstraction and its ability to practice rational inference can pose problems for religious traditions if they are employed in a "freethinking" spirit, but it is the third order's embeddedness in roles and relationships that can help to make it less of a danger and to channel the energies of inquiry into supporting rather than seriously questioning the intellectual presuppositions of the tradition. A value system also begins to emerge in the third order, but it remains largely implicit and tends to be based on interpersonal relations rather than universal principles. Beliefs and values are felt and dwelt in—that is, one is embedded in them. They cannot yet be objectified and thought about systematically. Meaning is contained in symbols felt to be inherently sacred, and the sacred itself is closely tied up with the interpersonal—all of which helps to support one's commitment to the conventions of the religious group. In the third order, formal operational thinking begins to develop but still remains somewhat rudimentary and hence unlikely to feel compelled toward a systematic critique of traditional patterns of thought.

Kegan's "modern" consciousness, the fourth order, on the other hand, is bound to have a more ambiguous relation to religion, since here formal operational thinking enables critical reflection, which can question conventional formulations and also conceive of other perhaps preferable systems, both cognitive and sociopolitical, than the one the religious group advocates in its doctrines and embodies in its organization. Ideology, formulation, and relations between abstractions are features Kegan highlights as characteristic of his fourth order, and they give it a power of critique that can break the hold of traditional patterns of thought, loyalty, and authority. But at the same time, Kegan's fourth order can also suffer from a certain narrowness and rigidity through its embeddedness in the systems it constructs and in the mental procedures by which it constructs them.

Excursus: James W. Fowler and Stages of Faith Development

Here it will be worth considering the parallel between Kegan's idea of a fourth order of consciousness and the individuative-reflective stage of faith development in the scheme of stages of faith worked out by James W. Fowler, a psychologist-theologian who, like Kegan, also worked with Lawrence Kohlberg and drew on Kohlberg's studies of moral development as well as Piaget's of cognitive development. I do not want to burden the reader with the details of too many stage theories, but Fowler's stages, as worked out in *Stages of Faith: The Psychology of Human Development and the Quest for Meaning*, are so pertinent to the development of religious thought as well as to some of the problems Kegan addresses that they are worth a brief account.

The ones most directly relevant are mythic-literal faith and what Fowler called synthetic-conventional faith, followed by individuative-reflective faith and conjunctive faith. The first two of these, mythic-literal and synthetic-conventional, are what one would expect to find in a religious person operating in Kegan's third (or "traditional") order of consciousness. The mythic-literal hardly needs explanation; it is a mode of faith that takes sacred stories for historical accounts and tends to think of the relation to the divine in terms of concrete reciprocity: God demands certain things from us, rewards us if we give them, and punishes us if we don't—very much the way a young child thinks of parental authority. To develop beyond that pattern of faith requires at least the beginning of a capacity for what Piaget called formal operational reasoning, and since this develops late, if at all, it is not surprising that Fowler's mythic-literal mode of faith is so common that many simply identify religion as such with it.

Fowler says that synthetic-conventional faith, which usually first begins to develop in the teen years, is stimulated when people start to notice contradictions or conflicts among their authoritative stories and to ask the kind of questions that represent the first movements of formal operational thinking, which at this stage, however, still remains rudimentary. What he means by "synthetic" is nonanalytical: although meaning begins to be abstracted from the concrete details of narrative, it still tends to come to the mind as a global whole. Meaning is still closely tied to symbols, which are felt to be inherently sacred. For a person at this stage of faith, demythologizing or even the discussion of alternative possibilities of interpretation would feel like a radical threat to meaning and an attack on the sacred as such. Also at this stage an implicit value system begins to emerge based on interpersonal relations (which begin to take on a new intensity with adolescence), but it is not yet explicit as something that can be reflected on. As in Kegan's third order, beliefs and values are felt and dwelt in; they cannot be objectified and thought about, and they are closely tied up with interpersonal relations and loyalties.

Synthetic-conventional faith brings with it a particular development of the ideas of God and of the religious community. From being the authoritative legislator of mythic-literal faith, God for the synthetic-conventional becomes a supremely personal other who cares about the individual and grounds the caring community of fellow believers. Right in this context becomes personal loyalty and fulfilling the expectations of significant others. One effect of this strong connection between convention and the interpersonal, says Fowler, is that synthetic-conventional faith "constructs social relations as extensions of interpersonal relationships. It does not think of soc iety in terms of a network of laws, rules, roles, and systematically determined patterns."[32] All of this makes for a strong commitment to the conventions and institutions of one's religious group, but just as conflict among authoritative stories is an important factor in preparing the transition from mythic-literal faith, so conflicts among authoritative leaders and institutional policies or practices can disturb the equilibrium of synthetic-conventional and prepare for the next transition.

As its name indicates, Fowler's individuative-reflective faith involves emergence from the group as an individual critically reflective thinker. It comes about in part because dissatisfaction with conventional answers calls it forth and also because here Piaget's formal operational thinking matures, producing a greater awareness of one's interpretative and cognitive processes. One can

32. Fowler, *Stages of Faith*, 162.

begin to understand, for example, what it means to ask Bernard Lonergan's questions about what one is doing when one is knowing, why doing that is knowing, and what one knows when one does it. (In fact, Lonergan's emphasis on explicit rationality in *Insight* seems predominantly an expression of Fowler's individuative-reflective faith, compared, as we will see, with his later writings.)

In contrast to synthetic-conventional faith's way of binding meaning and symbol together, individuative-reflective faith regards meanings as separable from symbols and seeks to translate them into propositional form. A person operating at this stage of faith tends to distrust any meaning that cannot be propositionally formulated. Demythologizing comes to feel imperative, even redemptive, not the threat it seemed to mythic-literal faith. Authority is relocated from external sources to one's own intellectual and moral conscience. Fowler also says that since the new identity that takes shape at the individuative-reflective stage is no longer defined by the roles one plays for others, to sustain it one now puts together a "meaning frame" that is "aware of itself as a 'worldview.'"[33] Both one's self and one's outlook become differentiated from those of others. This demands systematizing reflection, leading to the formulation of an explicit ideology regarding both the social environment and the ultimate environment the social is set in. To put all of this in Piagetian terms, formal operational thinking (explicitly self-aware cognitive operations) takes shape as a subjective structure and produces as its corresponding objective structure an explicit, consciously developed and articulated worldview.

Along with such reflectiveness and critical distance, however, comes a limitation: conscious thinking and explicit meaning may become so highly valued that a person at Fowler's individuative-reflective stage of faith can tend to overlook the influence of unconscious factors on thinking and behavior and to neglect or dismiss meaning that cannot be explicitly formulated—the tacit dimension of consciousness that Michael Polanyi argued could never be fully reduced to an object of focal attention.[34] I mentioned that Lonergan's thought in *Insight* might exemplify Fowler's individuative-reflective faith, and perhaps it can serve also to illustrate the limitations of this stage. In *Insight*, Lonergan treated myth as simply the opposite of critically reflective knowledge and equated mythic consciousness with the absence of self-knowledge, that is, in Piaget's terms, with the absence of formal operational thinking. One of Lon-

33. Ibid., 182.

34. See, for example, Polanyi, *Personal Knowledge: Towards a Post-critical Philosophy* and *The Tacit Dimension.*

ergan's sympathetic critics, Robert M. Doran, spoke of this narrowness in his thought and suggested that Lonergan's view of myth and the existential subject could fruitfully draw on the complementary insights of Carl Jung and Paul Ricoeur. In particular, Doran suggested that "mediating between judgments of fact and judgments concerning what is good and worthwhile, is the apprehension of potential values and satisfactions in feelings," which may be expressed in a not fully paraphrasable way in imaginative symbols. Lonergan took this criticism seriously and began himself to move in that direction in his later writings, such as "The Subject" and *Method in Theology.* In the latter, for example, he defines *faith* not as a claim to objective "knowledge" in the sense in which he used that term in *Insight* but as "the knowledge born of religious love," saying that "besides the factual knowledge reached by experiencing, understanding, and verifying, there is another kind of knowledge reached through the discernment of value and the judgments of value of a person in love."[35]

This example may also serve to illustrate the factors leading to the transition from Fowler's individuative-reflective stage of faith to what he calls conjunctive faith. As Fowler puts it, "Images and energies from a deeper self" and "a gnawing sense of the sterility and flatness of the meanings one serves" along with "recognition that life is more complex than stage four's [individuative-reflective faith's] logic of clear distinctions and abstract concepts can comprehend" are what "press one toward a more dialectical and multileveled approach to life truth." Fowler himself, explaining his idea of conjunctive faith, invokes Paul Ricoeur's idea of a "second naïveté" as a postcritical desire to go beyond demythologizing and resubmit to the initiative of the symbolic. Conjunctive faith comes to recognize that there may be depths of meaning in symbols that can never be rendered fully explicit and can be discovered only by attentive listening for further disclosures. He uses the example of a person who has learned to read scripture using critical tools but who now also listens meditatively for what further meanings the text itself may be able to suggest. Fowler refers to the cognitive mode of conjunctive faith as "dialogical knowing," a willingness to engage in a mutual "speaking" and "hearing" in dialogue with the text.[36]

At this stage of faith, says Fowler, one also develops a critical recognition of the influence of one's culture, one's "social unconscious," on the ways one

35. Lonergan, *Insight,* 542–43; Doran, *Subject and Psyche: Ricoeur, Jung, and the Search for Foundations,* 97; Lonergan, *Method in Theology,* 115.

36. Fowler, *Stages of Faith,* 183, 185.

may interpret symbols and construct a worldview. One recognizes the need to come to terms "with [one's] own unconscious—the unconscious personal, social and species or archetypal elements that are partly determinative of our actions and responses." Balancing one's now well-developed critical faculties with a new humility of meditative hearkening, one can develop a capacity for "ironic imagination"—the ability to dwell appreciatively in the symbols of one's culture while simultaneously recognizing that they can never be more than partially adequate, that they not only *reflect* a reality that transcends them but also *distort* it.[37] This results both in respect for tradition and in recognition of the *partiality* of all traditions. This in turn can make for openness to encounter with other traditions and to recognition that they may contain meanings that can complement or correct one's own.

The Ambiguous Potential of "Postmodern" Consciousness

Comparing Fowler's stages of faith with the cultural eras with which Kegan associates his later orders of consciousness, Fowler's synthetic-conventional faith would seem to correlate with "traditional" culture and Kegan's third order, his individuative-reflective, with "modern" and the fourth order. It may be less clear how Fowler's conjunctive faith would connect with the idea of "postmodern" culture, especially since the idea of postmodernism as a theme in contemporary culture is so often associated with criticism of tradition. But Kegan's way of discussing postmodernism in connection with his fifth order of consciousness does try to associate it, if not exactly with a recovery of tradition through a Ricoeurian second naïveté, at least with a liberation from the self-imposed limitations of rationalistic thought. Kegan describes his fifth order of consciousness as "trans-ideological" or "post-ideological" in relation to the fourth order's abstract systems or ideologies, from which the fifth order disengages its subjectivity in order to place them over on the side of the object. As in many discussions of postmodernism as well as in Fowler's discussion of conjunctive faith, Kegan speaks of an awareness of paradox that characterizes the fifth order and helps it to break out of fixation on the neat formulations of the fourth.

The relation of Kegan's fifth-order consciousness to what Fowler calls conjunctive faith is made still clearer in the distinction Kegan makes between

37. Ibid., 186, 198.

"deconstructive" and "reconstructive" postmodernisms. Deconstructive postmodernism, he says, is simply antimodern; it considers reason, freedom, rights, equity, self-determination—all the major achievements of the modern mentality—to be uncritically ideological concepts. Kegan considers this sort of negative critique to be an early step toward moving from fourth-order to fifth-order consciousness, but he thinks it still remains itself uncritically ideological, an incomplete transition.[38] Reconstructive postmodernism, on the other hand, seeks to rethink and reappropriate modern conceptions of reason and justice, though in a less absolutistic way.

Considered from this point of view, the movement known as deconstructionism that was popular in some academic circles in the late twentieth century might be described as an expression of the growing pains of transcending the fourth order of consciousness.[39] Deconstructionism's idea of the tendency of all meaning to subvert itself might be understood as an ideologization of the sort of transitional disorientation that is likely to accompany the process of differentiation that must precede the new integration that properly constitutes the fifth order. Since Kegan's fifth order of consciousness is a recent historical development that even those in its vanguard may still be struggling to complete, it should not be surprising that the social discourse of what is called "postmodernism"—much of which may be uttered by people who themselves have little notion of its psychological dynamics—should take on a primarily negative, often seemingly antirational tone. What the effects of such rhetoric will lead toward on the level of the general culture remains to be seen. Kegan himself sounds at times as if he is groping for the possibility of a positive development coming out of the vague turmoil that currently goes by the name of postmodernism.

Or perhaps one might say that like a good therapist, Kegan holds fast to the hope of a leap in development that will carry the patient beyond the current confusion. His own conception of a genuine (fifth order) postmodernism is not at all antirational and embraces everything that was a source of real strength in the fourth ("modern") order of consciousness. "Reconstructive postmodernism," he says, "reopens the possibility that some kinds of normativeness, hierarchizing, privileging, generalizing, and universalizing are not only compatible with a postideological view of the world, they are necessary for sus-

38. Kegan, *In over Our Heads*, 324.

39. I do not mean to imply, however, that all of what has gone by the name of "deconstruction" is reducible to this, even if statements by some of its proponents sometimes suggest that.

taining it," and he appeals to those who think of their thought as postmodern to consider the possibility that "a theory such as the one I have outlined in this book—in spite of the judgments, generalizations, and claims to universality it makes and in spite of its unabashed privileging of 'complexity'—is at least potentially an ally, not an enemy of postmodernism."[40]

Whether it is to be called postmodern or simply a further development in the differentiation of consciousness, Kegan's conception of his fifth order is a fleshing out of the idea—which is applicable to all levels of development—that each of us remains always a combination of both differentiation and embeddedness, and that we are never finished selves but selves in process. (There is more to be said both about this and about Kegan's fifth order of consciousness, but I will defer that discussion to Chapters 8 and 9, where the full importance of these ideas for understanding religious development will become clear.) What seems ultimately at issue in the controversy between fourth- and fifth-order thinking—quite apart from any associations with temporal epochs such as "modern" or "postmodern"—is the realization that subjectivity can never be reduced entirely to some kind of object—that there will always be a mysterious depth of subjectivity in consciousness, a point of emergence in the soul from which freedom, love, and all the potentialities of spirit can proceed and continue endlessly to unfold.

Lest speaking in such hopeful tones, however, about the possibilities of conscious human development seem to neglect the unconscious forces within us that can resist, impede, or deform that, I will turn in the next two chapters to consider some of those forces that seem especially pertinent to understanding the twists and turns that religious development can be subject to. It would nevertheless be misleading to think of them only as negative, regressive forces. On the contrary, we will see that they have evolved with us every step of the way as fundamental building blocks of our humanity. They may be largely involuntary, functioning as virtual mechanisms underlying our thought, feeling, and behavior, but whether that will function for possible good or possible ill in the life of any given person or community will depend on how we relate to them and to the possibilities they lead or push us toward, on how we succeed or fail in integrating them into actively conscious, reasonable, responsible existence.

40. Ibid., 331.

4

Death Anxiety and Symbols of Immortality

Ernest Becker

Ernest Becker's work, in such writings as *The Denial of Death* and *Escape from Evil,* explored the implications of the assumption that a major, but essentially unconscious and therefore highly problematic, motivation of all human beings is anxiety regarding one's own possible death. What makes this such a problem, he thought, is that beneath the surface of consciousness there always remains an immense force of repressed death anxiety that constantly shapes our thought and activity without our having any direct awareness of its doing so. Human beings have evolved to be self-conscious, but this consciousness itself has brought with it the awareness of possibility and futurity and therefore of possible future death. Following such revisionist Freudians as Otto Rank and Gregory Zilboorg, Becker thought that awareness of the possibility of death would produce crippling terror if it remained constantly in the forefront of attention. As he put it in *The Denial of Death,* "The fear of death must be present behind all our normal functioning, in order for the organism to be armed toward self-preservation. But the fear of death cannot be present constantly in one's mental functioning, else the organism could not function." Therefore, it must be "repressed," which means, he said, quoting Zilboorg, "more than to put away and to forget that which was put away and the place where we put it. It means also to maintain a constant psychological effort to keep the lid on and inwardly never relax our watchfulness."[1]

This almost superhuman effort requires instruments that cultures must evolve to provide, and these are essentially religious. What people need most basically to sustain them in this effort of keeping the terror of death at bay, said Becker, is existential self-esteem, the confidence that even in the face of death life is inherently valuable and that their own personal lives can be meaningful and of worth in the service of life, that their lives can have "cosmic significance." What a society that is itself capable of surviving must provide, therefore, is a cultural worldview that offers its members a script for what Becker called a hero project. Existential self-esteem depends on a heroic enterprise to carry out, which in turn means that there must be a worldview that embraces heroic values and interprets the cosmos as a theater for heroic action. "Society itself," said Becker, "is a codified hero system, which means that society everywhere is a living myth of the significance of human life, a defiant creation of meaning"—which means in turn that "every society is thus a 'religion' whether it thinks so or not."[2]

Perhaps I should explain before I go further, since it often becomes a source of misunderstanding to readers of Becker, that when he spoke of the fear of death as the fundamental human motive, he was not conceiving of death only as simple physical extinction. If that were all he meant by "death," his ideas about the power of the fear of death would be in obvious conflict with the idea cited from Peter Berger in the introduction that "anomy is unbearable to the point where the individual may seek death in preference to it." Certainly, we do fear death in the physical sense, but Becker would say that we can also fear it even more in its symbolic sense. He cited Erich Fromm to the effect that "the essence of man is really his paradoxical nature, the fact that he is half animal and half symbolic." "Man," said Becker, "is not just a blind blob of idling protoplasm, but a creature with a name who lives in a world of symbols and dreams and not merely matter." Physical death threatens us as animals, but it is not simply as animals that Becker thought we are driven fundamentally by the fear of death. The death that really grips us and holds us in a state of terror is symbolic. "The knowledge of death," he said, "is reflective and conceptual, and animals are spared it." Perhaps one might say more exactly that when an animal reacts to a threat of death, it is simply an immediate instinctive re-

1. Becker, *The Denial of Death*, 16, 17 (quoting Zilboorg, "Fear of Death," 467).
2. Becker, *The Denial of Death*, 3, 7.

sponse rooted deep in the primitive parts of the brain, whereas in a human, a fear of physical death may be triggered initially in the primitive parts of the brain (the medulla or the amygdala) by some physical threat, but as a constant underlying anxiety, it is generated by higher brain functions involving imagination and thought. "Death," Becker said is "a complex symbol" with many possible meanings varying from person to person and from culture to culture, with the various symbolic hero projects that cultures develop to manage that fear.[3] So it is not a contradiction to say that although we fear death, we might prefer death to anomie—that is, we might prefer a quick, straightforward physical death to the haunting symbolic death of loss of meaning, loss of world, loss of identity, by the defeat of our imaginative hero project. We do everything we can to repress our fear of both physical and symbolic death, but sometimes the only way one might feel able effectively to avoid the latter is by taking a quick leap into the former. If Becker were alive today, he would probably think the motivation of a religious suicide bomber was perfectly intelligible as a hero project with, for the bomber, cosmic significance. Physical death would in this case be the price of symbolic victory.

Becker modeled much of his thinking on Sigmund Freud's theory of repression and "the return of the repressed" in the form of symptoms, various sorts of behavior we cannot adequately explain in terms of any of our conscious motives, and also on Freud's later thinking about the balance between two great biological drives, Eros and Thanatos (Freud's hypothesized death drive). Despite the explicit line of descent from Freud, however, Becker cannot be considered a Freudian. In fact, his characterization of eros as much more than sexual libido links him with the broader philosophical heritage of the image of Eros that Jaspers also drew on. And his treatment of the death theme is actually quite the opposite of that of Freud, whose concept of Thanatos Becker saw as an attempt to mask the anxiety of death by interpreting death as a positive motive parallel to the sex drive rather than as an object of aversion and a source of terror.

Ultimately, Becker found more inspiration in Otto Rank and Søren Kierkegaard than in Freud. From Rank he took the ideas of repression as "character armor," a necessary "vital lie" used to keep terror at bay, and of society as a "hero system" in which one seeks through symbolic projects to triumph over death. Drawing on Rank, and other Freudian heretics such as Sandor

3. Ibid., 26 (referring to Fromm, *The Heart of Man: Its Genius for Good and Evil,* 116–17), 3, 27, 19.

Ferenczi, Fritz Perls, and Norman O. Brown, Becker discarded the biological emphasis of Freud and reinterpreted his themes existentially, interpreting the Oedipal motive, for example, as an "Oedipal project" of becoming one's own father, that is, one's own self-generating cause and thereby becoming immune to the power of death. The problem for the neurotic comes when the vital lie of character goes too far and becomes a prison of repression and when the hero systems of traditional culture no longer function effectively to sustain the conviction that death is not simply the negation of all meaning in our lives. "Neurosis," said Becker, "is another word for describing a complicated technique for avoiding misery, but reality is the misery." To come out of neurosis into the fullness of experience is to come face-to-face with terror in the face of possible death: "Full humanness means full fear and trembling, at least some of the waking day."[4]

The mention of "fear and trembling" is, of course, an allusion to Kierkegaard. The reason Becker considered Kierkegaard the greatest of psychologists is that he was absolutely clear about this point and also that he recognized—as most others, Becker thought, did not—that the only way one can endure reality without neurotic defenses is through a courage sustained by some form of faith. Kierkegaard, too, thought of character as a vital lie that can become a "philistinism" that "tranquilizes itself in the trivial," but his analysis of the ways human life can fail when it closes itself against reality was in the service of a positive aim beyond the diagnoses of the psychoanalyst. Kierkegaard wanted "to be able finally to conclude with authority what a person would be like if he did not lie," as Becker put it. As such, said Becker, Kierkegaard was "a theorist of the open personality, of human possibility," and this is something that "leads man beyond himself." The way Kierkegaard urges us to pursue this is to study in "the school of anxiety," facing *into* the terrors of finitude instead of building up defenses against them. But no one can find the courage for this without a basic trust that that possibility is more than an abyss: "Without the leap into faith the helplessness of shedding one's character armor holds one in sheer terror." This is why Becker wrote that in *The Denial of Death* he was "arguing for a merger of psychology and mythico-religious perspective."[5]

But that remained in the end something Becker could only point to. He was not a theologian, and whatever ideas he might eventually have wanted to develop on this subject were cut short by his death not long after the book's pub-

4. Becker, *The Denial of Death*, 36, 57, 59.
5. Ibid., 74, 85, 86, 90, xi.

lication. At the time he died he was working on another book, *Escape from Evil,* published posthumously, that did not pursue that particular direction further but did explore the ways repressed anxiety could generate deadly worldviews by paying for such faith with the dark side of heroism, namely, its polarizing implications as a combat, an agon, between protagonist and antagonist, hero and nemesis. (A classic example would be the Bible's divinely decreed eternal enmity between Israel and Amalek. The Jewish tradition's effort to wrestle with the sinister implications of this particular element of their ancestral story will be discussed in Chapter 6.)

Becker's central assumption in all his work was that by generating and maintaining self-esteem, our hero projects enable us to feel immortal. In order to endure the terror of living in the ever present face of death, we draw on worldviews that tell us life is more powerful than death and that we have a permanent place in the drama of its triumph. In *The Denial of Death,* Becker had emphasized as a fairly unambiguous value the cultural hero projects that can provide us this hope. At the beginning of *Escape from Evil,* on the other hand, he said that his previous works "did not take sufficient account of truly vicious human behavior." Instead, he asserted that in this one he would "attempt to show that man's natural and inevitable urge to deny mortality and achieve a heroic self-image are the root causes of human evil."[6]

This is not to say that Becker ceased to believe that effective hero projects did not remain an important need, but the later book shows a greatly increased sensitivity to their possible costs and destructiveness:

> If you talk about heroics that cost mountains of human life, you have to find out why such heroics are practiced in a given social system: who is scapegoating whom, what social classes are excluded from heroism, what there is in the social structure that drives the society blindly to self-destructive heroics, etc. Not only that, but you have to actually set up some kind of liberating ideal, some kind of life-giving alternative to the thoughtless and destructive heroism; you have to begin to scheme to give to man an opportunity for heroic victory that is not a simple reflex of narcissistic scapegoating. You have to conceive of the possibility of a nondestructive *yet victorious* social system.[7]

Following the tradition of Freud, *The Denial of Death* places relatively greater, though not exclusive, weight on the psychology of the individual; *Escape*

6. Becker, *Escape from Evil,* xvii.
7. Ibid., 126; emphasis in the original.

from Evil, as the reference to scapegoating indicates, shifts the relative emphasis to social psychology. At the center there is still the idea that repression makes us unconscious of our deepest motivations and especially of "the twin fears of life and death"—we fear death, but we also fear life because it might lead us toward death—but the emphasis is on how these drive social institutions. Society is still a religious system, as it was in *The Denial of Death,* but here, in an explicit effort to merge Freud with Marx, Becker talked about repressed death anxiety as the root of economic activity, class distinctions, and ritual. Money is still an immortality symbol in the new book, but now it is also a surplus generated for the sake of supporting sacrificial rites, which (1) allay death anxiety by expiating the "natural guilt" of being alive and therefore vulnerable to death; (2) feed the gods so that we can draw on their power in the fight against death; (3) demonstrate that we are favored by the gods (since it was our victims who died, not us); and (4) buy off death by offering substitutes in our place.[8]

Becker also saw death as the source of the first class distinction, that between mortal humans and immortal gods, which in turn generates the distinctions between the rest of us and the priests and kings who are agents of divine power or the heroes whose glory makes them godlike.[9] Ultimately, he said, these break down into the distinction between sacrificer and sacrificed, scapegoater and scapegoat.

The capstone of Becker's "general theory of human evil" is that its root is "man's hunger for righteous self-expansion and perpetuation," the paradox that "evil comes from man's urge to heroic victory over evil." This is why human beings project their sense of guilt, inadequacy, and vulnerability onto scapegoats and then destroy them: they cannot endure these characteristics in themselves, and they hope, unconsciously and stupidly, that they can exterminate them with their victims. "From the head-hunting and charm-hunting of the primitives to the holocausts of Hitler, the dynamic is the same: the heroic victory over evil by a traffic in pure power. And the aim is the same: purity, goodness, righteousness—immunity."[10]

What, then, can we do, or do we dare try to do, if our evil is the result of our very effort to be good? Actually, Becker thought we can do quite a lot, and even if his positive suggestions remain somewhat sketchy, and perhaps

8. Ibid., 92, 85, 101, 102, 105, 109.
9. Ibid., 43.
10. Ibid., 135, 136, 150.

sometimes even naive—at least retrospectively, as when he said that Marxism "has already had an enormous influence for human survival: it stopped Hitler in Russia, and it eliminated the gratuitous and age-old miseries of the most numerous people on earth"—much of what he suggested seems clearly helpful. One may feel somewhat wary of his recommendation of what he called "objective hatred," the substitution of impersonal objects of hatred, such as poverty and disease, for human ones, since hatred of any kind usually proves to be a dangerous medicine. But he certainly hit home with his urgent appeal that we recognize "how men defeat themselves by trying to bring absolute purity and goodness into the world" and that we also recognize "the nonabsoluteness of the many different hero systems in the family of nations."[11]

When Becker called for "a nondestructive *yet victorious* social system," he put his finger on one of the core problems the present study is centrally concerned with. He suggested, rightly I think, that any worldview that is to be effective in eliciting human trust and loyalty must offer satisfaction to "the basic general motive of man—his need for self-esteem, for a feeling of primary value," by promising victory over "extinction with insignificance."[12] It must, in other words, offer something worth believing in and living for. But it must do so without tempting us to believe in utopian absolutism and without yielding to the allure of polarized visions of a world divided into heroes and eternal enemies. That is not an easy need to fill, but Becker recognized that, and some of his suggestions seem to point in a helpful direction.

Most important, Becker urged that, in light of his analysis of the role of unconscious motives in driving us to turn our best impulses to evil, we must learn to act consciously and carefully rather than unconsciously and stupidly. This requires an effort of demystification of socially constructed myths and hero systems, "the revelation of the lie," as he put it. But he thought it also requires a new formulation of religious sainthood, one that could join with psychoanalysis in seeking to uncover what is repressed and could counter our tendency to shrink artificially our intake of experience: "Both religion and psychoanalysis show man his basic creatureliness and attempt to pull the scales of his sublimations from his eyes. Both religion and psychoanalysis have discovered the same source of illusion: the fear of death which cripples life. Also religion has the same difficult mission as Freud: to overcome the fear of self-knowledge. . . . The

11. Ibid., 170, 145, 168.
12. Ibid., 139, 4.

ideal of religious sainthood, like that of psychoanalysis, is thus the opening up of perception: this is where religion and science meet."[13]

Becker placed great weight on the claim that his approach brings religion and science together. He believed religion is of fundamental importance as the principal vehicle and source of maintenance for cultural worldviews, but he was equally concerned with bringing all the resources of reason to bear on the issues religions are concerned with. Certainly, if it is possible to connect science and religion in such a way that they complement each other rather than compete, this could be of great value both for understanding the nature and role of religious worldviews and for making our ways of relating to them less problematic—especially since one of the main problems with religious worldviews has always been their tendency to assert themselves absolutely, disregarding critical questions and even sometimes denigrating critical inquiry as a value. If one of the major challenges facing religious traditions in the next centuries will be finding a way to encourage the highest possible level of psychological and intellectual development among their faithful, a way of thinking about religious worldviews that is fully respectful of the needs of critical consciousness will be imperative. One place to start developing this, since religion and psychology do find some degree of common focus in the study of human spirituality, would be to take advantage of whatever psychology may have to offer in the way of a scientific basis for that study.

One might wonder, however, precisely what sort of scientific grounding Becker thought psychoanalysis can offer—or even itself legitimately claim. Freudian theory has been extensively applied in clinical settings, but it is now widely recognized that the results have been ambiguous when compared with other forms of psychotherapy—and most important, with placebo therapies in which someone simply listens sympathetically to patients while offering no particular treatment—and there has never been much effort to subject Freudian theory to experimental testing. Becker seems to have taken Freudian claims to scientific status more or less at face value.

Becker's own ideas—which as I indicated above are actually quite distinct from Freud's—have, on the other hand, begun to be rigorously investigated by experimental psychologists, principally Sheldon Solomon, Jeff Greenberg, and Tom Pyszczynski, who have developed carefully designed experiments to test for what they call "mortality salience" (the unconscious fear of death) and its effects on worldviews and behavior.

13. Ibid., 125, 163.

Terror Management Theory

The testable hypothesis these psychologists have derived from Becker they call "terror management theory." It involves the following assumptions:

1. Humans have evolved with an instinctive propensity for self-preservation.

2. Cognitive complexity in humans makes them capable of regulating their behavior through the delay of responses and the consideration of alternatives.

3. The same cognitive complexity also makes humans uniquely self-conscious, explicitly aware that they exist and that one of their possibilities is nonexistence.

4. Self-consciousness produces a potential for both awe (regarding life's positive possibilities) and terror (in the face of its negative ones, especially the prospect of death).

5. This potential for terror before the ever present possibility of death could itself inhibit effective action and increase the danger of death unless means were developed to keep it under control.

The key idea of terror management theory, then, is that in the process of their evolution human beings drew on the same intellectual capabilities that made them susceptible to potentially paralyzing terror in order to develop an instrument to assuage it. This instrument, as Becker suggested, is cultural worldview. What worldviews offer us is assurance that the world we live in is not simply chaotic and dangerous but also orderly and that its dangers are therefore manageable if we live appropriately. The idea of living appropriately implies a standard of value that we are challenged to meet. If we can meet it, then our lives will be both secure and praiseworthy; we will be valuable members of a meaningful universe. Hence, the crucial importance of self-esteem—from this point of view, self-esteem is not only a matter of feeling good about oneself but also a participation in the symbolic immortality one gains through identification with entities more comprehensive and enduring than the individual self. It must be a *cultural* worldview because it can do its assuaging work effectively only in the context of a culture, supported by collective myths and rituals and culturally defined marks of success and embodied in the larger community that not only provides these supports but also functions itself as the vehicle of immortality identification.

People are therefore strongly motivated to maintain their self-esteem and the cultural worldview it depends on and to defend both of these against anything that might undermine them. As Sheldon Solomon and his colleagues put it, self-esteem can function as an effective "anxiety buffer" only to the extent that faith in the cultural worldview is preserved; self-esteem is, after all, primarily one's sense of success in meeting the qualifications of membership in the culture. Any challenge to worldview should trigger attempts to bolster it so as to prevent anxiety. Likewise, any reminder of the possibility of death should produce increased attachment to the worldview, as well as increased motivation to behave in a way that is consistent with it. This, then, is the point of purchase for empirical testing of the theory.

The experiments Greenberg, Solomon, Pyszczynski, and their colleagues in Germany and Israel have worked out fall into two general patterns: anxiety-buffer studies and mortality-salience studies. The first proceed from the hypothesis that if a psychological structure provides protection against anxiety, then augmenting that structure should reduce it; that is, strengthening either self-esteem or faith in the cultural worldview should reduce anxiety and anxiety-related behavior in response to threats. Various experiments were devised to first raise or lower self-esteem and then test for anxiety responses. Raising self-esteem was indeed found to reduce anxiety and anxiety-related behavior in response to threats (in comparison with control subjects). Reducing self-esteem was correspondingly found to increase them. Most significant for the theory, these effects were produced with respect to reminders of mortality, not to threats simply to self-esteem as such. They also found that high levels of self-esteem led to a reduction in the use of various types of vulnerability-denying defensive biases that presumably function to minimize anxiety.[14]

The mortality-salience studies are based on the hypothesis that if a psychological structure (in this case the cultural worldview) provides protection specifically against anxiety about death, then reminders of mortality should increase the need to maintain that structure. There have been many experiments demonstrating mortality-salience effects.[15] One asked municipal court judges to decide how much bail they would require for an accused prostitute. The hypothesis was that if the judges first experienced a triggering of

14. Greenberg et al., "Assessing the Terror Management Analysis of Self-Esteem: Converging Evidence of an Anxiety-Buffering Function"; Greenberg et al., "Effects of Self-Esteem on Vulnerability-Denying Defensive Distortions: Further Evidence of an Anxiety-Buffering Function of Self-Esteem."

15. For a review of these studies and their results, see Greenberg, Solomon, and Pyszczynski, "Terror Management Theory of Self-Esteem and Cultural World Views: Empirical Assessments and Conceptual Refinements."

mortality salience, they would find moral transgressors more threatening and anxiety-producing because they violate cultural values. The result was that such judges set an average bail of $455 as compared with $50 for judges who were given neutral topics to think about first. This effect was subsequently replicated by German investigators with university students as the subjects, but logically enough, the moral transgressions had to be different in Germany, to correspond to differences in the cultural worldview there. For example, a man abandoning his wife and children was judged harshly, but prostitutes were not, since prostitution is legal in Germany and is generally more socially acceptable there than in the United States.

Striking close to home at the time of this writing, a study published in 2006 found that mortality salience had the effect of heightening the sense of hostility on both sides of the conflict between the United States and the Muslim world.[16] One experiment investigated the effect of mortality salience on support by American college students for (1) preemptive attacks using nuclear and chemical weapons against Iran, Syria, or North Korea (even without evidence of any current threat from these countries); (2) their willingness to see thousands of innocent people killed as collateral damage in an effort to destroy Osama bin Laden; (3) the strengthening of the Patriot Act at the cost of relinquishing personal freedoms. The investigators found that mortality salience increased support for all such measures among students who identified themselves as politically conservative but not among politically liberal students—that is, it seems to have stimulated the conservative students to strengthen their commitment to their conservative worldview and to the conservative political leaders they look to for security. A contrasting experiment investigated the effect of mortality salience on the attitudes of students in two Iranian universities toward suicide bombers. Participants were first randomly assigned to answer questions either about their own death or about some other aversive topic unrelated to death. Then they were asked about their attitudes toward two hypothetical fellow students, one described as supporting martyrdom attacks against the United States and one described as opposing such attacks. The control participants (those who did not receive reminders of their own mortality) preferred the student who opposed martyrdom attacks; those reminded of mortality preferred the student who supported martyrdom and indicated they were more likely to consider engaging in such activities themselves.

16. Pyszczynski et al., "Mortality Salience, Martyrdom, and Military Might: The Great Satan versus the Axis of Evil."

As would be expected in the light of Becker's ideas about scapegoating as a defense against anxiety, mortality salience was also found in other studies to increase prejudice against foreigners generally as well as against anyone who could be perceived as advocating or even believing in a competing worldview. Adherents of different religions, even among members of one's own society, represent this sort of danger. For example, an experiment in Alabama found that mortality salience stimulated anti-Semitism among Christian subjects. Another experiment found that it increased the extent to which American college students agreed with the statement that "the Holocaust in Nazi Germany was God's punishment for the Jews." Another found that students shown graphic videos of automobile accident scenes (to sensitize them to their own mortality) and then asked to set damage awards in hypothetical accident cases were more severe if they thought the car was Japanese than if it was American.[17]

Especially significant was a finding that was predictable by the theory but might run counter to general expectations. Many studies not associated with terror management theory have focused on prejudice against black people stemming from the symbolic threat they pose to the white worldview. But the terror management theorists found that in cases of mortality salience, the prejudice depended on the relation of the black persons in question to the white subject's worldview. An experiment in 1996 found that white subjects whose mortality salience was triggered and who were then exposed to a black confederate of the researchers who dressed and behaved in either a stereotypic or a counterstereotypic manner actually reacted more favorably to the stereotypic model, even though that embodied values and attitudes quite different from those of the white subjects (while the counterstereotypic example dressed and acted like an intelligent, studious person of a sort they would normally respect).[18] Normally, this might seem a counterintuitive result, but since terror management theory holds that mortality salience produces a desire to bolster one's cultural worldview, and since stereotypes are a component of that, the theory predicts that mortality salience would make one prefer the black whose dress and manner reinforce the subjects' stereotyped negative expectations of blacks. The counterstereotypic example, on the other hand, could be expected to disturb the stereotype and thus challenge the worldview that includes it.

17. Greenberg, Solomon, and Pyszczynski, "Terror Management Theory," 81.

18. Schimel et al. "Stereotypes and Terror Management: Evidence That Mortality Salience Enhances Stereotypic Thinking and Preferences."

This could be expected to make the white subjects uncomfortable, and evidently it did.

In all the experiments, it was found that mortality salience effects were triggered only by reminders of one's own possible death, not by other sorts of anxiety-provoking events. In addition, it was found that these effects did not depend on any negative emotional state that the thought of death might arouse. On the contrary, effects like high bail for a prostitute were not accompanied by any special elevation of negative affect, whereas asking subjects to think about matters that did stimulate negative feelings (such as intense pain, a difficult exam, giving a speech in public) but that did not remind the subjects of their own possible death did not produce mortality-salience effects.

The general pattern of response to a direct reminder of the possibility of one's death was repression, which rendered death-related thoughts at least temporarily less accessible to consciousness than they were initially, and then subsiding of the effort to exclude them, accompanied by heightened accessibility of death-related thoughts just below the surface of consciousness. This in turn was followed by: defense of the subject's worldview and renewed efforts to live up to its values, and possibly denigration or aggression against others who might represent a challenge to the subject's worldview.

Where the reminder was not direct—that is, where the subject was not rendered explicitly conscious of possible death—the phase of repression and reduced accessibility of death-related thoughts did not take place; rather, accessibility was heightened immediately, and mortality-salience effects were increased. The less conscious and reflective the subject, that is, the more powerful the impact. It was also discovered, to the initial surprise of the investigators themselves, that the effects of thoughts of mortality on behavior and judgment are greatest when they are accessible to consciousness but no longer in focal awareness or working memory. It was a serendipitous accident of the early experiments that there was always a delay (involving some other mental tasks that distracted subjects from mortality) between the manipulation of mortality salience and the measuring of the relevant effects, because if there had been no delay, they later found, the effects would have been much less pronounced. They also found that after the initial triggering of mortality salience, asking the subjects to think further about their possible death and express their deepest fears about it led to significantly less defensiveness and hostility than when they were not asked to do this. In one experiment some subjects were given distractor tasks following the stimulation of mortality salience, while others were given tasks that kept them focused on death. Those given distractor tasks subsequently exhibited greater mortality-salience effects than those who kept conscious of the danger of death. Generally, it was found that indirect and subtle mortality-salience manipulations produced stronger effects than more overt ones and that symbolic terror management defenses, such as increased defense of the cultural worldview, occur only after individuals have been distracted from conscious thoughts of death.[19] Although this research was stimulated by the ideas of Ernest Becker, the results also therefore suggest the pertinence of Martin Heidegger's idea that human beings tend to flee from the thought of their own death into a diminished consciousness and that to live authentically, one should face death consciously and continuously.

Of special importance for the question of what might render worldviews less dangerous is the investigators' finding that mortality-salience effects were strongly affected by the mode of thinking that the subjects were encouraged to employ. Stimulated by the distinction in Seymour Epstein's cognitive experiential-self theory between rational and experiential thought as two fundamentally different types of thinking, Solomon and his colleagues developed experiments to see whether these types of thinking would make a difference in mortality-salience responses. Rational thinking is described by Epstein as a "deliberative, effortful, abstract system that operates primarily in the medium of language." What he calls "experiential" thinking, on the other hand, is "a crude system that automatically, rapidly, effortlessly, and efficiently processes information" and "is experienced passively and preconsciously," and its results are apprehended as self-evidently valid.[20] This also tends to be the system that is dominant in most circumstances, since it is both easier and quicker.

In one study they manipulated these modes of thinking by the appearance of the investigator. To encourage the rational mode in subjects, the experimenter wore a lab coat over trousers and black-rimmed glasses and sat formally behind a desk. To encourage the experiential mode of thinking, he wore shorts, a T-shirt, and Birkenstock sandals. In another study, written instructions were used. To encourage the rational mode of thinking, subjects were instructed to consider their answers carefully before responding and to be as rational and analytic as possible. To encourage the experiential, they were told to give their first natural response because what the experimenters were looking for was people's gut-level reactions. In both experiments mortality-salience effects were produced only in subjects thinking in the experiential, not the ratio-

19. Greenberg, Solomon, and Pyszczynski, "Terror Management Theory," 64.
20. Epstein, "Integration of the Cognitive and the Psychodynamic Unconscious," 715, 711.

nal, mode. (It was another lucky accident that the experimenters had always dressed and acted informally in their earlier studies, or else they might never have turned up any very strong mortality-salience effects to begin with.)

These findings suggest that if a religion is interested in developing and encouraging less dangerous worldviews, it will help if it can incorporate the values of rational thinking, open-mindedness, tolerance, respect for the rights of others, and benevolence—especially since mortality-salience effects include attempts not only to defend one's cultural worldview but also to live up to the values it enshrines. One might think in this connection, for example, of the Roman Catholic theologian Bernard Lonergan's effort to integrate theology and cognitional theory and his formulation of what he called the "transcendental imperatives": "be attentive, be intelligent, be reasonable, be responsible, be loving, develop and, if necessary, change."[21]

But the findings also suggest the dangerousness of cultural worldviews that encourage experiential thinking over rational, unthinking obedience to authority and tradition, and hostility toward people and groups with different views. In addition, they suggest reasons that some religious or political leaders might be tempted to encourage the experiential mode of thinking and to manipulate their followers by playing on their fear of mortal dangers from people who think differently. For a religious or political Machiavellian, this could be very useful knowledge, and there seem to have been some who have grasped this intuitively and put it to effective use. One might think, for example, of Charles Manson or the Reverend James Jones in California or Slobodan Milošević in Serbia—to mention only a few who seem to have operated as conscious Machiavellians.

A corollary implication of these findings, therefore, also seems to be that the social strength of a cultural worldview and its institutions cannot be a criterion of its ultimate value, since an authoritarian, illiberal, antirationalist worldview can be expected to be more successful at stimulating fervent devotion and strong adherence than one that encourages reflectiveness and open-mindedness. Or to put it the other way around, a cultural or religious organization that wants to encourage the latter qualities may have to be willing to sacrifice organizational strength for their sake.

The experimental results described above offer substantial confirmation for Becker's theory that fear of death is a fundamental human motive and that attempts to repress death anxiety can make human beings more dangerous

21. As phrased by his former student David Tracy in *Achievement of Bernard Lonergan,* 4.

through their relation to the worldviews they develop and defend. But they also show that the cultural worldviews people draw on from the milieu they happen to participate in can themselves have a major influence on the resulting effects. They show that mortality salience stimulates not only defense of one's worldview but also an effort to live up to its ideals, whether these are ideals of intolerance or tolerance, polarization of the world into "us" versus "them" or depolarization. Drawing out the social implications of Becker's theory and their own experimental findings, Solomon, Greenberg, and Pyszczynski suggest that "specific cultures can be judged in terms of the extent to which they (1) provide for the material needs of their members given their current level of technology and resources, (2) provide social roles that allow as many people as possible to obtain and maintain self-esteem, and (3) accomplish these first two goals without undue harm to others inside or outside of the culture." They also add that in light of what they found, the possibility of attaining all of these goals will be heightened where there is "a liberal worldview that places a high value on tolerance, open-mindedness, and respect for those who are different."[22] It will also be helpful, one might add in light of what they found regarding Seymour Epstein's ideas about "rational" as compared with "experiential" thinking, if the worldview places a high value on consciousness itself and on developing a capacity for careful, critical thought.

Becker's own contribution toward this goal, like that of Freud who inspired him, was to unmask and raise into the light powerful motives that work within us below the level of consciousness. Freud's basic hypothesis was that biological appetites (especially the sexual appetite) move us in ways we do not always consciously recognize. Becker's was that the fear of death also moves us in such ways, stimulating us to cultural hero projects and also to scapegoating. Both also assumed that the attempt to avoid recognizing these unconscious motives makes us more dangerous to ourselves and others and that bringing them to light would make us less so. They disagreed, of course, as to which motive is the most fundamental or the most important. Before returning our own focus to possible ways that rational consciousness may develop, we will consider one more school of thought that focuses on still another unconscious system of motivation: the mimetic psychology of René Girard and other mimetic theorists.

22. Solomon, Greenberg, and Pyszczynski, "Tales from the Crypt: On the Role of Death in Life," 40.

5

Mimetic Theory

René Girard and Mimetic Psychology

A broad-ranging school of thought, comprising theologians, political economists, and literary critics as well as psychologists, has developed around the idea of René Girard that the most important fundamental human motive is mimesis—by which he means not just the tendency to imitate others but specifically the tendency to imitate their desires, or at least what one perceives to be their desires.[1] This was a theme Girard developed initially in a critical study of the novel, from Cervantes to Dostoyevsky and Proust, *Deceit, Desire, and the Novel: Self and Other in Literary Structure* (or in the original French title, *Mensonge romantique et vérité romanesque* [Romantic lying and novelistic truth]). The "romantic lie" the title refers to is the naive belief that our desires originate spontaneously within what we think of as our "selves"; the "novelistic truth" is that we look to others to give us clues as to what is truly desirable. In particular, we look to prestigious others, figures who seem to possess a vitality or psychological strength beyond our own, and we imitate their desires in order to model ourselves on them and thus acquire their qualities. Girard terms this pattern of mimesis "metaphysical desire," because its real goal is the supposed "being" of the other. Behind all of our conscious

1. My earlier book *The Self Between: From Freud to the New Social Psychology of France* was a survey of these currents of thought as they developed in France from the 1960s through the 1980s.

desires for particular objects lies our real, but largely unconscious, desire for the sufficiency of being that the other embodies and exemplifies for us. "Imitative desire," says Girard, "is always a desire to be Another. There is only one metaphysical desire but the particular desires which instantiate this primordial desire are of infinite variety."[2]

Metaphysical desire as Girard describes it stems from the fear we each harbor that we are deficient in "being"—which on the most primitive level simply means to us "power." Each of us comes into the world utterly helpless, surrounded by powerful, godlike others, and we long to possess the ontological plenitude we see in them. Noticing that they desire various objects, we assume that they must want them in order to gain a still greater sufficiency of being than they already possess, and so we reach for the same objects in the hope of gaining that, too. But nothing ever assuages the vulnerability we feel, and so we continue throughout our lives looking for a model who can indicate where true "being" is to be found.

The reason we are addicted to lying about this, to repressing it, is that we are afraid to admit to ourselves the vulnerability we feel and the extent to which we feel dependent on our models of being. To acknowledge this would be to admit into consciousness that which we most flee: the fear of our own deep ontological lack. This is a point at which Girard and Becker overlap. Both see the fear of being nothing and nobody as our deepest repression, and both interpret it as driving us unconsciously to projects of becoming somebody, to hero projects, as Becker phrased it.

This fear and our tendency to imitate the desires of others in order to gain relief from it became the nucleus in Girard's thought of an intricate psychological and anthropological system. At its heart is the concept that he calls "mediation," a term for the way in which human beings model themselves on others whom they situate between themselves and their goals. Our model "mediates" for us between ourselves and our objects of desire and between our felt deficiency and the supersufficiency the mediator seems to embody and that we long to acquire. This can take the simple form of wanting what we think the other wants, but it can also go through various permutations. For example, it can become "double mediation," when the other whose supposed desires we imitate turns around and imitates ours in turn. An example Girard refers to in *Deceit, Desire, and the Novel* is the rivalry that develops in Stendhal's novel *The Red and the Black* between the Marquis de Rênal and M.

2. Girard, *Deceit, Desire, and the Novel,* 83.

Valenod, a rising bourgeois, over gaining the services of Julien Sorel. Rênal was only toying with the idea of hiring Julien as a tutor until Julien's father, sniffing the possibility of a good price, made up a story about their having a better offer. Rênal leaped to the conclusion that this must be from Valenod, a supposition that immediately turned his interest in Julien from a whim into a passion. Valenod, in Girard's terms, became the mediator of Rênal's desire to employ Julien. The real Valenod, as it happened, had never even thought about hiring a tutor, but when he subsequently heard that Rênal wanted to hire Julien, he in turn decided he must have him for himself—a perfect example of double mediation.

The truth Girard thinks a great novel discloses and that romantic lying conceals is that in human life all desire is "mediated," that is, stimulated by what we perceive as the desires of others. Several important consequences derive from this. The most obvious is that desires tend to clash and lead to conflict. If we learn what to desire by imitating the desires of others, then it is inevitable that our individual vectors of desire will sometimes converge on a single object; if that object is scarce or even unique, then competition will take place for it. When this happens, the model becomes what Girard terms a "rival model" or "model-obstacle," who not only teaches us what to desire but also tries to prevent us from attaining it. If an understanding of this principle is combined with the insight that all mimetic desire is also ultimately metaphysical and can therefore never be satisfied by the acquisition of particular objects but aims at the "being" (that is, the power) the model is felt to enjoy, then another likely consequence is that the competition of desires will become violent and even murderous as particular mundane objects become secondary and the real object, power itself, comes into view. No object can ever really satisfy our deep hunger for being, and no victory over any rival can ever provide effective assurance of our own power, since the very fact that we have defeated the rival will tell us he was not as powerful as we had thought. The inevitable trajectory of desire, therefore, according to this system, is to "escalate" as one proceeds in search of the unattainable sufficiency of "being" that could render us invulnerable.

Or if the relation to the mediator does not lead to simple rivalry, another consequence can be masochistic identification. In this case, the subject, seeking the plenitude of being he thinks he sees in the mediator, tries to gain it imaginatively by identifying with the mediator's power and subordinating his own vulnerable existence to it. This may seem a paradox, but psychologically it is straightforward: there is no need for an individual to identify simply with himself, and if one's present identity as a weak figure provides no possibility of satisfaction, there can be a genuine thrill as well as relief in yielding oneself to a powerful other in whose power one can participate imaginatively, even if it means the crushing of the worthless weakling one previously identified with.

This way of interpreting masochism runs counter, of course, to the more common way that associates it with specifically sexual pleasure derived from submission to domination, as depicted in Leopold von Sacher-Masoch's *Venus in Furs* and theorized as a syndrome by Richard von Krafft-Ebing in *Psychopathia Sexualis* in 1886. Girard considers that sort of explanation, focusing on the sensual pleasure supposedly sought by the masochist, to be itself a version of the "romantic lying" that suppresses the psychological truth of metaphysical desire. A person who holds this view, says Girard, "does not want to delve into the truth of desire to the point where he himself would be just as much involved as the subject of his observations. By restricting the deplorable consequences of metaphysical desire to an object which the masochist, and he alone, would desire, one makes an exceptional being of him, a monster whose sentiments have nothing in common with those of 'normal' people, i.e., our own." And he adds, "It is preferable, of course, not to know that the masochist desires exactly what we ourselves desire: autonomy and a god-like self-control, his own self-esteem and the esteem of others."[3] One might ask why Girard focuses on the masochist and not on the sadist. The reason is that he thinks masochism reveals the real truth of metaphysical desire. The sadist is a person still lost in the romantic dream of power to satisfy his desires. He has not yet realized that neither the power he longs for nor the satisfaction he would pursue with it is his to possess. The masochist does not yet realize the full truth, since he still believes in the power of the sadist, but realizing that power is not in himself, he is further along on the path to the truth that it will never be found anywhere.

For Girard, this truth is more than just psychological. It also has important theological implications, since to the ordinary religious mind divinity is closely tied up with the symbolism of power, and one might even say that before the truth about mimetic, metaphysical desire is realized, religion gravitates toward being masochistically structured. "In the experience which originates the mediation," he says, "the subject recognizes in himself an extreme weakness. It is this weakness that he wants to escape in the illusory divinity of the

3. Ibid., 183.

Other. The subject is ashamed of his life and his mind. In despair at not being God, he searches for the sacred in everything which threatens his life, in everything which thwarts his mind." This last point is why Girard says, "The truth of metaphysical desire is death. This is the inevitable end of the contradiction on which that desire is based." Hence, "the will to make oneself God is a will to self-destruction which is gradually realized."[4]

Violence and the sacred, therefore, go hand in hand, as the title of Girard's next major book, *Violence and the Sacred,* suggests: "Violent opposition," he says there, "is the signifier of ultimate desire, of divine self-sufficiency, of that 'beautiful totality' whose beauty depends on its being inaccessible and impenetrable." As long as he never realizes the insidious dynamics of the process he is caught up in, the desirer will proceed endlessly "to an even greater violence and seek out an obstacle that promises to be truly insurmountable." "Desire," says Girard, "clings to violence and stalks it like a shadow because violence is the signifier of the cherished being, the signifier of divinity."[5]

To the mind of desire—which is what the religious mind, like any other, ordinarily tends to be—God is the embodiment of supreme power, the ultimate owner and holder of all that is desirable. As a theological thinker, Girard, despite his own Roman Catholicism, resembles the Protestant Karl Barth, who distinguished sharply between "religion" and "the gospel" and said that religion is man seeking God, whereas the gospel is God seeking man.[6] What Barth meant is that human beings, governed by original sin, constantly manufacture divinity in their own image; the gospel, on the other hand, the message of who and what Jesus Christ is as one who did not seek power but "emptied himself" (Phil. 2:7), overturns human imagination and thinking. It is the communication of God's radical transcendence, his complete difference from every image of power and majesty that human beings tend to project onto him.

Girard's own version of this critique is that religion is the natural product of the mechanism of mimetic desire as, pursuing its natural trajectory, it accidentally stumbles on the device that delivers it from the self-destruction that by itself it hurtles toward. This device is the victimizing or scapegoat mechanism, another point at which Girard and Becker converge (see Becker's reference to "narcissistic scapegoating" in Chapter 4). Left prisoner to the de-

4. Ibid., 282, 287.

5. Girard, *Violence and the Sacred,* 148, 151.

6. For an explicit expression of Girard's Roman Catholic loyalty, see his *Quand ces choses commenceront . . . : Entretiens avec Michel Treguer.* For Barth on "the gospel" versus "religion," see *The Word of God and the Word of Man,* 41–50.

sires that drive them to seek unattainable objects and invincible rivals, human beings would generate such a chaos of violence that each would have died its victim long ago, and human life as such would have ended. But our early ancestors, Girard hypothesizes, were saved from this situation by the same mimetic tendency that got them into it: just as their mimesis of each other's desires produces general rivalry, so the mimesis of each other's hostility leads to the focusing of their violence on a common victim.

Chance, says Girard, will lead at some point to two or more fighting a single opponent, and this will attract the mimesis of others, so that eventually they will form a group, unified by their opposition to the individual or other group they gang up on. Collectively, they find themselves delivered by this from mutual random violence and united in solidarity with fellow enemies of the one whom the victimizing mechanism leads them to see as embodying all threats. Thus, the anarchic violence that might have destroyed them all becomes transformed in their experience into a creative struggle against "evil." Standing over the body of their victim, they feel blessed and at peace with one another through this "polarization of violence onto a single victim who substitutes for all the others."[7] The enemy who was first hated as the source of the evil among them thus becomes in their eyes the source of the peace and brotherhood they now experience.

Girard sees this as the moment in which religion, the sense of the sacred, sacrifice, and society are all born—and they go hand in hand. The ambiguous power of the scapegoat to generate both violence and peace, hatred and love, is the reason, according to Girard, for the ambiguity of the sacred analyzed by phenomenologists of religion such as Rudolf Otto and Mircea Eliade—as *mysterium tremendum et fascinans,* something beyond intellectual comprehension and simultaneously terrifying and powerfully attractive. Religion is born as the effort to preserve the reconciling (atoning) effect of this life-giving death by its commemoration through rites of sacrifice and by the prohibition of further violence among those it has united.

This means, of course, that Girard's attitude toward religion (as a human product) is more positive than Barth's, since he sees it as the source of peace and the foundation of society. But it remains a mask worn by violence, and the scapegoat remains a victim. As in the story of Israel and the Amalekites that was mentioned in the previous chapter in connection with Becker's critique of

7. Girard with Jean-Michel Oughourlian and Guy Lefort, *Things Hidden since the Foundation of the World,* 161.

scapegoating, the natural tendency of religion is not necessarily toward peace and universal love but quite commonly toward the kind of polarized violence that sets a divinely favored "us" against a "them" that is the embodiment of evil and the object of divine wrath. As it was for Barth, the Christian faith, for Girard, is in essence—and despite its historical accretion of a great deal of ordinary religiousness—the true opposite of this natural development. Girard considers Christianity, properly understood, to be completely *super*natural because its essence is inconceivable from the point of view of human desire, violence, and fascination with power. It entered the world in the person of Jesus as the one who with full consciousness saw through the scapegoat mechanism and unmasked it once and for all. This was the secret "hidden since the foundation of the world" referred to in Matthew 13:35 and Luke 11:50–51 (and alluded to, of course, in the title of Girard's *Things Hidden since the Foundation of the World*).[8] This secret was hidden because of the reluctance of human beings to face the reality of their own mimetic and violent motives, and the device for hiding it was the scapegoat on whom it was projected. It also had to be hidden in normal human life because as the source of society, religion, and culture generally, the victimizing mechanism had to be shielded from direct knowledge in order that it might perform its covert foundational work.

This, says Girard, is why Jesus was rejected and put to death: the truth he exposed would have undermined the world as the ordinary person knows it. This is also why the Gospels refer to Satan as the "prince of this world": he is the Bible's mythic image of conflictual mimetism and of the victimizing mechanism. Satan, the victim's "adversary" or "accuser" (the meaning of his name in Hebrew), is the source and ruler of the institutions and practices that hold together the world of our ordinary lives. As Girard put it in *The Scapegoat,* "The kingdom of Satan is not one among others. The Gospels state explicitly that Satan is the principle of every kingdom."[9] When Jesus refused to bow down to Satan, he was refusing to play the world's game, and when he taught that his own kingdom was not of this world, he threatened the world's very foundation. Jesus therefore became a scapegoat to those who crucified him, but it was a role he himself saw through and rejected.

For Girard this, then, is the heart of the gospel: the revelation of the role that violence and the victimizing mechanism have played in all human affairs and the announcement that there is another way, a way of nonviolence

8. See ibid., 159–60, 164.
9. Girard, *The Scapegoat,* 187.

without victimization. Girard sees this as the culmination of the entire biblical tradition, in which it was prefigured by the story of Job[10]—who rejected the suggestion of his "comforters" that he had somehow deserved to be the victim of the misfortunes that befell him—and by the gradually unfolding teaching of the prophets that God does not want sacrifice and that he has called his people Israel to stand on the side of the victim rather than on that of the victimizers. In all the religious history leading up to Jesus, says Girard, this message was effectively buried, but in the case of Jesus and the Gospels that re-present him, the dangerous truth cannot be fully obscured: "The Passion reveals the scapegoat mechanism, i.e., that which should remain invisible if these forces are to maintain themselves. By revealing that mechanism and the surrounding mimeticism, the Gospels set in motion the only textual mechanism that can put an end to humanity's imprisonment in the system of mythological representation based on the false transcendence of a victim who is made sacred because of the unanimous verdict of guilt."[11]

Girard thinks this revelation or exposure of the truth offers both hope and genuine danger. The hope is that when the mechanisms of mimesis and victimization are effectively unmasked, they will also be disarmed; the realization that desire is mimetic breaks its enchantment, and the realization that one is scapegoating makes it difficult to carry on doing so. The danger, however, is that as the scapegoat mechanism becomes more transparent it also becomes less effective at stopping the chain of violence that threatens society. In a world that has digested both too much and not quite enough of the truth revealed in the Gospels, there is an increasing danger of runaway violence. As Girard put it in *Things Hidden,* "Human beings, confronted with this situation, will be tempted to restore the lost effectiveness of the traditional remedy by forever increasing the dosage, immolating more and more victims."[12]

The modern world—seeded, ironically, by the Gospels it tends to reduce to just another myth—has destroyed religion, one might say, but has still failed to grasp the gospel. This deprives us, says Girard, of the only effective cultural device in history that has so far functioned to deliver us from runaway violence. Since those of us who have come this far can no longer return to our earlier naive belief in scapegoats, Girard believes that the only solution to our

10. The story of Job is the focus of Girard's book *Job: The Victim of His People.*
11. Girard, *The Scapegoat,* 166.
12. Girard, *Things Hidden,* 128.

dilemma will be to proceed forward to full consciousness of that which was hidden and is now revealed, to a truly radical renunciation of violence, and to transcendence of the mimetic mechanisms on which it is founded.

Mimesis and Human Evolution

In their highlighting of the problem of scapegoating, we can see that despite their basic differences of approach, Becker and Girard converge on a single problem: the tendency of worldviews, under some circumstances, to become polarized, dividing the world into a "their" side and an "our" side, a side of demonic evil and a side of the angels. Both thinkers describe human life as an imaginative project of, in Becker's phrase, "heroic victory over evil by a traffic in pure power."[13] For both, the fear of being or becoming nothing and nobody is a powerful psychological motive, and both think the half-conscious efforts we make to deal with that fear tend to lead toward victimization. For Becker, the victim is the object onto whom we project everything about ourselves that reminds us of our potential death; for Girard, the victim is the chance point of convergence of vectors of hostility growing out of a competition of mimetic desires. Both hope that knowledge of how these unconscious processes operate will help people to avoid letting their thinking and action be unconsciously controlled by them.

Becker's hypotheses have been tested experimentally, with results that offer strong support to the idea of an unconscious fear of death that leads us to become defensive about our own worldview and aggressive toward those who represent competing ones. No group of experimentalists has directly taken up Girard's hypotheses for testing, and his theory of society (and language, religion, and even human consciousness as such) as founded on victimization is so broad and speculative that it is hard to imagine how all of it could be tested—although the twentieth century offered plenty of evidence that scapegoating does take place on a massive social scale and at least circumstantial evidence that it can play an important role in generating class, party, or national solidarity.

Girard's hypothesis about mimesis as a fundamental human motive, on the other hand, has received considerable indirect experimental support in the work of people studying imitative behavior among children (and in the recent

13. Becker, *Escape from Evil,* 150.

neurological discovery of "mirror neurons," as will be discussed below).[14] Girard's associate Dr. Jean-Michel Oughourlian, a psychiatrist in Paris and one of his collaborators on *Things Hidden,* referred in his own book *The Puppet of Desire* to a study by Andrew N. Meltzoff and M. Keith Moore that reported on experiments showing that imitation of facial gestures, which Jean Piaget had thought could take place only after about eight to twelve months, could in fact take place within two to three weeks.[15] The same investigators have since found that the starting point for such learning is much earlier, within the first hour after birth. They consider this "the starting point of infant psychological development" and "an important building block for subsequent social and cognitive development."[16] Their subsequent research has followed up by studying the ways that infant imitation of the acts of others is integral to their forming an understanding of the world around them. Jean Piaget held that infants come to know things through acting on them; Meltzoff and Moore suggest that "imitation is to understanding people as physical manipulation is to understanding things" and that "infants see other people in terms of human acts and, in imitating them, intend to match these acts."[17]

Since this type of imitation is conscious—Meltzoff and Moore think "early imitation is a goal-directed, intentional activity"—it may not seem to connect directly with the focus of either Girard or Becker and the terror management theorists on unconscious motives. But if the motive to imitate is so fundamental and innate that it begins to operate immediately after birth and continues to expand its scope throughout early life, this suggests it may operate also below the level of consciousness, just as it also suggests that the tendency to imitate is there because it has played an important role in the evolution of our species.[18]

14. For a survey of biological research pertinent to the Girardian mimetic hypothesis, see William Hurlbutt, "Mimesis and Empathy in Human Biology."

15. Meltzoff and Moore, "Imitation of Facial and Manual Gestures by Human Neonates," 75–78, cited in Oughourlian, *Puppet of Desire,* 7–8.

16. Meltzoff and Moore, "Newborn Infants Imitate Adult Facial Gestures," 708; Meltzoff and Moore, "Imitation in Newborn Infants: Exploring the Range of Gestures Imitated and the Underlying Mechanisms," 954.

17. Meltzoff and Moore, "Imitation, Memory, and the Representation of Persons," 96; Meltzoff and Moore, "Infants' Understanding of People and Things: From Body Imitation to Folk Psychology," 54.

18. Meltzoff and Moore, "Infants' Understanding," 51. That a tendency to imitate is particularly strong in the human species due to its particular evolution is suggested by the research of psychologists comparing the learning behavior of chimpanzees with that of human three and four year olds. See Victoria Horner and Andrew Whiten, "Causal Knowledge and Imitation/Emulation Switching in Chimpanzees *(Pan troglodytes)* and Children *(Homo sapiens).*"

Another psychologist, Merlin Donald, independently of any of the above, has developed a theory of cognitive evolution, from primates through early hominids to *Homo sapiens,* that also hypothesizes a central and essential role for mimesis, which, like Meltzoff and Moore, he too conceives of as conscious and intentional but also considers innate. He thinks that the capacity to imitate evolved prior to linguistic ability and that it was an essential building block in the development of human cognition. He traces cognitive evolution through a series of stages beginning with episodic cognition among the great apes and other higher mammals and ending with mythic and theoretic cognition and culture in *Homo sapiens.*

Episodic cognition consists of the ability to grasp a concrete situation and remember it, but with little or no grasp of abstract pattern in that situation, which tends to be remembered with pattern and detail indiscriminately mixed. Accompanying episodic memory there is also procedural memory, which is still more primitive and is shared with lower species as well. It consists of memory of how to perform operations that have been learned. Apes are able to employ episodic and procedural memory to solve problems—as in the case of Wolfgang Köhler's famous experiments with chimpanzees that learned to use boxes and poles to reach bananas. But with episodic cognition alone, they have a very limited ability to abstract a pattern from the mass of detail it is embedded in. (One can get a good sense of what episodic cognition is like from listening to the way a young child recounts a story.)

Mythic cognition, of which we find the first evidence in *Homo sapiens,* uses narrative structure to organize its data. Every human mind that reaches later childhood learns to think by way of narrative, and this always remains the most common medium for thought and communication (notice how much of the conversation around a typical kitchen table consists of narrative).[19] The further transition to theoretic thinking is challenging and in most lives is not even necessary except for special purposes; in evolution, theoretic thinking is both late and rare. The real problem in cognitive evolution is how to account for the millennia-long transition from episodic cognition to mythic. Donald thinks there is a need for an intermediate developmental step to link that first stage with the later ones. This is where mimesis comes in.

19. For a full exposition of the idea that the basic form of human thought is narrative, see Mark Turner, *The Literary Mind.* Turner is a literary scholar who has been working in collaboration with cognitive scientists on this topic.

The first hominid species, *Australopithecus afarensis*, appeared in Africa about four million years ago, where it lived in the same small region for millions of years—suggesting it had no special cognitive abilities beyond those of the apes it lived among. *Homo erectus*, which appeared about one and a half million years ago and survived until about three hundred thousand years ago, was quite another matter. This hominid developed a variety of sophisticated tools and spread widely over the Eurasian landmass, adapting to a wide variety of climates and living in complex societies in which cooperation was essential. It engaged in cooperative hunting, and it used fire and cooked food. Its extensive use of tools indicates it had a technique for training others in their use. Since *Homo erectus* seems not to have had language with which to do this, it must have had some other system of communication.

Donald therefore offers the hypothesis that *erectus* used imitation as a means of communication and that this became the basis of a mimetic culture that functioned for more than a million years. Although there is no way it could be proved that mimetic skills served as the basis of the culture of *Homo erectus*, Donald thinks that without this as a hypothesis there would be no way, in view of the absence of language, to account for the vast differences between *erectus*'s achievements and those of prior hominids and apes. Imitation clearly would have a great deal to contribute as a means of rehearsing and refining a skill on the part of an individual and of teaching and training skills to students. Its utility for these purposes is indicated today by the fact that the pedagogy of tribal societies is still primarily mimetic in character, as is instruction in manual skills even in our own culture. (Would you prefer to learn something by reading an instruction manual or by watching it done?)

Even more important, mimesis could make representation possible through the invention of symbolic gestures, the gesture serving as a representation of what it imitates. Although mimesis is a more primitive form of symbolic representation than language, it would make possible the ability to reflect on the representation and to abstract patterns from it, distinguishing between essential and accidental features, selecting the essential for miming and ignoring the rest. Also, miming is referential. When one uses it, one recognizes the difference between the mimetic act itself and the acts it mimes. (A dog's episodic cognition enables it to recognize a fight episode when it sees one, but a dog cannot tell the difference between a play fight and a real one.)

Mimetic culture would also make new forms of social organization possible. Ritual is an inherently mimetic activity, and since ritual is a basic instrument of social organization in all known human societies but is not necessarily dependent on language, it might account for how prelinguistic *Homo erectus* was able to develop forms of social organization much more elaborate than anything found among species with strictly episodic cognitive capacities.

Another valuable contribution mimesis could make to this is music. Melody, harmony, and rhythm are all essentially mimetic and do not depend on language. One of the main effects of music easily noticeable today is its power to conform members of a group to a common pattern of feeling (that is, induce inner mimesis of each other's feelings) and thereby to instill a sense of group identity. There are tribal groups in our own world who "own" songs and identify themselves through them.

Although Donald concentrates on imitation as a conscious, intentional activity, his hypothesis does not imply a need to limit mimesis to it, especially since to perform all its prelinguistic functions it seems logical that it would have to be deeply rooted in our biology, and as in the case of Becker's hypothesis there are now experimental studies that support that theory. That there is in fact a biologically rooted capacity for preconscious imitation has been shown by the discovery of "mirror neurons" in monkeys in 1996 by a team of researchers led by Giacomo Rizzolatti, a neuroscientist at the University of Parma, and by the subsequent discovery that humans have an elaborate network of systems of mirror neurons located in several areas of the brain, including the premotor cortex, the posterior parietal lobe, the superior temporal sulcus, and the insula. Extensive research since then has shown that these systems of mirror neurons play an essential role in enabling humans, through inward neurological imitation, to understand and empathize with the actions of others, their intentions, and the social meaning of their behavior and their emotions.[20] Patricia Greenfield, a psychologist who studies human development, has said that mirror neurons provide a powerful biological foundation for the evolution of culture. Until now, scholars have treated culture as fundamentally separate from biology, she says, "but now we see that mirror neurons absorb culture directly, with each generation teaching the next by social sharing, imitation and observation."[21]

20. See Mirella Dapretto et al., "Understanding Emotions in Others: Mirror Neuron Dysfunction in Children with Autism Spectrum Disorders"; Marco Iacoboni et al., "Grasping the Intentions of Others with One's Own Mirror Neuron System"; and John P. Murray et al., "Children's Brain Activations while Viewing Televised Violence Revealed by MRI." Sandra Blakeslee summarizes this research in "Cells That Read Minds" (*New York Times*, January 10, 2006).

21. Quoted in Blakeslee, "Cells That Read Minds," n.p.

These forms of neurological mimesis take place automatically within the brain, prior to any conscious intention. If one can think of this type of inward mimesis as operating preconsciously in ways that range widely with regard to learning and empathy, mimesis would explain something that sociologists of knowledge, such as Peter Berger and Thomas Luckmann, have described but not explained: that confident belief in a worldview depends to a large extent on social confirmation. In *The Social Construction of Reality: A Treatise in the Sociology of Knowledge,* Berger and Luckmann analyze most of what people believe in any given society (their cultural worldview) as made up not of knowledge in the strict sense (that is, knowledge based on methodical procedures of observation, interpretation, and verification) but of "knowledge" in a phenomenological sense. As Berger phrases it in *The Sacred Canopy,* this is "the cognitive and normative edifice that passes for 'knowledge' in a given society." Strictly speaking, it is not *known* as true (rationally) but only *perceived* as true (phenomenologically). That is, it is taken for true, not on the ground that it can stand up to critical inquiry but only that it somehow feels right because it is what "everyone" thinks. It is, in Berger and Luckmann's terms, a social "objectivation" that the members of society "internalize."[22] Social belief is a function of the strength of this internalization—and internalization is difficult to do as an isolated individual. As Berger explains it:

> Man's world-building activity is always a collective enterprise. Man's internal appropriation of a world must also take place in a collectivity. . . . [T]he internalization of a world is dependent on society . . . because . . . man is incapable of conceiving of his experience in a comprehensively meaningful way unless such a conception is transmitted to him by means of social processes. . . . The world is built up in the consciousness of the individual by conversation with significant others (such as parents, teachers, "peers"). The world is maintained as subjective reality by the same sort of conversation. . . . If such conversation is disrupted . . . the world begins to totter, to lose its subjective plausibility.[23]

This idea also finds an echo in Jean-Michel Oughourlian's theory of "universal mimesis" as a form of social gravitation, which he describes as a "natural force of cohesion, which alone grants access to the social, to language, to

22. Berger and Luckmann, *Social Construction of Reality,* 1–3, 19–28; Berger, *Sacred Canopy,* 20; Berger and Luckmann, *Social Construction of Reality,* 129–73.

23. Berger, *Sacred Canopy,* 16–17.

culture, and indeed to humanness itself . . . simultaneously mysterious and obvious, hidden in and of itself, but dazzling in its effects—like gravity and the attraction of corporeal masses in Newtonian space."[24] Mimesis would explain psychologically why a collective belief is easier than individual judgment: from the point of view of mimetic psychology, the preconscious imitation of others' attitudes would automatically draw us into thinking the way others around us think, and if the others constituted a community of belief (or even of convincingly apparent belief), it would take effort to resist believing along with the group. Oughourlian likens mimesis to the gravitational pull of mass: "Mass correlates closely with quantity. The mimesis that a crowd triggers, the power of influence a group has, is proportional to the number of individuals in it. It is this prodigious magnification of the force of mimesis that explains the difference between the psychology of individuals and mob psychology and the stupendous transformations that the former can undergo when influenced by the mimetic power of a group, a crowd, or a mob." This is why he speaks of psychology and sociology as "two sciences that are artificially separated, but which in reality make up a single science."[25] Oughourlian himself uses the idea of mimesis as a fundamental psychological motive to explain the phenomena of possession, exorcism, and hypnosis as well as what Freud called the psychopathology of everyday life. But as his analogy to gravitation indicates, he does not consider it responsible only for pathology. Without mimesis and its effects, it would be difficult to understand how either learning or empathy could ever develop.

The importance of mimesis for learning and empathy is indicated by many experimental studies in addition to those mentioned earlier. Mabel Rice and Linda Woodsmall, for example, report that children learn new words more easily when they see them being used by others on television. Richard J. Davidson and Nathan A. Fox studied human infants by measuring the brain waves of ten month olds watching videotapes depicting an actress acting out the expression of various emotions by laughing, crying, and so on.[26] The children's

24. Oughourlian, *Puppet of Desire,* 2. Oughourlian wrote this book before the discovery of mirror neurons, but his more recent book, *Genèse du Désir,* devotes a chapter to the subject. I am currently preparing a translation of the latter for publication by Michigan State University Press.

25. Oughourlian, *Puppet of Desire,* 3–4, 7.

26. Rice and Woodsmall, "Lessons from Television: Children's Word Learning When Viewing"; Davidson and Fox, "Patterns of Brain Electrical Activity during Facial Signs of Emotion in 10–Month-Old Infants."

brain waves showed that as they watched, they experienced inwardly the emotions they saw enacted. As was the case in the studies of Meltzoff and Moore, Davidson's and Fox's purpose was simply to find a way to see if children so young could learn something from watching television, but they found also that babies had emotional reactions that mimicked the ones they watched.

Other researchers have found that a virtually automatic inward imitation of the feelings of others occurs even before a child acquires the sense that it exists apart from other people at all. Leslie Brothers notes, "Studies of human and non-human primate infants reveal the presence of innate and early responses to facial expressions."[27] Brothers has been especially interested in identifying the brain circuits and neurons essential to these emotional responses and has shown in the process that monkeys, too, are evidently capable of empathy, since particular neurons in their brains are triggered by their seeing facial expressions.

The regions of the cortex where these neurons are located is an area where there is a particularly dense network of links to the amygdala. This suggests that the ability to mimic inwardly the feelings of others is hardwired into the system by evolution in such a way that it can operate with maximum speed and minimal need for the sort of analytic reflection that the cortex makes possible. The amygdala, bypassing reflective consciousness, is able to sort out its impressions and deliver responses much more quickly. But as Daniel Goleman points out in *Emotional Intelligence,* "If the amygdala senses a sensory pattern of import emerging, it jumps to a conclusion, triggering its reactions before there is full confirming evidence—or any confirmation at all. . . . The amygdala can react in a delirium of rage or fear before the cortex knows what is going on because such raw emotion is triggered independent of, and prior to, thought." Paul D. MacLean dubs this system the "reptilian brain," which he considers the remnant of an early stage of evolution that continues to function in us and to which we can regress, especially when heightened anxiety triggers it.[28] As the terror management theorists found in the experiments described in Chapter 4, what the "gut" thinking of the lower brain generally is not good at is protecting us against oversimplification and polarized worldviews, but as

27. Brothers, "A Biological Perspective on Empathy," 17.

28. Goleman, *Emotional Intelligence,* 24; MacLean, *The Triune Brain in Evolution: Role in Paleocerebral Functions.* MacLean's thesis is that the human brain consists of three distinct systems, which evolved at different stages of our animal history (reptilian, paleomammalian [the limbic system], and neomammalian [neocortical]) but in a way that keeps them interdependently connected.

they also found, higher-order, cortical, functioning can also be evoked, and when it is it *can* help protect us against such reptilian regression.

Both death anxiety and mimesis seem to be lower-order functions that have played an essential evolutionary role in enabling human beings to survive and reproduce, and without them our lives would be impoverished—especially if, as Brothers argues, mimesis plays an essential role in empathy. But death anxiety and mimesis are at least half-blind and are likely, given time, to lead us into the pitfalls Becker and Girard describe unless a more actively reflective mode of consciousness is cultivated.

From Psychology to Theology

The Limits of Psychological Theory

As we prepare to turn from the preceding survey of psychological factors that may shape minds and influence worldviews to an examination of patterns of religious thinking in light of these factors, it will be helpful to reflect on some of the problems of applying psychological theories to the analysis of religious phenomena. One obvious problem with theories focused on the psychology of the unconscious is that they may reduce religious thought, aspirations, and behavior to mere epiphenomena of impersonal forces that are thought to drive religion, as it were, from behind. They may even attempt to explain religious thought and aspirations as mere "symptoms" of an underlying psychological disorder. Freudian approaches have been notorious for this, which is one reason that in my consideration of psychologies of the unconscious, instead of discussing Freud in particular, I have focused on other figures with less tendency to reductionism. (I will, however, give more attention to Freud's thought and some of his specific criticisms of religion in what follows, especially in Chapter 8, on religion and personhood.)

Discussing psychologies of consciousness, I focused on thinkers in the tradition of Piaget who discuss the development of consciousness through stages. Here too there could be potential problems. One is that religion itself might be thought of as a stage that one either grows into after developing through other earlier ones or that one grows out of, depending on whether a particular theorist might view religion favorably or unfavorably. Sometimes Freud, who also thought about developmental stages, hoped religion might be outgrown, and at other times he despaired of humanity ever being able to outgrow it. Lawrence Kohlberg, on the other hand, began with a set of six stages he thought of as strictly psychological, but eventually found himself led, as will be discussed below, to speculate about a further seventh stage that began to look more theological than psychological.

Still another potential problem is that if the idea of psychological stages is applied too rigidly, it may entail the supposition that everything about a given religious person, movement, or group may be thought explicable as the expression of a developmental stage that is assumed to be massively deterministic in its functioning. A given phenomenon might be assumed, that is, to be the necessary result of the way a "stage X" person could be expected to think—as though a person who has developed to a certain stage must always think in a particular manner characteristic of that stage.

To interpret developmental stage theory in such a way may seem all too natural when one thinks of stages, in Piaget's manner, as rooted in structures as distinct and inevitable as those exhibited in the development of, say, a caterpillar into a butterfly or an acorn into a sapling. Piaget's own original training was not in psychology but in biology, and it is worth remembering that his notion of a psychological structure is a metaphorical adaptation of the structures he first encountered in the study of insects and plants. This, coupled with the general prestige in our culture of the "hard" sciences, may have led Piaget and some of those who came after him to conceive of developmental stages less flexibly than is really appropriate for human development.

Lawrence Kohlberg said that, like Piaget's, his own was a "hard structural stage" model in which each stage is founded on "an organization of manifest thought operations."[1] He therefore began by looking for "hard" structural stages, although over time he found that he eventually had to reduce these to something "softer" in order to take account of the human reality he and his associates actually observed. According to hard structural stage theory, as new thought operations become possible, a new psychological structure develops as a transformation of an earlier one, with the operations of the old

1. Kohlberg, *Essays on Moral Development,* 2:244.

one "hierarchically integrated" into the new one in combination with new operations employed to new purposes.[2] As Kohlberg himself described it:

> Within the Kohlberg model, the interiorized forms of action that the operations represent are prescriptive forms of role-taking in concrete moral situations. The Kohlberg stage model, then, represents the different hierarchically integrated forms of the operations of reciprocity, equality, and equity. For Piaget and for ourselves, justice is the structure of conflict resolution for a dilemma of competing claims between or among persons. It is the parallel in the social world to the structure of logical thought in the physical world. The justice operations of reciprocity and equality in social interaction parallel the logical and mathematical operations of reciprocity and equality in science and mathematics. In both the logical and justice domains, the use of operations imply equilibrated or reversible systems which we call hard structures.[3]

Kohlberg insisted on the distinctness of his psychological stages even more emphatically than did Piaget. Just as Piaget had preoperational, concrete operational, and formal operational stages, Kohlberg's six moral stages fall into a larger grouping of three levels that he called preconventional, conventional, and postconventional.[4] Kohlberg considered each successive stage to represent

2. "Soft stages," as compared with "hard" ones, add new developmental elements to earlier ones but do not fundamentally transform a person's mental organization.

3. Ibid., 244–45.

4. I do not want to burden the reader with too many stage theories, but the following, purposely simplified, table (based on his own summary in the appendix, "The Six Stages of Moral Judgment," in ibid., 1:409–12) may help the reader who is interested in the particulars of Kohlberg's stages:

Preconventional level
Stage 1. Punishment and Obedience
Stage 2. Individual Instrumental Purpose and Exchange
Conventional level
Stage 3. Mutual Interpersonal Expectations, Relationships, and Conformity
Stage 4. Social System and Conscience Maintenance
Postconventional, Principled level
Stage 5. Prior Rights and Social Contract and Utility
Stage 6. Universal Ethical Principles

The preconventional level comprises two stages. The first, "Punishment and Obedience," involves no reciprocity at all; the child is completely egocentric and has no sense of the interests of others. In the second stage, right is serving one's own needs while letting others do the same and making fair deals in terms of concrete exchange, the most rudimentary form of reciprocity.

The level of conventional morality also has two stages. In stage 3, "Mutual Interpersonal Expectations, Relationships, and Conformity," there is a more developed awareness of and concern for the feelings of others. The principle of action becomes what Kohlberg called "the concrete

an advance building on the lower ones in a necessary sequence, and he considered their distinctness and sequentiality to be proven by empirical studies.[5]

Kohlberg did, however, revise his interpretation of his findings over the course of time. Early on, he thought he had found examples of all of his six stages among children and adolescents. Later he reconsidered this, deciding that no subject exhibited his stage 5 thinking before age twenty-four and that only 5 percent did by age twenty-five, with only 13 percent reaching it by age thirty-two.[6] In the case of his sixth stage, that of universal ethical principles, not only its developmental timing but even the question of its empirical reality eventually disturbed Kohlberg's schema. He thought at one time that he had found stage 6 even among adolescents, but he later said that he incor-

---

Golden Rule," putting oneself in another's shoes. (It is concrete in that the imaginative role taking it involves is limited to the particular instance—how this particular other would feel if I did or failed to do this particular act.) What is right is living up to the particular expectations of those close to one or to what is generally expected of people in the socially defined roles one fills. There is no "system" perspective in the moral framework of this stage, and obligations are primarily personal.

The difference that comes with stage 4, "Social System and Conscience Maintenance," is the expansion of perspective to include the social order as a whole. Laws, contracts, and other forms of general obligation come to seem important as a system that serves the general welfare, and justice is thought of as living up to such obligations in order to contribute to society. (Kohlberg also came eventually to speak of a stage 4.5 that is transitional between the conventional and the postconventional levels of moral thinking—which further complicates, of course, the question of how many stages he thought there were. This transitional stage involves the realization that there can be other general perspectives than that of one's own society, but it does not yet include any basis other than arbitrary personal preference for choosing which social values to choose and which to reject.)

Kohlberg considered the truly postconventional level of moral thinking to be characterized by principled choice falling under some general rule, not just social norms. His stage 5 takes a "prior-to-society" perspective, one aware of values and rights more fundamental than social attachments and contracts. Stage 6, "Universal Ethical Principles," "assumes guidance by universal ethical principles that all humanity should follow." It "takes the perspective of a moral point of view from which social arrangements derive or on which they are grounded. The perspective is that of any rational individual recognizing the nature of morality or the basic moral premise of respect for other persons as ends, not means" (ibid., 412). The Kantian echo here is significant, because the very idea of the sixth stage in Kohlberg's schema is based on the logical implications of the Kantian deontological approach to ethics, as I will explain below.

5. Such as a study done in 1983 that, Kohlberg said, showed downward stage movement in only 4 percent of cases and at most by only a half stage, with not a single instance of stage skipping (ibid., 2:208). On average, 67 percent of an individual's thinking was found in this study to exhibit the characteristics of a single dominant stage, with the rest showing those of an adjacent stage. Cross-cultural studies of stages in Turkey and Israel showed results similar to those among American subjects. Kohlberg said that research in the United States, Britain, Turkey, Taiwan, and Yucatán found that moral thinking takes the same six forms everywhere and that their forms "constitute an invariant sequence of stages in each culture" (1:40).

6. Ibid., 2:458.

rectly attributed this stage to some of them because it shared some features with his stage 4. In the introductory note to part 1 of the first volume of his *Essays,* Kohlberg said that he had come to believe stage 6 was "a rare stage of adult development." Still later he questioned even this, saying, "We no longer claim that our empirical work has succeeded in defining the nature of a sixth and highest stage of moral judgment. The existence and nature of such a stage is, at this moment, a matter of theoretical and philosophical speculation and further empirical data collection." His further data collection seems to have produced no evidence, however, because still later again he said, "Stage 6 has disappeared as a commonly identified form of moral reasoning as our stage-scoring concepts and criteria have developed from the continuing analysis of our longitudinal data. None of our longitudinal subjects in the United States, Israel, or Turkey have attained it."[7] Although he continued to say that on both philosophical and psychological grounds he and his coworkers still hypothesized a stage 6, he also acknowledged they could not verify it empirically.

Why, then, did Kohlberg think his sixth stage had to be postulated? One reason, more philosophical than psychological, is that he was studying moral development in particular and that the very idea of the sixth stage in Kohlberg's schema is based on the logical implications of the Kantian deontological approach to ethics. Like Piaget in his own work on moral development, Kohlberg began his investigations and carried most of them out with Kantian moral assumptions.[8] He wrote, for example, "Like most deontological moral philosophers since Kant, I define morality in terms of the formal character of the moral judgment, method, or point of view, rather than in terms of its content." He said that it was on this basis that he judged stage 6 as the most adequate: because it is the most universal and prescriptive in character.[9]

Formalistic deontology, however, is only one of several ways ethics can be conceived, whether in philosophical or in religious thinking. Its major historical competitor in both domains has been the eudaemonistic ethic deriving from Aristotle, which focused on the importance of forming good habits ("virtues") conducive to a satisfying life and ultimate happiness. Deontology conceives of the good in terms of duty, eudaemonism in terms of fulfillment

7. Ibid., 1:5, 2:215, 270.

8. See Piaget, *The Moral Judgment of the Child.*

9. Kohlberg, *Essays on Moral Development,* 1:170. "I am claiming that developmental theory assumes formalistic criteria of adequacy, the criteria of levels of *differentiation* and *integration.* In the moral domain, these criteria are parallel to formalistic moral philosophy's criteria of *prescriptivity* and *universality*" (171).

or the enjoyment of well-being. Kant argued that since to be human is to be rational, it is a demand of our nature as rational beings that we should always be governed by reason, and since desire is nonrational, its satisfaction and the enjoyment deriving from that can never be a properly ethical motive. In his early writings, Kohlberg explicitly espoused deontology and rejected the Aristotelian idea of virtue.

In this, too, however, as with the question of the existence of his stage 6, he seems to have softened his position over time and to have become more flexible about the need to fit his material into a framework both of hard structural stages and of Kantian deontology. He later wrote, "We cannot claim either that there is a single principle which we have found used at the current empirically highest stage [that is, stage 5], nor that that principle is the principle of justice or respect for persons. There may be other principles," which he listed as agape (a theological term for the self-giving love of God), benevolence, or utility. He also wrote at that time that "our assumption of cognitivism, unlike Kantian rationalism, does not deny affect as an integral component of moral judgment or justice reasoning," and he went on to say that affect in the form of empathy with both the agent's motive and the persons affected is essential to the role-taking process on which moral psychology is based.[10]

Both the logic of deontological ethics and concern with empathic love therefore led Kohlberg to speculate, beyond any empirical cases, about a sixth developmental stage that began to border on the religious, associated as it was with the idea of agape and existential questions about potentially self-transcending selfhood. A still further speculation that clearly crossed that border was the idea of a possible seventh stage of development, the essence of which, he said, "is the sense of being a part of the whole of life and the adoption of a cosmic, as opposed to a universal, humanistic stage 6 perspective."

10. Ibid., 2:273, 291. This more positive attitude toward the role of affect in ethical thinking may have developed in part in response to criticism from Carol Gilligan, who suggested that in addition to Kohlberg's morality of justice there is a morality of caring and responsibility in which decisions are not impartial and universalizable. Kohlberg accepted her point in part, saying that it would be best to think of justice and caring not as two different moralities but as poles of a continuum in which both are always interwoven. He then said, "We see justice as both rational *and* implying an attitude of empathy," and he suggested distinguishing between two types of moral judgment: "justice judgments" and "responsibility judgments," which "consider fulfilling the other's need when it is not based on a right or claim or where it is not a matter of preventing harm" (232 [emphasis in the original], 234). Responsibility judgments also consider the implication of the self in the action—the questions of the kind of self one wants to be and the kind of relationships one wants to cultivate. In practice, he said, people operating at his conventional and postconventional levels usually try to integrate both justice and care in their morality.

In the chapter devoted to stage 7, he said, "This chapter's central claim is that religion is a conscious response to, and an expression of, the quest for an ultimate meaning for moral judging and acting."[11]

One might ask, however, why this idea of a cosmic perspective should be thought of as precisely a seventh "stage." Kohlberg considered his moral stages to develop from one to the next in a logical process, and his reason for hypothesizing a stage 6 was that it seemed logically implied by the Kantian assumptions about prescriptiveness and universality that his analysis of morality is founded on: stage 6 was simply the maximum point of that line of development. To speak of the cosmically religious as a *seventh* stage, on the other hand, would seem to imply that it forms a part of the same developmental sequence, although as Kohlberg worked out his schema of the *six* moral stages, there can be no place for further moral development after the sixth, since that stage is supposed to constitute the full unfolding of the prescriptiveness and universality the previous five were developing toward.

One answer to the problem this poses might be that his stage 7's cosmic perspective does represent a type of developmental advance, even if not a *logical* or even perhaps *psychological* development but one of another kind. Kohlberg drew at one point on the language of gestalt psychology to say something of this sort:

> The center of the highest stage is experiences that are most distinctively religious experiences of union with deity, whether pantheistic or theistic. These experiences we do not interpret in a reductionistic psychological manner, as does the Freudian theory, of mystic experience as a survival of an early feeling of union with the mother. We treat it instead as both arising from, and contributing to, a new perspective. We term this new perspective "cosmic" and "infinite," although the attainment of such a perspective is only an aspiration rather than a complete possibility. The attainment of this perspective results from a new insight. Using Gestalt psychology language for describing insight, we term it a shift from figure to ground, from a centering on the self's activity and that of others to a centering on the wholeness or unity of nature or the cosmos.[12]

Another reason Kohlberg stated for thinking about a seventh stage is that at stage 6, "universal ethical principles cannot be immediately justified by the realities of the human social order." A person might wonder why it makes sense

11. Ibid., 1:345, 336.
12. Ibid., 370–71.

to obey universal moral prescriptions in a world in which, as the proverb goes, the good die young and the evil flourish like the green bay tree. Reflecting on the metaethical question "Why be moral?" someone thinking within Kohlberg's stage 6 would become aware that the universal prescriptions need some ultimate ground beyond their mere logical form, some specifiable reason for their imperative character. One traditional way of thinking in religious terms about such a ground for morality has been in terms of divine command, but Kohlberg rejected this as exogenous and heteronomous and therefore not truly ethical. Rather, he said, "we use a metaphorical notion of a 'Stage 7' to suggest some meaningful solutions to this question that are compatible with rational universal ethics. The characteristics of all these solutions is that they involve contemplative experience of a nondualistic variety."[13]

For examples of such experience he referred to philosopher Baruch Spinoza and Catholic theologian Pierre Teilhard de Chardin. In both Spinoza's and Teilhard's cases, Kohlberg asserted (as though echoing Becker) that the challenge that served as the stimulus to the development of a cosmic perspective was the inexorable fact of death. For Spinoza, hc said, our normal joys are the results of our self-actualization, but the prospect of death makes this finally unsatisfying unless we shift to the cosmic perspective: "But if we are aware of the relationship of all people and things to the whole of Nature or to God, then we continue to love the whole in spite of the disappointments and losses. And if we love life or nature, we are even able to face our own death with equanimity, because we love life more than our own particular and finite life."[14]

Teilhard, who was deeply affected by the deaths of friends, was also motivated in his cosmic theological vision by struggle with the problem of death. Kohlberg quoted Teilhard's friend Henri de Lubac as saying, "There would be no exaggeration in presenting the whole body of his work as one long meditation of death."[15] He said that Teilhard's answer to despair in the face of death was faith in his "cosmic Christ" as the embodiment of perfect love and the culminating point of divinely inspirited cosmic evolution.

The key idea in Kohlberg's conception of the seventh stage is self-transcending love. One can see, then, why his seventh would have to stand in an ambiguous

13. Ibid., 344, 337, 345.
14. Ibid., 364.
15. Lubac, *The Religion of Teilhard de Chardin*, 56, quoted in Kohlberg, *Essays on Moral Development*, 1:365.

relation to the six deontological moral stages. The golden rule only demands that you do unto others as you would have them do unto you. To love the source of all being with all your heart, soul, mind, and strength and love your neighbor as yourself is not exactly something that can be deduced as an ethical principle or a duty. Kohlberg himself realized this: when one critic of his work suggested that an alternative way to conceive of the sixth stage would be to think of it as centered on the idea of love as agape, Kohlberg responded that "agape is not a principle of justice competing with the principle of fairness as reversibility" and that "rather than replacing principles of justice, agape goes beyond them in the sense of defining or informing acts of supererogation (acts beyond duty or beyond justice)."[16] Kohlberg wanted both to analyze justice in strictly rational terms and to supplement justice with a love that respected justice but also went beyond it.

One might, however, ask why a cosmic perspective as such would lead to the birth of love. Evidently, Kohlberg assumed that confrontation with ultimate loss (that is, death) would lead through despair to a break with the perspective of self-interest and that this would be the beginning of radically self-transcending love—that the death of ego would release love to burst forth as a new life and create a correspondingly new worldview, the cosmic perspective. Comparing Spinoza and Teilhard, he said, "The personal history and thought of our examples suggests that the transition to Stage 7 begins with despair; that is, with the consideration that human life and action is in the final analysis meaningless and doomed to extinction. The experience of despair calls into question the fundamental worth of human activity. The only response to the radical questioning inherent in despair is the construction of a metaphysics capable of reaffirming what has been denied."[17]

Kohlberg thought of the ascent to stage 7 as rooted, like his own moral stages and Piaget's cognitive ones, in cognitive development. He quoted Teilhard as saying:

> Union can only increase through an increase in consciousness, that is to say, in vision. And that, doubtless, is why the history of the living world can be summarised as the elaboration of ever more perfect eyes within a cosmos in which there is always something more to be seen. . . . To try to see more and better is not a matter of whim or curiosity or self-indulgence. To see or to perish is the

16. Kohlberg, *Essays on Moral Development,* 1:351.
17. Ibid., 368.

> very condition laid upon everything that makes up the universe, by reason of the mysterious gift of existence.[18]

But it is clear that the sort of cognitive development Teilhard was referring to was different from the logical progression involved in Kohlberg's six deontologically conceived moral stages. As Teilhard described his own experience of it, it involved developing a "perception of being" that was like a sort of "touching" or "tasting": "A transformation had taken place for me *in the very perception of being.* Thenceforward being had become, in some way, tangible and savorous to me; and as it came to dominate all the forms which it assumed, being itself began to draw me and intoxicate me."[19]

The reference to a taste for being—what I termed *existential appetite* in Chapter 2—as having the power to draw someone, and even to do so powerfully enough for it to be called an intoxication, fits rather oddly into Kohlberg's thinking, since it clearly conflicts with his Kantian deontological approach to ethics. Teilhard was talking in a eudaemonistic manner reminiscent not only of Aristotle but also of Dante, Bonaventure, Aquinas, and much of the rest of his own Christian tradition. That Kohlberg quoted this passage from Teilhard with evident approval suggests that he was beginning to feel he had come to the limit of deontological and psychological reasoning and needed to look elsewhere for an answer to the metaethical question of why one should be moral or do one's duty. This answer was universal love, not as a rule to be obeyed but as an experience that can be tasted and enjoyed.

The cosmic perspective and its corresponding agape seem to have occupied a place in Kohlberg's thinking somewhat like that which holiness—defined as perfect accord between one's own will and the moral law—did in Kant's, except that Kant did not try to integrate holiness into his moral theory. Kant not only thought that duty was a rationally self-justifying end in itself but even considered holiness, or inherently good will, irrelevant to ethics except as a goal that is humanly unattainable but that we are nevertheless obliged to strive toward. To do the good because, out of love, one enjoys doing good rather than because it is one's duty would not be an ethical act, for Kant, even if it leads one to do the ethically right thing. Kant's ethical ideal of rational

18. Teilhard de Chardin, *The Phenomenon of Man,* 31, quoted in Kohlberg, *Essays on Moral Development,* 1:365 (quotation corrected to agree with Teilhard's original text).

19. Teilhard de Chardin, *The Divine Milieu: An Essay on the Interior Life,* 129 (emphasis in the original), quoted in Kohlberg, *Essays on Moral Development,* 1:366.

autonomy is that one should be governed by reason alone, not by any appetite—even if that appetite might be love for the true good or a longing for true being.

Kohlberg does not seem to have fully grasped the philosophical implications of his divergence from Kant on this point. One of the critics Kohlberg responded to objected that his deontological ethic was an example of what Alasdair MacIntyre called "the Enlightenment project," that is, the project of an independent rational justification of morality after it had become separated as a distinct cultural sphere from the theological, the legal, and the aesthetic.[20] Kohlberg said MacIntyre did not understand the issues he was concerned with, since his own idea of a seventh, religious, stage of moral development was meant to make up for the lack of an independent, purely rational justification of morality. But it also looks as if Kohlberg did not himself understand that MacIntyre's critique had important implications for the formalistic way in which he had conceived of his first six stages. There are, as was mentioned earlier, other ways of thinking about ethical issues and the moral life than the deontological, the most important of which historically has been the eudaemonistic idea that moral development consists of the elucidation and education of desire so that in addition to serving a good beyond itself it may also arrive at its own true fulfillment.

That, however, raises still another question about the problem of thinking in terms of clearly delineated stages, which is that agape, self-transcending love, even if its movement of self-transcendence may involve development through stages, cannot be tied to a particular stage—as though one would first have to develop through all the stages leading to universal rational ethical principles before beginning to be moved by self-transcending love. It may be true that the love of someone whose ethical thinking is limited to a preconventional notion of concrete reciprocity (I'll do what you want if you'll give me what I want in return) will be essentially egoistic, but it can make as much sense to think that self-transcending love, present in some form at any stage of development, may be what moves the transition from simple concrete reciprocity to a more universal ethic as to think that this transition must derive from rational deduction prior to any real intention of love for the other.

Just as Kohlberg found his ideas of development leading him beyond psychology into areas of questioning usually associated more with theology and

20. Kohlberg, *Essays on Moral Development,* 2:320–26. See also MacIntyre, *After Virtue: A Study in Moral Theory,* 39.

then found that this in turn raised questions about how to relate that to his scheme of stages, so also James Fowler discovered problems incorporating the ultimate possibility of development into his own scheme of stages as something that could be studied psychologically. In addition to Fowler's stages of faith discussed in Chapter 3—mythic-literal faith, synthetic-conventional, individuative-reflective, and conjunctive—Fowler felt his scheme would not be complete without a further stage that he called universalizing faith. But after conceiving it and then looking for empirical instances in the populations he studied, he had to face the fact that he never actually found one in his interviews. In his later book *Becoming Adult, Becoming Christian: Adult Development and Christian Faith,* Fowler accepted the suggestion of Gabriel Moran that his stage of conjunctive faith be taken as the normative end point of development, but with the reservation that even if that may be the end of natural development, universalizing faith may exist as a matter of grace, since "movement to the universalizing stage . . . seems to require a disruption of or a disjunction from the 'natural'" and that even if it leaves psychology behind, it is necessary to imagine this as the theoretical ultimate goal of religious development.[21]

Fowler suggested that a good account of this highest level of faith development can be found in H. Richard Niebuhr's idea of "radical monotheism," a faith relationship characterized by trust in and loyalty to the principle of being. Since he did not himself go into what this might involve, it may be helpful to look directly at Niebuhr's *Radical Monotheism and Western Civilization* for an explanation. As Niebuhr described it, "For radical monotheism, the value center is no closed society or the principle of such a society, but the principle of being itself; its reference is to no one reality among the many, but to One beyond all the many, whence all the many derive their being and by participation in which they exist."[22] Faith in this context "is the confidence that whatever is, is good, because it exists as one thing among the many which all have their origin and their being in the One, the principle of being which is also the principle of value. In Him we live and move and have our being not only as existent but as worthy of existence and worthy in existence." Radical monotheism, as Niebuhr conceived it, leads to universal loyalty, which "expresses itself as loyalty to each particular existent in the community of being and to the universal community."[23]

21. Fowler, *Becoming Adult, Becoming Christian,* 73.

22. Niebuhr, *Radical Monotheism,* 27–28. The theme of "participation" ("in being" or "in God" or both) that Niebuhr referred to will be developed at greater length in the next chapter.

23. Ibid., 28, 30.

In Niebuhr's thought, this idea of the radical source of being as the root of value is not connected with deontological ethics. Rather, it recalls the thinking of the eudaemonistic Saint Thomas Aquinas, who spoke in similar terms of God as not "a" being but "Ipsum Esse" (Being Itself).[24] In Fowler's thought, on the other hand, the explicit link of his scheme of stages with Kohlberg's suggests that he conceived its implications deontologically. As examples of figures who looked to him as if their lives expressed this pattern of faith, Fowler offered Mahatma Gandhi, Martin Luther King Jr., and Mother Teresa of Calcutta.

These may indeed be good examples of a universalizing faith, but the differences among them also suggest some of the difficulty of thinking about either Fowler's or Kohlberg's sixth stage. As we saw above, Kohlberg considered his own sixth stage to be the logical culmination of all moral stage development because in his deontologically based scheme it was the most universal and prescriptive in character. That is, its actions could be understood as proceeding from a process of formal moral reasoning about universal moral obligations. Like Kant, Kohlberg had difficulty making a place in his deontological scheme for feeling and desire. It may have been the case, although we would probably need more biographical information than is available to know it, that each of the figures Fowler cited as examples went through a Kohlbergian process of deontological reasoning to reach the mode of universalizing religious faith he saw in them, but it is also possible that a theory of obligation may not have been all that was involved. In Gandhi's case there seems to have been some possibly rather egoistic spiritual ambition as well as an affective kindling through the symbols of both Hinduism and Christianity. In King's case there was probably also some of the same sort of affective stimulation by traditional religious symbols and also by more particular symbols that awoke feelings in him about the history and experience of his own African American community. In the case of Mother Teresa (not to mention the others as well) there is even the possibility of the "holiness" that Kant considered nonethical, however admirable it might be. Mother Teresa may, that is, have cared for the dying in Calcutta not simply out of a belief in duty but because she loved them and actually wanted to care for them.

Perhaps it was possibilities of this sort that led Fowler later to speculate that his level of universalizing faith may be a matter of grace and not a stage of natural development at all—especially since in the Kohlbergian framework

24. This is a topic that will be discussed in detail in the next chapter.

he began with natural psychological development was closely involved with deontological thinking. The traditional discourse of "nature" versus "grace" supposes, however, that there is a discontinuity between natural stages of development and some supernatural addition to human life that may be given to some but withheld from others. Again, that may be the case, but we should at least recognize that thinking this way may itself be both historically conditioned and the result of a pattern of development; it may be the expression of a particular cultural worldview corresponding to a particular subjective developmental structure. Other views of the relation between nature and grace may also be possible, and deciding which makes more sense may require mental operations that can only themselves be understood as the possible result of further processes of development.

Perhaps it will help if we conceive of human development in general—psychological, philosophical, and spiritual—as a process in which new operative capacities and skills are added incrementally to a repertoire of capacities. New ones, when added, may lead to new patterns of mental organization, both subjective and objective—that is, to new habits of mental operation, on the one hand, and to a new or at least significantly modified worldview, on the other. To the extent that the new patterns of thinking developed become habitual, they will seem to have a stability and an apparently irreversible status, like the physiological structure Piaget saw in the butterfly. There is no way a butterfly could return to living as a caterpillar. Among humans, however, a person who develops a capacity for one pattern of mental operation may still remain capable of operating, thinking, and feeling in a different way, and one may under some circumstances—when thwarted by recalcitrant material or tempted by special interests—tend to revert to a less developed mode of thinking than that which one usually operates with, or at least that one tends to operate with at one's best. Or one may apply different modes of thinking in different areas of one's life. We could imagine, for example, a person who in her professional life and relations with colleagues always employs carefully critical methods of inquiry, consciously balancing probabilities and adroitly weighing potential outcomes. And one could imagine the same person, in her dealings with people who think less carefully, depending on institutional arrangements to bring the unpredictability of their motivations and social behavior under control. Or one could imagine the same person, when hit suddenly by the death of a parent, surprised by feelings of dependency and anxiety that may even temporarily produce behavior and patterns of thinking that would no longer be characteristic of her under normal circumstances.

If that can happen in the life of an individual, it can certainly happen all the more in a diverse population. Simply to identify a religious movement or a given religious form with a particular stage of development would be to ignore the fact that as an inherently social phenomenon religion will always involve people who are at different points in their lives, from youth to old age, and who may also have developed in different ways at any given age. As we saw Kegan say in *In over Our Heads,* not everyone living in an advanced industrial society at the beginning of the twenty-first century can be assumed even to have a "modern," let alone a "postmodern," mentality.

On the other hand, religious developments can be expected to have at least some relation to the patterns of psychological development that are both humanly possible and, in some cases, already actualized. Piaget and Garcia's study of the relation of the development of science to psychological development did not assume that all people in a given historical epoch were capable of the operations the scientific pioneers of their period employed, or that those pioneers were in any way typical of their time. Nor does the fact that modern science began to develop only around the time of the Renaissance mean that the operative capacities that began to produce it then had not already been developing, perhaps for millennia, among our ancestors. It also seems reasonable to assume that the same operative capacities developed and functioned among the spiritual explorers of religious traditions. To understand how this has worked out in the practice of actual religious thinking and how psychology can lead directly into theology, it will be helpful to pursue a bit further the ways in which Piaget's genetic epistemology and his reflections on the relation between psychogenesis and the history of science dovetail with the cognitional theory Lonergan worked out in *Insight* and *Method in Theology.*

From Developmental Psychology to Cognitional Theory

As we saw in Chapter 2, Piaget mapped out systematically the formative stages of the course of development that can culminate at its highest levels in the philosophical processes analyzed by Lonergan, and he did that mapping in a way that was complementary to the critical realist cognitional theory Lonergan advocated. Setting aside any questions about the relative "hardness" or "softness" of Piaget's structural stages, his developmental perspective has important implications for an understanding of the possibility of religious worldviews as interpretive structures built up not only on the basis of cultural habits, inherited beliefs or prejudices, scapegoat mechanisms, and so on but also, at least for some religious thinkers, on the basis of careful, conscious thinking grounded in the sorts of psychological structure that Piaget studied.

Cognitional theory could perhaps seem a digression from the topic of religious worldviews, but since much of the conflict between and within religions grows out of different interpretations and beliefs, the pertinence of considering what authentic knowing can be, in both psychological and philosophical terms, should be fairly obvious. Something that may be less obvious but is equally important for understanding what religions can and sometimes do reach toward is the pertinence of authentic interpreting and believing to the development of religious personhood, a topic that will be discussed in some detail from a theological point of view in Chapter 8. The desire to know may not be as universal as Aristotle asserted in the famous opening sentence of *Metaphysics,* since as Freud, Becker, Girard, and countless others have shown, the desire *not* to know may often be even stronger, but I think it must be recognized that at least some religious believers, at least some of the time, do wish actually to know in some manner the objects of their belief and to do so authentically.

Like Piaget, who believed we experience a basic psychological urge to exercise our operational capacities, Lonergan believed, as was mentioned in Chapter 2, that at the root of all our cognitive development and concrete inquiry there is in every human person the "Eros of his mind" that functions as a universal and fundamental human motive: "To inquire and understand, to reflect and judge, to deliberate and choose, are as much an exigence of human nature as waking and sleeping, eating and drinking, talking and loving." Beneath all its concrete expressions, even before it can express itself at the level of the higher operations and whether or not it ever sufficiently overcomes any impeding inertia or aversion to do so, this existential eros constitutes a "primordial drive" that Lonergan termed the "pure question": "It is prior to any insights, any concepts, any words, for insights, concepts, words have to do with answers; and before we look for answers, we want them; such wanting is the pure question." This, said Lonergan, is the wonder that Aristotle claimed is the beginning of all philosophy, but it is present in the life of a child just as in that of a philosopher. It is latent at all times, until it is triggered by experiences that it reaches out to understand. The pure question first expresses itself as something like "What is this?" Responding to experiences, it forms images of them, then probes the images in order to grasp a pattern. When it succeeds, this is what Lonergan called "insight," which he termed the "pivot between images and concepts."[25] (Piaget discussed this as the transition from "figurative" to "operative" thinking.)

Confronted with something circular, for example, and wondering how it might be understood, one constructs something like the image of a cartwheel. Then, considering that image, one may grasp that the spokes, all radiating from the center toward the circumference, are of equal length. This is the insight. Its formulation in language provides the definition of a circle. The definition formulates the concept (the intelligible pattern) implicit in the initial insight and makes it explicit. The process begins with data of experience and organizes them into a patterned image, but ultimately leaves the image behind: "But, while the cart-wheel was imagined," Lonergan said, "the circle consists of a point and a line, neither of which can be imagined."[26]

To phrase it in the language we saw Piaget using, the data are "represented" in a process of "inward imitation" (the initial image of something vaguely circular), then formed into a group (the image of the cartwheel and its components). Then there is a further elaboration and grouping as one grasps the possibility of a universal pattern (the concept of a circle) characteristic of all members of the group of groups that would contain all particular circles. This produces abstract categories that can themselves be operated on without reference to the initial image in which they nevertheless remain rooted. One can proceed, for example, to an analytic geometry of circles.

What philosophers call the process of abstraction is the grasping and identifying of the pattern that insight discovers in the image. Abstraction is sometimes thought of as a merely negative activity, as if reality were reduced or even excluded as abstraction proceeds, but the important point is that abstraction—that is, insight and its articulation—adds a further level of operation to what would otherwise be only blank attention soaking up experience as a buzzing, blooming confusion. "So far from being a mere impoverishment of the data of sense," wrote Lonergan,

> abstraction in all its essential moments is enriching. Its first moment is an enriching anticipation of an intelligibility to be added to sensible presentations; there is something to be known by insight. Its second moment is the erection of heuristic structures and the attainment of insight to reveal in the data what is variously named as the significant, the relevant, the important, the essential,

25. Lonergan, *Insight,* 474, 9, 10.
26. Ibid., 16.

> the idea, the form. Its third moment is the formulation of the intelligibility that insight has revealed. Only in this third moment does there appear the negative aspect of abstraction, namely, the omission of the insignificant, the irrelevant, the negligible, the incidental, the merely empirical residue. Moreover, this omission is neither absolute nor definitive. For the empirical residue possesses the universal property of being what intelligence abstracts from.[27]

One can always return, that is, to the experience and image to try to discover further patterns there.

Once one has grasped a pattern of meaning as a possibility, the force of the "pure question" can go on to express itself as a question for critical reflection, such as, "Is it really that?" or "Is it really so?" This question in turn generates its own heuristic procedures as it reaches for what might satisfy it. It determines, that is, what conditions have to be met for assent, for "answering 'Yes' or 'No' to a question for reflection."[28] In the knowledge not of abstractions (as in mathematics) but of concrete reality, the fulfilling conditions are found on the level of past and present experience. In a typical case, one considers the experiential foundation of the insight again to see if its interpretation adequately takes account of the data of experience. If it does not, one considers other possibilities until an answer turns up that is at least relatively adequate—sufficiently so to bring the restless striving of the question, at least temporarily, to rest—at least until a further interpretation occurs to one or new data call the old answer into question. This coming to rest in a yes or no regarding relative adequacy is what Lonergan called "judgment."

Since inquiry always begins with the stimulus of experience and proceeds by way of insight and abstraction, it always has two dimensions, which Lonergan called classical and statistical heuristic procedures. These are simply the combination of conceptual articulation and logical analysis, on the one hand (what Piaget termed "hypothetical-deductive" reasoning), and the return to empirical observation of concrete instances, on the other. To speak of these two types of procedure is simply to speak of how critical reflection culminating in judgment (the yes or no to a proposition) combines the formulation of a general proposition with observation of the frequencies with which the general description fits particular instances. In Lonergan's own formulation, "while classical investigations head toward the determination of functions and their systematiza-

27. Ibid., 88–89.
28. Ibid., 272.

tion, statistical investigation clings to concrete situations. Hence, while classical conclusions are concerned with what would be if other things were equal, statistical conclusions directly regard such aggregates of events as the sequences of occasions on which a coin is tossed or dice are cast, the sequences of situations created by the mobility of molecules."[29] Working together, the two procedures provide us with probable knowledge of the real world—which is the only knowledge possible with regard to contingent reality.

There are, however, two different types of probable knowledge: scientific knowing and commonsense knowing.[30] The difference between them does not lie in their structure, which consists in both cases of experience, understanding, and judgment as a cumulative, integrated pattern of interrelated operations. The difference lies in the ways they carry out their operations and in their focus. With regard to the first: science could be described simply as the careful exercise of the same cognitive operations that common sense employs less carefully and usually with less self-awareness. With regard to their focus, common sense is rooted in ordinary perception and describes things as they appear to us and relate to our concerns, whereas science focuses on the way things relate causally to one another.

So, the story goes, the apple fell on Newton's head. From the point of view of his common sense, he may have thought something like "It fell down on me," but from the point of view of his interest in explanation, he began to wonder what "falling" is and how it takes place: why down, not up? What brought that questioning to rest for Newton, and for the scientific world in general for several centuries, was his theory of gravitation. But that state of what John Henry Cardinal Newman, in his *Essay in Aid of a Grammar of Assent,* called "certitude," or "a specific sense of intellectual satisfaction and repose," was nevertheless temporary.[31] It lasted until Albert Einstein thought of a new and different way to look at the same issues and until astronomers established that there were further empirical data that could not be explained in Newtonian terms (the apparent shift of stars in connection with the solar

29. Ibid., 53.

30. There is also another type of knowledge, in Lonergan's schema, though it is not probable knowledge in the sense that common sense and science are. This he referred to as "'knowing' in the elementary sense in which kittens know the 'reality' of milk," a type of knowing that "is constituted completely on the level of experience" (ibid., 252). This, too, has its own validity as a type of knowledge, as its survival value for cats attests.

31. John Henry Newman, *Essay in Aid,* 196. Newman's conception of "certitude" and the process of arriving at "intellectual satisfaction and repose" will be discussed at greater length in Chapters 8 and 9.

eclipse in 1917) but could be explained by Einstein's theory of relativity. All knowledge of the real world, both scientific and commonsense, is inherently open-ended, subject to revision when new information or new interpretative possibilities call for it.

It is not uncommon to hear common sense and science contrasted as though they are simply opposites. According to Lonergan, this is a fundamental misunderstanding. They certainly differ in methodical carefulness and in focus, but they both employ the same operations, and they both inquire into the same reality. What they actually are is complementary, "functionally related parts within a single knowledge of a single world." "All the affirmations of empirical science," said Lonergan, "contain the qualifying reservation, 'from the viewpoint of explanation.' Similarly, all the affirmations of common sense contain the qualifying reservation, 'from the viewpoint of ordinary description.'"[32]

The recognition of the structural parallel between the different types of knowledge, and the relative validity of each, is important for several reasons. For one thing, it can be a basis for resolving what is often taken to be an inherent conflict between religious and scientific thinking when religious thinking operates in an imaginative, mythic version of the commonsense mode. For another, it eliminates some of the classic pitfalls of the philosophical tradition, such as the empiricist claim that only sensory observation constitutes genuine knowledge of reality and the Kantian claim that there is no way to get behind phenomena to discover the noumenal reality of the "thing-in-itself." From the point of view of Lonergan's cognitional theory, all genuine human knowledge is made up not merely of sensory observation but of a compound (that is, a hierarchical integration) of experience, interpretation, and critical reflection and judgment. Because it overlooks the role of judgment and supposes that knowledge "simply is attained by taking a good look at the 'real' that is 'already out there now,'" empiricism, Lonergan maintained, "is a bundle of blunders, and its history is their successive clarification." And the Kantian distinction between phenomenon and noumenon is simply a way of talking about the relation between commonsense description (things "for us") and scientific explanation (things "in themselves"). Another reason recognition of the structural parallel between common sense and science is important is that it makes clear the genuine, even if relative, validity of our cognitive operations on the various levels on which they may be performed. Commonsense observation, interpretation, and judgment may err, but they do not do so necessarily, and

32. Lonergan, *Insight,* 297, 295.

for most of us most of the time, they serve us fairly well. "The intelligibility that science grasps comprehensively," as Lonergan put it, "is the intelligibility of the concrete with which common sense deals effectively."[33]

The complementarity of scientific and commonsense thinking also makes clear the continuity of cognitional process on the various levels of human development and explains the structural relation between our acts of knowing and the content of what we know in a way that harmonizes with Piaget's analyses. Like Lonergan's cognitional theory, Piaget's genetic epistemology sees the cognitional process as a dialectic between experience and interpretation that proceeds toward a state of satisfaction (Piaget's "equilibrium") corresponding to Lonergan's (and Newman's) coming to rest in a judgment. Piaget's general term for the process of reaching this state was *equilibration,* which he defined as "a process that leads from a state near equilibrium to a qualitatively different state at equilibrium by way of multiple disequilibria and reequilibrations." That is, a hypothetical initial state of blank, unquestioning consciousness encounters something in experience that stimulates it to questioning ("disequilibrium") until, through hypothesis and testing, it arrives at a satisfactory answer (a new equilibrium). The response to a stimulus proceeds through "optimizing equilibrations" that successively correct and complete previous equilibriums until a wider and more stable equilibrium is reached. What Lonergan called the "sublation" of experience into interpretation and of interpretation into critically reflective knowledge is what Piaget called "hierarchical integration" as "the conservation of subsystems in systems." Cognitive structures resemble biological equilibriums (rather than mechanical or thermodynamic), according to Piaget, because the system and subsystem help to conserve each other rather than destroy each other, which means that "equilibrium is due, among other things, to a close association of differentiation and integration."[34]

This is to describe the process in terms of its subjective pole, that is, the subjective structure of the process of knowing. Corresponding to that is its objective pole, the structure of the known. Piaget described his cognitional process of optimizing equilibration as a movement toward relative adequacy in the relation between interpretation and experience: "Knowing reality means constructing systems of transformation [that is, interpretations] that

33. Ibid., 412, 297–98.

34. Piaget, *The Equilibration of Cognitive Structures: The Central Problem of Intellectual Development,* 3, 21, 4.

correspond, more or less adequately, to reality. They are more or less isomorphic to transformations of reality. The transformational structures of which knowledge consists are not copies of the transformations in reality; they are simply possible isomorphic models among which experience can enable us to choose. Knowledge, then, is a system of transformations that become progressively adequate."[35]

Lonergan described the same process in terms that are similar but make clearer its philosophical implications. On the subject of "the isomorphism that obtains between the structure of knowing and the structure of the known," he wrote: "If the knowing consists of a related set of acts and the known is the related set of contents of the acts, then the pattern of the relations between the acts is similar in form to the pattern of the relations between the contents of the acts." These acts are hierarchically integrated for Lonergan, just as for Piaget. This means that at the subjective pole of conscious operation, "every instance of knowing proportionate being consists of a unification of experiencing, understanding, and judging." Correspondingly, at the objective pole, "it follows from the isomorphism of knowing and known that every instance of known proportionate being is a parallel unification of a content of experience, a content of understanding, and a content of judgment."[36] ("Proportionate being" is being that is proportionate to human cognitive operations, that is, whatever is capable of being known through these processes of critical inquiry.)

To state the principle of isomorphism another way, to every cognitional theory and epistemology there must correspond, at least implicitly, a metaphysics. As Lonergan used that term, metaphysics is the analysis of the general structure of what "the related set of contents of the acts" that constitute the known must be if knowing consists of the particular "related set of acts" that are attention to experience, construing or interpretation of experiential data, and critical reflection on the adequacy of the construing to the set of data it tries to take into account. To use the traditional Aristotelian metaphysical terminology of potency, form, and act:

> Potency denotes the component of proportionate being to be known in fully explanatory knowledge by an intellectually patterned experience of the empirical residue.

35. Piaget, *Genetic Epistemology,* 15.
36. Lonergan, *Insight,* 399, 400.

> Form denotes the component of proportionate being to be known, not by understanding the names of things, nor by understanding their relations to us, but by understanding them fully in their relations to one another.
>
> Act denotes the component of proportionate being to be known by uttering the virtually unconditioned "Yes" of reasonable judgment.[37]

A "substance," in the traditional metaphysical language, is the unit constituted by these three. As Lonergan explained, "It follows that potency, form, and act constitute a unity. For what is experienced, is what is understood; and what is understood, is what is affirmed. The three levels of cognitional activity yield a single knowing."[38] The main difference, Lonergan said, between Aristotle's metaphysics and his own is that Aristotle's approach is descriptive whereas his own is explanatory—that is, it explains how and why the structural pattern of the objective contents of cognitive acts must correspond to the structure of the cognitive acts themselves and to their relations to one another.

In anticipation of the discussion of religious worldviews in the next chapter, I would like to mention one other aspect of Lonergan's discussion of metaphysics that shows its possible implications for a theological worldview. He spoke of potency as including finality or teleology, since "just as intellectually patterned experience heads toward insights and judgments, so potency heads toward forms and acts," and he said that proportionate being itself, therefore, exhibits an incompleteness and a "dynamic orientation towards a completeness that becomes determinate only in the process of completion." This theory about the teleological character of being, he asserted, "affirms a parallelism between the dynamism of the mind and the dynamism of proportionate being. It affirms that the universe is not at rest, not static, not fixed in the present, but in process, in tension, fluid."[39] Aristotle had mixed teleologi-

37. Ibid., 432. For a reader not familiar with Aristotelian metaphysics, or in Aristotle's own term for it, "first [that is, fundamental] philosophy," reality is made up of "substances," things that are real in themselves and capable of existing independently of their "accidents" (such as their particular color). A "substance" is composed of a fundamental "matter" and a "form." Aristotle's "matter" is a substratum capable of taking on any "form"; the "form" is the active organizing principle that gives the "substance" its particular characteristics, that makes it to be the kind of thing it becomes through the "form." Thus, "matter" is "in potency" to any possible "form," and the particular "form" (of dog, for example, or of cat, or of ball, pencil, and so forth) is what makes the "substance" the kind of thing it actually is. "Form" and "matter" are both only "potential" until they are united as the actual "substance," but it is "form" that is said to give "matter" its actuality, to "reduce it from potency to act."

38. Ibid.

39. Ibid., 444, 445.

cal thinking with a static ideal of cognition that resulted from the projection of his logical categories into reality as such. Lonergan tried to move from a descriptive metaphysics to something like a scientific, explanatory one by integrating it into the higher viewpoint of cognitional theory, and in the process he found that it pointed toward a dynamic, developmental worldview with a corresponding theology that points toward and complements the theological vision of his fellow Jesuit Pierre Teilhard de Chardin, whose thought, as we saw, drew the interest of Lawrence Kohlberg because of the way it pointed toward an ultimate telos of spiritual development that Kohlberg thought was needed to make full sense of the possibilities of psychological development.

The Sociological Dimension

Before proceeding into the theological development of religious thought, however, it will be appropriate to stop briefly to consider the ways in which social forces as well as psychological ones can affect religious thinking. When I told a professor of sociology once that I was working on a study of the psychology of worldviews, he asked why psychology, why not sociology? The question is worth considering, because religion is a social phenomenon and social forces play a powerful role in shaping it. However spiritually enriching may be the insights brought to the world by an original spiritual explorer, the religion that develops around those insights can be expected to operate to a large extent according to the dynamics of a group formed of people who do not always find it easy to follow where the explorer trod and who can be expected to adapt the originating insights to fit the purposes of those who presently carry the most weight in the group.[40] Sometimes a religion develops along lines that clearly serve the power interests of the elite that controls its institutions, and some versions of the sociology of religion focus on that sort of development to the exclusion of any other. Others focus on the way religion is used among social groups to keep anomie at bay, constructing a "sacred canopy" under which to shelter from any challenges to belief in the orderliness of the cosmos. One historian of religion, Erwin R. Goodenough, developed a

40. Eric Voegelin spoke of the problem of a "secondary symbolism" that develops when those who hear the "primary symbols" developed by an original thinker on the basis of his or her spiritual or philosophical experience can find nothing comparable in their own experience to connect those symbols with and therefore associate them with different experiences that give them a different meaning. See especially the introduction to Voegelin, *The Ecumenic Age*, 96–107.

theory of religion according to which, although human beings are confronted at all times by a *tremendum* ("that which is to be feared") that threatens to undermine their confidence in cosmic and social order, they are rescued from anxiety and anomie by heroic individuals who dare to peek from time to time behind the canopy, get a glimpse of the chaos beyond, and then make adjustments to the canopy's fabric of images so as to make them more socially effective for a while.[41]

Depending on those daring few is the nervous multitude, which usually does not want to look very closely at how the canopy was woven. When a group feels the heroic status of its deliverers is impugned, even tangentially, its reaction can become deadly. Consider, for example, an incident in contemporary Pakistan. On August 20, 2001, the *New York Times* reported that a physiology teacher, Dr. Younus Shaikh, was sentenced to death on charges of blaspheming the Prophet Muhammad because some students in his class said he had told them that the Prophet had not become a Muslim until the age of forty and that before then he had not followed specifically Muslim practices. Since Muslim tradition itself has always held that the first revelation did not come to Muhammad until he was around forty years old, and that he too, like any other Muslim, had to make the decision to accept and obey the revelation, what Dr. Shaikh said should hardly seem even surprising, let alone disturbing. If one reads the account in the Qur'an, in the "Blood Clots" sura, of Muhammad's first experience of revelation, it sounds as if that was as disturbing to him as what Goodenough called the experience of the *tremendum.* That he was uncertain how to interpret the revelation or even whether to trust it as coming from the supreme God rather than from a jinni or from his own imagination is clear from the tradition that it was his wife Khadijah who persuaded him it sounded genuine. If one thinks of Muhammad as one who dared to face into the mystery of radical transcendence and found the courage to put his trust in that experience and its transcendent source, then those who denounced Dr. Shaikh and the court that sentenced him would seem more motivated by fear of anomie than by reverence for the faith of the Prophet.[42]

41. See Goodenough, *The Psychology of Religious Experiences.*

42. The reader will be pleased to know that, although Dr. Shaikh was held in solitary confinement in a death cell in the Central Gaol of Rawalpindi from the time he was found guilty on August 18, 2001, he was retried and eventually acquitted on November 21, 2003. Still, he subsequently had to flee Pakistan because of continuing threats against his life. For good or ill, the social force of religion is immensely powerful.

I hope citing such an example will not appear prejudicial, especially at a time when the Islamic tradition seems to be receiving rather widespread negative treatment in the Western press in the aftermath of the events of September 11, 2001. I do not think Islam as such is inherently more susceptible than any other religion to the problem Dr. Shaikh's story illustrates. Other religious traditions have their own catalogs of horrors, some on a much more massive scale. Nor, unlike many contemporary critics of religion such as Daniel Dennett, Richard Dawkins, or Christopher Hitchens, do I think religion as such is the source of the problem. Rather, what we see illustrated with striking clarity in this particular story is something that can happen among any group of people who let a group dynamic take hold of them and overcome their ordinary capacity for measured thought.

I expect that any faithful Muslim, in the normal light of his or her own best understanding, would recognize that the tradition itself holds that Muhammad was not born a Muslim but became one through a decision to submit to the calling of the God who revealed himself in the Qur'an. But there are many in the Muslim world at present who understandably feel that their religion is not receiving sufficient social confirmation and that it needs to be defended against anything that might even look like doubt or might remind them that their own adherence to the Muslim worldview, like the Prophet's, has to be a personal commitment, not just an inevitability. An unwelcome reminder of this can lead, as in this instance, to a mob mentality taking over and looking for someone to attack—exactly the sort of response that would be predicted by the Beckerian terror management theorists discussed in Chapter 4.

If we want to understand what motivates a crowd when it feels what Peter Berger calls its *nomos* threatened, it is helpful to have someone like Ernest Becker to tell us about the power of anxiety to trigger mortality-salience effects or someone like René Girard to tell us about the universal human tendency to imitate, wittingly or unwittingly, the passions and hostilities of the people around us—and to tell us, as both of these thinkers do, about the tendency of the mass mind to seek out scapegoats. When one considers a phenomenon like the case of Dr. Shaikh in this perspective, the dividing line between sociology and psychology seems rather blurred, and both seem equally relevant to making sense of it. There are social phenomena that can be understood simply in terms of rational conscious interests, but there are also others that seem to call for psychological explanations in terms of nonrational motives working below the threshold of awareness and that become particularly powerful when the individual mind yields to the undertow of a group. This is one of the reasons, besides their relative freedom from reductionism, that I have drawn on the thought of Becker and Girard rather than some of the other well-known psychologists of the unconscious who tend to give more attention to the psychodynamics of the individual.

Both sociological and psychological approaches can be helpful in understanding religion as a social phenomenon, but both also involve the inherent limitations of their strengths. Sociology focuses on groups and tends to emphasize statistical method in studying them. This offers it great power for the analysis of the group effects it studies. But to gain that power it has to narrow its focus to what can be statistically analyzed. Two anecdotes may illustrate the problem such a focus brings with it. Both recount actual incidents. One involves a sociologist telling a literary scholar that a book he had written on the religious thought of a number of major modern authors could have little relevance for the understanding of religion, since the authors in question, admittedly important as they might be as literary figures, were all "intellectual virtuosi," who as such are inherently rare and therefore statistically insignificant. The other is a story told by an anthropologist who went to Thailand to study contemporary Buddhist political movements. While there he heard about a monk who had a large following despite the remoteness of his forest monastery. The monk was known for his social teaching but was also reputed to be able to intuit winning lottery numbers. The anthropologist decided to make the journey to see what this was all about. He found a large crowd gathered in the forest to hear the monk's dharma talk, and when he listened, he noticed that, along with dharma and Buddhist social teachings, the talk was sprinkled with references to numbers, to which the audience was listening with keen attention.

The two stories converge, I think, on an interesting question that has no simple answer but does illuminate a fundamental problem: what is religion really? Is the real phenomenon that which has the greatest statistical weight? The sociologist's critique of the negligible statistical mass of intellectual virtuosi makes a valid point. If one were to try to argue that the real Christian religion, for example, is that of elite figures such as T. S. Eliot or W. H. Auden, or of Saint Thomas Aquinas or Saint Gregory Palamas, or of Karl Rahner, Bernard Lonergan, the Niebuhr brothers, or Paul Tillich, one would have to ignore the great mass of Christians who not only have never read such figures or perhaps even heard of them but would also probably have little use for them if they had. Daniel C. Dennett said to me in conversation after his book *Breaking the Spell: Religion as a Natural Phenomenon* was published that "the only people who read theologians are other theologians."[43] He knew he was exaggerating, I'm sure, but his serious point was the same as that of the sociologist who dismissed intellectual virtuosi as statistically insignificant. Theologians themselves also recognize the seriousness of that point. One of the most eminent of them, H. Richard Niebuhr, said in *Radical Monotheism*, "The sociological analysis of religion is . . . so persuasive because the kind of faith most frequently associated with religion is of the social sort."[44]

But the other story raises a counterquestion: is a religion really about only what those with substantial statistical mass seem to be most focused on in it? I doubt if any serious Buddhist would want to argue that what the Buddhist religion is really all about is how to find winning lottery numbers. In fact, all traditions of Buddhist teaching emphasize seeking freedom from the desire for the sort of worldly goods that those who bet on lottery numbers usually want to spend their winnings on. Those who have actually understood well through study and meditative practice the Buddha's dharma and have taught it on that basis through the centuries may have been numerically rare followers of a statistically insignificant individual, the Buddha himself, and the Buddhist religion as a historical phenomenon may have involved vast numbers of adherents who were more interested in improving their worldly situations either in the present life or in a future incarnation than in breaking free altogether from the cycle of rebirth as the Buddha advocated. But even these individuals, if asked in a sociologist's survey what they thought the Buddhist religion is really about, would probably try to say something about the four noble truths (of the inherent unsatisfactoriness of a life of craving) and about the noble eightfold path (of meditation, wisdom, and right action) that leads to liberation from craving and therefore from reincarnation—even if some of them, while answering, might also begin wondering if numbers like four and eight combined in some way could be useful clues for quite a different purpose. Similarly, the Christian laity in the pews may not often study the major thinkers of their own tradition, but most of them probably hope they are being led by pastors who once did so in seminary.

What is the corresponding limitation of the focus of psychologies of the unconscious? These focus on nonrational forces that drive human beings

43. In his book Dennett says somewhat less pithily, "This earnest intellectual exercise [theology] scratches the skeptical itch of those few people who are uncomfortable with the creeds they were taught as children, and is ignored by everybody else" (*Breaking the Spell*, 208).

44. Niebuhr, *Radical Monotheism*, 19.

without their being aware of what is moving them. Certainly, these psychologies are helpful for understanding the dynamics of the uncritical mass mind. I said in the Introduction that my focus would be on two central questions, one of which is "What subjective factors sometimes render religions harmful not only to nonmembers who might become objects of aggression but also to their own adherents by stifling their development toward full personhood?" One answer to this question is that religions can be dangerous when they generate polarized worldviews, that is, when they divide the social world into a good "us" and an evil "them" whom we interpret ourselves as having a sacred obligation to destroy. Death anxiety, the effects of mimetic psychology, and the fear of anomie can all work together to produce this sort of reaction in the mass mind.

The other question has to do with what conditions might foster less aggressive and dangerous, and even perhaps helpful, forms of religiousness, and here psychologies of the unconscious are of more limited even if real value. The limitation is that they do not address the question of how a mind might develop to become reasonable and responsible and what sorts of worldview might support that development and, through it, the full development of human persons. This is why I have given so much attention to theories of developmental psychology and to cognitional theory. On the other hand, that limitation is a function of their focus on factors that inhibit development and need to be raised into consciousness if development is to take place. Before the members of a religious group can learn to resist the pull of polarized worldviews or to resist the temptation to stifle questions that might arouse anxiety, they first need to become aware of those tendencies and the danger of yielding to them.

René Girard's critique of what in *Things Hidden since the Foundation of the World* he terms "historical Christianity" calls our attention both to the need for developing this awareness and to the force of resistance to it. As we saw in Chapter 5, Girard argues that the heart of the Christian gospel is the revelation of the role that violence and the victimizing mechanism have played in human affairs and in religion, and the principal vehicle of this revelation is the story of the crucifixion of Jesus. Religion, Girard says, including the religion of "historical Christianity" that developed in the centuries after the founding events and insights, has tended to take the form of a sacralization of victimizing, but the gospel is the unmasking of this, forcing the realization that the victim is innocent and that the violence comes not from him but from ourselves. Christianity began, in Girard's interpretation, with a radical critique of sacrificial religion, but in its subsequent historical development, even though the originating antisacrificial insight was preserved in the story for those with ears to hear, "historical Christianity" largely reverted, among the many, to a religion of the standard sacrificial type. Jesus, whose victimization should have exposed once and for all the psychological mechanism of scapegoating, became interpreted as having cooperated voluntarily with his victimizers in order to offer himself as a sacrifice to appease a violent God. The efforts of Christian theologians to explain Jesus' death as a sacrifice, Girard thinks, "only result in absurdities: God feels the need to revenge his honour, which has been tainted by the sins of humanity, and so on. Not only does God require a new victim, but he requires the victim who is most precious and most dear to him, his very son."[45] Girard does not mean that such absurdity has ever been the whole of the Christian religion; he thinks there have always been Christians with ears for what he believes is the authentic original revelation, even if they have been statistically few. Rather, his point is that the history of Christianity has involved a continual dialectic between the sacrificial and antisacrificial readings of the story, and that the truth of the religion is preserved by the few who are able to understand the antisacrificial revelation of the gospel.

There has been a similar dialectic in the Jewish tradition. The story of Amalek as the archetypal enemy of Israel illustrates this well, both because it has always had a central place in the story the ancient Israelites and later Jews have told themselves about their divine calling and because the obvious difficulties it poses for conceiving of God as merciful have given rise to searching efforts of interpretation.[46] The key biblical passages are Exodus 17:8–16, Deuteronomy 25:17–19, and 1 Samuel 15:1ff. The Exodus passage describes how the Amalekites attacked the Israelites as they were passing through on their way to the Promised Land and how the Israelites did well in battle against them as long as Moses could stand with his arms raised (with Aaron and Hur on each side helping him hold them up). After the victory, Moses declared that God said, "I will utterly blot out the remembrance of Amalek from under heaven" and called for "war with Amalek from generation to generation." This enmity is evoked again in Deuteronomy, as Moses says, "Remember what Amalek did to you on the way as you came out of Egypt, how he attacked you on the way,

45. Girard, *Things Hidden*, 182.

46. I am indebted for the Jewish sources in what follows to my colleague Professor Martin S. Jaffee, who discussed the biblical story of Amalek and its later interpretation in a lecture, "Remember Amalek! The Eternal Antisemite and the Politics of Apocalypse in Contemporary Judaism," presented at the University of Washington on February 8, 2006.

when you were faint and weary, and cut off at your rear all who lagged behind you; and he did not fear God. Therefore when the LORD your God has given you rest from all your enemies round about, in the land which the LORD your God gives you for an inheritance to possess, you shall blot out the remembrance of Amalek from under heaven; you shall not forget."

Later, as the story goes, a time came to fulfill this command when Samuel anointed Saul as Israel's first king and told him that Yahweh's command to him was, "Now go and smite Amalek, and utterly destroy all that they have; do not spare them, but kill both man and woman, infant and suckling, ox and sheep, camel and ass." When Saul carried out the order in a general way but spared Agag, the Amalekite king, and saved the best of their sheep and oxen to sacrifice to God, God's response was to reject Saul and declare him deposed. Samuel then ordered Agag brought forth and after hacking him to pieces with his own sword said to Saul, "Has the LORD as great delight in burnt offerings and sacrifices, as in obeying the voice of the LORD? Behold, to obey is better than sacrifice, and to hearken than the fat of rams"—a passage that sounds like a preparation for the eventual antisacrificial interpretation that Girard sees developing in the prophetic tradition but also shows how long the road to that would be.

Amalek reappears in the Bible centuries later in the Book of Esther, where Haman, the evil prime minister of Persia who vows to "destroy all the Jews," is identified as "the Agagite," that is, an Amalekite and presumably a descendant of the King Agag whom Samuel slew. He is defeated, of course, by Queen Esther, an event that is celebrated annually in the Feast of Purim.

In these stories we find a polarized religious worldview in which Israel has an everlastingly evil enemy, Amalek, whose utter obliteration is decreed by God. But by the time the rabbinic Jewish tradition developed, the depolarizing of the religious vision of the Jews had progressed to the point that some other way of reading the story had to be sought. The memory of the command to destroy Amalek was preserved as sacred tradition by the ritual of reading it aloud at a Sabbath prior to Purim, but the rabbis also said in the Talmud that because of the genealogical confusion among Middle Eastern peoples since the conquest of the northern kingdom of Israel by the Assyrians in the eighth century, it is no longer possible to identify Amalek with any particular nation or person.[47] Moreover, even if Amalek could be identified in the present, any

47. Babylonian Talmud, Tractate *Yoma*, folio 54a.

attempt to fulfill the commandment to destroy the Amalekites must wait until the messianic age, since only then would the condition be fulfilled that was specified in Deuteronomy as "when the LORD your God has given you rest from all your enemies round about, in the land which the LORD your God gives you for an inheritance to possess."[48] The command still stands, but Jews are not only no longer obliged to carry it out in the present world but actually forbidden to try to do so—but with the awkward implication that the messianic age will be a time of bloodshed.

The Kabbalah carried this process of depolarization a step further by interpreting Amalek as a kind of metaphysical principle of opposition to God rather than a real people on earth,[49] and Hasidism subsequently interpreted the enmity with Amalek as a metaphor for the spiritual battle within each person between the desire to be obedient to God's commandments and his or her own impulse to rebel.[50] Thus, the Jewish tradition gradually worked out the idea that it is *tshuvah*—an act of penitential self-critique—that constitutes the true fulfillment of the commandment to obliterate Amalek.

The development of this theme in Jewish thought illustrates how psychologies of the unconscious and sociologies of culture can illuminate but also need to be complemented by psychologies that consider developmental possibilities. The rabbis, the Kabbalists (who were sometimes the same people), and the Hasidim stepped back from the mythic agon with Amalek and developed an awareness of the way a polarized worldview can develop from and feed irrational and largely unconscious forces within us. These Jewish traditions, working out the logic of their conception of God's calling to Israel to be a light to the nations, developed the idea that this calling would require transcending, through a heightening of differentiated self-awareness, the temptation to polarization. This became for them an imperative for the sake of their mission to draw all peoples into a right relationship with God.

This does not mean, of course, that such depolarizing of worldviews is an inevitable evolutionary development in the life of a religion. Depolarization is not a one-way street. The revival of militant versions of messianism among some Jewish groups today, accompanied by the demonizing of new incarnations of Amalek, as in Rabbi Meir Kahane's proposal for the forcible deporta-

48. Babylonian Talmud, Tractate *Sanhedrin,* 20b.
49. *Zohar* 3:65a and 3:291b.
50. For example, Elimelekh of Lizhanzk, *Noam Elimelekh,* 1:40b; and Nahum of Chernobyl, *Me'or 'Enayyim,* 2:379a–b.

tion of all Arabs from Israel and the extension of the boundaries of modern Israel to encompass all the territory thought to have once been part of the kingdom of David and Solomon, is sufficient evidence to the contrary. This "repolarization," as one might perhaps call it, is even echoed and endorsed by some Christian groups that think reoccupation of all of ancient Israel's biblical territory will help prepare for the Second Coming.

Nor should any of this be surprising. Religions do evolve, but evolution is simply change in response to changing conditions, not an inexorable climb toward the higher and better, and it does not involve every member of a population. Rather, what is remarkable and precious is the slow and precarious development of a radically depolarized religious vision among at least some Jews and some Christians over the centuries. In the chapters that follow I will explore ways in which both psychologies of the unconscious and developmental psychologies of the sort represented by Piaget and his successors can elucidate the possibilities in religions for transcending polarized worldviews and fostering the development of reasonable and responsible persons.

The Philosophical Dimension

Before turning to that, however, there is a further question to be considered: since the development of such persons must involve development of the capacity for critical reflection and careful, conscious interpretation and deliberation, in what ways does the development toward critically reflective theology also constitute a movement beyond psychology and toward philosophical reflection? This, I think, is an even more fundamental question than that about the relative importance of sociological or psychological approaches to the topic. As I mentioned in Chapter 1, Sigmund Freud said that the goal of his own psychology of the unconscious, as expressed in his injunction, "Wo Es war, soll Ich werden" (Where "it" was, there should be "I"), was to lead beyond the twitches of unconscious mechanism toward the development of a free, conscious person: instead of blind mechanism, a conscious, critically reflective interpreter and actor. But if that is the goal, how much can psychology or psychotherapy simply as such do to help us toward it?

A friend of mine, a retired psychotherapist with several decades of clinical experience, has told me that during the course of her career she became increasingly convinced that what really lay at the root of the problems her clients brought to her was that they had never learned to think clearly and critically and that something they all needed was a basic course of philosophical training. She did not mean philosophy as the formal analysis of arguments, but rather the sort of careful, attentive exploration of existential questions depicted in the Socratic dialogues of Plato—when they are read as genuine dialogues, as processes of reflection led by open-ended questions, rather than as collections of arguments intended to bring dialogue to an end by the force of formal logic. My friend was a reader of both Ernest Becker and Bernard Lonergan, and she had especially in mind something like Lonergan's grounding of the philosophical fields of metaphysics and epistemology in a cognitional theory consistent with Piaget's ideas about the dependence of thought on the capacities for mental operation developed by the thinker. Of course, it would be inappropriate to suggest that a psychotic or a person suffering from a neurologically based disorder simply needs to develop skills in critical thinking, but those were not the sort of people she, or psychotherapists generally (as compared to psychiatrists), have as clients.

I am reminded in this connection of a story told about D. W. Winnicott by Masud Khan in the introduction to Winnicott's *Holding and Interpretation: Fragment of an Analysis.* A group of young Anglican priests once asked Winnicott "how to differentiate between a person who seeks their help because he is sick and needs psychiatric treatment, and one who is capable of helping himself through talking with them." "Telling this story to me," says Khan, "Winnicott said that he had been taken aback by the awesome simplicity of their question." Then after a long pause for thought he told them, "If a person comes and talks to you and, listening to him, you feel he is *boring* you, then he is sick, and needs psychiatric treatment. But if he sustains your interest, no matter how grave his distress or conflict, then you can help him alright."[51] The person who bores is stuck; a person whose thought is led by a genuine question is in movement—and, as philosopher Hans-Georg Gadamer has said, it is their sharing in the felt force of a dynamic question that overcomes, in genuine dialogue, what might otherwise be the isolation of both speakers within separate mental horizons. Gadamer formulated this conception of philosophy eloquently:

> The art of dialectic is not the art of being able to win every argument. On the contrary, it is possible that someone who is practicing the art of dialectic, i.e. the art of questioning and of seeking truth, comes off worse in the argument in the eyes of those listening to it. Dialectic, as the art of asking questions, proves

51. Winnicott, *Holding and Interpretation*, 1.

> itself only because the person who knows how to ask questions is able to persist in his questioning, which involves being able to preserve his orientation towards openness. The art of questioning is that of being able to go on asking questions, i.e. the art of thinking. It is called "dialectic," for it is the art of conducting a real conversation.[52]

In the chapters that follow I will try to work out some of the implications of the profound truth in Gadamer's conception of dialectic. If religions can become aggressive toward outsiders and inhibit the openness of questioning among those within their fold, and then if they are to become less dangerous and even perhaps helpful, that can happen only if religious persons break free from the constraints both inward and outward that make them want to suppress anything that conflicts with the received ideas of their group. These conventional ideas constitute what, as was explained in Chapter 5, Peter Berger and other sociologists of knowledge call "socially objectivated 'knowledge,'" with the word *knowledge* in quotes because it is not knowledge of the sort that is developed through critical reflection on the relative adequacy of interpretations in relation to experience but rather what official sources approve or just what "everybody says." Uncritical as it is, it is the latter that constitutes what Berger calls "the cognitive and normative edifice that passes for 'knowledge' in a society." As he also goes on to say, "Most socially objectivated 'knowledge' is pretheoretical."[53]

Berger does not attempt to explain the mechanism underlying the force of this sort of "knowledge," although he does say, as we saw in the Introduction, that it involves "a human craving for meaning that appears to have the force of instinct." My own suggestion, as I indicated in Chapter 5, would be that the principal mechanism making the social construction of objectivated "knowledge" and its successful internalization possible is what Girard and Oughourlian call "mimesis," the innate preconscious tendency to imitate the desires and attitudes of others. Such mimesis operates, as Girard puts it, "with a quasiosmotic immediacy," absorbing what is around it in the social atmosphere prior to any consciousness of doing so.[54]

52. Gadamer, *Truth and Method*, 330.
53. Berger, *Sacred Canopy*, 20, 21.
54. Ibid., 22; Girard, *"To Double Business Bound": Essays on Literature, Mimesis, and Anthropology*, 89.

For a pretheoretical mind, I suggest, assent is usually not rational but mimetic. One of the most powerful and disturbing features of the modern world for people with such minds, which is to say, for the great majority of humankind even today, is that it undermines the confident certitude of mimetic assent. This is one of the ways in which many people find themselves, as Kegan phrased it, "in over their heads." As long as there are dissonant voices able to be heard, the pretheoretical mind cannot easily come to satisfying rest in the conventional interpretations that shelter it from anomie. There may have been religious explorers into the *tremendum* who have had a higher degree of tolerance for uncertainty, but this has not generally been the case among their followers any more than it has among the rest of humanity. To the extent that they become socially effective for large numbers, religious worldviews are usually developed on the basis of very limited rationality and maintained with a comfortable sense of certitude by the suppression of dissent.

But that is not the whole of the story. Religions are not monolithic. Nor, as I said above, do I think religion as such is the problem. Religious traditions have many streams, and some of these, recognizing the mystery inherent in transcendence, encourage openness to uncertainty and to exploratory questions. Before considering what might lead beyond the problems and conflicts that religions can give rise to, it will be worthwhile to consider in the next chapter both the diversity of worldviews *within* religious traditions and the possibilities such diversity opens up for the development of alternative, less dangerous ways of being religious.

The Dynamic Diversity of Religious Worldviews

Conceiving the Divine

In *The God We Never Knew: Beyond Dogmatic Religion to a More Authentic Contemporary Faith,* New Testament scholar Marcus Borg tells how he did not discover until he was in his thirties that there were two very different Christian Gods. The first was the one he learned about as a child. This was "a supernatural being 'out there' who created the world a long time ago and had occasionally intervened in the aeons since, especially in the events recorded in the Bible," and who was not "here" but "somewhere else" and would take us to that place someday after death, "provided that we had done or believed whatever was necessary to pass the final judgment." The second was a God who was very much "here," active within the world and in the depths of each person within it, who was not concerned with judging and rewarding and punishing but who willed life and growth for every person and willed it for the present, not just for an "afterlife." Borg's book is mainly about how the second God can be found in various parts of the Bible and the theological tradition of Christianity, but it also describes the difficulty he had himself in seeing that alternative theological conception because, he says, "the notion of God I received as a child stood in the way."[1]

1. Borg, *God We Never Knew,* 1.

Borg's own emphasis in discussing this is on the picture he received of the first God, but perhaps equally important, from the point of view of developmental psychology, would be the age at which he received it, exactly the age James Fowler associated with his stage of mythic-literal faith.[2] Going through the list of beliefs (about God, the Bible, humanity, Jesus, the way of salvation, faith, and the afterlife) that constituted what he calls his "childhood package," Borg concludes with this observation: "Heaven and hell were central. Salvation meant going to heaven, but some people would go to hell. So fundamental was this notion that if somebody had been able to convince me at age ten or twelve that there was no afterlife, I wouldn't have had any idea why one should be a Christian. It was all about going to heaven."[3]

We saw in Chapter 3 that these years are also the age of what Robert Kegan called "the imperial self," the stage at which the child, embedded in its "needs," is concerned only with what will satisfy them and thinks of others primarily in terms of how useful they can be for assisting in that aim.[4] The parents, for that stage as for the earlier "impulsive self," are still authority figures who have the power to grant or withhold satisfactions as well as to punish infractions of the rules they impose. The "imperial self" has learned to control and contain its impulses in order to manipulate the powerful others to win satisfactions. It was such a child's interest in the sort of rudimentary morality implied in this behavior (the "fair play" of doing this in order to get that) that led Lawrence Kohlberg to turn from Freud to Piaget to understand the way a young child makes sense of its world: "There is an impulsive morality, but it is still a morality, not an 'id'; there is a rational cognitive morality, but it is still a morality, not an ego."[5]

What makes Borg's story especially significant for what it can tell us about religious development is that in his case the ten year old's way of thinking about God acquired sufficient habitual force in his mind to shut out any other conception until he was in his thirties and had already been through a seminary. He suggests a psychological reason for this: "Because this image of God and the Christian life was presented to me as divine revelation of the way things are, it went much deeper into my psyche than much of what I learned as a child."[6] This interpretation seems reasonable from a developmental point

2. See Chapter 3.
3. Ibid., 18.
4. See Chapter 3 and Kegan, *Evolving Self*, chap. 6.
5. Kohlberg, *Essays on Moral Development*, 1:378.
6. Borg, *God We Never Knew*, 19.

of view, since a child of that age has not normally developed the capacity for the reflective operations that would be needed to question a claim to "divine revelation," and the child's susceptibility to the logic of reward and punishment could be expected to give it the feeling it had better submit obediently and unquestioningly to that claim lest it suffer punishment.

Borg's description of his childhood experience shows that his package of beliefs was clothed with the aura of what Rudolf Otto and Mircea Eliade called "the sacred"; he speaks of how closely his childhood image of God was tied up with the image of the imposing Pastor Thorson who shook his finger at the congregation as he preached: "The finger-shaking God was God the lawgiver and Judge. Pastor Thorson's unadorned black robe drove the point home: Who else in our experience wears a plain black robe? Moreover, God as the big eye in the sky and God the finger-shaker went together very well: as all-knowing, God the lawgiver and judge knew everything we thought or did."[7] It might take courage for a child under the spell of such a figure even to allow doubts to enter his consciousness, and for critical reflection even to get started it would require, as Kegan would say, sufficient differentiation of consciousness to step back from the aura of feelings associated with the sacred and take them as object. One can understand the concern about such a pattern of thinking and feeling that would lead a Daniel Dennett to urge "breaking the spell"—but perhaps that is also the limitation of Dennett's critique: its focus is essentially on the God of ten year olds, even if, as happened in Borg's case, many of those who retain that image of God may be quite a bit further along in actual years.

It was not, of course, that Borg continued to believe until his thirties in the childhood package and its God. Rather, when he ceased to believe, as he did by the time he was in college, the God of his childhood retained its hold on his imagination as the one that he *no longer* believed in and the only God he thought anyone had ever believed in. He says, "Though I no longer visualized God with Pastor Thorson's face, I still thought the word *God* referred to a personlike being 'out there.'" What brought his own belief to an end, he says, was "a collision between two worldviews," that of his childhood package (which is probably close to that of people of all ages in many traditional cultures) and what he calls "'the modern worldview' . . . the image of reality that emerged during the Enlightenment."[8] This, he says, was simply the opposite of the old

7. Otto, *The Idea of the Holy: An Inquiry into the Non-rational Factor in the Idea of the Divine and Its Relation to the Rational;* Eliade, *Sacred and Profane;* Borg, *God We Never Knew,* 17.

8. Borg, *God We Never Knew,* 23 (emphasis in the original), 19, 20. Borg defines *worldview,*

one; where the old one had been spiritual and arbitrary, the Enlightenment worldview was materialistic and deterministic. He did not find that one satisfying for long, either, and his studies eventually led him to the discovery that there had been another Christian worldview all along and a different God that went with it.

Borg, like many others today, uses the term *supernatural theism* for the worldview he rejected, centered on God conceived as an omnipotent, omniscient lawgiver and enforcer, who was one being among other beings even if vastly more powerful than the others. The alternative worldview he later became aware of he calls "panentheism" (literally, from Greek, "all-in-God-ism"), a term coined by German theologians in the early nineteenth century to speak of the idea expressed in Acts 17:28, where Paul says of God, "In him we live, move, and have our being."[9] Panentheism refers to a God that is not "*a* being" but "being itself," and it holds that all particular things exist "*within*" God, who as being itself transcends all the particular, finite beings that exist in "him" (to use the traditional anthropomorphic language, which becomes rather stretched in this context). Borg says he first learned about this other way of conceiving God from Bishop John A. T. Robinson (the author of *Honest to God*) and Paul Tillich, who often spoke of God as "Being-Itself" or "the ground of being" and said that God does not "exist"; rather, God *is.*[10] But the way of thinking that now goes by the name of panentheism is much older and more closely involved with the Christian theological tradition than Borg indicates in his book (Borg's own focus is more on biblical sources). Saint Thomas Aquinas in the thirteenth century formulated it in metaphysical terms in the language of "*Ipsum Esse subsistens*" (Being Itself subsisting) in his *Summa Theologica,* and Thomas's innovation was not this way of thinking but only the Aristotelian conceptuality that he brought to it.[11] The same pattern of thinking was shared by Thomas's contemporary Saint Bonaventure, even though Bonaventure used the more traditional Neoplatonic language for it, and it can

---

helpfully I think, as "a culture or religion's taken-for-granted understanding of reality—a root image of what is real and thus of how to live" (19–20).

9. The word, perhaps I should note for those to whom it is unfamiliar, is *panentheism,* not the more familiar *pantheism,* which simply identifies the divine with the totality of finite things.

10. Borg, *God We Never Knew,* 24. We also saw in Chapter 6 another formulation of this way of conceiving God in H. Richard Niebuhr's discussion of what he called "radical monotheism."

11. See Aquinas, *Summa Theologica,* pt. 1, questions 2–3, especially question 3, article 5, "Whether God is contained in a genus?" and question 13, especially article 11, "Whether this name, *He Who Is,* is the most proper name of God?"

be traced all the way back through Augustine and the Greek patristic theologians to the earliest years in which Christians began to look for philosophical language to express what had before been spoken of only in biblical narrative and poetic imagery.

For an audience not familiar with any conception of God other than the one Borg calls the finger-shaker, Borg's book is a good introduction to a broader picture, although it simplifies the real complexity of the Christian question of God by reducing it to just two conceptions.[12] Simplification is useful, and I don't mean to criticize Borg for it, especially since it was appropriate for the audience he was addressing and since I want myself to try to avoid getting more involved in the intricacies of that history of ideas than is needed for my purpose at this point, which is to call attention to the diversity of worldviews that can be found within each religious tradition and make for different possible lines of development within them.

There is an inherent dynamism in religions, I would like to suggest, that gives any religion a tendency toward inner diversity; religious conceptions grow out of questions, and the answers to questions tend to give rise to new questions in turn. Religious questions are never simply theoretical speculations. On the contrary, they are existential.[13] Religious questions look for meaning that offers orientation in a bewildering universe in which we need to know not only what to think but also how to live, what to do, and how to relate to one another, to ourselves, and to our and the world's possibilities. Every crossroads on the paths of questioning opens ways that some within a tradition may feel offer promise. Sometimes elaborate institutional systems form to protect certain answers and close off further questions, but existential questions are not easy to stifle.

I will come back later to the diverse worldviews that fall under the general umbrella of "Christianity," but for the moment I will mention just one additional complication about that tradition that also has a bearing on the contemporary international scene: there are deep differences between Western

12. For a more extensive historical and theological exploration of these issues, see William C. Placher, *The Domestication of Transcendence: How Modern Thinking about God Went Wrong.* It is perhaps worth mentioning that the single greatest division within the historical Christian tradition, the split between the Eastern and Western churches over different conceptions of the doctrine of the Trinity, involved major differences between two essentially panentheistic patterns of theological thinking. On this, see Webb, "Augustine's New Trinity: The Anxious Circle of Metaphor."

13. For a profound discussion of existential questioning as it can unfold on various levels and in various modes from mythological to theoretical, see Voegelin, *The Ecumenic Age,* 388–410.

Christian worldviews and those of the Eastern Christian world, and also very different experiences of historical development between them. I will not try in this book to go into those differences, but it is at least worth noting, since they have played a historic role both in the distant and in the recent past, and they may become salient again at some point in the future. As I write this now, the differences between the Western world and the Islamic world are the ones that seem to cry for attention, but not long ago the major conflict attracting the world's attention was in the former Yugoslavia, where Eastern and Western Christians were struggling with each other as well as with the Muslim people of Bosnia and Kosovo. At the time it seemed few in the West were giving much consideration to the idea that understanding the religious histories of those various traditions could help one to understand something important about the roots of that conflict, but since the events of September 11, 2001, and the U.S. occupation of Iraq, with the Muslim sectarian conflict that has since broken out in that country, it has become clear that religious differences are worth serious attention.

Islamic Worldviews: Sunni and Shiite

Let us turn then to the consideration of Islamic worldviews. I hope I may be forgiven for speaking anecdotally about some of this, but since even as I write we are in the midst of a great deal of discussion among the broad North American and European public of just these matters, it seems appropriate for me to speak of what I have been encountering in the way of people's efforts to get a handle on them in the aftermath of 9/11. They have not found it easy. There are plenty of good books on Islam and Muslim history, but few seem to have the time to read them, and some hope to get better information by listening to actual Muslims rather than by reading scholars of Islam, who are largely, even if not exclusively, non-Muslim. This can make for some difficulties, especially when the Muslim informants represent different types of Islam while typically considering their own type to be the only authentic one (a problem not unknown, of course, among people who speak for other religions).

On one occasion, in the winter of 2006, I participated in an interfaith discussion in which the Muslim informant, the imam (the prayer leader) of a mosque in Seattle, was asked about Shiite Islam. He answered that the difference between Sunnis and Shiites is simply political, explaining that after the death of Muhammad in 632 CE there was a discussion of who should be his successor as the head of the Muslim community and that although the majority decided in favor of Abu Bakr, a minority, the Shiites, preferred a different candidate and refused to accept the majority vote. From the Sunni point of view, this really is all there is to it, and hence the difference seems only political. But the Shiite point of view is quite different—so different in fact that in such a discussion Sunnis and Shiites could only talk past each other, because they speak out of different imaginative universes.

Boiled down to bare essentials, the Sunni way of understanding Islam is, as was mentioned in the preceding chapter, that Muhammad (beginning in 610 at around the age of forty) received the revelation of the Qur'an and was called to accept and submit to it like any other human being.[14] He had to figure out what it might mean, he had to decide whether the meaning made sense and was believable, and he had to decide whether to believe and obey it. Muhammad in the Sunni worldview was a man like any other, and therefore in his submission (which is the root meaning of the word *islam* in Arabic) to the will of God as expressed in the Qur'anic revelation he became a model for every other Muslim (that is, "submitter"). In principle, every person can become like Muhammad by doing as he did. The community of Muslims is made up of people who interpret, believe, and heed the commands of the Qur'an, people who are equals in the sense that they are all in the same position before the revelation from God, of which Muhammad had been in no sense the author but only the deliverer.

From the Sunni point of view, Muhammad was one of those equals, even though his role as receiver and reporter of the divine message and his personal capabilities also led to his playing an extensive role as leader of the community of the faithful during his lifetime. This was a much more comprehensive leadership role than is the pattern in most other religions: Muhammad was not only the spiritual leader of the Muslim community but also its political leader, its military leader, and its highest legal adjudicator. Because Muhammad had served as this sort of leader (imam) for the community (the *ummah*), it was

14. In what follows I will be presenting the standard historical account of the events. I should mention that there is a revisionist school of thinking among some Western scholars engaged in a "quest for the historical Muhammad" that interprets most of this history as mythic, but they remain a minority among Islamicists. What matters for the present purpose is that, whatever the historical truth may be, the main outline of events as I will recount them is accepted as accurate by both Sunni and Shiite Muslims, and it serves as the story on which both base their interpretations of what true Islam is. The holy book believed by Muslims to record the revelations received by Muhammad I will refer to as the *Qur'an,* the transliteration currently favored by most Islamicists, though it is also often transliterated as *Koran.* The word *Sunni* derives from *sunna,* which refers to the path of tradition deriving from Muhammad's practice and example.

natural to look for another who could play that role after his death in 632 CE.[15] The followers sought a leader appropriate to succeed Muhammad in all those roles—the only exception being that the successor (*khalifa*, "caliph") would not receive further revelations from God. This exception made emphatic the equality of all believers before the Qur'an, the full and final revelation. Therefore, any good Muslim with leadership ability could in principle serve as caliph.

Various candidates were considered, but the one with the most support among those with influence at the time and place was Muhammad's father-in-law, Abu Bakr, an early and well-respected follower of the Prophet. Hence, from the Sunni point of view the question of succession was a political issue, a decision to be made by the community through majority choice. Sunnis constitute the great majority, usually estimated at roughly 85 percent, of Muslims worldwide. and so from their point of view Shiite resistance to the Muslim community's decision is a rejection of the divinely willed unity of the *ummah*.

The minority that became the Shia agreed with the others on the need for an appropriate successor, but they had a different idea not just of who in particular that should be but also of what should be the criteria of appropriateness.[16] The minority believed that Muhammad had been not simply first among equals but had also received special charismatic qualities from God that raised him above other human beings, and that these qualities could be inherited by his male descendants.[17] Consequently, they thought that the leader of the *ummah* should be a male descendant of Muhammad. None was available at the time, because the Prophet had left only daughters, but the minority believed that the most appropriate candidate for first caliph was Ali,

15. I am simplifying here, but this is the way Muslims themselves have told the story for centuries. In fact, not everyone agreed that there should be one successor for the Muslim community as a whole; there were some who thought there should be separate leaders for Medina, Mecca, and other places, and the eventual unified Islamic state had to be imposed by force on dissident tribes. See Marshall G. S. Hodgson, *The Venture of Islam: Conscience and History in a World Civilization*, 1:197–200.

16. The word *Shia* comes from a word meaning "division," "party," or "sect," a name applied to the Shia, as one might expect, by Sunnis.

17. Or at least this is what later Shiite traditions interpreted the early minority position to be. It is also possible that they were simply legitimists, that is, that they simply preferred hereditary succession to election as a political principle and that Shiite thinking in the proper sense as it later developed has been projected back into the time of origins, as often happens among religious groups. What is important to bear in mind is that, whatever the actual historical facts, it is the story told in the tradition that functions to define a religion for its believers.

Muhammad's cousin and son-in-law and the father of his grandsons Hasan and Husayn.[18] They thought that Ali, whom they also believed to have special spiritual gifts of his own and to have received secret instructions on the faith from his father-in-law, should have been the first caliph and then should have been succeeded by his sons, the true descendants of the Prophet.

As it happened, Ali eventually did become the fourth caliph, although with some serious opposition, but he was assassinated in 661 by some in his own camp who objected to his willingness to negotiate with his opponents. I do not wish to burden the reader with too much detail, but some of the details are of interest since they indicate the nature of the differences of worldview that developed between Sunnis and Shiites. Ali succeeded the third caliph, Uthman, after he had been murdered by some opponents of his own who then installed Ali. The legitimacy of Ali's caliphate was consequently questionable from the start, since from the point of view of Sunni Muslims, Uthman's murder was a crime against the legitimately chosen head of the community, and it should have been followed by another community deliberation about his appropriate successor. Sunni tradition recognizes Ali as the fourth caliph, but with all the ambiguity entailed by these circumstances.

From the Shiite point of view, on the other hand, Ali's ascension to the caliphate was justified whatever the circumstances, because it was in accord with God's will and was the righting of an original wrong, and his subsequent assassination was just one more expression of human failure properly to submit to God, that is, to be truly *muslim,* a "submitter." Ali was not, from their point of view, the fourth in the line of successors to Muhammad, but really the first. (There was even one early Shiite sect that claimed the angel Gabriel should be cursed for misdelivering the Qur'an to Muhammad rather than Ali, who should have been the leader of the community from the very beginning.)[19] Shiites generally have come to use the term *Imam* (meaning "leader") rather than *caliph* for the true successors of Muhammad.[20] This is the same term as that generally used among Sunnis for the person who leads prayers in the mosque on a Friday, as mentioned above, but without the idea

18. Since Arabic names have to be transliterated to be rendered in the Roman alphabet, one sees them spelled in a variety of ways. *Husayn,* for example, is also written as *Husain* or *Hussein.* I will use the transliteration *Husayn* so that it will be clear that I am not referring to any of several modern Husseins.

19. See Patricia Crone, *God's Rule: Government and Islam,* 82.

20. I will capitalize the word *Imam* when referring to the Shiite use to distinguish it from the Sunni use, which is more general and has no sacred connotations.

of a special charismatic status. Sunnis have no ordained clergy in the sense in which Christian ministers or priests or Jewish rabbis are officially ordained. Rather, any reputable and knowledgeable member of the *ummah* can serve as imam during Friday prayers. Among Shiites, on the other hand, *Imam* has a very special meaning: an Imam for Shiites is one of the male descendants of Muhammad who has inherited the sort of special spiritual qualities that distinguished him and who is therefore suited to serve as a guide for the *ummah* as a whole.

The Shia divided over the centuries into different streams of tradition, generally around the particular Imams thought to be the last in the true line of succession. Hence, there are what are known as Fiver, Sevener, and Twelver Shiites—generally after the number of Imams they believe constitute the true succession—or as they are also called, *Zaydis, Ismailis,* and *Imamis* after the Imams they believe were last in the true line. Twelvers, for example, believe that the twelfth and last Imam did not die but withdrew into "occultation" or "hiding" (hence the term *hidden Imam*) and still communicates spiritually with certain eminent individuals, such as ayatollahs and perhaps other prominent clerics.

There are nevertheless considerable differences among Shiite groups. To simplify, one important difference is that although the Shia began with the claim that the rightly guided Imam should be the political as well as the religious leader of all Muslims, the movement of the Twelvers, who are now the largest Shiite group and have been dominant in Iran for centuries, originated from among earlier Shiites when the eleventh Imam in their line died in 874 without a successor. The original Twelvers claimed that the eleventh Imam had had an infant son, Muhammad al-Mahdi, who was his rightful successor but was taken by God into hiding after disappearing during the funeral of his father in the great mosque in Samarra (the mosque that was blown up in February 2006, setting off widespread conflict between Shiites and Sunnis throughout Iraq). This twelfth Imam is identified by them as the "Mahdi," the messiah-like figure widely expected among Muslims generally to come (along with Jesus) at the end-time and play a major role in the events that will wind up the course of history. This had the effect of making the Twelvers into an eschatological movement and leading them to withdraw from politics while waiting for the Imam's return from hiding—until the Ayatollah Khomeini developed a new religiously quite revolutionary (for Twelvers) way of thinking in the 1980s that brought them back into political life in Iran. Until Khomeini, Twelvers had believed the true faithful should keep aloof from the impurity of the political world and wait for the return of the hidden Imam. Khomeini developed a radically different conception of the Shiite purpose as a calling to become directly involved in politics in order to prepare for the Imam's return. (It was his rejection of this religiously revolutionary political activism that led Ayatollah Ali al-Sistani to leave Iran and move to Iraq.) Ayatollah Khomeini's transformation of the Twelvers' traditional passive eschatology into eschatological activism is not unlike some of the eschatological activisms that erupted in Europe in the later Middle Ages and Reformation and that shaped the thinking of many early settlers in New England about establishing a New Jerusalem to prepare for the Second Coming of Christ.[21]

The Seveners originated around the same time as the Twelvers, as a reaction against the Twelver idea that the Imam was to be a spiritual leader but not a political one, and they have subsequently divided into many groups, some of the best known of which are the Nizar Ismailis (who follow the Agha Khan as their Imam), the secretive Druzes, and the medieval group known as the Assassins. Both the Twelvers and the Seveners believe their "rightly guided" Imams to be infallible. Many also believe them to be sinless. Some Seveners have even claimed that their Imam is a manifestation or incarnation of God, a claim that is blasphemy to Sunnis and that even most Shiites would consider extreme.[22]

The important implication of all this is that, as Patricia Crone, puts it, "With the Shi'ites . . . we encounter a thinking that can only be described as authoritarian."[23] The search for a true successor to Muhammad and to Ali was a search for someone who could guide the faithful with such sureness that there could be no doubt either about him or about the direction he would give the Muslim community. The logic of trying to find that in an individual person was worked out in different ways by different groups, but the general direction in which it led was toward a person who could be deemed to have superhuman qualities such as infallibility and sinlessness or even to be divine in his very being. The difference of worldview that this implies between Shiites and Sunnis should be clear, along with its social and political implications.

It would be too simple, however, to say that whereas Shiite Islam has an in-

21. A late medieval example would be Cola di Rienzo and an early Reformation one would be the Anabaptist movement in Münster led by John of Leiden in the sixteenth century.

22. This is also the claim of a group known by their opponents as the *ghulat* (extremists). As Heinz Halm explains: "The Imams are not human individuals for the *ghulat,* but rather are only 'veils' in which the deity constantly reclothes himself" (*Shi'ism,* 154).

23. Crone, *God's Rule,* 70.

nate propensity toward authoritarianism, Sunni Islam, because of its belief in the equality of all believers, is inherently democratic. The reality is more complex, for several reasons. One is that the reality of Islam in practice is not made up of watertight compartments with Sunni thought in one and Shiite in the other. Shiite themes and imagery can also be found running through the Sunni imagination, such as devotion to local holy men or the idea of the special honor due to a sayyid or sharif, that is, a descendant of the Prophet through Husayn or Hasan. Despite the Sunni idea of the equality of Muslims before the God-given law of the Qur'an, some of the faithful can stand distinctly above others. In Sunni Morocco, for example, all three patterns are combined: the sultan is elected by a council of ulema (men learned in the Qur'an and Muslim traditions), but to be eligible for election he is also supposed to be both a charismatic holy man and a descendant of the Prophet. Clifford Geertz describes this as exhibiting "the contradictions of an Islam scriptural in theory but anthropolatrous [man-worshiping] in fact."[24]

It would also be too simple, I should add, to try to explain the conflict in Iraq between Sunnis and Shiites in the first decade of the twenty-first century only in terms of the differences in worldview just sketched. Prior to 1991, when President George H. W. Bush urged Iraqis to rebel against Saddam Hussein and many Shiites did so, the religious differences between Sunnis and Shiites in Iraq did not on the whole seem particularly urgent to either group, even if there was tension present in their historical memories of how the Arabian Sunni caliphate had opposed the Shia led by Husayn, Muhammad's grandson, who was killed at Karbala in 680 in a failed rebellion against the Umayyad caliphate. The fierce repression and persecution of Shiites in the aftermath of the 1991 rebellion, however, began stimulating the sort of polarization effect that thinkers like Girard, Becker, and the terror management theorists describe, and this effect has been immensely exacerbated since America entered Iraq in 2003 and produced the sort of situation that Girard calls a "sacrificial crisis," in which people threatened with chaos defend themselves against that by seeking a common enemy (a potential sacrificial victim) to unite against.[25] It is not differences in worldview as such that cause the polarization; rather, the crisis itself causes a frantic search for differences of any kind (which could be of religion or worldview, of skin color, of class, of cultural ethnicity, or even Dr.

24. Geertz, *Islam Observed*, 53.

25. See Girard, *Violence and the Sacred*, chap. 2, "The Sacrificial Crisis," and chap. 4, "The Origins of Myth and Ritual."

Seuss's stars on bellies) around which a group can form and define itself as the polar opposite of some other group.

Although one might expect a tradition that believes in equality before the Qur'an to be open to diversity of interpretation, Sunni thinking has tended in recent centuries to stick to a very conservative standard reading. In the first centuries of the Muslim era there was extensive dialogue about how to understand the Qur'an and its implications for practice, especially with reference to situations that, due to the rapid Muslim conquest of surrounding territories, were not present at the time of the original revelation. What eventually became the favored way of dealing with such questions, however, was following the teaching and example of the Prophet as supposedly recorded by observers. (Muhammad's teaching was distinct from the Qur'an, which came directly from God by the transmission of the angel Gabriel. The tradition holds that Muhammad was always careful to distinguish his own views from the truth that was revealed.) Traditions (known as "hadith") about what Muhammad said and did (his practice, or "sunna") were collected during the first two centuries or so, until so many diverse and even contradictory hadith had accumulated that scholars had to begin a great winnowing to identify the more reliable ones. Where neither the Qur'an nor the hadith provided clear answers, interpreters were expected to reason by analogy from material in these sources, or as a last resort to employ *ijtihad,* the effort of individual reasoning. In the early Muslim centuries there were also very lively schools of thought that tried to deal with questions of interpretation and practice by reasoned discourse informed by the study of Greek philosophy, but those were eventually eclipsed by the power of the developing consensus *(ijma)* founded on the hadith accepted as genuine. The eventual outcome was what we now know as Sunni Islam, based on the consensus among the hadith party as to how Islam should be understood and the Muslim world ordered. The "gates of *ijtihad*" were said to be shut.

Many questions that were originally open therefore became closed. For example, one that was actively debated in the early centuries had to do with whether the Qur'an was created or eternal. To the advocates of reasoned interpretation it seemed that to interpret the Qur'an as uncreated would be equivalent to identifying it with God, so they thought it should be considered created. The consensus of the ulema, however, became that it is uncreated and eternal, and that position remains firmly dominant today. Then there was the question of literal or metaphorical interpretation of the many passages that refer to God as having bodily parts, sitting on a throne, and so on. To those influenced by Greek philosophy those ideas taken literally seemed to conflict with the idea of God's infinity and eternity, but the ulema decided even such passages must be interpreted literally.

Then there are passages that seem ambiguous but regarding which the consensus settled on a single interpretation that has since remained unquestionable, such as the idea that Jesus was never crucified and did not die but was assumed into heaven. The Qur'an has a passage that describes the Jews as saying, "Lo, we slew the Messiah, Jesus, the son of Mary, the Messenger of God," and then comments, "yet they did not slay him, nor did they crucify him, but doubt was sown among them. And those who differ therein are in doubt because of him. They have no knowledge concerning him, but only follow an opinion. In truth they did not slay him, but God raised him up to Himself." Robert Charles Zaehner wrote that it would be more logical to interpret this statement in a way that would parallel another Qur'anic passage about the Muslim victory at the Battle of Badr, where God says, "Ye slew them not, but God slew them; and where thou (Muhammad) didst throw, then thou didst not throw, but God threw," that is, it was God who caused the events to happen, not human power or design.[26] Such an idea regarding the possible death of Jesus is no longer open to discussion, however, for Sunni tradition.

According to the hadith, Muhammad is supposed to have said that the Muslim community will never agree on an error. Consequently, once a consensus forms, however tenuous might be its cognitive foundations, it becomes virtually impossible to reopen a question, since that would raise the possibility that both Muhammad and the community's consensus could be fallible. In this respect, both the Sunni and the Shiite traditions might be said—at least to one looking at them from the outside—to have fallen captive to a fundamental human proclivity to flee from the dynamism (and anxiety) of questioning into premature closure. Both Sunni and Shiite Muslims understand their relation to God as one of submission (which, as mentioned above, is the Arabic meaning of the word *islam*). Submission to God tends to become mediated for Sunni tradition by submission to the consensus of a particular time and culture, and for Shiite tradition by submission to the authority of a sacrosanct leader.

The Shiite tradition, precisely because of its authoritarian tendency, actually has more built-in possibility to change direction. The Shia also has its own hadith and its own consensus of scholars, but the possibility of authoritative lead-

26. Surahs 4:156 and 8:17, quoted in Zaehner, *The Comparison of Religions*, 211, 212.

ership from an Imam, whether hidden and mediated by learned and inspired representatives (the ayatollahs), as for the Twelvers, or continuously present, as for the Nizar Ismailis, makes for the possibility of considerable innovation. There has been a long tradition among Twelver Shiites of recognizing as *mujtahids* those authorized to exercise *ijtihad*, the power to reason on the basis of their own thinking and of their spiritual attunement to the wisdom of the hidden Imam. The Ayatollah Khomeini's revisionist interpretation of the relation between the Shiite leaders and the state is an example, and there is no reason there could not be other abrupt changes in Shiite thought in the future. A community loyal to infallible consensus is much harder to turn around than one following an infallible leader, but exploratory questioning and dialogue become difficult in either.[27]

Conceptions of Authority and Interpretation

I am sure the reader has already begun to think about parallels in Christian tradition, and as I said, the problem is rooted in a fundamental human proclivity, not just a particular religious culture. The Roman Catholic Church, especially since the declaration of papal infallibility in 1870, has a highly authoritarian structure, at least in principle, and considerable Catholic controversy since that time has had to do with trying to figure out how to interpret its implications. It may even be that the hesitance of Catholic theologians to identify any particular papal pronouncement as infallible and the difficulty they have had deciding what precisely would constitute the criteria of infallibility function as a kind of parallel to the hiddenness of the Shiite Imam: it offers the advantages of believing there is certainty while keeping a safe distance from its actual effects.[28] If one were to look for a Christian

27. There have, however, been interesting reports recently of some Muslims actually converting from Sunni to Shiite (something rarely known in the past) because they believe Shiism offers greater room for *ijtihad* and therefore for more flexible adaptation of Islam to modern conditions. See Andrew Tabler, "Catalytic Converters."

28. Regarding this particular issue, however, it is probably important to bear in mind that the meaning of such an idea as "infallibility" may differ considerably in different cultural contexts. Anglo-Saxon and northern European ways of thinking about law, for example, are very different from those in Italy, where "I was in a hurry" is not an excuse that would be dismissed out of hand by a traffic policeman. A Jesuit friend told me that when he was studying in Rome a prohibition was issued against Catholic clergy appearing at public "spectacles," which included theatrical events. The cleric who made that decree, a great opera lover, was seen that very night at the opera and was asked how he could be there. He answered that the ban was "in principle," but if one had a good reason, such as a night at the opera, one could ignore it. It may be that the dogma of papal

parallel to the Sunni emphasis on infallible consensus, the clearest example would probably be Eastern Orthodoxy, where no one bishop has authority to impose his interpretations and where the consensus of the faithful holds the ultimate authority—even to decide which decisions of councils of bishops can be considered to have ecumenical validity.[29] It may take centuries for that consensus to become clear, but when it does, it tends to be strongly resistant to change. A tradition with a strong central authority can change quickly, as happened with the abrupt (and for some Catholics jolting) shift from the Latin mass to vernacular masses immediately after the Second Vatican Council, or as could happen if a future pope should decide, perhaps in the face of continuing decline in the number of male priests, to permit priests to marry or even to permit women to be ordained. Another example would be the decisions of presidents of the Church of Latter-day Saints since 1890 to end the practices of polygamy, prohibition of interracial marriage, and the exclusion of people of African descent from Mormon priesthood.

If Roman Catholicism has sought certainty in the infallibility of the pope and Eastern Orthodoxy in conciliar consensus, the traditions that grew out of the Protestant Reformation tended to seek certainty in the text of scripture, and some Protestant groups today still maintain emphatically the idea of "the inerrancy of scripture." Much of the history of Western Christianity since the Reformation, however, on the part of both Catholics and Protestants, has consisted of working out other ways of interpreting the nature of scriptural authority. Ulrich Zwingli, at the very dawn of the Reformation, wrote a book called *The Clarity and Certainty of the Word of God* (1522) in which he claimed not only that the Christian scriptures were inspired truth but that their meaning was so clear that interpretation was unnecessary. A few years later, however, he and Martin Luther clashed over the interpretation of Christ's presence in

infallibility has really meant, in its cultural setting in Italy, only that once the supreme pontiff has terminated a discussion on some point, the members of the flock are not to persist in publicly arguing it, whatever their actual views about the truth of the matter might be.

29. To mention a few examples of the determining role of consensus of the faithful in the Eastern Christian tradition: on the negative side, the failure of the Council of Ephesus in 449 to win acceptance and the rejection of the reunion of the Eastern and Western churches formalized at the Council of Ferrara-Florence in 1439 (despite the fact that it had the support of the emperor and the patriarch of Constantinople and all Eastern bishops present except one), and, on the positive side, the wide acceptance by Eastern Orthodox of the ecumenical standing of the councils in Constantinople in 1341 and 1351 that settled the Hesychastic Controversy, despite the fact that these were small, local events in what was by that time a greatly shrunken eastern Roman Empire.

the eucharist. Prince Philip of Hesse, in an effort to promote unity in the camp of reform, brought Luther and Zwingli together in Marburg in 1529 to discuss their differences, but they were unable to reach agreement on how to interpret biblical references to the eucharist as the "body" and "blood" of Christ. Literal meaning turned out to be more elusive than either anticipated, and with that began centuries of biblical interpretation and hermeneutic theory that Christians of all denominations have since either had to take into account or try to ignore. For many Christians it has been either a wrenching or an exciting experience, and sometimes both. Islam has not yet gone through anything like this, but it is likely that eventually it will, especially since many Muslims now live in Western cultural milieus and are exposed to the force of the same sorts of question that precipitated the hermeneutic crises of the West. Considering the centrality of the Qur'anic text for both Sunni and Shiite Islam, the opening up of the Qur'an (not to mention the hadith) to something like the range of interpretation the Hebrew and Christian scriptures have undergone among Jewish and Christian scholars could be expected to have earthshaking consequences, especially if the rapidity of modern communications forces it, once it starts, to take place during a much shorter time span than was afforded to Christians and Jews.

If this does take place, there is another element in the mix that will also play a role: the mystical tradition in Islam. Where an emphasis on institution or text tends to externalize authority, mysticism tends to put more emphasis on the authority of inner divine presence, and this can foster and legitimate departures from fixed traditions. In Islam the mystical side of the religion usually goes by the name of Sufism, although that word involves other connotations as well.[30] To simplify, after the solidifying of the ulema tradition Sufism took shape as what Fazlur Rahman has called "the Sufi challenge of love and pure devotion to the legists' concept of obedience and observance of the Law." It is not surprising that conflict would develop between Sufism's profession of an "inner way" of trust in and love for God and what Rahman calls "the charge of the 'Ulema' that, should the Sufi claims be granted, a door would be opened to spiritual anarchy because of the impossibility of regulating, controlling, and indeed, predicting the course of the 'inner life.'" Some Sufis were even exe-

30. Geertz says of Sufism: "In the Middle East, this seems mainly to have meant reconciling Arabian pantheism with Koranic legalism; in Indonesia, restating Indian illuminationism in Arabic phrases; in West Africa, defining sacrifice, possession, exorcism, and curing as Muslim rituals. In Morocco, it meant fusing the genealogical conception of sanctity with the miraculous—canonizing *les hommes fétiches*" (*Islam Observed*, 48).

cuted in the early centuries of Sufism for what sounded like extreme claims to have experienced "annihilation" of self and to "subsist in" God, but eventually an accommodation was worked out, principally through the influence of Abu Hamid al-Ghazali (1058–1111 CE), who said that Sufism and sharia (the tradition of law worked out by the consensus of the ulema) were complementary: that Sufism is the inwardness of Islam and sharia the outwardness, and that both are needed.[31] Sufism has given rise to its own forms of externalization, through the preeminence it sometimes accords to saints, living and dead, but it also undermines them even as it does so by legitimating claims to illumination from within.

Islam might be compared in this respect to Buddhism. Buddhism was born with an emphasis on the need for individual meditation practice if one is to become free from the desires that bind humans to an egoistic conception of existence, but Buddhist traditions have taken many forms in different cultures, some of which involve cultivating a sense of reliance either on a supernaturalized interpretation of the founder, Gautama Buddha—complete with descent from heaven and miraculous birth—or on a virtual pantheon of Buddhas and bodhisattvas. Vipassana and Ch'an (Zen) concentrate on the practice of sitting meditation and insist that one must break free from illusion by one's own efforts; Jodo devotees, on the other hand, chant endless prayers to the bodhisattva Amitabha. There is no need here to go into detail about the different forms of Buddhism, but it is worth bearing in mind that these divergent patterns of relation to transcendence represent fundamental possibilities that are likely to be realized in any religious tradition. Jewish tradition has both scholarly rabbis and charismatic rebbes, and Christian parallels probably leap by themselves to the reader's mind.

I will return for the moment, however, to the discussion of patterns of thinking in Islam, since the question that seems most urgent today is the potential for different sorts of development within the Islamic tradition. I should mention that Sufism constitutes a current running (often against some resistance, despite the synthesis of al-Ghazali) through Shiite as well as Sunni Islam. Haydar Amuli, for example, a fourteenth-century Shiite, proclaimed that "the true Shi'ism was Sufism and that reciprocally the true Sufism was Shi'ism."

31. Rahman, *Islam,* 130, 135. A prominent Sufi in the following century, Umar Suhravardi (1145–1234), said that God appointed Adam to propagate the sharia and his son Seth "to propagate the Sufi way as the inner truth of the Shar'ia," a division of labor that Ismaili Shiites attributed to Muhammad and Ali respectively and that they "projected back to all the great prophets" (Hodgson, *Venture of Islam,* 2:283).

So whatever potential Sufism might offer for more flexible interpretation is available to both Muslim traditions. Henry Corbin speaks of the connection between Sufism and the Shiite idea of *ta'wil* as a spiritual hermeneutic according to which "every exoteric meaning *(zahir)* has an esoteric meaning *(batin);* the book 'descended from Heaven,' the Koran, limited to the apparent letter, perishes in the opacity and servitude of legalistic religion." For the Qur'an to be truly revelatory, "it is necessary" through *ta'wil,* Corbin goes on to say, "to bring out the transparency of its depths, the esoteric meaning. And that is the mission of the Imam, the 'spiritual Guide,' even if in the present period of the world he is in 'great Occultation'—or rather, this meaning is himself, not to be sure his empirical individuality, but his theophanic Person."[32]

The reference to theophany (manifestation of the divine in some finite form) indicates the source of tension between the more standard versions of Islam, Sunni especially, and Sufism. One of the most famous incidents in Sufi history is the execution of the Persian Sufi al-Hallaj in Baghdad in 922 CE for proclaiming himself to be one with God in such statements as, "I am the Truth" ("al-Haqq," one of the ninety-nine names of God). As Corbin indicates, there is an affinity for theophany in Shiite Islam, since many Shiites think of their Imam as manifesting the divine, but for Sunni Islam the difference between God and creation is absolute. Shiites tend to see the gulf between God and creation being bridged at least partially in the person of the Imam, but they usually limit theophany to that one point. The Sufi strain within each of the two streams stretches them in the direction of something like a belief in universal incarnation as a process gradually being realized in persons open and responsive to the pull of the divine drawing.

The mainstream of Islamic thought has always been wary of such thinking, interpreting it as pantheistic. Although the origins of Sufism are historically obscure, one of the principal historical speculations has been that it derives from pre-Islamic pantheism either in Arabia or in central Asia in the region somewhat to the northeast of Persia. If Sufis used the terminology of Christian theologians that we saw Marcus Borg drawing on when he spoke of "panentheism," they might use that term too in defending themselves against the charge of pantheism. The difference between pantheism and pan*en*theism is that in the former there can be no transcendence, since "God" becomes simply the name for the sum total of all finite reality. For panentheism, on the other hand, the syllable *en* (in) functions metaphorically to indicate that the infinite be-

32. Corbin, *Creative Imagination in the Sufism of Ibn Arabi,* 26, 28.

ing of God radically transcends all "participated being," whether one seeks to explore that in the outward or the inward direction. Just as the Jewish tradition may speak of God as "at once above the Universe and the very soul of the Universe," what the Sufi contends is that in the mystery of God divine transcendence is complemented by divine immanence: the divine Beyond is also a divine Within.[33]

The language of divine union is used by Sufis, as also by Christian and Jewish mystics, to refer to the terminal point of their process of spiritual striving, the goal of their deepest longing. In a simple pantheism there would be nothing to strive toward or long for, since all that exists would be flattened out into a world without transcendence. One might strive, as Spinoza seems to have, for the serenity that would come with knowing that the finite is all there is, but that is not the aspiration to which Rumi, the thirteenth-century Sufi poet, gave expression when he wrote:

> This is how I would die
> into the love I have for you:
> as pieces of cloud
> dissolve in sunlight.
>
> or
>
> No longer a stranger, you listen
> all day to these crazy love words.
> Like a bee you fill hundreds of homes with
> honey, though yours is a long way from here.[34]

Such language, as long as it makes clear that it is not crossing over into simple pantheism, has resonance for Muslims generally, since one of the most basic principles of all Islam, urged throughout the Qur'an, is what is called *dhikr,* the constant remembrance of the presence of God and of the calling to inward as well as outward *islam* ("submission" to God). *Dhikr,* one might say, is

33. This last phrase is an echo of Eric Voegelin, commenting on the Apocalypse of Abraham: "Since God is present even in the confusion of the heart, preceding and motivating the search itself, the divine Beyond is at the same time a divine Within" (*The Ecumenic Age,* 398). See also Abraham Cohen's *Everyman's Talmud:* "However reluctant the teachers of Israel were to identify God with His Universe and insisted on His being exalted high above the abode of men, yet they thought of the world as permeated through and through with the omnipresent *Shechinah.* God is at once above the Universe and the very soul of the Universe" (47).

34. Maulana Jalal al-Din Rumi, *The Soul of Rumi: A New Collection of Ecstatic Poems,* 32, 63.

where Sufism overlaps with both Sunni and Shiite Islam, and this is probably the reason for the wide acceptance among many Muslims of the synthesis of al-Ghazali.

That synthesis may constitute a basis for future development in the Muslim world, as may also the regard in Sunni tradition for another complementary figure, the important tenth-century Sunni thinker al-Ashari. Like al-Ghazali, who began as a legal scholar but later became a Sufi and worked out a way of combining Sufism with the legal tradition, al-Ashari began as an advocate of philosophical critique and rationalizing interpretation of the Qur'an, but later converted to the position of the ulema regarding the importance of staying as close as possible to a literal interpretation. However, in his working out of the conservative position to make it more defensible as well as more palatable to those who were hesitant about overly literal interpretation, he taught that although statements in the Qur'an that attribute bodily parts to God are to be interpreted literally, what those literal interpretations may mean is beyond human comprehension: what it means to say that God sits, sees, and so on does not mean what we normally understand as sitting or seeing. Another position of the consensus of the ulema that al-Ashari interpreted in a way that opened it up for possible development was belief that the Qur'an is uncreated and eternal. Advocates of philosophical critique objected, as was mentioned above, that this would make the Qur'an identical with God. Al-Ashari worked out an interpretation according to which the words of the Qur'an, as ideas in the mind of God, are uncreated and eternal, but the words read or recited are created and temporal and are produced in part by human effort.

The Islamic world has not yet experienced anything like the vast enterprise of scriptural critique that the Jewish and Christian worlds have since the Middle Ages, but when it does, it may be that al-Ashari's recasting of the medieval consensus, which remains widely respected in the Muslim world, will serve as a preparation for it. If Islam eventually does go through that sort of critical reflection on its sources and their possible meanings, Sufism's tradition of inwardness and al-Ashari's recognition of the limitations of human understanding as it reaches toward God may together serve as a basis for recovering the intellectual openness Islam had in its early centuries.

Different Christian Gods

That kind of critical reflection is still going on, of course, in the West, and to understand what it involves here and could also eventually involve for the

Islamic world, it may be useful to consider more carefully the case of Christian thought and the question of its different Gods with which this chapter opened. I said above that the question of Christian conceptions of God was more complex than Borg had time to address in *The God We Never Knew,* although he does an excellent job of opening up the topic. It will be worth looking a little more deeply into the history of Christian thought on this subject because that tradition has probably articulated more fully and in more explicit detail than any other so far the range of ways, present in all three of the monotheistic faiths, that it is possible to interpret the idea of God or a God.

Perhaps I should address a question that may arise in some readers' minds as to why I, like Borg in *The God We Never Knew,* speak of different Christian Gods: are not Christians, Jews, and Muslims supposed to believe there is only one God? Why not speak simply of different ways of understanding that one God? To speak in that manner, however, would beg several major questions. It would assume that there is a single real entity named "God" who is simply interpreted in different ways by different people. Or it would assume that whether or not that God really existed, there is a single ideal conception of the divine that is only articulated in different ways. It would also deflect attention from important differences of theological conception by treating them as secondary and accidental, while assuming that the one either real or ideal entity is what matters, whether we understand it well or not. As I will explain, the differences among some of these conceptions are quite deep, and to believe in and seek to serve the God defined by one of them may mean to oppose the God defined by another. A still more important reason for taking a phenomenological approach to the question of God—that is, an approach that steps back from the question of reality and simply considers ideas as ideas—is that one of the deepest and most divisive questions in theology is whether what the tradition calls "God" should be conceived as a particular entity at all or whether that God should be conceived, as in Aquinas and most earlier Christian thinkers, not as an entity but as Being Itself.

This last issue can lead to pitfalls if it is not well understood. An example, I think, is the position advocated by Daniel Dennett that God can be legitimately conceived only as a supernatural individual entity. Defining what he means by religious belief, Dennett says, "If what they call God is really *not* an agent in their eyes, a being that can *answer* prayers, *approve* and *disapprove, receive* sacrifices, and *mete out* punishment or forgiveness, then, although they may call this Being God, and stand in awe of *it* (not *Him*), their creed, whatever it is, is not really a religion according to my definition." Later he says more pointedly, "If what you hold sacred is not any kind of Person you could pray to, or consider to be an appropriate recipient of gratitude (or anger, when a loved one is senselessly killed), you're an atheist in my book. If for reasons of loyalty to tradition, diplomacy, or self-protective camouflage . . . you want to deny what you are, that's your business, but don't kid yourself."[35] Explaining his reasons for this view, Dennett draws on what he calls the "useful if philosophically misbegotten terminology," of the sociologist of religion Rodney Stark, who "distinguishes two strategies: *God as essence* (such as Tillich's God as the Ground of All Being, entirely nonanthropomorphic, not in time and space, abstract) and *God as conscious supernatural being* (a God who listens to and answers prayers in real time, for instance)."[36]

The reason Dennett considers Stark's terms "philosophically misbegotten" is probably that the term *essence* is used in philosophy (as in theology) to refer to the "nature" or intelligible structure of a thing, whereas Stark's definition of it for his own purpose is cosmic or universal "principle." To quote Stark himself, "In some religions the supernatural is conceived of as an omnipresent *essence* or principle governing all life, but as impersonal, remote, and definitely not a being." He gives as an example the Chinese concept of "the Tao" and then likens that to some Western ways of thinking about the divine: "However, religions based on essences are not found only in the East. Many western intellectuals, including some theologians and bishops, have reduced their conception of 'God' to an essence as impersonal as Immanuel Kant's . . . of which he wrote: 'God is not a being outside me, but merely a thought in me . . . God must be represented not as substance outside me, but as the highest moral principle in me.'" Stark goes on to say, "At a minimum, the term 'God' ought to refer to *beings*. Hence: *Gods* are *conscious supernatural beings*."[37]

Dennett does find Stark's distinction "useful" enough that he proceeds to use it a great deal, and Stark would probably be indifferent to the idea that it might be "philosophically misbegotten," since his own focus is sociological, and his point is that religions (such as Taoism, Buddhism, and Confucianism) that do not involve gods have little sociological impact. Unlike Dennett, Stark does not deny the name "religion" to a religion without a "conscious super-

35. Dennett, *Breaking the Spell,* 10 (emphasis in the original), 245. Even more pointedly, he quotes H. L. Mencken: "The only really respectable Protestants are the Fundamentalists. Unfortunately, they are also palpable idiots" (190).

36. Ibid., 266, 191.

37. Stark, *One True God: Historical Consequences of Monotheism,* 9–10 (emphases in the original). He quotes Kant in *Kant Selections,* 373–74.

natural being," but says that "Godless religions are unable to gather a mass following, always being limited in their appeal to small, intellectual elites," because "divine essences can do nothing on behalf of humans."[38] I see no reason to object to Stark's use of his terms for his purpose, which is more narrowly and precisely focused than Dennett's, but if either's way of using some of these terms were to be taken as normative for understanding religious thought more broadly considered, it could be seriously misleading, so I will try to clarify the issues and the history of the terms as they have been used by serious religious thinkers over the centuries.

Since it will help to clarify other terms as well, let me start by discussing one Dennett, Stark, and Borg all use in a modern colloquial sense but which has had a precise technical meaning in theology that is quite different: *supernatural.* As we have seen all three of these thinkers use the term (as I too, somewhat reluctantly following Borg and popular use, have also used it in the phrase "supernatural theism"), it refers to whatever might be conceived of as above the level of human beings in the order of nature. So the type of "supernatural being" Dennett and Stark refer to would be a particular entity possessing greater powers than human beings have. Neither talks about angels, but if they did, they would probably consider angels, too, to be supernatural beings, since angels are thought of (by people who think angels exist) as higher in the order of nature than humans or any other kind of earthly being. But in the theological tradition that developed in the Middle Ages to talk about them and about God in a systematic way, angels were not considered supernatural at all, because they had natures. The term *nature* meant that which defines an entity as belonging to a certain type and thereby sets the ontological boundaries of the entity, that is, limits it to having the characteristics of its type of entity and not of some other. Every entity was said to be bounded (limited or defined) by its nature: a human is bounded by human nature, an animal by animal nature (which includes the properties of human nature except for rationality), a vegetable by its vegetable nature (which includes the animal's capacity for self-nurture and propagation but lacks consciousness and the capacity for locomotion), minerals are bounded by their own still more limited nature, and angels are both limited and differentiated from one another by their particular angelic natures. God, on the other hand, has no limits at all to his being and is therefore "supernatural," that is, he has no "nature."

38. Stark, *One True God,* 10.

Another term closely related to *nature* in medieval thought was *form.* The form of a thing was what gave it the characteristics of its type, and in the case of incarnate entities (the highest or least limited of which is the human being), what made it possible for more than one instance of the type to exist simultaneously was what was called its "matter," its "principle of individuation."[39] Each incarnate entity was interpreted as made up of form and matter. So there could be several dogs, for example, each having a canine nature, or several human beings, each having a human nature. One of the implications of this pattern of thought was that there could be no two angels with the same nature, since angels were understood to be incorporeal beings.[40] They had natures and limits and were individual, but because they had no matter to individuate their form, they had to have different forms, or as Aquinas put it, they had to "differ in species" since "such things as agree in species but differ in number, agree in form, but are distinguished materially," and since "angels are not composed of matter and form . . . , it follows that it is impossible for angels to be of one species."[41] What this means in simple English is that like anything else other than God, an angel is a "natural" being; it differs from other ones only in that unlike them, an angel cannot share in a common nature with other angels but each must have a unique nature all its own. In Aquinas's terminology, an angel's act of being (its *actus essendi*) is limited by the defining characteristics of its particular nature, and therefore it is a natural entity, included in the order of nature as a whole; it is not something "supernatural." Aquinas does speak of God's essence or nature, but uses those terms in a metaphorical sense, since unlike natural essences God's essence is simply "to be," not to be an entity of a particular kind.

The word *supernatural,* in that tradition of thought, has only one proper reference, and that is to God. God alone is supernatural in the precise sense that his *actus essendi* (his act of being) is not bounded by the limits of a circumscribing nature. To say that God is "supernatural" is to say the same thing as that God is "infinite" (literally, without limits) and "eternal" (without the sort of limits that constitute time). In theological usage, *infinite* is not a quan-

39. The difference between form and nature (or essence) is that in the case of a material being, the latter term also includes a reference to matter. "Human nature" involves having a material body, and therefore materiality is included in the essence of a human being, but not in its form; rather, form is what joins with matter to make the individual human. In the case of an incorporeal being (an angel), on the other hand, *form, essence,* and *nature* are all equivalent terms.

40. Aquinas, *Summa Theologica,* pt. 1, question 50, articles 1 and 2.

41. Ibid., question 50, article 4.

titative but strictly a qualitative term; it does not mean "extremely large" as in colloquial language; it means without any limits at all, not even the very expansive limits that make the extremely large larger than something else. The same is true of the term *eternal.* "Eternity" is not, as in colloquial use, a very long time, or even "endless" time, but a quality of being that is beyond time. Hence, in theological terms, to say that God is infinite and eternal is to say (negatively) that he is not limited in his being and (positively) that in God all possible fullness of being is actual.

It is perhaps worth mentioning that although many Christians tend to think of eternity as "endless time," probably because they read translations of the New Testament and see references there to a promise of "eternal life" or "everlasting life" for those who follow Christ, that is not the actual meaning of the phrase in the Greek original. The translation "eternal life" can be misleading if read as referring to temporal quantity; the actual phrase in the New Testament is "zoe aionios," which means literally "the life of the age" (the age to come), that is, the kind of life that first-century Jews expected in the coming messianic age. This referred to a new quality of life, life in fullness as God intended it to be before, as the biblical story goes, humanity went astray, wandering away from life toward death. That "life of the age" was expected to be endless, but simple endlessness was not its defining characteristic; endless life of a lesser quality might only be endlessly unsatisfying.

The idea of God as alone infinite and eternal (that is, "supernatural" in the traditional theological sense) is not limited to Christian or Jewish theology; it is why a Muslim thinker like al-Ashari had to address the question of the "eternal Qur'an" and find a way to talk about it that could differentiate the Qur'an as it is eternally in the mind of God and the Qur'an as read and recited by humans in time. Theologians may have a limited audience among the large population of the faithful, but their role in shaping religious thought is not negligible, and they *do* read each other—not only within their own tradition but also across traditions. Muslim and Jewish thinkers both played a role in relaying theological questions and terminology to Aquinas and his tradition, and subsequent Christian theology, both Catholic and Protestant, generally continues to use with similar meanings many of the terms and concepts that developed in the Middle Ages. It may be true that if one wants to understand a religion it is not enough to attend only to its tradition of reflective thought, but it is not enough either simply to dismiss that as of interest only to specialists.

So to continue, one problem with dividing concepts of the divine into God as agent or supernatural individual and God as essence is that the terms *supernatural* and *essence* have had quite different meanings for people who have participated actively in the tradition of religious thought than they do in modern colloquial use. Another problem is that it draws an unnecessary dichotomy between the personal and the supernatural (in the proper theological sense); that is, it assumes too simply that if God is not conceived as a kind of superhuman individual, this implies God must be impersonal and, as Dennett says, incapable of agency and therefore of responding to prayer. Earlier in this chapter I referred to Aquinas's argument that God is not *a* being but Being Itself, but in the tradition Aquinas spoke for, to say that did not mean God was impersonal.[42] In fact, it meant quite the opposite: that all of the qualities we associate with personhood are contained in God "formally and eminently"—that is, in their true and proper signification but without the limitations they have in even the highest creatures. As one modern commentator on Aquinas's thought explains it:

> Absolute perfections . . . existence, for example, and truth, goodness, wisdom, love, are found formally in God, because they are in him essentially and properly. . . . Further, these perfections are in God properly speaking, that is, not metaphorically, as when we say "God is angry.". . . [T]hese absolute perfections . . . do not in their inner formal meaning imply any imperfection, although in creatures they are always found to be finite in mode and measure. . . . Absolute perfections are found both in God and in creatures, not univocally, and not equivocally, but analogically. This is the precise meaning of the term *formaliter eminenter,* where *eminenter* is equivalent to "not univocally but analogically."[43]

What this means is that from the point of view of theological tradition, God can be understood as eminently personal, in that God possesses *in eminent degree* (that is, in a less limited manner) all the qualities (such as consciousness, intelligence, wisdom, love) that we ordinarily think of as characteristic of persons, but God is not, strictly speaking, a "person" in the sense in which we ordinarily use that word. To be a person is to be an individual entity with some finite version of those qualities. This does not mean God could never appropriately be spoken of as a person, but to do so would be to speak ana-

42. For Aquinas's argument that God is not a being, see ibid., question 3, article 5.

43. Reginald Garrigou-Lagrange, *Reality: A Synthesis of Thomistic Thought,* 88–89, with a further reference to Aquinas, *Summa Theologica,* pt. 1, question 13, article 5. *Formaliter* is Latin for "formally," and *eminenter* for "eminently." The topic of univocal or analogical conceptions of "being" became a major issue a generation after Aquinas, as will be explained below.

logically or metaphorically—and much religious language in any tradition is analogical in just that way. It also does not mean God could not be spoken of as an agent, since unlimitedness does not imply an inability to act; it only implies that the agency of God is not that of a superhuman individual but that of the radically transcendent source of all that is. I have drawn on Aquinas to articulate this pattern of thought, since he worked it out with special explicitness. But Aquinas's version of it is akin to those of the Jewish Maimonides and the Muslim al-Ashari, al-Ghazali, and Ibn al-'Arabi, to name just a few, so for anyone who wants to understand what is involved in the encounter of these great traditions in our own time, it is worth understanding that this pattern of thinking has a substantial presence in each and may still play a significant role in future developments within them.

If this tradition of divine "eminence" is so well established, however, where did the idea of God as a superhuman individual come from? There are several answers to this question. One, of course, is that suggested by Borg: from the imaginations of ten- to twelve-year-old children. This is not a trivial answer, since for many religious people the idea of the divine they received as children, in pretty much the only way a child is developmentally capable of conceiving it, still retains its grip on their imaginations even well past the age Borg discovered another way to think about it.[44] Another answer suggested by evolutionists such as Richard Dawkins, Scott Atran, David Sloan Wilson, Justin Barrett, and others is that it is an accidental by-product—either unhelpful (Dawkins, Atran) or adaptive (Wilson, Barrett)—of the way the human mind evolved to tend to assume agency and causality in virtually everything around it.[45]

Still another answer, closer to the religious mind's home ground, is that it comes from the Bible; the God who demanded the utter destruction of the Amalekites does not look like a God whose anger is only metaphorical. A person of any age who simply reads or hears the stories about God in the Bible will imagine him as a dramatic character of the sort one encounters in any story. But the Bible is a book with many historical layers, each with its own version of God, and to read it as a whole is to retrace a millennia-long process of imaginative interpretation in which the biblical God moves, in a first

44. In his *Toward a Mature Faith,* historian of religion Erwin Ransdell Goodenough tells a similar story in his account of his own upbringing as a conservative Methodist in northern New York in the late nineteenth century.

45. A survey of such evolutionist theories can be found in Robin Marantz Henig, "Darwin's God."

transformation, from being one god among many, even if the most powerful member of the genus, "a great God and a great king above all gods," as in Psalm 95, to being the only real member of the genus.[46] Eventually, in a more radical transformation, the Yahweh of the Israelites moves, in some of the later prophets such as Jeremiah, Ezekiel, and the second Isaiah, toward being conceived as radically transcendent, beyond the cosmos and even, as Aquinas later argued, beyond the genus of gods altogether.[47] The Bible, that is, moves by fits and starts from what was essentially polytheism in the beginning (Israelites had one deity and their rivals had others) through henotheism (God is the preeminent entity, or perhaps even the only entity, within the category of divine beings) to monotheism (God is beyond the category of gods altogether).

As Jewish and Christian interpreters grappled with this change over time, one idea developed to explain it was "accommodation." This is the idea that God wanted from the start to communicate himself as he truly is, but he had to "accommodate," that is, adapt, that revelation to the receptive capacity of his hearers.[48] So he began with stories of himself as a dramatic character like any other and then over the centuries gradually led Israel to a deeper understanding of his transcendence. Viewing the process from another angle, the worldviews inscribed in the Bible can be seen to move from outward to inward, from heteronomy in relation to divinely given laws written on tablets of stone to the hope of theonomy, that is, guidance from within by the Spirit of God in accord with a law of love written on the heart (Ezek. 11:19; 2 Cor. 3:3). So from these points of view, another answer to the question of where the idea of God as superhuman individual came from would be that the "finger-shaker" is the God one sees if one focuses on earlier rather than later and theologically deeper layers of the biblical text. (It is in this connection, by the way, that one can see the theological significance of the difference between the deontological and eudaemonistic approaches to ethics discussed in Chapter 6. The deontological strategy assumes the need to impose a rule on someone who has not developed, or perhaps cannot develop, the capacity to

46. Perhaps I should note that in the quotation from Psalm 95, the original Hebrew has no capital letters to distinguish "God" from "gods" (majuscule and minuscule were invented in the Middle Ages).

47. Aquinas, *Summa Theologica,* pt. 1, question 3, article 5, "Whether God is contained in a genus?"

48. See Stephen D. Benin, *The Footprints of God: Divine Accommodation in Jewish and Christian Thought.* For a discussion of John Calvin's use of the principle of accommodation, see Placher, *Domestication of Transcendence,* 55–60.

appreciate and actually desire and enjoy the true good; the eudaemonistic assumes the possibility that the good could be desired for its own sake if that capacity develops in the heart.)

But there is still another culturally very important answer to where the idea of God as superhuman individual came from; although that conception may be theologically a relatively late development, it too has had a theological tradition. As a theological formulation, it derives principally from William of Ockham in the fourteenth century, about a generation after the death of Aquinas. Aquinas himself did not produce a radically new theology; he simply found a way to express the traditional one using an Aristotelian metaphysical conceptuality. To see what the traditional theological language looked like before Aquinas, one might look at the *Itinerarium mentis in Deum* (The Journey of the Mind into God) of his contemporary, Saint Bonaventure. The characteristic feature of that worldview (as of the Neoplatonic worldview before it) is the idea of "participation in being": the idea that creaturely existence is a greater or lesser participation in what being can be in its fullness. Existence, that is, takes place by degrees; an entity can "be" more or less. Fullness of being is what is found in God; the creature can, to speak metaphorically, move "toward" or "into" that fullness. This pattern of thinking about being as participation was the philosophical and theological lingua franca of the Western world from late antiquity through the thirteenth century, and was shared by Jewish and Muslim as well as Christian thinkers. When its prevalence began to fade, it became known as the *via antiqua,* in contrast to a *via moderna* that developed in the fourteenth century and called into question its most fundamental assumptions.

The leading figure in this *via moderna* was William of Ockham, who lived from sometime in the late thirteenth century until 1349. His response to Aquinas's system illustrates what I spoke of at the beginning of this chapter as the dynamism of questioning that drives change in religious worldviews. Aquinas invoked Aristotle, but an Aristotle strongly colored by the Neoplatonist language of participationism. Ockham too adapted Aristotle for theological use; his starting point, however, was not Aristotle's metaphysics but his logic. Aristotelian logic had as a fundamental principle the law of the excluded middle, which posits that whatever can be logically affirmed either is or is not; there can be no middle ground between existing and not existing. This, of course, negated the cornerstone of the earlier way of thinking, since if there is no middle ground between existence and nonexistence, to speak of degrees of being would be nonsensical. Instead of a universe of being, in which many beings participate to varying degrees in Being Itself, Ockham's universe is made up of individual entities, each of which has an existence all its own. Ockham's God, therefore, can only be one entity among others. He may be the greatest and most powerful of entities, but there is one sense in which all other entities are God's equals: they exist in exactly the same sense in which God exists. The technical term for this is *univocity of being,* the idea that "to be" has only one meaning (that is, is univocal) no matter what it is used to refer to.

To be, for Aquinas, was an analogical term: to say that a flea is, that a human being is, or that God is was to use the word *is* with three similar but still rather different meanings. The flea's being is like that of the human, but more circumscribed; there are reaches or depths to the being of a human person that exceed those of the flea. According to the principle of eminence, as was explained above, all the perfections of being that are present in the flea are also to be found in the human, but eminently, that is, in a less limited form. And all the perfections of being that are to be found in both are present in God eminently, in absolutely unlimited form. The word *is,* therefore, when applied to each of the three, has analogous rather than identical meanings. In Ockham that entire pattern of thinking is simply set aside: the word *is* has exactly the same meaning, whether it is applied to God or to the most limited of creatures. What exists simply exists, and what does not exist simply does not.

Ironically, therefore, there is a sense in which Ockham's thought, despite its revolutionary character in relation to the main tradition of theology, can be said to have been the logical next step on the very path that Aquinas pioneered when he tried to "Aristotelianize" theology. But to say that only touches the surface of a revolution in thought that both Aquinas and Ockham were caught up in.

A question that may probe the dynamism of the larger process more deeply is, "Why did Aquinas think it would be advantageous to integrate Aristotelian thought and theology?" The answer is that he believed doing so would make it possible to convince religious opponents of correct theological positions through the force of reason alone. This was something quite new, as can be seen from a closer comparison with Aquinas's Franciscan contemporary Bonaventure. Bonaventure and Aquinas taught during the same era in Paris, both dying in the same year, 1274, a dual passing that marked a theological epoch. Even though they shared, as was mentioned above, the traditional idea of God as Being Itself and of existence as participation in being, there is a deep difference between them that indicates what was revolutionary in Aquinas: the idea that a person could be brought to correct belief through the force of logic. The earlier spiritual tradition, which Bonaventure's *Itinerarium* exemplifies, had always seen faith as closely related to love. The way to bring a person to true faith was to elicit love—to show, by life as well as by teaching, that the object of faith was beautiful and truly worthy of love and loyalty. The *Itinerarium,* like Dante's *Commedia* (which expresses a synthesis of Bonaventure and Aquinas), is an imaginative journey in which the reader is led up a ladder of loves to the contemplation of God as both love itself and the highest object of love. Such faith is not something that can be coerced, even by the gentle force of logical argument. Rather, it is more like a sort of falling in love. In Bonaventure's words: "That this transport may be perfect, it is necessary that all intellectual operations be abandoned within it, and that the peak of the affections be as a whole transferred and redirected towards God. This is, however, something mystical and most secret, *which no man knoweth but he that receiveth it;* and only he receives it who desires it, and only he desires it whom the fire of the Holy Spirit, sent by Christ to the earth, inflames to his very marrow."[49]

This has important implications for the question of what one may mean by "faith" or "belief," but I will leave further consideration of that for the next two chapters, since this one is already long and the question bears more directly on the topics of those. In the consideration of worldviews, as in the case of any other phenomena of consciousness, one may distinguish between their objective and subjective poles. The objective pole is what is believed or held, the worldview's content. The subjective pole is the manner in which it is held, the operations of constructing it, weighing it, and affirming it, whether reflectively or uncritically, wholeheartedly or only tentatively. The present chapter is concerned primarily with the objective contents of religious worldviews and the way their implications and ambiguities can unfold over time and generate an inner diversity that brings with it a dynamic tension eliciting new questions and possibly leading to further developments. I am using Christian thought here as an example in which this sort of process can be seen working itself out over time.

For now, therefore, I will try simply to sketch the implications for the objective pole of the Christian worldview of the shift from the earlier love-centered spirituality of the *via antiqua* to the logic-centered theology of the *via moderna.* The point at issue is that Aquinas's adoption of Aristotelian reasoning in theology was already a major step in the direction of what came later with

49. Bonaventure, *Itinerarium mentis in Deum,* chap. 7, para. 4, quoted in *The Wisdom of Catholicism,* ed. Anton Charles Pegis, 286. The biblical quotation in italics is from Rev. 2:17.

Ockham and his heirs. This would probably have surprised Aquinas, but there was a dynamism to the process that is clear in retrospect, and this dynamism was not only logical but also social and political.

What motivated Aquinas in trying to turn theology from spiritual evocation to logical argument? The key factor is that Aquinas was a Dominican, and the central purpose of the Dominican order was intellectual polemics. It was founded in 1216 (eight years before Aquinas's birth) by Saint Dominic for the purpose of converting the Albigenses in southern France, against whom Innocent III had declared a crusade. The crusade against the Albigenses was not simply a religious affair; it was a war of northern France against the Languedoc. Its religious purpose was to reassert Catholic doctrine against the Catharist movement and to ensure the delivery of tithes to Rome, which the Catharists did not believe in paying since they considered the Roman hierarchy to be corrupt, heretical, and illegitimate. The kings and nobles of France, however, also saw this as a golden opportunity to gain political possession of the southern territory. Dominic organized his new order to serve as the propaganda wing of this war, which continued through Aquinas's lifetime and beyond. Dominic and his successor as head of the order, Albertus Magnus, believed that argument could be as effective as the sword in destroying Albigensianism. It was Albert who initiated the use of Aristotelian argumentation as an ideological weapon in this war, and it was for the same purpose that Albert's student Thomas Aquinas developed that weapon in its full systematic form.

If Thomas was a Dominican and an agent of what might be called imperializing ecclesiasticism, William of Ockham, on the other hand, was a Franciscan and throughout his life an advocate of individual and ecclesiastical liberty and a critic of papal claims to excessive authority. Politics was also as important a factor in his thinking as the logic of ideas. He defended the Franciscan order's practice of voluntary poverty (which was under attack by the papacy), advocated conciliar church government instead of papal monarchy, and spent the last two decades of his life as a fugitive from papal authority.

What were the major differences in worldview that grew out of Ockham's critique of the *via antiqua*? The most obvious was that God ceased to be Being Itself in which particular entities participate and became simply one more particular entity among others, even if the most powerful of all. Other less obvious differences probably had even greater impact on future Christian thought in the West. Perhaps the most important of these had to do with the question of the ground of value. One of the most fundamental philosophical and theological questions is what makes the good good? Is it good intrinsically, or is there some extrinsic cause that the goodness of the good depends on? Another closely related question is what is God's relation to the good? Does God will the good because it is good? Or is the good good because God wills it? That is, does the good become good simply by divine decree? And if so, does that mean that values are ultimately arbitrary, that the good is whatever the most powerful being simply declares it to be—that might, as it were, makes right? To put the issue in the simplest, most essential terms, does God first *be* and then will whatever he might happen to will, or is what God wills an expression of what God essentially *is*?

For Aquinas and the entire tradition of the *via antiqua,* values could not be arbitrary, because they were grounded in the very being of God. God could not change fundamental values any more than he could change what he is. God could will only the good, and true values were therefore eternal. To many religious people this pattern of thinking would seem both obviously true and deeply reassuring, and it has had many partisans, even among the nonreligious who seek to understand what religion must mean to the religious—as in the case of the anthropologist Clifford Geertz, who says that the heart of the religious perspective is "the conviction that the values one holds are grounded in the inherent structure of reality, that between the way one ought to live and the way things really are there is an unbreakable inner connection." Explaining this idea, Geertz goes on virtually to define religion in terms of that linking of reality and value:

> In anthropology, it has become customary to refer to the collection of notions a people has of how reality is at base put together as their world view. Their general style of life, the way they do things and like to see things done, we usually call their ethos. It is the office of religious symbols, then, to link these in such a way that they mutually confirm one another. Such symbols render the worldview believable and the ethos justifiable, and they do it by invoking each in support of the other. The worldview is believable because the ethos, which grows out of it, is felt to be authoritative; the ethos is justifiable because the worldview, upon which it rests, is held to be true. Seen from outside the religious perspective, this sort of hanging a picture from a nail driven into its frame appears as a kind of sleight of hand. Seen from inside, it appears as a simple fact.[50]

50. Geertz, *Islam Observed,* 97.

That, however, remains *one possible* religious worldview, not simply *the* religious worldview, and if there were no other exception to prove that, Ockham alone would suffice.

To Ockham, Aquinas's grounding of value in the being of God seemed to diminish the divine majesty, subjecting God to the necessity of always willing what he had to will. Ockham took seriously the biblical image of God as absolutely sovereign, and he believed in God's omnipotence and radical freedom. He seems to have viewed Aquinas's theology not only as an intellectually questionable reification of abstractions (which is what the famous "Ockham's razor" is about)[51] but also as the reduction of divine freedom to mechanical necessity. Ockham's God was free to will anything whatever, and whatever God willed was good, simply because God willed it. As Frederick Copleston summarizes:

> For Ockham . . . the divine will is the ultimate norm of morality: the moral law is grounded on the free divine choice rather than ultimately on the divine essence. . . . By the very fact that God wills something, it is right for it to be done. . . . God can do anything or order anything which does not involve logical contradiction. Therefore [for example] . . . God could order fornication. . . . Hence, if God were to order fornication, the latter would be not only licit but meritorious. Hatred of God, stealing, committing adultery, are forbidden by God. But they could be ordered by God; and if they were, they would be meritorious acts.[52]

And of course, a supreme entity with this kind of arbitrary freedom would always be free to change his mind and reverse all the values he had previously decreed.

One can see how a worldview based on such a conception of the divine would make for a sense of insecurity, and it certainly did two centuries later for Martin Luther. By Luther's time, the *via moderna* had become the prevalent theological framework in most of northern Europe. It was the school of thought Luther was educated in, and Luther's theology of gratuitous salvation

51. Although we cannot be certain that Ockham himself formulated this maxim, his name has long been associated with it, and it does express a principle central to his thinking. The maxim is "Entia sine necessitate non multiplicanda sunt" (Beings must not be multiplied without necessity); that is, one should not casually suppose that there are actual entities corresponding to abstractions such as the scholastic *materia prima,* vegetative, animal, and intellectual "forms," separate faculties of "intellect" and "will," *intellectus agens* and *intellectus possibilis,* and so on.

52. Copleston, *A History of Philosophy,* 3:104–5, citing Ockham, *Super quattuor libros sententiarum subtilissimae quaestiones,* pt. 2, 19P, 19O.

was intended as an antidote to the anxiety generated by belief in a God whose will was so arbitrary. He once wrote, "Ockham, my teacher, was the greatest of dialecticians, but he was not skilled in preaching," that is, he did not effectively present what Luther considered to be the gospel ("good news") of equally arbitrary forgiveness.[53] Calvin's doctrine of double predestination—the idea that God arbitrarily, even before creating the world, determined to create some individuals for salvation and others for damnation—is another branch from the same root. Much of the theology of the Reformation was an attempt both to take seriously and to tame this God of unlimited and arbitrary power, either through a version of Luther's solution or through the idea that God voluntarily limits his own freedom by binding himself to a covenant.[54] To the modern reader these issues may seem a bit antique—even if they have modern echoes in Ivan Karamazov's claim that if there is no God everything is permitted—but they also lie in the background of some Christians today who emphasize the role of the Bible as a sort of law book communicating arbitrary divine commands.

Another important element in the heritage of the *via moderna* that remains a live issue today is the insistence of some modern Christians on literal interpretation. This, too, probably derives much of its force from Ockham's insistence on the idea that the only reality is the existence of concrete, particular entities. Literalism can grow in part out of limitations of imagination, but Ockham's critique of what the *via antiqua* called "the analogy of being" has remained its principal theoretical source ever since. Aquinas still thought theologically in terms of metaphor. In his treatise on the names of God, Aquinas works through a series of questions to show that God is not a god, but rather the name "God" functions as a metaphor for something for which all analogies ultimately fail.[55] The highest of analogies is "Being," hence Aquinas's reference to God as *Ipsum Esse* (Being Itself). But even that remains an analogy. A better name than either "God" or "He Who Is," he says, is the name that was never pronounced, the Hebrew consonants Yod He Vaw He (transliterated later by German biblical scholars as YHWH, or YHVH in English, and written out as the familiar but really quite modern and artificial name "Jehovah"). In Aquinas's own words, "still more proper is the Tetragrammaton [YHVH], im-

53. Quoted in Steven E. Ozment, *The Age of Reform (1250–1550): An Intellectual and Religious History of Late Medieval and Reformation Europe*, 238.

54. See Francis Oakley, *Omnipotence, Covenant, and Order: An Excursion in the History of Ideas from Abelard to Leibniz.*

55. Aquinas, *Summa Theologica*, pt. 1, question 13.

posed to signify the substance of God itself, incommunicable and, if one may so speak, singular."[56] YHVH is not an analogy but an indicator that with the symbol "Being," one has reached the ultimate limit of metaphors; the tetragrammaton is the jumping-off point into absolute mystery.

Ockham's logical critique of the language of participation in being was as much an attack on the idea of metaphor as a genuine, even if limited, form of knowing as it was an attack on Aristotelian metaphysics. Consequently, ever since the shift to the *via moderna* it has been difficult for many religious people in the Western Christian tradition to remember something that seems still to have felt quite natural to earlier Christians, as it is to most traditional religious people: how to read a story as a story—not as a factual history in the modern sense, or a treatise on cosmology, or a code of laws.

This factualist literalism regarding scripture that developed during the late Middle Ages and the Reformation eventually led to another revolution in Christian thought: the development of historical and textual criticism of the Bible. Luther and other early reformers made the Bible the central authority for Protestant Christians in place of the ecclesiastical hierarchy and theological tradition of the Roman Catholic system, but they did not at the time realize that this would bring with it the question of how the text should be interpreted. As I mentioned earlier when comparing Sunni Muslim and Shiite ideas of authority with Protestant and Catholic ones, both Luther and Zwingli believed that the meaning of scripture was so straightforward that interpretation was unnecessary, but this did not prevent their interpretations colliding at Marburg in 1529. Subsequent generations of Protestant scholars found more and more questions that demanded research and debate about both the meaning and the factual historicity of the biblical narratives. Over time this forced both biblical scholars and theologians to reflect carefully on methods of inquiry. The Catholic Church tried for a while to avoid getting caught up in the turmoil; between 1907 and 1943 Catholic scholars were prohibited by papal decree from publishing in this field. But in the second half of the twentieth century, Catholics became as active in biblical research as Protestants, and Catholic theologians such as Karl Rahner and Bernard Lonergan, partly in recognition of the complexity of interpretive processes, began to shift the emphasis of theological discourse to reflections on method, an emphasis clearly reflected in the titles of Lonergan's two principal works: *Insight: A Study of Human Understanding* and *Method in Theology*.

56. Ibid., question 13, article 11, reply to objection 1.

Luther might have been dumbfounded to hear the twentieth-century Lutheran theologian and biblical scholar Rudolf Bultmann claim, in his lectures at Yale and Vanderbilt universities in 1951, that his method of "demythologizing" the New Testament was the fulfillment of Luther's theological program:

> Indeed, de-mythologizing is a task parallel to that performed by Paul and Luther in their doctrine of justification by faith alone without the works of law. More precisely, de-mythologizing is the radical application of the doctrine of justification by faith to the sphere of knowledge and thought. Like the doctrine of justification, de-mythologizing destroys every longing for security. There is no difference between security based on good works and security built on objectifying knowledge. The man who desires to believe in God must know that he has nothing at his own disposal on which to build this faith, that he is, so to speak, in a vacuum.[57]

During much of the mid-twentieth century, Bultmann was probably the single most influential biblical theologian, at least in North America and northern Europe. That he could speak in this way and not only continue to be recognized as Christian but also as a leading theologian indicates what a profound impact the questions growing out of the *via moderna* and the Reformation have had, and how much the focus of Christian thought has shifted from the question of what one can know to how one knows and how one should relate to the how and the what of faith—from the objective pole of worldview, that is, to its subjective pole.

Eventually, the Muslim world can be expected to feel the impact of similar kinds of questions about the Qur'an and hadith, and when it does, that will probably be an even more stressful experience than it has been for Christians and Jews, who began asking critical questions about the Bible even before their Christian neighbors did. Christians and Jews have had from approximately the eleventh century until now to raise and ponder such questions and begin to digest their implications. They also have had the advantage of living in a more slowly paced world in which communications were not instantaneous; they were not bombarded with one question after another along with demands for immediate answers. Anyone suffering such an intellectual and spiritual bombardment today deserves sympathy and a greater effort of understanding than those of us in the West have usually been inclined to give.

57. Bultmann, *Jesus Christ and Mythology*, 84.

As a Muslim speaker who participated with me in a lecture series on Islam in the winter of 2007 said, "We are going through a painful process right now." Difficult as this process may be, however, it can lead, in both East and West, for those who can muster the courage and trust to pass through it, to growth and discoveries—not the least of which is the self-discovery of the theological subject, the inwardness of the person of faith.

Religion and Personhood

Critiques of Religion

We turn now to the subjective pole of worldviews. As we saw in Chapter 1, Karl Jaspers took a first step in analyzing the psychology of worldviews by dividing *Weltanshauungen* into attitudes or dispositions *(Einstellungen)* on the subjective side and particular world pictures *(Weltbilder)* on the objective. It is easier to grasp the objective pole of worldview than the subjective, even if, as we saw in the last chapter, that too can be complex and even ambiguous. The objective pole of a worldview is the set of ideas it contains about fundamental reality: about how the world is structured, where it came from, what are its possibilities, how one should live in it to fulfill its best possibilities, and so on. Or to put it another way, the objective pole is the set of answers that people who hold the worldview have worked out for the questions they consider basic about the meaning of their lives. Some, like Clifford Geertz, distinguish between "worldview" as a set of ideas about reality, on the one hand, and "ethos" as a set of ideas about values, on the other. Others, like Jaspers, combine the two under the general heading of worldview, but one way or the other, fundamental conceptions of reality and value go together and constitute a picture of their total framework of life for the people who hold them.

The idea that the objective content of a worldview consists of a set of answers to fundamental questions says something already about the nature of its subjective pole. Whatever else it may be, this is at the very least a dynamism of questioning that generates, or unfolds as, a process of interpreting something in experience that elicits a desire to understand. Processes of questioning and interpreting may be more conscious and careful or less so. I said in the last chapter that the subjective pole of a worldview also includes the manner in which it is held. A worldview can be held critically or uncritically, anxiously or confidently, mournfully or enthusiastically. What is held as a worldview and how it is held are major constituents of the persons who hold it. Not only do our worldviews shape our phenomenological reality, that is, the perceived world we live in and relate to either as a group or as individuals, but they also shape as persons those who live in them. To the extent that one has the ability to choose a worldview, doing so will also be a choice of what kind of person one wants to become and live as.

Freud's principle is again pertinent: "Where 'it' was, there should be 'I.'"[1] To the extent that we live unreflectively, or even resist consciousness, we function as mechanisms driven by unconscious forces of the sort that Freud and other psychologists of the unconscious studied. One might even say that our life is lived between the poles of "it" and "I": we are never fully either one or the other, simply unconscious mechanism or fully personal. We feel the pull of both poles, and we have to decide to which we are going to commit ourselves. Freud's dictum, in the original German, is not a scientific statement of fact (as the English translation in the Standard Edition tries to make it sound) but an injunction, an ethical appeal for commitment to conscious personhood as a good worth striving toward and worth fighting for against the inner forces that pull us toward being simply an "it."[2]

Freud's main work was the analysis of those forces in their manifold forms, and he viewed religion, at least in the forms with which he was familiar, as one of them: "Its method consists in decrying the value of life and promulgating a view of the real world that is distorted like a delusion, and both of these imply a preliminary intimidating influence upon intelligence. At such a cost—by the forcible imposition of mental infantilism and inducing a mass-delusion—religion succeeds in saving many people from individual neuroses. But little more."[3] Even if one may think that there can be more to religion than this,

1. "Wo Es war, soll Ich werden." See Chapter 1, note 4.

2. Cf. Paul Ricoeur's way of speaking about the self as "person," discussed in Chapter 2, as rooted in an experience of "tendency and tension" between Pascal's twin poles of God and nothing, while personhood itself "is given first in an intention."

3. Freud, *Civilization and Its Discontents,* 776.

anyone who takes religion seriously, either as a sympathetic investigator or as a believer, should acknowledge that Freud made some penetrating criticisms of ways of being religious that can stand in the way of developing full human personhood—and also, as spiritual directors might add, of living up to the full potential of their own religious lives. Every religion has its own tradition of critique from within, and anyone attempting to practice that might well learn from an observer as astute and perceptive as Freud. Since Freud's critique of religion focuses on its relation to some of the deep unconscious sources of deformed subjectivity that drag us toward "it" and obstruct our movement toward "I," it is a good place to begin a consideration of how that movement might progress and how religious thinking might help or hinder it.

Following Ludwig Feuerbach's earlier suggestion that God and the gods are idealized human projections, Freud suggested that religion is a recapitulation on the societal level of the process by which a child idealizes its parents and develops dependency on them: "Psychoanalysis has taught us the intimate connection between the father complex and belief in God. . . . In the parental complex we thus recognize the roots of religious need; the almighty, just God and kindly nature appear to us as grand sublimations of father and mother, or rather as revivals and restorations of the infantile conceptions of both parents. Religiousness is biologically traced to the long period of helplessness and need of help of the little child."[4] In *The Future of an Illusion,* Freud developed this idea further and also stated explicitly that what is involved is not a healthy process but at best a kind of sheltering neurosis that may help for a while to shield someone from still greater neuroses or psychoses but should ultimately be outgrown:

> We know that the human child cannot well complete its development towards culture without passing through a more or less distinct phase of neurosis. This is because the child is unable to suppress by rational mental effort so many of those instinctual impulsions which cannot later be turned to account, but has to check them by acts of repression, behind which there stands as a rule an anxiety motive. . . . In just the same way one might assume that in its development through the ages mankind as a whole experiences conditions that are analo-

4. Freud, *Leonardo da Vinci: A Psychosexual Study of an Infantile Reminiscence,* 103–4. Cf. Ludwig Feuerbach: "The Divine Being is nothing else than the human being, or, rather, the human nature purified—i.e., contemplated and revered as an other, a distinct being. All the attributes of the divine nature are, therefore, attributes of the human nature" (*The Essence of Christianity,* 14).

> gous to the neuroses, and this for the same reasons, because in the ages of its ignorance and intellectual weakness it achieved by purely affective means the instinctual renunciations, indispensable for man's communal existence. And the residue of these repression-like processes, which took place in antiquity, has long clung on to civilization. Thus religion would be the universal obsessional neurosis of humanity. It, like the child's, originated in the Oedipus complex, the relation to the father. According to this conception one might prophesy that the abandoning of religion must take place with the fateful inexorability of a process of growth, and that we are just now in the middle of this phase of development. . . . [T]he true believer is in a high degree protected against the danger of certain neurotic afflictions; by accepting the universal neurosis he is spared the task of forming a personal neurosis. . . . [A]nd now we may say that the time has probably come to replace the consequences of repression by the results of rational mental effort, as in the analytic treatment of neurotics.[5]

Freud makes four main points in these passages, which I will summarize so we can consider them more closely.

1. The idea of God is a projection based on an idealized image of the parent.
2. Just as with the parent, the relation to the projected God is fraught with anxiety and repression growing out of Oedipal conflict.
3. Religion functions as a sort of collective neurosis that may offer some protection against even more serious neurosis, but at the cost of cognitive delusion in the objective pole of consciousness and "the forcible imposition of mental infantilism" in the subjective.
4. Religion should and eventually will be outgrown.

To some religious believers, the assertion that the idea of God is a projection might seem a direct attack on belief itself, but if one remembers the preceding chapter's discussion of theological metaphor in the thought of Aquinas, it is easy to see that much of what Aquinas said could also be recast in the language of Freud and Feuerbach. He would not have used it to draw the same conclusion—that is, that the metaphorical language of theology points toward no truth—but in speaking of the ultimate inability of any analogies to reach the divine mystery toward which they point, Aquinas could well, in a later generation, have drawn on the idea of projection in critiquing their

5. Freud, *Future of an Illusion,* 75–77.

inadequacy. When the prophets of Israel, such as Amos, Hosea, Jeremiah, or Isaiah, denounced as idols the Baals and Astartes worshiped not only by their pagan neighbors but also all too often by erring Israelites, they too, in a later generation, might have drawn on the concept of psychological projection to talk about how the worshipers of idols cast them in their own image rather than that of the One whose name is not to be pronounced.

One might also consider projection from a developmental point of view, seeing it as the externalization of something one is not yet able to apprehend except by imagining it as outward. Bernard Lonergan, for example, wrote in *Method in Theology:* "In the earliest stage, expression results from insight into sensible presentations and representations. . . . Only in so far as the temporal, generic, internal, divine can somehow be associated with or—in the language of the naive realist—'projected' upon the spatial, specific, external, human, can an insight be had and expression result. So it is by associating religious experience with its outward occasion that the experience becomes expressed and thereby something determinate and distinct for human consciousness."[6] Or one might imagine a law intrinsic to one's own being or to the order of nature as though it were a command from an external entity. So, for example, the fulfillment of one's own potential for psychological and spiritual growth might require fulfilling demands that can only be imagined by a child as imposed by the parent—such as, to use Freud's example of the Oedipus complex, bringing under control one's murderous impulses toward a frustrating parent in order both to avoid the burden of guilt and to gain the benefits of parental protection while it is needed.

Or one might believe in rules of hygiene or diet that may incidentally benefit health but are imagined to have been dictated for quite different reasons by a deity or divinized ancestor. Or one might believe in rules about keeping categories distinct so as to reduce the anxiety that can arise from their blurring (this, not hygienics, is Mary Douglas's suggestion for the origin of the idea of clean and unclean foods in ancient Israel).[7] Laws of the latter type might include not only such benign rules as not to eat shellfish (because they blur the categories of fish and stone) but also such less benign practices as the killing of twins, whose very existence can raise disturbing questions about identity, seniority, property, and so on. Most ethnologists today treat fear of twins as arising in this way from the problem of classification; René Girard,

6. Lonergan, *Method in Theology,* 108.
7. See Mary Douglas, *Purity and Danger: An Analysis of Concepts of Pollution and Taboo.*

on the other hand, suggests that it has more to do with fear of the rivalry that could arise between siblings with minimal social difference and could spread from them to others: "It is only natural that twins should awaken fear, for they are harbingers of indiscriminate violence. . . . When faced with biological twins the normal reaction of the culture is simply to avoid contagion."[8] Whichever explanation applies—and again there is no reason both might not be pertinent—the taboo against twins might look, from the point of view of our own culture, like the sort of irrational externalized laws that call out for either rational or prophetic critique.

In a society that still feels the force of such a taboo, it seems likely that critique in the form of prophecy, such as an announcement by a charismatic voice that a divine being revokes the old law and prohibits the practice, would be more socially effective than an appeal to reason.[9] In such circumstances, projection might be a helpful device for apprehending the notion of a higher good in a real if rudimentary way through the imagination and feelings. In this respect, such externalized imagery of divine command might serve in a given community as a feature of what in Chapter 3 we saw D. W. Winnicott call a "holding environment" and Robert Kegan a "culture of embeddedness," that is, an imaginative context that can nurture possibilities of further development and encourage transition to some still more adequate way of thinking that might reach beyond externalizing imagery. Of course, it is also possible, as Kegan said, for a culture of embeddedness to try not just to *hold* (in the nurturing sense) the developing person but to *hold on to* him or her, or, as Freud put it, to impose "mental infantilism."

That is an important problem, to which I will return shortly. For the moment, however, let us consider further the question of the relation between projection and reality. Is projection inherently false, a generating of illusion or even delusion? Peter Berger addresses this question in *The Sacred Canopy*, where he says that "sociological theory must, by its own logic, view religion as a human projection, and by the same logic can have nothing to say about the possibility that this projection may refer to something other than the being of its projector." Berger suggests that another reasonable way to look at the question would be to say that "man projects ultimate meanings into reality be-

8. Girard, *Violence and the Sacred*, 57.

9. A modern example might be the declaration in 1890 by President (and Chief Prophet) Wilford Woodruff of the Church of Jesus Christ of Latter-day Saints that Mormons should no longer practice polygamy.

cause that reality is, indeed, ultimately meaningful and because his own being (the empirical ground of these projections) contains and intends these same meanings."[10] As an example he refers to mathematics, which projects into the world mathematical ideas that modern science finds "have turned out to correspond to something 'out there.'" Freud himself, suspicious of religion as he was, acknowledged the same possibility when he distinguished illusion from delusion: "In the delusion we emphasize as essential the conflict with reality; the illusion need not be necessarily false, that is to say, unrealizable or incompatible with reality," so that even if "religious doctrines . . . are all illusions," nevertheless "of the reality value of most of them we cannot judge; just as they cannot be proved, neither can they be refuted."[11]

Freud's own estimate of the truth value of religious ideas was entirely negative, but as a critical thinker he also recognized the methodological limits that prevented his judgment from claiming absolute certainty. Perhaps the simplest way to state the difference between Freud's view and that of a methodologically aware theologian like Aquinas or Lonergan is to say that both Freud and the theologians understand religious ideas as the imaginative projection of analogies by which to explore ultimate questions, but whereas Freud's guess is that the analogies point to no reality, the theologians' hope and trust is that they do. Theologians, too, recognize that religious imagery and ideas can be misleading, since all theological language must fall short of the transcendent reality it points toward, but analogy, with all its limitations, is the only cognitive instrument we have with which to think about ultimate questions. The important thing is to use it carefully, with a recognition of its limits and of its analogical character.

Freud also postulates that religion is psychologically rooted, like everything else in human psychology, in the Oedipal conflict: that the idea of a God whose help we need developed in part on the basis of the sense of vulnerability that we all felt acutely in early childhood and that persists in some form throughout our lives and that the anxiety that motivates religious projection grows not only out of such feelings of vulnerability but also out of inner conflict, as the child feels a complex mixture of dependency on the father, desire

10. Berger, *Sacred Canopy*, 180. Berger goes on to say that "such a theological procedure would be an interesting ploy on Feuerbach—the reduction of theology to anthropology would end in the reconstruction of anthropology in a theological mode" (ibid.). (See the quotation from Feuerbach in note 4 above.)

11. Ibid., 181; Freud, *Future of an Illusion*, 54–55.

to displace him in the mother's affection, and fear of the father's punishment of that desire.

The question of the centrality of the Oedipus complex to all psychological disturbance is one of the more debated points of Freudianism, but there is no need to enter that debate here, since I see no reason Oedipal conflict could not be one factor among others in generating anxiety and motivating beliefs and repressions designed to reduce it. It is easy to see how a child's limited ability to step back from such conflicting impulses and work out a rational way to deal with them would heighten the anxiety already present as a result of the natural vulnerability of the childhood state, and when such feelings are present they can be expected to color the entire imaginative life of the child, including its images of transcendence.

In Chapters 4 and 5, we saw that Ernest Becker and René Girard posit two quite different primary unconscious motives: death anxiety and mimetic desire. Again I see no reason that both death anxiety and the need to imitate powerful others should not also be counted as major factors in shaping the personality. Perhaps what is more significant is that Freud, Becker, and Girard all believe that the child's or adult's sense of radical vulnerability is the underlying source of whatever unconscious psychological motive is really fundamental. It is only to be expected that unconscious motives would be a tangle, since it is precisely the lack of intelligent deliberation, making such a tangle possible, that reduces us at times from person to mechanism, or, in Freud's terms, from "I" to "it."

What I would like to probe further is the question Freud raised about the ways in which religion may impede the development of rational consciousness by imposing "mental infantilism" and "inducing a mass-delusion." That this *can* happen is hardly questionable, since history is replete with examples. One that stands iconically for them all in modern memory is the case of Galileo under the Roman Inquisition in the seventeenth century. Freud would probably himself have considered it sufficient to establish his point. Most readers must already be familiar with it, but to summarize briefly, Galileo argued for Copernicus's hypothesis that the sun rather than the earth was the center around which all the planets, including the earth, revolved, and he was consequently accused of denying the truth of the Bible, which speaks in various places about the sun revolving around the earth. On June 16, 1633, the Congregation of the Inquisition in Rome decreed that "Galileo Galilei . . . as decreed by his Holiness, is to be interrogated concerning the accusation, even threatened with torture, and if he sustains it, proceeding to an abjuration . . .

before the full Congregation of the Holy Office, sentenced to imprisonment at the pleasure of the Holy Congregation, ordered in either writing or speaking, not to treat further in any way either the mobility of the Earth or the stability of the Sun; or otherwise he will suffer the punishment of relapse." Under this threat Galileo submitted abjectly, signing the statement, "I do not hold and have not held this opinion of Copernicus since the command was intimated to me that I must abandon it; for the rest, I am here in your hands—do with me what you please."[12] What they did was ban his previous writing on the subject, forbid him to write further about it, and place him under house arrest until his death in 1642.

A few other details are worth mentioning both because they illustrate Freud's point and because they can help us to understand the nature of the "mental infantilism" and "mass-delusion" that Galileo's opponents were trying to impose. One is that the controversy was not simply or even primarily about Copernicanism but rather about the nature of authority, both the church's and the Bible's. In his defense Galileo argued that even if the book of scripture was dictated by God, it remains ambiguous, whereas the book of nature can be probed and tested. The Bible "told how to go to heaven," he said, "not how the heavens go."[13] To see how the heavens go, on the other hand, one could look through the telescope Galileo invented, and if one did, one could see that many sacrosanct assumptions about the heavens were simply false, such as that the moon, being unaffected by Adam's Fall, must have an unblemished, perfectly spherical surface or that other planets could not have moons, since the earth was the only center of motion. On one occasion, Galileo took his telescope to Rome to demonstrate it to the College of Cardinals; some looked through it with interest, but there were others who simply refused to do so lest it tempt them to embrace untraditional views.

Galileo was indeed trying to persuade them to look at conventional assumptions about the heavens with new evidence and from new angles and to change their views if the evidence warranted, and in his defense before the Inquisition he tried to persuade his accusers that the Bible too could be approached from different angles that would open it to new interpretations. Those who opposed him were trying to enforce uncritical belief in particular ideas about astronomy and the meaning of biblical passages that made reference to astronomical phenomena, and they tried to do so by stifling the pro-

12. Quoted in Owen Gingerich, "The Galileo Affair," 142, 143.
13. Ibid., 134.

cess of questioning itself so as to prevent efforts at critical reasoning.[14] Their reason for this was probably not simply the desire to maintain their institutional power but also sincere pastoral concern. They seem to have feared that if people were allowed to question and investigate freely, they might go astray, with terrible consequences for their eternal destiny. Or to put it more bluntly, in terms that echo Freud's and illustrate his point, they considered the laity of the church to be mental infants who needed to be protected for their own good from the possibly dangerous consequences of trying to use their minds like mental adults.

Critical Reflection in Religion

It is clear that the rejection of scientific truth and the suppression of critical inquiry *can* take place in the name of religion. But one can still ask whether that *must* take place in connection with religious belief or under what circumstances it may. Freud seems to have thought that it must happen wherever religious belief is involved, but a cursory glance at theological literature is sufficient to show that this is not the case, since even a single theologian who advocated critical judgment rather than blind faith would be sufficient evidence against that, and their number is actually legion. There is, of course, Bernard Lonergan, with his "transcendental precepts"—"Be attentive, Be intelligent, Be reasonable, Be responsible"—which he described as the necessary means to "subjects being their true selves," by which he meant very much the opposite of mental infantilism.[15] But there are also the Niebuhr brothers (Reinhold and H. Richard), Paul Tillich, Rudolf Bultmann, Karl Rahner, John Courtney Murray, and many other prominent figures, Protestant, Catholic, and Jewish.

Of course, the names just cited are all from the twentieth century and from Europe and North America, and this is not accidental. Even if it began being voiced in the Middle Ages, especially by Jewish thinkers, the idea that each

14. Cf. Robert Towler in *The Need for Certainty: A Sociological Study of Conventional Religion:* "The implicit plea which underlies traditionalism is not for questions to be answered, but for all questioning to be taken away and put under the lock and key of a trustworthy authority" (91).

15. Lonergan, *Method in Theology,* 53. John F. Haught, adapting Lonergan for his own use in *Is Nature Enough? Meaning and Truth in the Age of Science,* suggests reformulating the third precept from "Be reasonable" to "Be critical," but only to make Lonergan's meaning clearer for his audience (33). Cf. also David Tracy's own version of the precepts (cited in Chapter 2), probably based on what he heard Lonergan say in his classes when he was his student: "be attentive, be intelligent, be reasonable, be responsible, be loving, develop and, if necessary, change" (*Achievement of Bernard Lonergan,* 4).

person has a religious responsibility to think carefully and critically became a prominent theme of Western religious thought only gradually in the past few centuries. One sociologist of religion, Robert Towler, writing about how Ernest Renan had felt obliged to leave the Roman Catholic Church in 1845 because of his ideas about the life of the historical Jesus, says, "It is important to recognize that the views which compelled Renan to leave the Church came slowly, via the Modernist controversies of the turn of the century, to be not unusual among people who remained in the Church. Private judgment, the error which more than any other Pius X sought to stamp out, has become a religious imperative even in the Church of Rome."[16]

Perhaps the representative figure for the beginning of the shift in Catholic thinking on that subject would be Cardinal Newman, who wrote of the act of judgment in *An Essay in Aid of a Grammar of Assent* in 1870, "Certitude is not a passive impression made upon the mind from without, by argumentative compulsion, but in all concrete questions . . . it is an active recognition of propositions as true such as it is the duty of each individual himself to exercise at the bidding of reason, and, when reason forbids, to withhold. . . . Every one who reasons, is his own centre; and no expedient for attaining a common measure of minds can reverse this truth."[17]

Not that Newman's argument found a ready audience at the time in the church to which he had converted. The year of the work's publication, 1870, was the very year Pius IX (to Newman's distress) arranged for the proclamation of papal infallibility at the First Vatican Council. From that time through the effort to suppress the modernist controversy in the early twentieth century, the Vatican authorities did all they could to prevent the spread of the kind of thinking Galileo had threatened them with and that was continuing to plague them in the form of critical biblical scholarship and evolutionary thinking about both biology and the history of theological ideas. It is probably significant that Newman learned first to think independently and only later converted to the Roman obedience as a result of following out a line of reasoning he articulated earlier in *Essay on the Development of Christian Doctrine* (written before his conversion) and defended later in *Apologia pro Vita Sua.* The idea that Christian doctrine went through a historical evolu-

16. Towler, *Need for Certainty,* 20–21. Towler also notes Peter Berger's discussion of this phenomenon of modern Christianity in Berger, *The Heretical Imperative: Contemporary Possibilities of Religious Affirmation.*

17. Newman, *Essay in Aid,* 262.

tion was not welcome in Rome at the time, and especially not the idea, on which Newman based his conversion, that even if the papal primacy did not descend from the earliest years of the Christian religion, it was nevertheless a legitimate later development. The opposition to such critical thinking probably reached its peak with Pius X's condemnation of "modernism" in 1907 in the encyclical *Pascendi Dominici Gregis* and the prohibition against the publication of critical biblical scholarship by Catholics from that time until it was lifted by Pius XII in 1943. Newman's influence nevertheless took root and grew, inspiring Lonergan, John Courtney Murray, and enough others that the Second Vatican Council eventually endorsed freedom of inquiry and did away with the Index of Forbidden Books, which had been binding on Catholics from the time of the Council of Trent in the sixteenth century.

I have focused on the historical record of the Roman Catholic Church to explore the question raised by Freud about the way religion can attempt to suppress the development of critical reason and the mature personhood that requires it, but I do not mean to imply that this is primarily a problem of that one ecclesiastical tradition. There have been similar efforts on the part of various Protestant churches and movements, and they continue today in the form of attempts to suppress science in favor of biblical literalism, especially in certain parts of the United States where the teaching of Darwinian evolutionary theory and scientific cosmology are still under attack. The Catholic case is useful as an example, I think, both because that church's institutional centralization makes for a less amorphous narrative and because one can see from it very clearly that the course of a religious stream may involve not only a current of intellectual repression but also a countercurrent of intellectual liberation that can encourage the development of critically reflective, intellectually responsible personhood as itself a religious goal.

A Protestant figure, to cite just one, with some explicit thoughts on "mental infantilism" and on the relation of religion to stages of life is Søren Kierkegaard, whose life (1813–1855) overlapped for a while that of Newman. Kierkegaard was very different from Newman in his relation to the institutional aspect of Christianity—some have said he was so Protestant no church could contain him—but he shared Newman's belief that authentic religion could proceed only from authentic personhood by way of the capacity and willingness to think for oneself, and he recognized that the effort toward that goal can meet with strong resistance, both from without and from within. I quoted in Chapter 2 a passage from Kierkegaard's *Concluding Unscientific Postscript* in which he distinguished between authentic subjective existence and merely objective, which he referred to as "existence in a loose sense of the word."[18] He distinguished, that is, between, in Freud's terms, the mode of existence of an "I" and that of an "it."

In the conclusion of that book, Kierkegaard also talked about what he called "childish Christianity," saying, "The Christianity which is taught to a child, or rather what the child pieces together for itself when no violence is used to force the little exister into the most decisive Christian determinants, is not properly Christianity but idyllic mythology." Idyllic mythology is not in itself, however, the problem from Kierkegaard's point of view. In fact, he seems to have thought that in the case of a child, such mythology could serve as a kind of holding environment, to use Winnicott's phrase again. The real problem arises with adults who make the child's version of faith their model:

> There are not lacking instances of people who previously were not religiously moved and first became so through the child. But this piety is not properly the religiousness which should belong to older people, and it is no more reasonable that the mother should be nourished by the milk which nature provides for the babe than that the religiousness of the parents should find decisive expression in this piety. . . . Childish Christianity, which is lovable on the part of a little child, is in the case of an adult the childish orthodoxy which has been rendered blissful in the medium of fantasy and has contrived to introduce the name of Christ into it. Such an orthodoxy brings everything to confusion.[19]

There is a type of religiousness suitable for children, he thought, a sort of proto-Christianity that may prepare them for the stronger medicine to come later, and there is the real thing, which is appropriate only for those who are ready for it:

> Just as Christianity did not come into the world during the childhood of mankind but in the fullness of time, so, too, in its decisive form it is not equally appropriate to every age in a man's life. . . . To cram Christianity into a child is something that cannot be done, for it is a general rule that everyone comprehends only what he has use for, and the child has no decisive use for Christianity. As indicated by the coming of Christianity into the world after a foregoing preparation, the invariable law is this: *No one starts by being a Christian, everyone becomes such in the fullness of time . . . if he does become such.*[20]

18. Kierkegaard, *Concluding Unscientific Postscript,* 276. See Chapter 2, note 3.
19. Ibid., 523, 527.
20. Ibid., 523; emphasis in the original.

Intellectual and Spiritual Development

This must remind us, of course, of the developmental thinking we saw in Piaget, Kohlberg, Fowler, and Kegan. Kierkegaard was saying, like them, that human life develops through stages and that the quality of a form of religiousness can correlate with levels of development. That, however, opens up a whole new set of questions that are bound to seem even more controversial than questions about the objects of religious belief. Does thinking about developmental possibilities in connection with religion, for example, imply that religion is to be understood simply as a function of stages of development? To answer that question with a simple affirmative might be as reductionistic as would treating it as a neurotic symptom, since it could imply both that the pattern of one's religion is determined by one's stage and that some religions are superior or inferior to others on the basis of the stage of development they correlate with. As a Lutheran pastor of my acquaintance put it, the problem with discussing religion in terms of stages of faith is that there is a tendency for the speaker to assume that he or she represents the highest stage and that those who differ on some point do so because they are at a lower one.

Here, I think, one can see the great advantage offered by Kegan's shift from talking about psychological development in terms of stages to talking about orders of consciousness. Stage theory was appropriate for his *Evolving Self* because that book traced biologically based development from infancy to adulthood. But the mind of a biologically mature adult can organize itself in a variety of ways, each of which may be suited to the circumstances of a particular adult milieu. Kegan's main point in *In over Our Heads* was that fully developed adults in the modern world now find themselves having to struggle to adapt their resources of affective and operative capacity to conflicting demands and multiple milieus. It is not that there is some "right" order of consciousness that everyone should develop toward. Rather, adult orders of consciousness (or patterns of mental organization) constitute multiple possibilities for the fully mature person; they are not directly connected with maturational levels but constitute a variety of ways a mature person can deal with diverse situations and their challenges.

To separate religion from questions of development and claim that all ways of being religious are therefore equal, on the other hand, would be just as reductionistic. This would not just ignore but also suppress the religiously central question of whether biologically and psychologically mature adults stand in no need of developing further. All of the world's major religions assume that they do, and each tends to think that its own reason for being is to make people aware of that need and to offer valuable guidance toward it. Buddhist teaching, for example, assumes that there are people suffering from a false understanding and mistaken way of life but who are capable of developing insight that will liberate and transform them if they practice the eightfold path of the Buddha. Islam counsels the practice of *dhikr* (remembrance of God) and the five pillars of *Din* (the key religious observances: witness, prayer, almsgiving, fasting, and pilgrimage) as a process by which one moves gradually toward becoming not only outwardly but inwardly *muslim* (one who truly "submits" to the reign of God). Every religion has its own version of Kierkegaard's distinction between a "childish," or at least less intellectually and spiritually mature, way of grasping the meaning of the religion and a deeper meaning that the faithful are called to grow into.

Perhaps it can help to sort out these issues if we distinguish questions about organic and intellectual development from those about spiritual development. Piaget, beginning as he did with biological science, studied human development as that of an organism. Just as there is an organic development from crawling to walking as the bones, muscles, and motor nervous system mature, as the endocrine system and the cerebral cortex mature the human organism develops mental capacities that make it capable of different kinds of interpretative and critical operation, and these are hierarchically integrated, in the sense that those that develop later require and build on those that developed earlier.[21] So, operations in the proper sense, which Piaget said transform objects or states, build on preoperative figurative functions that imitate states taken as momentary or static. Operations in turn then expand and transform themselves as they move from concrete operations carried out only on objects to "formal" or "hypothetical deductive operations" that can operate on operations, construct abstract representations of alternative possibilities, and deduce their implications. Just as a child matures physically through puberty to biological adulthood, so one gradually develops one's capacity for a full range of mental operations. The latter may take a somewhat longer period, but once it is complete, the question is not whether the operating person has completed his or her organic development but what he or she is going to do with those operative capacities.

21. For an argument that the endocrine system plays as important a role in human thinking as the brain, see Antonio R. Damasio, *Descartes' Error: Emotion, Reason, and the Brain.*

This is where intellectual and spiritual development comes into play as a lifelong process. It is also where religious leaders can begin to disagree about how much such development should be encouraged or which forms of it are beneficial and which may be dangerous. I mentioned above that the ecclesiastical authorities who condemned Galileo, when they tried to stifle questioning that threatened their traditional worldview, were probably also motivated (whatever other motives they may also have had) by sincere pastoral concern for the spiritual well-being of their flock. So, I am sure, are the *mujtahids* and ayatollahs of Shiite Muslims and the ulema of the Sunnis when they try to impose strict limits to Muslim behavior and bind the faithful (including themselves, to be sure) to a consensus of interpretations that developed centuries before the range of possible questions that could now be asked were even thought of. It is not my purpose here to make religious judgments about whether such pastoral concern, even if genuine, is really wise or possibly misguided. That is something the members of a religion must do for themselves—and over time, they do tend actually to do that. That is how religious development takes place. Just as sincerely religious people believe there can be more or less intellectually and spiritually mature ways of understanding and living their religion, so religious traditions do actually grow and change because at least some of their adherents believe that their religion itself calls the faithful to develop its best possibilities.

The subsequent story of the Galileo case is an example. Galileo was silenced in 1633 in the manner I described above, and the Catholic Church continued to make serious efforts for another century or so to suppress the questions he raised as well as those raised later by other scientists and by biblical scholars. But eventually the countercurrent that developed among thinkers such as Newman, Lonergan, Rahner, John Courtney Murray, Raymond E. Brown, and others began to gain influence and draw the Catholic conscience. On October 31, 1992, Pope John Paul II publicly retracted the condemnation of Galileo, saying that in consequence of that affair the church had developed a more correct understanding of the proper nature of its authority and that "from the Galileo case one can draw a lesson which applies to us today, in view of analogous situations which come forth today and which may come forth in the future."[22]

22. John Paul II, "Discourse to the Pontifical Academy of Sciences," no. 11, para. 1. I am indebted for this citation to Fr. George V. Coyne, S.J., director of the Vatican Observatory, who was a member of the papal commission appointed to review the Galileo case.

Those who are concerned about the integration of the Islamic world into modernity should find this story a source of hope, but they would also do well to remember that the Galileo case took the Vatican almost four hundred years to resolve and that the Islamic world has scarcely begun to encounter and digest the implications of the type of critical inquiry of which that affair was only the bare beginning for the West. Just as a ten year old, an adolescent, or even a young adult might still need guidance by clear and simple, externally imposed rules—deontological ethics functioning as a holding environment, one might say—so some ecclesiastical authorities could perhaps make a reasonable argument that for the church to have yielded without any resistance to the claims of a Galileo in the sixteenth century might have led at the time not to intellectual and spiritual development among the great mass of Catholics but to intellectual confusion and spiritually dangerous religious chaos.

I do not bring this up in order to endorse such an argument, but rather to draw attention to the fact that real development tends to be slow, difficult, and erratic and to suggest that people who view a religious tradition from outside may need to exercise some patience and understanding with regard to the way people within it wrestle with their challenges. Again, it is not my purpose to judge traditions or to suggest solutions for their problems; rather, what I hope to do is to clarify the nature of religious development and uncover principles of understanding that may help us to see those problems in a broader perspective and perhaps understand better how they may pertain to some of the problems confronting us in the twenty-first century.

Let us consider further, then, the questions of what sorts of development religious traditions may undergo or even seek and value and what sorts of impediment might stand in their way, and also of what intellectual development in the area of religion may have to do with specifically spiritual development. Even to broach the idea of religious development, of course, is to tread on sensitive ground. I mentioned earlier that stage theories can be both pertinent and problematic in connection with religion; equally problematic, but inescapable, is the question of how developments might be evaluated. To decide whether a development is of greater or lesser value implies some sort of normative standard, so there is the question of what that standard might be. Then if the idea of a normative standard is accepted, and with it the implication that some ways of being religious might be superior to others, another question begins to loom: does that lead toward the idea that one religion can be superior to others, and if so, does that imply that its members have a religious obligation to try to convert those of other religions or that the adherents of other religions ought to convert to the superior one?

Certainly, many people in various religious traditions would answer yes. There has always been a strong tendency among religious people to gravitate toward the idea that one way of being religious should apply to all and to fear that even to speak of the value of another way is a threat to the security of belief. This may be because, as a sociologist of knowledge like Peter Berger would put it, effective internalization of beliefs depends on powerful, socially supported objectivations. Or to put it in psychological terms, it may be caused by what Girardians would call mimetic factors, that is, because when the mind is functioning more in Freud's "it" mode than in the "I" mode, belief tends to derive its felt cogency from imitation, below the level of conscious awareness, of the attitudes of others. Members of a group who all say the same thing can, with little or no real thought, feel confident of it because it is "what everyone thinks." For a person who operates in that sort of unthinking mode, religion and belief tend to merge in the mind in such a way that even small differences in religious belief or practice can undermine confidence about beliefs. Also, people who incline to the idea that one way of being religious should apply to all are likely to fear that even to speak of the value of another set of beliefs implies a threat to impose it universally.

Although such a felt need for religious uniformity is widespread among many religious groups, it is not, however, universal. Buddhists think enlightenment is preferable to illusion, and many of them do try to bring the message of enlightenment they believe in to non-Buddhists, but their focus tends to be on the message rather than on the religion as such. One useful way of understanding religion is to think of it as a set of practices intended to support a faith, with the implication that a particular faith could be supported by diverse practices. For Buddhism, for example, the faith is centered in the message about enlightenment as a possibility, open to all, that can deliver human beings from unfulfillment and help them to live with compassion for others. Its practices involve regular meditation, retreats, the chanting of sutras, and so on, which Buddhists believe are helpful but which they also generally recognize as being secondary to the message itself. Both the Dalai Lama and Thich Nhat Hanh, for example, have spent a great deal of time trying to share the Buddhist message widely in the West without any attempt to persuade anyone to change his or her religion; rather, they encourage people to practice their own religions with the sort of insight and detachment that Buddhism tries to foster.

Islam, to take another example, has the reputation among many non-Muslims today of being aggressive and intolerant, but its history indicates something very different. The impression of intolerance probably derives largely from Muslim reactions to the feeling that they are under attack by people who are seeking to undermine their faith and destroy their religion. In the early years of Islam in the Arabian peninsula during the lifetime of Muhammad there were powerful efforts on the part of Arabian polytheists to destroy the Muslim community and faith. This was how the idea of jihad, or holy warfare, arose. Jihad was the effort of the Muslim community to defend itself against violent destruction by those opposed to its faith. There is an important religious symbolism in the fact that Muslims date their calendar from the Hijrah, the flight of the early Muslim community from Mecca to Medina in 622 CE. According to the tradition, there was widespread opposition in Mecca to the new religious vision Muhammad was spreading, even among members of his own tribe, the Quraysh. The Quraysh could not kill him because he was a fellow tribe member, and the other tribes could not kill him either, because the Quraysh, even if many of them would prefer to see him dead, would be honor bound to avenge him. So, as the story is told, the leaders of all the other tribes in Mecca compacted to assassinate him together and simultaneously so that the Quraysh would be unable to take revenge on any one other tribe but would have to fight all of them at once. Muhammad, after getting wind of the plot, fled to Medina to be joined there by his followers as they slipped in small numbers out of Mecca. Once safely harbored in Medina they managed to fight off Meccan attacks. That is what Muslims look back on as the beginning of the *ummah,* the community of the faithful as a new society that had broken irrevocably with the traditional tribal system of social organization and was thenceforth bound together by loyalty to the one God as revealed in the Qur'an. The *ummah* was thus born in the experience of the first jihad as Muhammad and his earliest followers fled from persecution and successfully defended themselves from those who wished to destroy both them and Islam itself.

After the Muslims defeated those who threatened them, even conquering Mecca itself in 630 CE, they became fairly generous toward the members of other faiths they did not consider threatening. Historically, the Muslim attitude toward Christians and Jews was comparatively tolerant—much more tolerant than that of European Christians in those centuries toward either Muslims or Jews. As long as the adherents of those faiths living within the Islamic world were willing to allow Muslims to govern it, as Muslims believed God intended, they were not expected to convert. What Muslims consider all people called to by the one God is, one might say, not Islam the religion but *islam* with a small *i,* that is, submission to God's righteous will as revealed in the various scriptures he has given. Jews and Christians also have, from the Muslim point of view, authentically revealed scriptures that, even if they reveal the one God less adequately than does the Holy Qur'an, are capable of guiding Jews and Christians to genuine submission (*islam* with a small *i*) to the true God.

To state this in terms of the distinction I drew above between a religion and a faith, what Islam thinks God calls for is monotheistic faith, that is, belief in, trust in, and loyalty to the one God, who has revealed himself in the Jewish, Christian, and Muslim scriptures. Muslims consider Islam to be the best religion, because it is the one that has grown out of the final culminating revelation, but the Muslim tradition also holds the belief that the religions developed around the earlier revelations are also legitimate because they too are usable to sustain genuine monotheistic faith. Under current conditions, on the other hand, with non-Muslims invading and taking control of Muslim lands and with all the cognitive dissonance brought by modern science and pluralistic culture and by the modern communications that intrude them constantly on Muslim attention, it is easy to see how the sociological and psychological impact of these factors would make tolerance seem to many Muslims to be almost akin to apostasy. But however powerful that effect may be, it is an accident of circumstances, not an inherent feature of the Muslim religion itself.

The Jewish tradition, to consider still another example, has never involved the idea that the calling of the Jews was to convert the world to their religion. In its earliest years, the religion of Israel seems to have been simply a tribal religion for Israelites, without implications for others, who were considered to have their own tribal gods. Over a period of centuries the prophetic movement brought into it the idea of a call to righteousness from a universal God to all people, not just Jews, but this was thought of simply as a call to ethical practice, not to the specific practices of the Jewish religion. Especially around the time of the Babylonian Exile, prophets such as Isaiah began to talk about a calling of the Jews to be a light to the nations (42:6, 49:6), to make God's ultimate purpose and his call to righteousness known to the whole world. During the Middle Ages, thinking about how to understand the relation of Jews to both Christians and Muslims as fellow monotheists who had received light from the Jews and were trying to live by it, the rabbis began to speak of two covenants, the Mosaic covenant between God and the Jews as a distinct people, and the Noachic (or Noahide) covenant, the covenant God made with

Noah, prior to Moses, that applies to the entire human race and involves not the hundreds of commandments that apply specifically to Jews but only seven: to refrain from idolatry, profaning the name of God, unchastity, murder, robbery, cutting off flesh from a living animal, and the general command to practice righteousness in relation to all people. Jews have never held the idea, which some (even if far from all) Christians and Muslims *have* held, that only members of their religious community will be eligible for a blessed afterlife; the only requirement for that is an ethical life in this world. Jews will be expected to keep faithfully the mitzvoth (commandments) that were given to them through God's revelation to Moses, but that will be expected only of Jews, and even a Jew will also have other more important criteria to meet, such as brotherly love and the love of truth. One of the well-known sayings of the rabbis is that when a man appears before the throne of the Holy One, one of the first things he will be asked is, "Did you look deeply into things?"

So it is easy to see that although religions generally do involve normative standards, the demand for conversion to one particular religion is not always or even usually seen as a necessary implication (the impression that it *is* probably derives mainly from the attitudes of some Christian groups). Self-transcending love and looking deeply into things, on the other hand, are widely shared values among the world's religions, so it seems appropriate to begin with them in considering what normative standards might be appropriate for evaluating religious ways of thinking, and this fits well into the pattern of developmental thinking extending from Piaget to Kegan and Lonergan.

It would be possible, of course, to interpret the idea of looking deeply into things as meaning simply to come up with and hold fast to the right answers, but that is not at all what it has meant in the Jewish use of that phrase. Rather, it has meant questioning and disputation in a continuing dialogue about the appropriate ethical conduct for different situations—that is, how best to live the calling to self-transcending love. The Talmud is mainly a record of rabbinic deliberations about questions posed to them regarding situations that called for some sort of action, and in that tradition the deliberation itself is considered a value. That is why minority positions were always recorded in the Talmud as well as the opinions that prevailed. It is also in the search itself for understanding that righteousness is enacted.

Christian thinking has, of course, been rather different on the whole regarding disputation; the church councils that formulated the orthodox creeds in the fourth and fifth centuries did not try to preserve minority views but ended their sessions with pronouncements of anathema on anyone who might disagree with the view finally settled on. The emphasis of the bishops in council in those early centuries was definitely on the objects of belief rather than on belief as a process in the life of a subject. Nevertheless, the latter has gradually come to be recognized in later Christian tradition as spiritually as well as intellectually important.

We saw Newman speak in his *Essay in Aid of a Grammar of Assent* of "an active recognition of propositions as true such as it is the duty of each individual himself to exercise at the bidding of reason, and, when reason forbids, to withhold." He also discussed there the psychology of belief in a way that helps to clarify the relation between its intellectual aspects and its spiritual dimension. Central to this is the distinction Newman makes between certitude and certainty and his analysis of how each is developed. "Certitude is a mental state," he said. "Certainty is a quality of propositions." A proposition is certain if it can be proven to the satisfaction of a rational thinker, that is, when the conditions for reasonable assent have been found to be fulfilled. In the case of deductive propositions, the fulfillment is principally a matter of formal coherence among the ideas that make it up (as in the case of the Pythagorean theorem, which is proven simply from the idea of a right triangle and does not depend on measurement of actual physical specimens). In the case of inductive propositions, propositions about matters of fact in the empirical world, assent never becomes certain in the formal sense but is arrived at by, as Newman says, "the cumulation of probabilities, independent of each other, arising out of the nature and circumstances of the particular case which is under review; probabilities too fine to avail separately, too subtle and circuitous to be convertible into syllogisms, too numerous and various for such conversion, even were they convertible." In both deduction and induction, conditions for assent are determined in the course of investigation, and "certitude," as Newman used the term, is the subjective state that recognizes the fulfillment of those conditions. The questioning mind, guided by intellectual conscience determining the conditions for assent, follows out the path of investigation and proof until it comes finally to rest "accompanied by a specific sense of intellectual satisfaction and repose."[23] Or at least that is what happens when the intellectual conscience is open and honest and when the process of inquiry is allowed to pursue fully its proper course.

This is where the spiritual dimension of inquiry becomes an issue. The intellectual dimension of inquiry is that which has to do with the object inquired

23. Newman, *Essay in Aid,* 262, 219, 196.

about, the problem to be solved, the answer to uncover. The spiritual has to do with the relation of the inquirer himself or herself to the inquiry and with the ways that can challenge one with questions of how *to be.* Authentic inquiry demands not only attentiveness and mental effort but also courage and humility. It requires love of truth and the continuous exercise of intellectual conscience energized by that love. Intellectual conscience is faithful sensitivity to the question of truth and to the possibility of further discovery and more adequate interpretations.

There can be no intellectual openness without spiritual openness, and without both together, intellectual conscience will lose its vital principle.[24] Inquiry is not always subjectively open to the full range of questioning and all possibilities of truth. Sometimes the intellectual conscience is dull and undeveloped; sometimes it is stifled by fear of disturbing possibilities; sometimes it lets itself be intimidated by authorities who tell it to leave the thinking to them; sometimes, as Freud, Becker, and Girard say, it wants simply to hide from reality by repressing awareness of it and overlaying it with palliative or self-serving myths. Looking deeply into things requires the courage to step out as an individual thinker and take risks, both intellectual and spiritual, for the love of truth. It also requires the honesty to recognize ulterior motives that might subvert that love from within. The inquirer's soul, to use the language of spiritual discourse, may live in openness, or it may let fear overcome love and close itself against both truth and love.

When the process of questioning, investigation, and critical testing is carried out in openness of soul with fidelity to the intrinsic norms of critical inquiry, the result is what Newman called "certitude": "the perception of a truth with the perception that it is a truth, or the consciousness of knowing, as expressed in the phrase, 'I know that I know.'" Accompanied as it is by its "specific sense of intellectual satisfaction and repose," this is a "tranquil enjoyment" of truth that contrasts with the "intellectual anxiety" that goes over and over arguments to assure itself or tries to argue others into supporting those arguments, as if "appealing to others for their suffrage in behalf of the truths of which we are so sure; which is like asking another whether we are weary and hungry, or have eaten and drunk to our satisfaction."[25]

24. For a discussion of the relation between intellectual and spiritual openness, see Eric Voegelin's essays "The Eclipse of Reality," "On Debate and Existence," and "Reason: The Classic Experience." See also Webb, *Eric Voegelin,* 147–48, 234–36, 271–73.

25. Newman, *Essay in Aid,* 149, 152, 153.

Religion and Orders of Consciousness

This indicates the intimate relation between intellectual development and spiritual. But what about their relation to Kegan's orders of consciousness? I mentioned above that the idea of orders of consciousness had the advantage over stage theory that it is open to the possibility of alternative ways a fully mature adult mind might organize itself to deal with the demands of various milieus and situations. It is not that one order of consciousness is "right" and the others wrong, even if some do have advantages in particular situations. Perhaps thinking further about these issues may also open another helpful angle on how different religions might relate to one another.

I would like to begin by approaching orders of consciousness as involving the development of capacities for operation. I have talked already about Piaget's developmental sequence as a hierarchical integration (later operations building on previously acquired ones) moving from "concrete" operations on objects to "formal" ones that not only bear on objects but also reflect on the subjective pole of consciousness. Lonergan's analysis of intentional consciousness, as discussed in Chapters 2 and 6, was inspired in part by Piaget's approach and involves a similar hierarchical integration of operations corresponding to his transcendental precepts ("Be attentive, Be intelligent, Be reasonable, Be responsible"): first there is attention to experiential data, then interpretation (a construing of the data in some pattern of interrelations), then critical reflection on the relative adequacy of the interpretation, leading to a judgment regarding its degree of relative adequacy, then consideration of what to do in the concrete situation if the interpretation is judged correct or at least probable. When the full process is carried out in sequence and with proper care on each level of operation, the result should be what Newman described as coming to rest in judgment and decision with a sense of satisfaction and repose.

Obviously, of course, certitude in the sense of satisfaction regarding the truth of some account of reality does not guarantee that the account will be really adequate. The ability to arrive adequately at that rest requires careful thought and sensitivity to intellectual conscience. And, of course, adequacy regarding an account of objective reality can never be more than a relative matter. It may be possible to attain complete certainty with regard to analytic propositions, such as proofs in geometry, but the most one can hope for regarding propositions that refer to a factual state of affairs is *relative* adequacy—relative, that is, to the availability of relevant data and the attentiveness with which they are collected, to the quality of the interpretations developed, and to that of the critical testing they are subjected to before the inquiry comes to rest in judgment. Part of what makes knowledge adequate is its own recognition of its relativity and an openness to further questioning, to further relevant data that may subsequently be noticed, and to further possibilities of interpretation. Adequate knowing must involve, that is, a willingness, and ideally even an eagerness, to see one's proudest accomplishments in knowing corrected and surpassed.

Again, this is not just an intellectual matter but also a spiritual one. The cognitive humility that recognizes the relativity of knowledge and the heuristic humility that values the search for adequate knowledge above any particular claim to its attainment are spiritual qualities without which any heuristic effort will be subverted. One cannot pursue knowledge effectively without the noetic differentiation of consciousness that realizes and appropriates the distinct interrelated operations that constitute the process of coming to know, but doing so also has to involve what one might call a spiritual differentiation of consciousness that distinguishes among what in Chapter 2 we saw Lonergan call the "transcendental notions" of the intelligible, the true, and the good; recognizes their distinctness from any particular object of understanding, judgment, or decision; and pursues them with constant fidelity to the openness of critical questioning.

The reason Lonergan used the term *transcendental* in connection with the transcendental notions and the complex of operations he called transcendental method that guides them is that they are absolutely fundamental and universal: any genuine knowledge is precisely that because it is constructed using those operations. Their integration is the bedrock of cognitive reality; they are the subjective pole of which the only reality proportionate to human knowing is the objective pole.[26] To use the language of Noam Chomsky's theory of generative grammar, one might describe the noetic operations of transcendental method as the *intellectual* deep structure of the human mind and their relation to the transcendental notions as its *spiritual* deep structure. Together they generate all the particular fields of the natural, historical, and social sciences, as well as literature, the arts, philosophy, and theology—all of which relate collectively to that deep structure the way all the particular languages

26. Hence the "isomorphism" between knowing and the known that both Piaget and Lonergan talk about. See Piaget, *Genetic Epistemology*, 15; Lonergan, *Insight*, 399–400; and Chapters 2 and 6.

with their various syntaxes do to the deep structure of possible meaning that Chomsky's theory interprets as hardwired in the human brain.

A similar analogy might be drawn regarding the relation of the orders of consciousness analyzed by Robert Kegan to that same intellectual and spiritual deep structure. In developmental terms, it takes something like the full course of organic maturation for a person to acquire the capacity to perform consistently and well the full range of noetic operations. Unless there is some sort of neurological deficit, however, that is normally accomplished by the time a child grows into adulthood. Whether that capacity will actually be used depends on all the psychological and spiritual factors described above—openness, courage, freedom from intimidation and repression, and so on—but above all love of truth and love of the good that will motivate one to try not to leap to conclusions or settle too quickly for comforting or conventional answers but really look deeply into things. Once the capacity for those operations has developed, and assuming the love to energize them is present and active, there are many ways they can be put to use. The adult orders of consciousness Kegan discusses are some of those ways.

The orders of consciousness are hierarchically integrated in the sense that they build on the capacities developed in the sequence of the orders as Kegan numbers them, from the first through the fifth. But at least with the last three, the orders of adult consciousness, this does not imply that further orders are intrinsically superior to earlier ones (the fourth to the third, or the fifth to the fourth), any more than calculus, say, could be said to be superior to algebra (even if it may build on algebra and be uniquely adapted for the particular kind of mathematical analysis it was developed for), or to use a linguistic analogy, any more than French, say, could be judged inherently superior to the Latin it grew out of or Latin to Indo-European.

The capacities added as one progresses through the orders of consciousness are not for new fundamental types of operation but for the application of the same fundamental types analyzed by Piaget and Lonergan to new material. As one progresses through the orders of consciousness, the source for that new material is the kind of progressive differentiation of consciousness that Kegan describes as the "disembedding" of subjectivity: something in which one was subjectively embedded in an earlier order becomes differentiated as an object of consciousness for the later one.

In Kegan's third order, for example, the developing person learns to step back from simple immersion in his or her own feelings and desires and recognize that there are other people with different feelings and desires of their own. A person who can operate skillfully in the third order of consciousness has learned to hold both his or her own and others' feelings and desires in the imagination simultaneously and reflect on them with a measure of detachment—which is precisely what we commonly mean by developing "objectivity." When one's own feelings and desires become differentiated (when one becomes disembedded from them), then one becomes capable of relating both to one's own and to those of the other in a new, more flexible way. When one remains embedded in one's own desires, on the other hand, the relation to those of others is virtually bound to become conflictual whenever the two do not exactly coincide. The ability to step back from both and work out a nonconflictual resolution makes it possible to develop a civil society, whether on the level of the family or that of a nation or civilization.

Here too, I think, there is a spiritual dimension. Just above I spoke of the intellectual and spiritual dimensions of inquiry. In the process of disembedding that Kegan talks about, there is a dimension that is psychological, the simple becoming aware of psychic contents as possible objects of awareness and operation. But the process of stepping back from one's impulses, desires, and identities can call one's being itself profoundly into question and demand a choice of how to be, of what kind of person one wants to become, of what spiritual possibilities one wants to love and serve. I will soon explore these implications further in connection with the question of radical self-transcendence. For now, however, let us continue with the relation of Kegan's orders of consciousness to one another.

The advantages of the third order of consciousness over the first two are so obvious that it seems completely natural to think of it as superior to the first and second. Certainly, no mature person would choose to give up those advantages, and their acquisition is probably what most of us think of as the mark of psychological adulthood. But there is a difference when one compares the third order with the fourth or the fifth. The latter two involve capacities that an adult capable of functioning well in a peaceful civil society could easily feel no need for and could even quite reasonably prefer not to be bothered with. A person with a third-order mentality might dwell in, or at least aspire to dwell in, a world with stable and well-functioning institutions, clear rules of conduct, and social networks maintained by people whose identities have settled into habitual shape so that they identify simply and completely with their social roles and always act in accord with them.

In the history of Christianity, Saint Augustine of Hippo might serve as an example. Augustine, living in the late fourth and early fifth centuries under an imperial system that was rapidly deteriorating in the Latin West, converted to Christianity and found in his new religion a worldview that he believed offered a practical alternative to the world of the Western empire he saw winding down toward collapse. Still, his Christianity had a structure very like that of the deteriorating empire he lived in, with a chain of command extending from God in heaven down through the institutional hierarchy of the church to its lay foot soldiers. Augustine's own position within that chain of command was that of a bishop acting as the local plenipotentiary for the church in his part of North Africa on behalf of the God that church represented. Augustine became firmly embedded, one might say, in this role, which he exercised in as authoritarian a manner as might a commander in the imperial army, introducing as a theological innovation (disturbing to many of his fellow bishops at the time) the idea that heresy should be forcibly suppressed by military action.[27] Seeing the whole structure of reality as he did through the lens of an imperial-military metaphor, it would probably never have occurred to Augustine to step back from his role as enforcer of orthodoxy to ask whether greater freedom of interpretation might be tolerated, and if it had even occurred to him to think about that possibility, he might well have interpreted it as a temptation to betray the responsibilities of his office as well as his personal loyalty to the Lord he served.[28]

Kegan's fourth order develops only when a person becomes aware of problems that cannot be adequately handled by identifying with the conventional roles, rules, and personal loyalties of the third order and simply barreling ahead with them. One begins to feel the need to step back and think about where the whole system is heading. A strong impetus to this can come from conflicts within the traditional system. One example of the beginning of fourth-order religious thinking may be seen in Dante Alighieri. Dante is in many respects a culminating figure in the development of traditional Christianity in the Middle Ages, but one does not have to be a rebel against tradition to step back from it. Rather, in order to take stock of the tradition and help keep it on a promising course, Dante felt the need to step back from the struggles between the heirs of Augustine, the followers of Saint Thomas

27. Cf. Peter Robert Lamont Brown, *Augustine of Hippo: A Biography:* "Augustine, in replying to his persistent critics, wrote the only full justification, in the history of the Early Church, of the right of the state to suppress non-Catholics" (235). The particular heresy in question was Donatism.

28. For a more extensive discussion of Augustine's embeddedness in his culture, with the implications for the way his thought developed, see Webb, "Augustine's New Trinity."

Aquinas and Saint Francis, the power of the papal center (which had begun an ongoing institutional revolution in the eleventh century), and the humanist aspirations of early Renaissance figures he admired, such as Brunetto Latini or Arnaut Daniel. His ability to reflect judiciously on the points of view of all of these and hold them in balance with a generosity of vision new to medieval Christianity is what makes his *Commedia* perhaps even more comprehensive and effective a *Summa* than that of Saint Thomas but also one of the first signs of a new era.

Or turning to a figure closer to our own time, one might take Cardinal Newman as an example of a person powerfully motivated like Augustine to connect with and involve himself (even "embed" himself, perhaps) in a strong tradition but who also, living mentally as he did in the nineteenth century, had ineluctably become historically minded and therefore had to step back and reflect on the church's life as a historical process—in a way that his more culturally insulated, and comfortably "embedded," contemporary Pope Pius IX could probably not even have begun to imagine.

Among the religious figures we have considered so far in the present study, the one who seems most clearly to represent the beginnings of a fifth-order mentality would probably be Bernard Lonergan, with his intensive reflection on method and his emphasis on the isomorphism of the objective and subjective poles of consciousness. The hallmark of the fifth order (or "postmodern") mind, as Kegan discusses it, is its ability to reflect on subjectivity as such, with recognition that it cannot be reduced entirely to an object. The fifth order, aware of the problems that grow out of the "modern" fourth-order mind's effort to see itself as a detached Cartesian ego, fully transparent to itself and in effective control both of itself and of its objective situation, recognizes that to be a person is to be always a combination of differentiation and embeddedness. Reading Lonergan's works from *Insight,* through the essays in his series of collections, to *Method in Theology,* one can see him gradually yielding an effort to objectify everything possible, including the subject as such, and coming to terms with a realization that subjectivity will always have depths that remain mysterious because consciousness will always retain what Michael Polanyi calls its "subsidiary," or "tacit," dimension.[29]

The fifth order's awareness that subjectivity can never be fully objectified and brought under control—and that it can consequently involve factors that

29. See, for example, Polanyi, *Personal Knowledge* and *The Tacit Dimension.* For a discussion, see Webb, *Philosophers of Consciousness,* 36–46 on Polanyi and 102–5 on Lonergan in relation to this.

sneak up on thinking from behind, as it were—has led many contemporary religious thinkers beyond Lonergan's methodological reflections to a searching ideology critique bearing on their own traditions. Two that come to mind in Lonergan's own Catholic tradition, and who both show signs of having read and digested his work, are Elisabeth Schüssler Fiorenza and Garry Wills. Schüssler Fiorenza writes about what she calls "kyriarchy," the tendency to see all of life unreflectively through the lens of domination.[30] Wills tries in his *Papal Sin: Structures of Deceit* to open up the perspective of a constructive postmodernism that can both preserve what is valuable in tradition and critique the unconscious structural sources of self-deception and blindness that he thinks have undermined the church hierarchy's efforts to deal effectively with the challenges of modernity. There is no need to go into detail about such critiques here, but that they have become an important feature of the theological scene in the past half century or so says something about the evolutionary trajectory of orders of consciousness—that is, that just as organisms evolve in relation to such factors as changes in climate, new orders of consciousness develop because they are better adapted to changes in their social and cultural environment and to the questions that move it.[31]

So even if Kegan's three adult orders may be equal insofar as each may be well adapted to the milieu to which it is appropriate, the possibilities of deeper reflection that the successive orders open up may offer important advantages in dealing with problematic situations that might arise. For some of the world's religions today the religious, cultural, and cognitive pluralism of the modern world is just such a situation. One common way of dealing with such challenges in traditional societies was ghettoization—either sequestering oneself from alien influences or sequestering the aliens. Another was inquisition and purging. But neither of those approaches can remain effective for long in a world in which instant worldwide communication has virtually become a structural necessity—as the increasingly desperate but only partially effective efforts of the Communist government in China to bring the Internet under strict party control demonstrate. For religions, the challenge of finding a better way to relate to a religiously pluralistic milieu than defensive mutual antagonism has clearly become urgent.

30. See, for example, Schüssler Fiorenza, *Jesus and the Politics of Interpretation.*

31. On the relation between physical and mental evolution and climate change, see William H. Calvin, *A Brain for All Seasons: Human Evolution and Abrupt Climate Change* and *A Brief History of the Mind: From Apes to Intellect and Beyond.*

Anyone interested in the possibility of peace among different religions should find in the development of fourth- and fifth-order possibilities of reflection a basis for hope. The ability of a religious person to step back from his or her own religious tradition and consider it, like other traditions, a partial, relatively adequate way of relating to transcendent ultimacy may be what will enable the various religions of the world eventually to develop a way of living together with mutual appreciation and respect. So may the ability to think seriously about the ambiguities of one's own tradition and about both one's tradition's and one's own possible unconscious subversions of the religion's deeper purpose.

The capacity to develop that sort of reflective distance should be welcomed by religious people as a spiritual as well as an intellectual advance, since it can enable the members of religious traditions to pursue more effectively the spiritual goals intrinsic to their religions. I earlier brought up the question of what criteria might be used to evaluate religious developments. Even if it may not be possible to find one criterion that would be recognized as valid by the members of all possible religions, I think there is one that could be acknowledged at least by the religions that today are playing the most prominent roles on the world scene—Christianity, Judaism, Islam, Buddhism, and some of the Vedic religious traditions of India. That criterion is radically self-transcending love. I will explain what I mean by that term and its qualifying adjectives.

The word *love* can mean various things to different people in different contexts. There are people for whom love denotes simply sexual appetite. There are others for whom it connotes also feelings of mutual affection between sexual partners, family members, and friends. There are others for whom its meaning extends to members of a clan, a political party, a church, or a nation. As love moves beyond simple gratification of individual appetites to concern for and empathy with others, it can be said to be at least relatively self-transcending. Looking back at Kegan's analysis of the stages of development, for example, the movement from the "imperial self" to the "interpersonal self" shows the beginning of self-transcendence: instead of identifying itself simply with its desires, the developing adolescent begins to identify with some of its personal relationships. But this is only a relative self-transcendence. It is *self*-transcendence in that it involves the centering of concern in a relation with another. The reason it is only *relative* is that it remains bound to the self constituted by an identification, even if that may be a new, more differentiated self. At the "interpersonal" stage the self is constituted by that interpersonal relation and enclosed within it. The further developments toward what Kegan calls the "institutional" and the "interindividual" stages involve further steps in relative self-transcendence. We saw Kegan say that "if one can feel manipulated by the imperial balance, one can feel devoured by the interpersonal one"; it is only as one transcends identification with the interpersonal relationship that the partners are given space to exist as distinct persons.[32]

Some forms of love, even if they might be considered the supreme value in some communities, can fuel the problem of religious strife rather than help to solve it. Love of neighbor might in some contexts mean love of the members of one's own group and imply hostility toward nonneighbors outside it. Religious suicide bombers probably think of themselves as motivated by love of their religion and of the neighbors they think they are defending against the group whose members they bomb. Or, lest it sound as if I may be criticizing one religious tradition and sparing another, the Catholic inquisitors who silenced Galileo and those who tortured and condemned many others to death probably thought they were acting out of love for their God and for those the heretics might lead astray. So, probably, did the Protestant judges of the Salem witch trials. Love of a group may be relatively self-transcending, leading a person to sacrifice his or her own desires for the welfare of the group, but to the extent that one's identity is closely tied up with the group, that very self-transcendence may lock one into a new group self-centeredness in the form of religious nationalism or ethnocentricity.

Religion as a "Holding Environment"

Here again we can see the problem of embeddedness and differentiation and the question of whether religion can serve as a needed holding environment that preserves a fragile sense of self while preparing for further differentiation and self-transcendence or whether, fueled by anxiety about loss of self and threats to one's worldview, it can bind one in identification and stifle the very possibility of transcendence. I am reminded of a conversation a friend of mine, an Eastern Orthodox Christian, told me she had with her aunt. My friend was very serious about her faith and interested in the history and theology of her tradition, in which she was well read. Her aunt, however, warned her that studying such things would lead her to ask questions, and asking questions might make her doubt her faith, and if she lost her Orthodox faith,

32. Kegan, *Evolving Self*, 97.

she would lose her Russian identity. For the aunt, it was identity that was the bottom line.[33]

Religion is inherently ambiguous: it can either provide a holding environment for the sake of growth or try to "hold on to" one, as Kegan puts it, and stifle growth. This ambiguity is rooted, however, not in some weakness inherent in religion as such but in humanity itself. Just as social scientists say that the quality called charisma is not a property inherent in the charismatic individual but a relation between that individual and the people who endow him with charisma by seeking it in him and projecting it onto him, so it is not simply that religion holds on to a person. Rather, the "holding on to" tends to be reciprocal. The leaders and other members of the group try to hold the potential deviant back from dangerous thoughts, but unless they have the sort of physical power of incarceration and torture the inquisitors had over Galileo, the social and psychological power they have must derive in part from the desire of the potential deviant himself to be held on to. As I mentioned in the Introduction, Peter Berger says that "anomy is unbearable to the point where the individual may seek death in preference to it," and anomie is a powerful threat to anyone who ventures beyond the beliefs of a group, even when there are no inquisitors to keep him in line. Berger also says that religious and other social influences do not work by a sort of mechanistic determinism: "The individual is not molded as a passive, inert thing. Rather, he is formed in the course of a protracted conversation (a dialectic, in the literal sense of the word) in which he is a *participant.* That is, the social world (with its appropriate institutions, roles, and identities) is not passively absorbed by the individual, but actively *appropriated* by him."[34] The religious person, that is, like anyone else, reaches out for an identity and a world to take hold of, and one of the great attractions of religion for many is that it provides these and thereby protects them from anomie. A given religious person, fleeing anxiety over uncertainty and existential vulnerability, may actually want to be "held on to" and held back and may want others held back too, so as to avoid losing the support of mimetic belief. But just as a child may want both to be held and to be let go and may feel torn between the two, so the same religious persons may seek in their religion both comfort and challenge. As

33. To put this in James Fowler's terms, one could say that my friend's aunt was trying to hold her in the synthetic-conventional faith of the era of adolescence and prevent her from moving on to individuative-reflective, conjunctive, or universalizing faith.

34. Berger, *Sacred Canopy,* 18; emphasis in the original.

Kegan said about the function of a holding environment or culture of embeddedness, what that can do at its best is nurture the developing person to the point that further development becomes possible, encourage transition to the next stage, and encourage reintegration in a new form of what has been transcended.[35] So cultural and religious pluralism can stimulate both anxiety and also, when circumstances favor it, the development of further ways of thinking that might be able to embrace pluralism without fear.

Psychological development through the various stages and orders of consciousness, then, can be understood as a sequence of steps in relative self-transcendence, and much religious development, too, may be little more than that if it is limited to cultivating the love of one's own group. But at least in their most developed forms, the major religions tend to strive toward not merely relatively but *radically* self-transcending love—not just love of one's coreligionists, fellow members of one's ethnic group, or even fellow members of the human race, but love of all beings and of being itself; not just love of particular goods but of the good as such; not just love of particular beliefs that may be comforting but love of truth as such, even if that may call one to face into the *tremendum*.

The Question of a Radically Self-Transcending "Self"

This, of course, raises a new and deeper question: what can it mean to speak of a radically self-transcending "self"? Freud said, "Where 'it' was, there should be 'I,'" but what is the "I" ultimately, or what can it ultimately become? Or to put it another way, what kind of self does the self strive to become when it tries to pass beyond itself absolutely, to become disembedded from every psychic content? Here one reaches the limits of psychology. Psychology cannot even ask such questions. But religions sometimes do.

Buddhism is one that asks it explicitly and insistently. Probably one of the most basic assumptions of the modern Western worldview is atomistic individualism, the belief that reality is made up of a vast number of indivisible units, and that the self is one of these. Buddhism, with its key doctrine of *anatman* (no self) calls this assumption into question in the most radical way. To elucidate the Buddhist critique of the idea of a substantial self, perhaps it will help if we begin by considering a Western analogue.

35. See Chapter 3, note 26.

David Hume, whose empiricism worked out the logic of atomism by reducing all reality to discrete data of consciousness that only appear unified through the association of ideas, found himself driven by that logic to doubt also the substantial reality of his own self—beginning with the question of whether we can claim even to have any real idea of such an entity:

> There are some philosophers, who imagine we are every moment intimately conscious of what we call our SELF; that we feel its existence and its continuance in existence; and are certain, beyond the evidence of a demonstration, both of its perfect identity and simplicity. . . . Unluckily all these positive assertions are contrary to that very experience, which is pleaded for them, nor have we any idea of self, after the manner it is here explain'd. For from what impression cou'd this idea be deriv'd? . . . It must be some one impression, that gives rise to every real idea. But self or person is not any one impression, but that to which our several impressions and ideas are suppos'd to have a reference. If any impression gives rise to the idea of self, that impression must continue invariably the same, thro' the whole course of our lives; since self is suppos'd to exist after that manner. But there is no impression constant and invariable. Pain and pleasure, grief and joy, passions and sensations succeed each other, and never all exist at the same time. It cannot, therefore, be from any of these impressions, or from any other, that the idea of self is deriv'd; and consequently there is no such idea.[36]

Nor is it only that we have no coherent idea of a self, Hume goes on to say. Rather, the pertinent observable reality suggests that not only is there no such idea, there is also no such reality:

> For my part, when I enter most intimately into what I call myself, I always stumble on some particular perception or other, of heat or cold, light or shade, love or hatred, pain or pleasure. I never can catch myself at any time without a perception, and never can observe any thing but the perception. When my perceptions are remov'd for any time, as by sound sleep; so long am I insensible of myself, and may truly be said not to exist. . . . I may venture to affirm of the rest of mankind, that they are nothing but a bundle or collection of different perceptions, which succeed each other with an inconceivable rapidity, and are in a perpetual flux and movement. . . . The mind is a kind of theatre, where several perceptions successively make their appearance; pass, re-pass, glide away, and mingle in an infinite variety of postures and situations. There is properly no simplicity in it at one time, nor identity in different; whatever natural propension we may have

36. Hume, *Treatise of Human Nature,* bk. 1, pt. 4, sec. 6, pp. 251–52.

> to imagine that simplicity and identity. The comparison of the theatre must not mislead us. They are the successive perceptions only, that constitute the mind; nor have we the most distant notion of the place, where these scenes are represented, or of the materials, of which it is compos'd.[37]

Hume drew no spiritual implications from this analysis of mental flux, but Buddhists do.[38] The Buddhist analysis of the idea of a self or soul is very similar in its basics to Hume's: what we think of as a unitary, perduring soul-entity is really an impermanent aggregation of constantly changing elements called *skandhas:* body, perceptions, feelings, thoughts, and *samskharas* (habitual tendencies or dispositions). It is the mix of these that constitutes the appearance we think of as the individual self during its lifetime, but each of them is in constant flux, and at death they disperse and the apparent unit dissolves. The purpose of Buddhist meditation practice is concretely to see through such illusory belief in the substantial existence of this self, which Buddhism believes both is rooted in and reinforces the craving one needs to break free from. The ultimate goal of Buddhism is both liberation *from* the suffering that craving causes and liberation *for* universal compassion, the radically self-transcending love that Buddhists identify with what they call Buddha-nature. To realize this, not as a theoretical idea but in a deep existential insight, is to discover one's true life in Buddha-nature. For Buddhists, Buddha-nature is ultimate reality, the truth of being that is hidden behind the illusion of egoistic existence. Buddha-mind, the compassionate mind of enlightenment, is the consciousness that emerges when that illusion dissolves.

This may sound, perhaps, like a way of thinking peculiar to Buddhism alone. Hume was not seeking deliverance from selfhood but found his theoretical insight into the insubstantiality of the self oppressive and felt relieved to be delivered from it by the habitual power of his illusions.[39] Vedic thought,

37. Ibid., 252–53.

38. The Buddhist thinker Thich Nhat Hanh, while studying for his master's in religion at Columbia University in the early 1960s, wrote his master's thesis on David Hume and the philosophy of Vijnanavada (the "consciousness-only" school of thought in Buddhism). There are many books by Buddhists dealing with the doctrine of *anatman.* An older classic is Daisetz Teitaro Suzuki, *The Zen Doctrine of No-Mind: The Significance of the Sutra of Hui-neng.* A very accessible more recent presentation of the topic by a Western psychiatrist is Mark Epstein, *Thoughts without a Thinker: Psychotherapy from a Buddhist Perspective.*

39. "Most fortunately it happens, that since reason is incapable of dispelling these clouds, nature herself suffices to that purpose, and cures me of this philosophical melancholy and delirium, either by relaxing this bent of mind, or by some avocation, and lively impression of my senses, which obliterate all these chimeras" (Hume, *Treatise,* bk. 1, pt. 4, sec. 7, p. 269).

rather than denying the *atman,* seems to affirm it as ultimate reality: "Thou art That," "Atman and Brahman are one." Christianity also probably seems closely tied in many minds to belief in the substantial existence of an immortal soul-self that can accumulate credit to its individual account by good deeds or the opposite by bad. When Western psychologists talk about the value of individuation, this too may sound like the very opposite of the kind of radical self-transcendence that Buddhism seeks. More closely examined, though, the differences are not as great as they might at first sound. In the case of Indian religions, there are strands of tradition, especially Jain and Samkhya, that do affirm the reality of an atomistic individual life-monad, sometimes called *atman* or sometimes *purusha* or *jiva,* and it was probably this pattern of thinking that the Buddhist doctrine of *anatman* was originally intended to counter.[40] But when the Upanishads or Advaita (that is, "nondual") Vedanta declare that Atman and Brahman are one, they seem to be saying something very like what the Buddhists mean when they identify ultimate reality with Buddha-nature and speak of realizing it in Buddha-mind.

Then again, this may all sound typically and exclusively Asian, but there are parallels in the mystical strains within Western religious traditions as well. Judaism has its Kabbala and Islam its Sufism, and both involve ideas about immanent divine presence and the discovery of one's true being in the One who alone truly is. Christianity may sound to many like the least-likely tradition in which to find something like this sort of radical self-transcendence, and it *has* tended toward atomistic individualism in some of the forms it has taken over time in the popular imagination, but there are also strong countercurrents to that within the Christian tradition itself. When Stephen Dedalus imagines a credit being rung up to his personal account at the great cash register in the sky, his author, James Joyce, is parodying a pattern of thinking that may be quite common, but few serious Christians would not see the humor of it and acknowledge the point of Joyce's satire, even if they might feel uncomfortable at the memory of times when they themselves have slipped into thinking of the spiritual path of their faith in terms of similarly naive and egoistic imagery.[41]

The widespread modern Christian belief in an individual, monadic soul that is immortal by its very nature seems to have come into Christian thinking

40. The term *life-monad* (as a translation for *purusha* and *jiva*) is from Heinrich Robert Zimmer, *Philosophies of India.* See, for example, pp. 229, 371.

41. Joyce, *A Portrait of the Artist as a Young Man,* 148. Cf. Fowler's finding that a substantial number of religious adults think largely in the mythic-literal mode and conceive of divine justice as concrete reciprocity.

mainly in the second millennium, partly from the influence of earlier classical Greek sources. The core belief of Christianity in its origin, as its classical creeds attest, was not immortality of the soul but resurrection, according to which the individual person was closely identified with the living but perishable body that could have a future life only if raised from death by divine power.[42] Nor did the early Christians seem to have identified simply and completely with that individual body. Rather, their earliest expressions of their worldview involved the idea of a transcendent, shared identity in which God, Jesus, and those who hear and heed him participate in one another, as when John's Jesus tells his disciples, "You shall know that I am in my Father, and you in me, and I in you" (14:20), or as when Matthew's tells them they will discover that "inasmuch as you have done it unto one of the least of these my brethren, you have done it unto me" (25:40).

If one looks at the oldest documents of the Christian tradition, the letters of Saint Paul, they are filled with references to "being in Christ" or "living in Christ."[43] Paul says in his Epistle to the Romans, "So we, being many, are one body in Christ, and every one members one of another" (Rom. 12:5), and in 2 Corinthians, "If any man be in Christ, he is a new creature" (5:17). The letter to the Ephesians speaks of how "we are [God's] workmanship, created in Christ Jesus" (2:10).[44] That to the Colossians speaks of "the mystery which has been hidden from ages and from generations, but now is made manifest to his saints . . . which is Christ in you, the hope of glory" (1:26–27), and of the calling of every person to become "perfect in Christ Jesus" (1:28). The Greek word translated here as *perfect* is *teleion,* which means complete, fully mature,

42. See Oscar Cullmann, *Immortality of the Soul or Resurrection of the Dead? The Witness of the New Testament.* Cullman argues that immortality of the soul was not part of the Jewish tradition at all, nor of early Christian. See also the discussion of this in John Dominic Crossan and Jonathan L. Reed, *In Search of Paul: How Jesus's Apostle Opposed Rome's Empire with God's Kingdom,* 343–45. For the view that immortality of the soul was an element in some strands of Jewish tradition even if belief in resurrection was more central for other strands, see Nicholas Thomas Wright, *The Resurrection of the Son of God,* 200–206.

43. See the discussion of this in Crossan and Reed, *In Search of Paul,* 278–79.

44. The reason I refer to the letter speaking instead of Paul speaking in the cases of Ephesians and Colossians is that the actual Pauline authorship of these ancient documents is not agreed upon by all New Testament scholars. There is, on the other hand, a very broad consensus on the Pauline authorship of the other letters I cite. Even in the cases of Ephesians and Colossians, sometimes referred to as "the Pauline School," there is no serious doubt that they come from a very early period, almost certainly in the first century, probably from Paul's lifetime, and perhaps even from Paul himself, even if they may have been edited to some extent in the course of transmission. Whether they are actually from Paul himself or not, Christian tradition has always treated them as though they were and considered them primary sources for the faith.

or having reached the culminating point (the telos) of a process—in this case, the process that God was believed to have begun with Adam, rebegun with the calling of Abraham and Israel, and brought to completion in the personhood of Jesus of Nazareth, who was intended by God to be "the firstborn among many brethren" (Rom. 8:29) who would come eventually to share in the full personhood first realized in him. When Paul says in 1 Corinthians 15:22, "For as in Adam all die, even so in Christ shall all be made alive," he sounds as if he is saying something not too different from what Buddhists mean when they speak of realizing the nonexistence of the self with which we normally identify and of coming to discover a new, true life in Buddha-nature. And when he says in Philippians 2:5, "Let this mind be in you, which was also in Christ Jesus," it sounds similar to the Buddhist idea of gaining release from the illusion of egoistic existence in order to come into Buddha-mind or the mind of enlightenment.

These images of "living in Christ" could be interpreted as merely metaphors for living in a new way as the same old individual, and there are probably many modern Christians who think this is the natural way to read them, because the worldview of atomistic individualism is so deeply ingrained in the modern Western mind that it feels simply natural (more than in Asia, but also more than in ancient Israel or in early Christian times). But these statements make more direct sense if interpreted as speaking of radical self-transcendence through union with the personhood of the divine Son, who incarnate in Jesus became the revelation of the true life intended by God from the beginning for all human beings as the ultimate fulfillment of providential history.[45]

This, at any rate, is how the classical Christian tradition subsequently interpreted the implications of Paul's language when it formulated the doctrine of the Triune God (in a way that corresponded to the panentheistic interpretation of Christianity discussed in the preceding chapter). There may be many Christians now who think of the doctrine of the Trinity as having to do with three individual entities, but Christian theologians have always rejected that as tritheism, even if they have sometimes found it difficult to find a way of talking about it that avoids suggesting that. The Jesuit theologian Karl Rahner said that "the real danger in the doctrine of the Trinity . . . in the average conception of the normal Christian . . . is the danger of a popular,

45. Cf. Saint Maximus the Confessor: "God the divine Logos wishes to effect the mystery of his incarnation always and in all things" (*Patrologia Graeca* 91.1084d, quoted in Norman Russell, *The Doctrine of Deification in the Greek Patristic Tradition*, 317).

unverbalized, but at bottom quite massive tritheism."[46] In modern English it is particularly difficult to avoid slipping into this because of the way the word *person* (*persona* in Latin, *prosopon* and *hypostasis* in the original Greek formulation) has taken on new meanings since the time of the Councils of Nicaea, Constantinople, and Chalcedon in the fourth and fifth centuries.

The doctrines of the Trinity and the Hypostatic Union and their terminology are technical subjects that there is no need to go into in detail here, but perhaps a few quotations from Karl Rahner and the Greek Orthodox theologian Metropolitan John D. Zizioulas may serve to illustrate what I think is the important point at their heart, which is the idea of coming into full personhood in love through radical self-transcendence.[47] Rahner says in his book *The Trinity:*

> When correctly understood and taken seriously, the thesis which we presuppose here as true states not some scholastic subtlety, but simply this: each one of the three divine persons communicates himself to man in gratuitous grace in his own personal particularity and diversity. This trinitarian communication is the ontological ground of man's life of grace.... [T]hese three self-communications are the self-communication of the one God in the three relative ways in which God subsists.... God relates to us in a threefold manner, and this threefold, free, and gratuitous relation to us is not merely a copy or an analogy of the inner Trinity, but this Trinity itself... freely and gratuitously communicated.[48]

Put in somewhat plainer terms, what Rahner is saying is that the meaning of the doctrine of the Trinity is that God is Love—not a kind of super life-monad who first exists as Supreme Being and then just happens to love, but who is Love itself as existential communion shared with the Other that is the necessary corresponding pole without which love could not be love. In Rahner's scholastic terminology, what the Christian idea of living in Christ means is living not just metaphorically but quite really in the second hyposta-

46. Rahner, *The Trinity,* 42. How easily many Christians slip into such tritheism is attested by Erwin Ransdell Goodenough: "I was brought up in practice a tritheist, for whom the three Persons of the Trinity were united only vaguely in monotheism" (*Toward a Mature Faith,* 80).

47. Some good sources on these doctrines and their history are Catherine Mowry LaCugna, *God for Us: The Trinity and Christian Life;* G. L. Prestige, *God in Patristic Thought;* Rahner, *The Trinity;* and Zizioulas, *Being as Communion: Studies in Personhood and the Church.* For a brief account of the pertinent terms and their history, see Webb, "The Hermeneutic of Greek Trinitarianism: An Approach through Intentionality Analysis."

48. Rahner, *The Trinity,* 34–35.

sis, in divine filiation, animated by the breath (the literal meaning of "Spirit") of the Love that is the divine life itself: "God's self-communication is truly a *self*-communication. He does not merely indirectly give his creature some share of himself *by* creating and giving us created and finite realities through his omnipotent *efficient* causality. In a *quasi-formal* causality he really and in the strictest sense of the word bestows *himself*."[49]

The radical self-transcendence that is rebirth in Christ is not in Rahner's understanding an arbitrary act from on high producing an instantaneous transition from one state to another, but what might be called creation-incarnation as a developmental process in which the divine life emerges from within as it is breathed in from beyond. Rahner says, "If there occurs a self-communication of God to historical man, who is still becoming, it can occur only in this unifying duality of history and transcendence which man is," and he goes on to explain that "the very acceptance of a divine self-communication through the power and act of freedom is one more moment of the self-communication of God, who gives himself in such a way that his self-donation is accepted in freedom."[50]

What should not be overlooked here is a seemingly small but immensely important shift from what had been for centuries the standard theological language, the language of Being Itself *(Ipsum Esse)* that was discussed in the preceding chapter. There I said that one of the deepest and most divisive questions in theology is whether God should be conceived as a particular being or whether God should rather be conceived, as in Aquinas and most earlier Christian thinkers, not as a particular supernatural entity but as Being Itself. I went on to talk about how Aquinas recognized that *Being,* too, like all other words applied to God—including the word *god,* capitalized or uncapitalized—is a metaphor; he said that the tetragrammaton, the name that was never pronounced, was the best name for God because it signified nothing in itself but only pointed beyond all language into absolute mystery. Still, some kind of language is needed if one is going to try to say anything at all, and Aquinas gave the highest place among forms of theological expression to the language of God as *Qui est,* He Who Is.

Something Aquinas did not discuss and would probably never have thought about, since even to think about it requires the kind of self-reflection that began with Marx, Nietzsche, and Freud on unconscious motives and the ide-

49. Ibid., 36; emphasis in the original.
50. Ibid., 92–93.

ologies they generate, is that the idea of "being" tends to be closely associated in the human imagination with power. (If he had been able to think about it, perhaps he might have been more suspicious of the polemical involvement of his own theology in the crusade against the Albigenses.) In Chapter 5 I mentioned Mircea Eliade's discussion of the sense of the sacred as *mysterium tremendum et fascinans.* Eliade believed all religiousness is rooted in this experiential pattern, combining awe and fascination (simultaneous fear and attraction) before what is felt to be mysterious, powerful, and radically beyond us. The dynamic core of the sense of the sacred, Eliade says, is "an unquenchable ontological thirst," a thirst "for *being.*" But what exactly is this thirst for being? Eliade's answer points to something like what in that same chapter we saw René Girard refer to as "metaphysical desire": "religious man deeply desires *to be,* to participate in *reality,* to be saturated with power."[51] As we saw there, Girard considers metaphysical desire to be rooted in our fear that we are deficient in "being": we feel from birth that we lack the power we think we see in the godlike others around us (our "mediators" of true being), and we long to possess the plenitude of being, that is, power, we attribute to them. For Girard, the ambiguous sense of terror and fascination we feel before the sacred is rooted in our fear of those powerful others and the longing we also feel to become what they are. The religious life, in turn, can become from this viewpoint a sacrificial self-abasement that is an act of surrender to the mediator and an attempt to merge with him and thereby participate in his power. The worship of a God of Being, that is, can easily slip into becoming a masochistically structured idolatry of power.

One could easily read Rahner without noticing the shift that is taking place in his thought from the language of being to the language of love, but in John Zizioulas it is explicit: "The substratum of existence," he contends, "is not being but love." This states succinctly the central point of his analysis of the process by which the patristic thinkers of the fourth and fifth centuries revised and deepened the meaning of the Greek philosophical and dramatic terms *(ho on, hypostasis, prosopon)* they appropriated to use as a language for understanding what it meant to say that God is love, that "God was in Christ" (2 Cor. 5:19), and that God also "abides in us, by the Spirit which he has given us" (1 John 3:24). The first of those terms *(ho on)* was the philosophical word for "being," the second *(hypostasis)* was the word for something that could be affirmed as real, the third *(prosopon* or, in its Latin translation, *persona)* referred to the

51. Eliade, *Sacred and Profane,* 64, 13; emphases in the original.

mask representing a character in classical drama. The patristic use of these terms shifted the meaning especially of the first and second from impersonal to personal by linking it with the third. *Hypostasis* had earlier been the Greek equivalent of the relatively impersonal Latin *substantia* (something with objective underlying reality), but for the Greek fathers it took on the qualities of the personal, making subjectivity and personhood the heart of the real. This, says Zizioulas, is the existential thrust of the doctrine of the Triune God: "The expression 'God is love' (1 John 4:16) signifies that God 'subsists' as Trinity, that is, as person and not as substance. Love is not an emanation or 'property' of the substance of God . . . but is *constitutive* of His substance, i.e. it is that which makes God what He is, the one God. . . . Love as God's mode of existence 'hypostasizes' God, *constitutes* His being." Love, that is, in the patristic vocabulary Zizioulas draws on, "hypostasizes" God (renders God substantially real and personal) as Father, the radically transcendent source of Son and Spirit, who are in turn hypostases (are personal reality) because they express and embody the love that proceeds from the Father. "Personhood," says Zizioulas, is "the total fulfillment of being." The purpose of creation, therefore, is not the production of entities whose existence could be grounded in impersonal being; it is the universal incarnation of love: "The incarnate Christ," says Zizioulas, "is so identical to the ultimate will of God's love, that the meaning of created being and the purpose of history are simply the incarnate Christ."[52]

In the fallen state of existence, he says, we identify personhood with the idea of an individual substantial "self" and with the qualities and experiences it possesses, with what we call its "personality." This is an expression of fallenness because it is moved by the will to dominate and to divide, "to seize, dominate, and possess being." Love is a relation with an Other. For the fallen, individualistic imagination, otherness is a function of division, but for Zizioulas, "in the context of personhood, *otherness* is incompatible with *division*." Rather, "the mystery of being a person lies in the fact that here otherness and communion are not in contradiction but coincide." He further states, "The only way for a true person to exist is for being and communion to coincide," and this is possible only in the Triune God. To be a "person," therefore, says Zizioulas, is to be "assumed" into and "hypostasized" (raised into true personhood) in Christ, that is, in the life of divine Sonship.[53]

52. Zizioulas, *Being as Communion,* 97, 46 (emphasis in the original), 47, 97, explicating the thought of Saint Maximus the Confessor. Cf. the quotation from Maximus in note 46 above.

53. Ibid., 106, 107, 106, 107, 56.

To be assumed into Christ *could,* if Christ were thought of as an atomistically conceived "individual," sound like the idolatrous, masochistic merging with the mediator of metaphysical desire described by René Girard, but what Zizioulas is talking about is quite the opposite.[54] The reason is that Christ, the incarnate second hypostasis, is not an individual in the atomistic sense: Christ, as true person, is not an individual instance of a "nature," but is a "mode of existence." That mode of existence is love, and love is what constitutes true personhood. For Zizioulas, "Christ, although a particular person, cannot be conceived in Himself as an individual"; rather, his "whole personal existence" includes his relation to his body, the church, to all those, that is, who through sharing his mode of existence become incorporated into the same personhood he embodies because, exactly as he is, they are animated from within by the dynamic love represented in trinitarian theology by the Holy Spirit. As Zizioulas puts it, "The Holy Spirit is not one who *aids* us in bridging the distance between Christ and ourselves," as would be the case for an individualistic Christology; rather, the Spirit "actually realizes in history that which we call Christ, this absolutely relational entity"—realizes it first in Jesus, that is, and then in those who follow him. When the idea of the Christ is understood pneumatologically, he says, "The Holy Spirit . . . is the one who gives birth to Christ and to the whole activity of salvation, by anointing Him and making him *christos* (Luke 4:13)," which means that "Christ *exists only pneumatologically,* whether in His distinct personal particularity or in His capacity as the body of the Church and the recapitulation of all things."[55]

Zizioulas might even sound as if he were commenting directly on Girard's critique of idolatrous mediation when he says,

> In a pneumatologically constituted Christology an event can never be defined by itself, but only as a relational reality. It is this that allows the Biblical notion of "corporate personality" to be applied to Christ: *Christ without His body is not Christ but an individual of the worst type.* Our continuity, therefore, with the Christ event is not determined by sequence or response based on distance; it is rather a continuity in terms of *inclusiveness:* we are *in* Christ, and this is what makes Him be *before* us, our "first-born brother" in the Pauline sense.[56]

54. Such modern, largely Western, "individualism" is fundamentally alien to the thought of Zizioulas's Eastern Christian tradition and also to Eastern thought generally. On this difference between Western and Eastern patterns of thinking, see Richard E. Nisbett, *The Geography of Thought: How Asians and Westerners Think Differently—and Why,* chap. 3.

55. Zizioulas, *Being as Communion,* 106, 110, 111 (emphasis in the original).

56. Ibid., 182; emphasis in the original. I should, of course, point out that Girard speaks of

For "Christ without His body" to be "not Christ but an individual of the worst type" would be for Christ to be conceived masochistically as a uniquely powerful individual before whom one must slavishly submit to domination and give up one's own personhood. Zizioulas's pneumatologically constituted Christ is the very opposite: the inclusive incarnation of corporate personhood in which all are invited to discover their own true life as free persons. The idea of salvation (from not loving into perfect love) through assumption into the hypostatic life of Christ, says Zizioulas, "means that Christ has to be God [i.e., Love] in order to be savior, but it also means something more: *He must be not an individual but a true person.* It is impossible, within our experience of individualized existence[,] to find any analogy whatsoever with an entity who is *fully* and *ontologically personal.*"[57] We only experience hints or inklings of what that might be, and the essence of faith is trust in the mode of existence that those hints disclose.

Earlier I raised the question of what it could mean to speak of a radically self-transcending "self," or with regard to Freud's "it" and "I," of what a true "I" might ultimately be or become. Here in this particular variety of Christian language, as in the Buddhist search for realization of true life in Buddha-nature, we find ways some traditions have tried to sketch out a possible answer. What the Eastern Christian Zizioulas and the Western Christian Rahner are both talking about in their interpretations of trinitarian theological language is coming into genuine personhood through radical self-transcendence. This is not easy to talk about even in theological language, let alone in psychological. In Chapter 6 we saw the difficulty Lawrence Kohlberg and James Fowler ran into in their efforts to define and empirically locate an ultimate stage of development that would transcend the self in universal love. Both recognized

---

Jesus only as an "external mediator" (that is, a mediator of mimetic desire who is external to the milieu in which we might be drawn into direct competition with him and who can therefore serve as a benign model for imitation, as compared with a mediator "internal" to one's milieu who can stimulate rivalry); he never speaks of Jesus as an object of masochistic identification. Jesus for Girard is what he says Amadis of Gaul was for Don Quixote, simply a model who inspires peaceful imitation. This does not, however, detract from the present point of comparison, since Girard's analysis of masochism in *Deceit, Desire, and the Novel* is not about "internal" as opposed to "external" mediation but only about what Girard calls "metaphysical desire" (as explained in Chapter 5 above), and there is no logical reason that the sort of desire to possess the "being" or "power" of an admired figure could not also be aroused without the rivalry of what Girard calls "internal mediation." In fact, since in masochism the subject feels no rivalry with the sadist but only identification with him, masochism would seem actually to be a version of "external mediation" gone bad.

57. Zizioulas, *Being as Communion,* 108.

that even the conception of such a stage had to do more with religion than with psychology, or perhaps that here psychology reached the limits of its scientific dimension while its spiritual dimension came into view. Kohlberg, as we saw, conceived his ultimate, seventh, stage as "the adoption of a cosmic, as opposed to a universal, humanistic stage 6 perspective."[58] He drew for the articulation of this cosmic perspective on the thought of Pierre Teilhard de Chardin, whose belief in the "cosmic Christ" as the embodiment of perfect love and the culminating point of divinely inspirited cosmic evolution was essentially the same as Zizioulas's belief in Christ as a "corporate person" incarnating universal love and potentially incorporating all who heed his invitation into his mode of existence.

As I mentioned in Chapter 6, Kohlberg explicitly identified his stage 7 with religion conceived as "a conscious response to, and an expression of, the quest for an ultimate meaning for moral judging and acting."[59] But as I also said there, one cannot simply identify religion as such with Kohlberg's seventh stage, since there are many ways of being religious and they can involve various levels of development. James Fowler worked out some of the implications of this by speaking not simply of psychological stages but of stages of faith that correlate with psychological stages like those of Kohlberg and Erik Erikson. In his empirical investigation of these stages Fowler found that his fifth stage (conjunctive faith) was far less common than the earlier ones and that the sixth (universalizing faith) remained, from a scientific point of view, purely hypothetical because he never found an actual instance in his interviews. Nor was Kohlberg able to find empirical instances of either his sixth or his seventh stage. For both Kohlberg and Fowler, their ultimate stages were theoretically necessary as indicators of what the processes of development they were trying to analyze and describe were moving toward, but in the final analysis both recognized that this was leading them beyond the limits of psychology as an empirical science.

Psychology tries to describe and explain empirical phenomena; theology tries to anticipate, evoke, and articulate an ideal. To cast the issue in theological language, the ultimate stages Kohlberg and Fowler speculated about theoretically were not empirical but eschatological. That is, they reach beyond psychology as science to sketch the spiritual telos that the psyche is drawn toward and that explains development by casting its light back over it, even if

58. Kohlberg, *Essays on Moral Development* 1:345. See also Chapter 6, note 12.
59. See Chapter 6, note 11.

that development may never actually in practice attain its culmination. Rahner, Zizioulas, and Teilhard interpret the incarnate Christ as the defining point at which the *eschaton,* the fullness of spiritual development, breaks into the present and illuminates its meaning. In Zizioulas's words, Christ "contains by definition the *eschata,* our final destiny, ourselves as we shall be; He is the eschatological Man—yet, let me repeat, not as an individual but as Church, i.e. because of our being included in Him."[60] Kohlberg and Fowler did not find an empirical instance of their ultimate stages of psychological and spiritual development; Rahner, Zizioulas, and Teilhard believed that there has been an actual instance of theirs in Jesus of Nazareth, just as Buddhists believe there has been one in Siddhartha Gautama, the historical Buddha.

This points toward the question of what religious belief is, and it raises further questions regarding how to understand what believing or even the idea of a believing "mind" could mean in the context of radical self-transcendence, with the tension it involves between psychological individuation, on the one hand, and transcendent personhood, on the other. We have seen Zizioulas using the term *individual* to designate a fallen selfhood that must be transcended in order to find one's true life in the transcendent personhood to which the term *Christ* refers. But we also saw Cardinal Newman speak of "assent," his word for judgment or belief, as "an active recognition of propositions as true such as it is the duty of each individual himself to exercise at the bidding of reason, and, when reason forbids, to withhold." In this, Newman almost echoes Martin Luther's famous, more pithy, dictum, "Every man must do his own believing, just as every man must do his own dying."

This in turn raises the question of whether religious belief must tend to be inherently divisive. If authentic faith requires individual belief, does this imply that each individual must pursue a path of belief that will lead in the direction of increasing particularity and potential conflict? If so, the multiple ways of being religious even within any one religious tradition would tend toward such potentially infinite multiplicity that no tradition could hope to survive as such—and the divisions between traditions would be utterly hopeless. We will turn in the next chapter to explore these questions and to consider the possibility that ways of being religious might develop that could reconcile the particularity of individual judgment with the potential universality of love.

60. Zizioulas, *Being as Communion,* 183.

Dialogical Faith

Faith and Belief

The last chapter ended with the questions of what believing as an act of authentic assent, or even the idea of a believing "mind," could mean in the context of radical self-transcendence, and whether the fact that authentic assent is an inherently individual act implies that religious belief must be socially divisive. These are closely related to the questions I brought up in the Introduction about what subjective factors might render religions conflictual and even aggressive and injurious not only to nonmembers but also to their own adherents, and what conditions might foster less dangerous, and even perhaps helpful and reconciling, forms of religiousness. The title of this chapter, "Dialogical Faith," points toward ideas that I think can not only help answer these questions but also resolve the underlying issues that make them problematic.

To approach those issues, we must first consider another fundamental question: that of how belief relates to religious faith. In the preceding chapter I said that a useful way of understanding religion is to think of it as a set of practices intended to support a faith. There my focus was on the way adherents of a particular faith might consider other religions to be legitimate if they could support the same essential faith—as in the case of Islam, which has traditionally considered both Christianity and Judaism legitimate religions because, even if incomplete, they derive from revelations of the one God and support monotheistic faith in him.[1] But what exactly is faith, and what role does belief play in it? Even if some Christians, Jews, and Muslims might consider themselves to share a common monotheistic faith, all members of those faith traditions would recognize that they divide substantially over many items of particular belief.

There are probably many to whom faith and belief seem simply identical, and the two words are in fact used interchangeably as translations for the Greek word *pistis* that appears so often in the New Testament, especially since the word *faith* in English—unlike *pistis* with its infinitive *pisteuein* in Greek—has no verbal form, so that to translate *pisteuein* there is no other word to use than *to believe.* The idea of faith is broader, however, encompassing along with belief the ideas of trust, loyalty, reliance, and in general everything that is connoted by fidelity or faithfulness.[2]

A good way of understanding faith, I would like to suggest, is to think of it as a deeply intended commitment involving basic trust in and loyalty to some comprehensive conception of the true and the good and to what one believes to be their source. This is a way of understanding the idea of faith that can encompass its use in any religious tradition, whether it uses theistic imagery to talk about what is ultimate (as in the cases of both monotheisms and polytheisms) or nontheistic imagery (as in the case of Buddhism). It is even broad enough to include nonreligious commitments and loyalties if they are deeply intended and pertain to some conception of ultimate truth and goodness. Daniel Dennett, for example, likens religion to a parasitic worm that can take over the brain of an ant, and he would like to see people cured of it, but his own commitment to rationality and ethics is deeply intended and expresses a basic trust in reason and loyalty to the good.[3] Dennett is clearly not religious, but he does have a kind of faith, in the broad sense in which I am using that word.

1. This does not mean, of course, that a Muslim would consider it legitimate for another Muslim to convert to one of those other legitimate religions; Christianity and Judaism may be acceptable for people who have not yet understood and committed themselves to the religion of the complete and final revelation, but once someone has made that commitment, Muslim belief is that to turn away from it would be apostasy, one of the most serious of possible sins.

2. Wilfred Cantwell Smith provides a thorough discussion of all aspects of this issue in relation to a variety of religious traditions in *Faith and Belief: The Difference between Them.* It is perhaps also worth mentioning that there is a clear affinity between the idea of faith, religious or nonreligious, and Erik Erikson's idea of basic trust as the fundamental existential challenge on which all further development builds. See his *Childhood and Society,* 247–51.

3. Dennett, *Breaking the Spell,* 3–4.

Religious belief is one of the practices (along with ritual—for example, prayer, meditation, community work, and so on) that can play a role in supporting faith. But what exactly *is* belief? This question is complicated by the fact that the word itself has had a history in the English language in which its meaning has gone through changes with far-reaching implications. As Wilfred Cantwell Smith has explained, the word *believe,* in its etymological roots, like its German cognate *belieben,* means "to hold dear" or "to cherish," and that was its main meaning in English too until a major shift took place during the seventeenth and eighteenth centuries, when it came to be associated primarily with cognitive claims, and especially claims that could not be proven.[4] It now sounds perfectly natural to us to say, for example, that a Christian might believe in God and also in the devil; we simply mean that a Christian might hold the opinion that both are real. In an earlier time, however, to say this might have sounded not just odd but nonsensical and even blasphemous. One of the earliest recorded instances in English of the word *belief* is a medieval homily that says Christians should not "set their belief" on worldly goods, meaning they should not make them the object of ultimate trust and loyalty, and that one who did so, would show himself to be the devil's child.[5] Smith comments:

> Since the preacher says that a Christian should set his heart on God, and that the person who sets his heart on things of the world is a child of the devil, we to-day would say that that preacher believed in the devil. In our sense of the word, undoubtedly he did believe in the devil; but in his sense of the word it would be an insult and a libel to say this of him. He recognized the existence of the devil, right enough; but the whole point of his homily was that one should, partly for that very reason, "believe"—that is, *belieben,* hold dear, love, give one's heart to—God alone. If he heard us speak of believing in both God and the devil simultaneously, he would think that we were mad—schizophrenic. . . . The question of import was, to which do you give your loyalty.

Talking about the shift that took place during the Enlightenment, Smith goes on to say that "the object of the verb begins by being almost always a person;

4. See Smith, "The English Word 'Believe,'" chap. 6 of *Faith and Belief,* and, for still more detail, his *Belief and History.* Smith also points out that the Latin *credo* (I believe) is formed from (*cor,* heart) and (*do,* I give), so that its root meaning is to give one's heart to what one believes in.

5. Cited in Smith, *Faith and Belief,* 111–12.

it ends by being almost always a proposition. That is, a shift has taken place from the verb's designating an interpersonal relation to its naming a theoretical judgment: from an action of the self, in relation to other selves, to a condition of the mind, in relation to an abstraction."[6]

I do not intend to quarrel here with modern usage, which itself has several centuries of acceptance behind it now. Today *believe,* in ordinary speech, means simply to affirm the reality of something or the truth of a proposition, and in what follows I will focus on the question of the role of belief in this narrower modern sense in religious faith—that is, the question of what are the possible ways a religious person can carry out the process of determining and holding fast to what he or she considers to be truth. It is differences over truth claims that seem to generate the most heat and precipitate the most violence among religious people today, both between traditions and within them. So the question of what conditions might foster less aggressive forms of religiousness is also a question of whether the practice of believing can be both fully critical and also vital and committed and of how that might take place.

The history of earlier meanings of the word *believe* is nevertheless important to bear in mind, for two reasons. One is that for religious believers even today, the earlier connotations of the word still contribute to its meaning in their personal lives of faith. A nonreligious investigator who does not understand this will miss a dimension that is important to the people he or she is trying to understand. The other is that even though the idea of believing has always involved a judgment of truth (an attitude of trust, after all, implies at least an implicit judgment regarding true trustworthiness), it also involves love. The mode in which belief takes place can vary according to the emphasis it puts on one or the other of those two aspects of the act of believing: truth or love. Daniel Dennett's hypothetical Professor Faith says that religious belief "isn't like accepting a conclusion; it's like falling in love."[7] Dennett thinks this is a bit of a dodge, and he has a point if the professor means that it involves no cognitive claims or that those it does have should not be critically examined (and of course, since the professor is hypothetical, he can mean whatever his author wishes him to mean). But the professor might have a point too, as I hope will become clear.

Perhaps the single biggest problem for most inquirers in approaching the topic of belief is that whereas believing is inherently a subjective act, our lan-

6. Ibid., 112, 118.
7. Dennett, *Breaking the Spell,* 250.

guage and most of our ordinary thinking are object oriented. Even to say that believing is a "subjective act" would probably imply to many at first hearing that it does not pertain to reality but involves entertaining fanciful ideas or arbitrary claims. But to say believing is inherently subjective refers simply to the fact that a judgment of truth—either about facts or about the true good—is a mental operation performed by a thinking person, that is, it is the act of what we call a subject. I am sure I do not need to rehearse at length the full discussion of cognitional theory pertaining to this presented in preceding chapters, but perhaps a brief summary may help.

We saw in Chapter 2 how Jean Piaget studied the way children gradually develop a range of figurative and operative capacities that enable them with increasing adequacy to interpret and come to know the world around them (the objective pole of their explorations) and also to reflect on and understand the mental acts by which they do so (the subjective pole). We also saw there how Bernard Lonergan worked out a concise formulation of these principles as a cognitional theory according to which inquirers begin with rudimentary operations on the level of attention to experiential data and then progress through interpretation (the construing of those data in intelligible patterns) and through critical reflection on the adequacy of an interpretation in relation to the data and to other possible interpretations. When the process of interpretation and critical reflection reaches a point of satisfaction that the investigation of both the data and their possibilities of interpretation has been carried far enough to determine a sufficient degree of relative adequacy in the interpretation, the mind comes to rest, as we saw Cardinal Newman put it, with "a specific sense of intellectual satisfaction and repose."[8] It is this coming to rest after attention, interpretation, and critical reflection that constitutes the judgment of truth. One judges that the interpretation is true (that is, that it has a sufficiently high degree of relative adequacy for the conditions of assent to be at least conditionally fulfilled) or false (that is, that it does not take into account enough of the pertinent data or does not do so as well as some competing interpretation).

All of the operations just rehearsed involve subjectivity. Sense data may be objective in the sense that they are what attention bears upon—that is, they are "objects" of awareness—but they could not be that unless an act of awareness were involved. The awareness is the subjective pole of which the datum is the objective pole. Attending to the data involves an effort to focus awareness,

8. Newman, *Essay in Aid,* 196.

and that takes place as a process of subjective life on the part of some attending organism.

The process of interpreting and of finding satisfaction in an interpretation is so obviously a subjective activity that few would object to calling it that, but there may be many who would think that it is precisely for that reason that believing as a cognitive effort goes astray. They might say that real knowing takes place only on the level of an immediate grasp of the data and that to interpret is to step away from that. Some who would say this may even be scientific specialists who are highly skilled in the interpretation of data and critical testing of interpretations but who, as we saw Piaget and Garcia suggest in Chapter 2, "are only partly conscious of what they do," with the result that "many . . . have made their discoveries by using procedures that run counter to [their] basic positivist tenets."[9]

Perhaps one reason for this sort of insistence on sensation as the criterion of truth is the structural "law of conscious awareness" we saw Piaget speak of in his *Psychology and Epistemology,* whereby subjective operations become noticed only when they run into obstacles that call attention to them. To use Robert Kegan's phrase, each person develops first as "a meaning-maker embedded in his perceptions."[10] Even at a fairly young age one learns an initial stepping back to notice perceptions as objects, but one may still remain embedded in the subliminal mental activities that construct the perceptions, and many probably do remain so all their lives.

Perhaps another reason, rooted not in our psychological structure but in our culture from the time of the first Greek philosophers, is the lingering idea that real knowledge must be certain, as in the formal proofs of geometry, so that other sciences bear the title *episteme* (knowledge) only by a kind of courtesy, since they offer only probabilities. In many minds the ideas of "objectivity," "truth," and "certainty" seem to be virtually fused and to depend on maximal closeness to sensation and distance from interpretative process. The idea of distinguishing, as in the last chapter we saw Newman do, between "certitude" as a mental state and "certainty" as a quality of propositions would therefore seem either a mere logical quibble or an evasion.

I hope, however, that a reader who has followed the discussion of these ideas in the present book will recognize how inadequate such an interpreta-

9. Piaget and Garcia, *Psychogenesis,* 24.

10. Piaget, *Psychology and Epistemology,* 104 (see Chapter 2, note 16); Kegan, *Evolving Self,* 32 (see Chapter 3, note 5).

tion of knowing really is. When we attempt seriously to understand and know something for ourselves, and not just by trusting some authority, we attend to experience, we interpret what we experience, we ask ourselves about the relative adequacy of our interpretations, and we make judgments regarding that when we are satisfied that we have noticed as much as possible of the pertinent data and assessed as carefully as possible the interpretations that might relate them adequately to one another. This entire process takes place as the subjective pole of our knowing or believing, and that is what it means to say that it is inherently subjective. On the other hand, when we speak of being "objective" in our inquiry, what we mean is that we carry out these subjective operations as carefully as we can and with maximum openness and freedom from bias. As Bernard Lonergan succinctly put it, "Objectivity is simply the consequence of authentic subjectivity."[11]

If we recognize that this interrelated pattern of operations indeed constitutes what we do as subjects whenever we seek actual knowledge, whether that is based on experiential data and their most relatively adequate interpretation or whether it looks simply for the formal coherence of deductive logic, geometry, or some other form of mathematics, then it should be clear why Newman's distinction is neither a quibble nor an evasion but a clarification of fundamental truth. If we want certainty, we can find it in the formal relations of abstract ideas—as Pythagoras derived his theorem from the abstract idea of a triangle—but we can find it only there. If we want to know the contingent reality of the concrete world we live in and of our own concrete lives within it, then the relative adequacy of a carefully considered interpretation of experiential data is the only real knowledge to be had.

By this point I hope the reader is willing to grant that to say believing is an inherently subjective act does not necessarily imply that it is uncritical—even if he or she may justly feel that as an account of religious belief it seems a little bloodless, an issue to which I will return in a moment. All interpretive operations are subjective; some are performed consciously and carefully, some uncarefully, and some even unconsciously (when we are so "embedded" in them that we are unaware interpretation is even going on). I am sure some readers will want to object that religious belief is not often done in the careful way I have described, and I grant that—but then neither are very many of the other ordinary acts of believing that make up much of our waking lives. Nor should this be surprising, since raising into reflective consciousness and

11. Lonergan, *Method in Theology*, 265.

critically examining all the ordinary interpretative processes by which we put together the phenomenological world we inhabit on a daily basis would slow our functioning down to a crawl that might even threaten our evolutionary survival. On the other hand, when we notice tangles and contradictions in our interpretations, we do try to slow down and untangle them so that we can better get on with our affairs after having done so. That is how philosophy and science were born.

Theology as a Mode of Inquiry

It is also how theology gets born. Religion first takes shape in the form of stories people tell about how the world and their own people within it came into being and why, and then rituals take shape around the meanings in the stories. When religious people begin to notice that some of those stories conflict with others or that a given story has ambiguous implications, they sometimes stop and ask if there isn't some interpretation that can help make better sense of them. In Chapter 7 we saw how the interpreters of Qur'anic statements about God sitting on a throne were driven to ask theoretical questions about whether this implied that God was a corporeal being. In Chapter 6 we saw how the heirs of biblical traditions have had to wrestle with the implications of the story of God's command to destroy Amalek and the way they conflict with the idea of a God who is supremely just and supremely loving. In Chapter 5, in the discussion of Merlin Donald's ideas about cognitive evolution, we saw how he traced it through a series of stages beginning with episodic cognition among the great apes and other higher mammals and ending with mythic and theoretic cognition and culture in *Homo sapiens.* I said there that theoretic thinking is a late and rare development, since in most lives it is not necessary or even useful except for special purposes. In religion, when an impasse arises on the level of mythic cognition, that can give rise to questions that become the special purpose of the sort of theoretic thinking that theology tries to be.

This may involve the adoption of an explicit philosophical framework, as in the case of patristic use of Neoplatonism, of Aquinas's use of Aristotelianism, or of Bultmann's use of Heideggerian existentialism, or it may involve simply a stepping back from the narrative framework of mythic cognition in order to work out a clearer statement of the spiritual purpose that framework is supposed to serve. Depending on how the theological enterprise is carried out, it can itself be naive or critical. It can either help to make religion less aggressive and dangerous or add fuel to the fire. One of René Girard's major points in his analysis of mythic thinking is that however benign it may appear on the surface or in an individual episode, myth always has an undertow of violence about it, because mythic narrative gravitates toward a polarized vision: the basic structure of narrative tends to involve a hero and a villain, or at least some force of evil, that threatens the hero and the community he fights on behalf of. Faced with an example of this, a theologian may either try to rationalize the mythic polarization, as apologists for crusades and the inquisitors of various traditions have done, or try to reinterpret the myth in a way that will defuse the polarization, as did the rabbis with the tradition about perpetual enmity with Amalek.

Or a religion can begin to split from within over how to engage such a problem. We can see being enacted before our eyes today a struggle within the Islamic world between those who are trying to interpret the Muslim tradition of jihad in radically conflicting ways, both of which can present problems for critical consciousness. Some Muslims have begun to claim that jihad has never been about physical warfare but only about inner spiritual struggle. Others, who are unfortunately becoming numerous and popular very rapidly, are interpreting suicide bombing as a legitimate form of jihad. The first group has to wrestle with the historical memory of the centrality of jihad as warfare in the founding events of Islam. As I explained in Chapter 8, jihad originated as a defense against historically concrete, living enemies who were trying to destroy Islam during the lifetime of Muhammad. I pointed out there that the Muslim *ummah* (the community of the faithful) was itself born in the experience of defensive jihad as Muhammad and his earliest followers fled from persecution and successfully defended themselves from those who wished to destroy both them and Islam itself. That is why the Muslim calendar dates from the flight to Medina and why some of the great events of Muhammad's leadership are believed to be his victories at the Battle of the Ditch, the Battle of Badr, and his final conquest of Mecca itself. The second group, the advocates of suicide bombing, have to suppress, or at least find a way around, the memory of centuries of Muslim interpretation of the laws of jihad that have prohibited both suicide and the harming of noncombatants.[12]

I do not mean to imply that such efforts of revisionist thinking must necessarily do violence to reason or involve a failure of logic, even if they may

12. For a concise account of this history and the present efforts to justify suicide bombing theologically, see Noah Feldman, "Islam, Terror, and the Second Nuclear Age."

have to stretch them. However execrable may be the motives and tactics of those who are trying to extend the concept of jihad to include suicide attacks and the mass killing of innocent bystanders, their interpretations and arguments involve basically the same sort of interpretative operations that Jewish thinkers have used to more peaceful purpose to defuse the violent potential of the story of Amalek. Modern jihadists argue that traditional injunctions against suicide were not necessarily intended in their time to prevent extreme measures in the defense of Islam when less extreme measures could not be effective against the kind of powerfully armed enemies Muslims are now facing. And they argue, by a somewhat greater stretch of interpretation but not necessarily a totally illogical one, that suicide bombers can be interpreted as martyrs and that innocent Muslim bystanders killed in connection with such attacks should also be interpreted as "involuntary martyrs" who will receive the heavenly reward due to those who die defending Islam. Other bystanders, they argue on the other hand, cannot be innocent but must be interpreted as enemies according to the premise (sometimes invoked by others as well) that "whoever is not with us is against us."

The cognitive process of attention, interpretation, critical reflection, and judgment, even if it is what makes the difference between authentic belief and its inauthentic imitation, is therefore neither the source of violence nor its inevitable cure—even if, as the experiments of the terror management theorists have shown, encouraging an atmosphere of rationality may reduce tendencies to violence. If one adopts the premise that there is a superhuman entity who may at least on some occasions demand and reward violence, and if one considers that premise from within the framework of a polarized mythic worldview, it is almost inevitable that one's religion will take a shape that will be aggressive and dangerous. It is all too easy to draw from the myths of almost any religion[13] the premise of divinely sanctioned violence against the enemies of the good, and once that premise is established, nothing can prevent logic, left to its own resources, from drawing out that premise's violent implications except a reconsideration of the premise itself.

Which brings us back to a point I mentioned above but set aside momentarily: that an account of religious belief entirely in terms of a theory of cognitive operations will probably seem a little bloodless to a reader who has any feeling at all for what religion can be to its faithful. Even if religious people

13. The obvious exceptions are Buddhism and Jain, since both believe that even if there are gods, they have no importance, and both make a religious principle of nonviolence.

sometimes use arguments to support their beliefs, it would probably be a rare religious person whose faith, or even whose more narrowly focused belief, was conceived in argument and terminated in its conclusions. And even if there were many such people among the religious, what they could try to prove with their arguments would certainly be much more restricted than what they actually believe in and care deeply about.

Faith and Love

This in turn recalls another idea mentioned earlier: that of Daniel Dennett's hypothetical Professor Faith, who said that religious belief "isn't like accepting a conclusion; it's like falling in love." Dennett introduced the idea of such thinking in *Breaking the Spell* in order to dismiss it, but as we saw in Chapter 7, Dennett also insists that religious belief can be genuine only if it asserts the existence of a supernatural individual entity, the God of what we saw Marcus Borg call "supernatural theism." A God of that sort would be an entity whose existence or nonexistence one could argue about, but as I explained in that chapter, that is not the only way to conceive of the divine, and theologically it is a relatively recent way of doing so. (It is also a way of conceiving of the divine that is particularly susceptible to assimilation to a polarized worldview, and the tendency of Dennett and other opponents of religious belief to identify religion with that sort of deity may be one reason they oppose it so strongly.) As we also saw in Chapter 7, Jewish, Christian, and Muslim theologians from ancient times through the Middle Ages all took very seriously the idea that God was not best thought of as a particular being (one member of the class of entities in general) but rather as Being Itself in whom all beings exist by participation.

An even more fundamental point is that neither polytheists nor monotheists, whether they are supernatural theists or panentheists, tend to be primarily interested in the question of whether their object of basic trust, loyalty, and devotion exists. Religious believers do believe in the reality of their God, but except in the case of a relatively new and rather anxious believer, that is only a starting point. Rather, their primary focus is on *what* their God is, not *whether*. It is on what it is about their God as they understand him that makes him what they long for, what it is that makes him supremely worth loving. What they care most deeply about, that is, is what their faith *reaches toward*, and they recognize that the God they reach for is not a problem to be solved but a mystery that calls them to dwell in its depth. As the modern Jewish philosopher Emmanuel Lévinas has said, "The relation to the Infinite is not a knowledge but a Desire."[14]

To *believe in* God is to love, trust, and give your loyalty to God above all else. The very idea of *believing that* there is a God in the same way one might believe that there is a devil, as we saw Wilfred C. Smith explain, is a comparatively recent way of conceiving of belief. Smith's twelfth-century homilist would have said (if he could even think in terms of the modern idea of *believing that*) that what matters is not to believe *that* there is a God but to believe *in* God, and to believe *in* God is to believe something about *what* God is, that is, that the infinite source of all being is worthy of love, trust, and loyalty.

This should make still clearer the pertinence of Aquinas's argument that begins from Aristotle's definition of the good as "what all desire"[15] and proceeds by saying that what all desire is "to be" and that what God is is precisely that: *Ipsum Esse,* true being.[16] God, therefore, is the supreme good, the ultimate goal of every longing. What Aquinas offers *is* an argument, but it is not an argument seeking to prove the existence of an entity; rather, it is an argument about the very structure of existence as we live and experience it. Its purpose is to clarify religious thinking that uses the symbol "God" as a pointer toward what is supremely worthy of love and the supreme source and goal of all love, whether that is consciously realized or not. Its conclusion is not that God exists as a particular entity but rather that if we have a sense of the ultimate intentionality of love, of what our love reaches toward at its maximum, this is what one properly means by the word *God.*

14. Lévinas, *Ethics and Infinity: Conversations with Philippe Nemo,* 92.

15. Aristotle, *Nicomachean Ethics,* bk. 1, sec. 1 (1094a3–4): "Every art and every inquiry, and similarly every action and pursuit, is thought to aim at some good; and for this reason the good has rightly been declared to be that at which all things aim" (*The Basic Works of Aristotle,* 935).

16. As Aquinas's argument goes in more detail, "being itself is the actuality of all things" ("ipsum esse est actualitas omnium rerum" [*Summa Theologica,* pt. 1, question 4, article 1, "Reply to Objection 3"]), and since God is being itself ("ipsum esse per se subsistens" [question 4, article 2, and question 3, article 4]), God is what all ultimately desire in every love they experience. See also question 5, article 1, "Whether the Good Differs Really from Being"; Aquinas argues that it does not. This principle applies not only to human loves, or even only to animal appetites as well, but it also includes vegetable and even mineral being. In Aquinas's theological vision, there is a ladder of loves running from the *inclinatio* of stones to gravitate downward toward their proper place in the great scheme of things and of fire to rise upward toward its place, and running through vegetative vitality and animal and human desires and *caritas* (the Latin equivalent of the agape discussed above in Chapter 6), through the love that, in Dante's poetic adaptation of Aquinas's thought, makes the heavenly angels circle the more swiftly about the still point of divine light the closer they are to God's perfection (Dante, *Paradiso,* Canto 28). For a discussion of the modes and degrees of love in the thought of Aquinas, see Albert Ilien, *Wesen und Funktion der Liebe im Denken des Thomas von Aquin.*

The implications of such a shift from God as an entity to God as perfect fullness of being and ultimately to God as Love will become even clearer if we consider the way Aquinas conceived the idea of faith. Far from understanding faith as simple belief in the fact *that* God is, Aquinas considered such belief, important as it may be as a preliminary for faith, to lack the essential element that makes faith salvific, or spiritually transforming. That missing element is both an understanding of *what* God is (infinite love) and an experiential participation in that *what,* that is, in the actuality of divine love.

Regarding that participation, Aquinas cites Isaiah 11:2, "The Spirit of the Lord shall rest upon him, the Spirit of wisdom and of understanding," and explains that "the word *intellectus* (understanding) implies an innermost knowledge *(intima cognitio),* for *intelligere* (to understand) is the same as *intus legere* (to read inwardly)," and that since "the natural light of our understanding is of finite power" and therefore is proportionate only to finite objects, the human believer needs to have the "supernatural light" of divine love bestowed on his intelligence if he is really to know God as God is in himself.[17] The understanding of what God is, therefore, must involve, through that bestowal, the living participation in divine love that makes faith truly living or salvific and that constitutes genuine knowledge of God.

The "innermost knowledge" *(intima cognitio)* in question, to make the matter more precise, is not a knowledge in the sense of *scientia*—knowledge that can be defined, proven, and taken possession of, the kind Lévinas had in mind when he said that our "relation to the Infinite is not a knowledge but a Desire." Rather, it is what Aquinas calls "wisdom" *(sapientia):* "The knowledge of divine things is called wisdom, while the knowledge of human things is called knowledge *(scientia),* this being the common name denoting certitude of judgment, and appropriated to the judgment which is formed through second causes."[18] *Scientia* is what might be called a "knowing from without"; *intima cognitio* and *sapientia* refer to the beginnings, at least, of a knowledge of God from within.

This does not mean that wisdom, as opposed to *scientia,* lacks real cognitive substance and its own kind of certitude (in the sense in which Newman used that term). The word *sapientia* in Latin derives from *sapio,* which refers to tasting. The *cognitio* of this *sapientia* is not theoretical, that is, but experi-

17. Aquinas, *Summa Theologica,* II-II, question 8, article 1. I hope the reader will remember here that Aquinas's use of the word *supernatural* is quite different from its modern use in the phrase "supernatural theism." See Chapter 7.

18. Ibid., question 9, article 2.

ential; it knows the divine love from within by "tasting" it, as it were. This is what we saw Pierre Teilhard de Chardin refer to as the experience of a sort of "touching" or "tasting," "a transformation in the very perception of being," in the passage cited by Lawrence Kohlberg discussed in Chapter 6.[19] Or as we also saw Bernard Lonergan put the same point (in Chapter 7), "Faith is the knowledge born of religious love." Commenting in this light on Blaise Pascal's famous saying that the heart has reasons that the reason does not know, Lonergan goes on to say, "The meaning, then, of Pascal's remark would be that, besides the factual knowledge reached by experiencing, understanding, and verifying, there is another kind of knowledge reached through the discernment of value and judgments of value of a person in love. Faith, accordingly, is such further knowledge when the love is God's love flooding our hearts."[20]

Faith that involves only belief *about* God rather than the actual participation that is belief *in* God is what Aquinas calls "unformed faith" *(fides informis)* and, following James 2:20, "dead" faith.[21] The faith that is truly "living," because it participates in the life of God himself, he calls "formed faith" *(fides formata).* For Aquinas, following Aristotle, the term *form* refers to the vital principle of something, that which takes hold of the elements of the thing and unifies them and, in the case of something living, breathes life into it. The essential point is expressed in his article on the question "Whether Charity [*caritas,* that is, supernatural love, agape] Is the Form of Faith?" To put this in modern English, the question is whether divine love is the vital principle of faith. Aquinas concludes that it is, that "the act of faith is perfected and formed by charity."[22] *Fides informis,* simple belief about God, useful as it may be in pointing the believer toward God's transcendence, is only an incomplete preliminary. *Fides formata,* faith animated by the divine love, which is God's own life breathed into it, actually touches and tastes its source and its goal, life in God—even if in this life as yet only partially and tenuously and even, one might say, rather blindly or obscurely, since the limitations of human knowing make it impossible to verify that the love we experience is actually the divine *caritas.*[23] Even if we live in faith, that is, we cannot know with objective

19. See Chapter 6, note 19.
20. Lonergan, *Method in Theology,* 115.
21. Aquinas, *Summa Theologica,* II-II, question 4, article 4.
22. Ibid., question 4, article 3.
23. "That, however, to which charity is ordered cannot be comprehended, because its immediate object and terminus is God, the supreme good, to whom charity unites us. Therefore, one cannot know from the act of love that he perceived in himself whether he has attained to the

certainty that our faith is truly living, divinely loving faith, but can only trust that, by the grace of God, it is that or is in the process of becoming that.

Aquinas is, of course, only one thinker from one tradition, but I hope this account of his analysis of the idea of faith will clarify the underlying issues involved in understanding how the word *faith* can be used by religious thinkers and how it may relate to *belief,* in the modern sense of that word. To put it simply, belief as we tend to use the word now, leaving out the element of loving that Smith says was once central to it, is only a part of faith, and a very limited part at that. Faith in its full form is not only a more comprehensive notion but also one different in quality.

This has several important implications for understanding religious thought in relation to psychological and spiritual development. One is that logical arguments of the sort academic philosophers tend to focus on regarding such a question as "the existence of God" have little bearing on what faith is actually about for many religious people and what sort of worldview might be implied in it. Such arguments, even if they were logically cogent, could never capture what the faithful believer reaches toward, which is not an idea or the truth of a theoretical proposition but a life.[24] The believer's question has to do with what that life could be in itself and whether it can be a real possibility for him or for her. Here, I think, one can see the real pertinence of what Dennett's Professor Faith said: that religious belief is not like accepting a conclusion but like falling in love. Aquinas's believer who lives in *fides formata,* does not *know,* in the strict sense of *scientia,* even that he does so. He is not, that is, in the position of being able to make a critical judgment regarding the adequacy of the interpretation that his belief is vitalized by the breath of divine love, because there is no way he can step back from it, if he *is* living in it, so as to render it an object for intentional consciousness. (This inability to step back and take as object a spiritual reality that can be known only from within, by immersion in its life, one might say, is precisely what is meant by the theological concept of "mystery.")[25]

---

stage where he is united to God in the manner necessary for the nature of charity" (Aquinas, *De Veritate* [On Truth], x, 10, quoted in Victor Preller, *Divine Science and the Science of God: A Reformulation of Thomas Aquinas,* 264).

24. Cf. Victor Preller: "In this life God is and remains *ignotum*—the Unknown God whom we cannot grasp or control in terms of the forms of intelligibility created by our intellects. In our language, *the intelligibility of God is not a syntactical matter*" (*Divine Science,* 265; emphasis in the original).

25. For a discussion, see Gabriel Marcel, *The Mystery of Being,* vol. 1, *Reflection and Mystery.*

Or to put the same issue in Robert Kegan's language, faith in its truly vital form is a matter of being "embedded" in a love that one could never differentiate oneself from, even if that were what one wanted. It is with that ultimate embeddedness that one reaches the limit of differentiation. And human limitations being what they are, not only cognitively but also existentially, even if one *is* living in that love to some degree, what it is in its fullness must extend beyond the form it can take in any individual person. This is, of course, part of what it means to call that love transcendent. If Professor Faith understands from experience the faith he describes, then he must know that it is not something he could grasp by "accepting a conclusion" but something he can only hope for more of—the way a person falling in love hopes this love will continue, grow, and be endless. Or as Emmanuel Lévinas put it in his further comment on the idea cited above that our true relation to the Infinite is by way of desire: "I have tried to describe the difference between Desire and need by the fact that Desire cannot be satisfied; that Desire in some way nourishes itself on its own hungers and is augmented by its satisfaction; that Desire is like a thought which thinks more than it thinks. It is a paradoxical structure, without doubt, but one which is no more so than this presence of the Infinite in a finite act."[26]

Faith as Inherently Dialogical

Another implication of the idea of "faith animated by love" *(fides formata)* for understanding religious thought in relation to psychological and spiritual development has to do with the structure of intentional consciousness and the way that is itself tied up with faithfulness in its most developed form. I spoke above about the inherent subjectivity of rational judgment as an act requiring radical openness to experience, interpretation, and critical reflection, and I quoted Lonergan's statement that "objectivity is simply the consequence of authentic subjectivity." Subjectivity can be open and authentic only if it is motivated by a genuine love of truth and of the good that is not subverted by self-serving biases that tempt one to premature closure. It can be authentic,

26. Lévinas, *Ethics and Infinity*, 92. What Lévinas means by "Desire" in this quotation is not at all, of course, what Buddhists call *tanha* (craving); it is what I referred to in Chapter 2 as "existential eros" or "existential appetite," and what Aquinas means when he argues that "good" (Being Itself, that is, God) "is that which all things desire" (*Summa Theologica*, pt. 1, question 5, article 4). See also Fowler on the importance of supplementing rationality with "passionality" (*Stages of Faith*, 102–3).

that is, only by being radically self-transcending, and this is itself an act of fidelity. Considering the structure of intentional consciousness from this point of view, it seems appropriate to describe it as animated by the same breath of life as the *fides formata* that Aquinas describes. It is the faithful love of truth that makes authentic judgment of truth possible, and it is faithful love of the good that makes authentic discernment of the true good possible. It is love, that is, that constitutes the essential subjective criterion of a good judgment.

And just as Aquinas's *fides* has to recognize that it cannot know with objective certainty that it fully attains what it reaches toward, so an authentic act of interpretation and judgment must recognize that its grasp of truth, even at its most confident, can never be judged to be final. As an act of interpretation and judgment, it is fully authentic only if its love of truth holds it continuously open to new experience, to new interpretations, to new possibilities of critical testing, and ultimately to new, more adequate understandings.

This has a further implication that is even more important for the present purpose: in its most authentic form, belief is not only inherently subjective but also inherently dialogical. To seek genuinely to critically verify one's judgments means to seek all the evidence that might be relevant and to be continuously on the lookout for any further interpretations that might be even more explanatory and better suited to verification—wherever these may come from. Any genuine inquirer who comes up with a new way of understanding reality seeks others to share it with so that they can confirm it, supplement it, or correct it. This is inherent to the dynamic of authentic inquiry. As finite experiencers, interpreters, and knowers, we know that we need the observations and insights of others to help us ensure we have not left relevant data unnoticed or that other possible interpretations cannot be found that might better take the available data into account.

It can happen, of course, that an inquirer may find his or her new interpretation rejected for reasons that are themselves inauthentic (one might recall Galileo's efforts to share his ideas in the Italy of his time), but that only means that a genuinely dialogical inquiry requires partners who are themselves open to dialogue. It also happens that people sometimes share their interpretations and conclusions, in an outward imitation of dialogue, but only with a wish to have them confirmed. That too only means there is a limit to the genuineness of their inquiry. In both cases what is lacking is faithfulness to the call of true being, both objective and subjective. Authentic dialogue requires a shared love of truth in a community of inquirers. When that is lacking, an individual inquirer may have to do the best he or she can without it, but that will impose a limitation on possible discovery, and any genuine inquirer knows that and will lament its absence.

Considering the ambiguous forms human motives can take, to maintain the openness required for authentic inquiry will always be a challenge. Perhaps the most successful effort in that direction has been the modern scientific enterprise, but even that has to struggle continuously against the undertow of inauthenticity, as numerous examples of scientific fraud have shown. The desire on the part of individuals to gain the appearance of scientific discovery and the rewards that go with it can still subvert the love of truth even when there are no religious or ideological institutions involved.

Then there is also the fact that the inquirers themselves may not think very explicitly about the norms of authentic inquiry or be primarily committed to them. I once had a conversation with the Nobel Prize–winning scientist John Polanyi about his father, Michael Polanyi, who had himself been an eminent scientist working in the same field of physical chemistry but had spent the last decades of his life writing on the philosophy of science. At the time I was in the process of writing about his father's thought, and he asked me to tell him about it, saying he had read his father's scientific papers but not his philosophical writings. One of the things I said about his father's idea of scientific knowing was that what the scientist desires above all is truth even if that means the disconfirmation of his own hypotheses. He laughed and said that what every scientist actually desires above all is "to be first." And of course he was right; I was describing the ideal, and he was describing human actuality.[27]

Nevertheless, it is the ideal that is the vitalizing principle of genuine inquiry, and when in any community of inquirers that ideal is abandoned, the enterprise must lose its purpose. In the community of scientists, however motivated each may be to be the first claimant to a discovery, the ideal of science as authentic inquiry continues to be upheld by the honesty that prevents most scientists from trying to make that claim fraudulently and by the self-correcting process of publication of experimental findings to be either replicated or proven false.

27. Peter Berger, on the other hand, suggests less disjunction between the ideal and the real when he says, "As I often tell my students, one of the pleasures of being a social scientist (as opposed to, say, a philosopher or theologian) is that you can have as much fun when you are proven wrong as when you are proven right" (introduction to *Many Globalizations*, ed. Berger and Huntington, 2). It is also possible, of course, that despite Berger's setting them to one side, there could even be philosophers and theologians who might consider truth more important than being considered right. See, for example, Robert Nowell, *A Passion for Truth: Hans Küng and His Theology*.

Religious communities, too, are susceptible to failing in commitment to the love of truth. If sociologists of religion are right, much, and perhaps even most, religion has probably been born out of a desire to legitimate a social system, dehumanize its enemies, and keep the *tremendum* hidden at any cost behind its "sacred canopy." This is why, as we saw earlier, Peter Berger puts the word *knowledge* in quotes in the phrase "socially objectivated 'knowledge'"; such "knowledge" is determined not by critical inquiry and the love of truth but by the fear of chaos and the desire to control truth rather than discover it. This was what choked the vitality of science both in Galileo's Italy and in Trofim Lysenko's Soviet Union. In the first case the dominant social ideology was religious and in the second antireligious, but in both the motive was ideological legitimation of an official worldview and a system of power, not desire for genuine understanding.

Still, the major religions of the world as we know them today have been shaped not only by such motives on the part of some of their adherents but also by a genuine concern on the part of others with transcendence and with truth. Human beings being what we are, both kinds of motivation can even do battle within a single breast, or within a single stream of religious tradition. As I mentioned in Chapter 8, the leaders of the church that condemned Galileo also came three and a half centuries later to feel the need to exonerate him and apologize for that condemnation, and on the basis of my own conversations with people close to the actual center of that decision, I believe they did so (even if with some struggle) out of conscience.

I hope that the above discussion provides sufficient answer for the question of what the idea of believing, as an act of authentic assent, could mean in the context of radical self-transcendence. It should be clear that it is precisely self-transcendence that makes authentic inquiry, and hence authentic assent, possible. With regard to the individual inquirer, self-transcendence is the necessary ground of the openness that is absolutely essential to authentic inquiry. Only if the inquirer is willing to overcome personal and group bias and to reach beyond familiar and comfortable interpretations and beliefs to engage new experience and possibilities of interpretation can new authentic knowledge develop. Beyond the individual inquirer, there is also a further social dimension to the self-transcendence that must be involved in authentic inquiry. This is implicit in its need for a community of inquirers, itself self-transcending in its love of truth, who can supplement and correct the limitations of any one inquirer and ensure that the process of inquiry remains always open and moves constantly forward. Both the individual and the community must subordinate egoistic self-interest to the radical love of truth and, through that love, to the dialogical community in which alone truth can fully flourish.

Dialogical Truth

This conception of faith as dialogical points also, therefore, toward a theological conception of what might be called "dialogical truth." The very structure of intentional consciousness requires fulfillment in a community of inquirers who both love truth and appreciate each other as partners in the search for ever deeper understanding of reality. Something else it means is that, because finite knowledge is always only partial, truth must always remain knowledge on the move, reaching endlessly toward still more adequate interpretations of a still further range of possible experience. The truth that can be known in this way is inherently dynamic, ever in movement. Newman spoke of inquiry coming to rest in assent, but his references to "tranquil enjoyment" of truth and to "a specific sense of intellectual satisfaction and repose" were not intended, I think, to imply the end of openness but only to contrast the satisfaction that comes from authentic inquiry with the intellectual anxiety that accompanies inauthentic inquiry. Perhaps a more precise metaphor than coming to rest, and one closer to Piaget's description of "equilibration," would be the dynamic equilibrium of a tightrope walker, who must balance inputs coming from all directions while continuing to advance forward.

This is what is really radical in the idea of dialogical truth. Dialogical truth demands both a full realization of the relativity of all objective knowledge and a full acceptance of its endless openness and ultimate finitude. To anyone approaching the idea of dialogical truth for the first time, it may look either like a simple philosophical relativism or like a kind of ascetic restraint that temporarily holds back from cognitive closure while waiting for a final fulfillment in just such closure. It may look, that is, like a relativistic throwing up of one's hands and concluding that there is no truth because all interpretations are equally valid as well as equally invalid. Or it may look like a strategy for avoiding both that pitfall and that of premature conclusion in order better to reach toward a grasp of reality that would no longer suffer from dialogical limits but would be able to possess and wield the power of a truth that would show itself finally to be monological.[28]

28. For those to whom the word *monological* may be unfamiliar, perhaps I should explain, as I mentioned briefly in the Introduction, that it refers to a mode of discourse dominated by

In reality, dialogical truth, while recognizing and appreciating relativity, is not a relativism, because it also recognizes that interpretations can be tested for their relative adequacy in construing the data of experience, even if further experience may discover more data or further interpretations may turn up still more (relatively) adequate ways of construing them. Authentic judgment, that is, is possible and is a requirement of authentic consciousness, but the authenticity of judgment requires recognition of its relativity. The ascetic restraint dialogical truth does require is not simply cognitive, not simply a strategy of holding out until really final cognitive mastery becomes possible; it is restraint from trying to overreach the ultimate finitude of objective knowing. Its asceticism, that is, is not simply a cognitive but also a *spiritual* asceticism that recognizes the temptation to power involved in cognitive overreaching and renounces it in favor of the endless, faithful, loving movement of dialogue with fellow finite inquirers. It is a matter, ultimately, of *living* dialogically—of dialogical truth as a mode of existence.

At the end of the last chapter I raised the closely related question of what it could mean to speak of a radically self-transcending "self," or in terms of Freud's "it" and "I," of what the true "I" might ultimately be or become. To put the question still another way, one might ask, what kind of "subject" begins to emerge in the quest for dialogical truth? The idea itself of dialogical truth points to one aspect of a possible answer to that question in that it suggests that the "I" that develops in authentic subjectivity cannot be identified simply with an individual inquirer but, by the very dynamism of intentional consciousness, extends beyond the individual to involve the community it needs for the fulfillment of its quest for ever more adequate understanding. Thinking is not a simply individual matter; there is a sense in which the inquiring "subject" is not just an individual inquirer or even a collection of those but the dynamism itself of the love of truth animating the community of authentic inquiry. But even to say that is to speak in terms of only one dimension of human intentionality, cognitive process. There is also the dimension of love in its full spiritual depth as love of the good in all its forms, especially the love of the

---

a single voice attempting to silence all other voices, or to the idea that only one angle of view on a given issue can be valid. The difference between "monological" and "dialogical" (open to multiple voices) discourse is a major theme of the influential literary critic Mikhail Mikhailovich Bakhtin. See, for example, his work *The Dialogic Imagination: Four Essays.* For studies of this theme in Bakhtin, see David McCracken, "Character in the Boundary: Bakhtin's Interdividuality in Biblical Narratives"; Gary Saul Morson and Caryl Emerson, *Mikhail Bakhtin: Creation of a Prosaics;* and Tzvetan Todorov, *Mikhail Bakhtin: The Dialogical Principle.*

neighbor and of the stranger. It is in this dimension that self-transcendence can become truly radical.

Perhaps it may open a further avenue into understanding what that might mean both in itself and in relation to the love of truth if we consider again the implications of Aquinas's panentheistic way of talking about God and about faith. In Chapter 7 we saw how in his treatise on the names of God Aquinas worked through a sequence of ever higher (because less limiting) analogical names toward the tetragrammaton (YHVH) as the jumping-off point into absolute mystery. Another designation he subsequently gives for God is the "first truth" *(prima veritas),* explaining that since "truth is found in the intellect according as it apprehends a thing as it is," and since "[God's] being is not only conformed to His intellect, but it is the very act of His intellect" and "He Himself is His own being and act of understanding," "it follows not only that truth is in Him, but that He is truth itself, and the supreme and first truth." God's being, that is, is the luminous actuality of divine life.[29]

By itself, Aquinas's reference in the treatise on God at the beginning of *Summa Theologica* to God as "the supreme and first truth" might seem little more than a pious abstraction, another superlative to attach to the supreme symbol Aquinas is trying to analyze logically. But a deeper implication appears when he brings the same phrase *(prima veritas)* back in the second part of the *Summa,* in his discussion of faith, to explain what it means for the author of the Epistle to Hebrews to say that "faith is the substance of things hoped for, the evidence of things that appear not" (11:1). Thomas's reasoning proceeds from the ideas that "the object of faith is the First Truth, as unseen, and whatever we hold on account of it" and that "we are accustomed to call by the name of substance the first beginning of a thing, especially when the whole subsequent thing is virtually contained in the first beginning" to the idea that "faith is a habit of the mind, whereby eternal life is begun in us, making the intellect assent to what is not apparent."[30]

29. Aquinas, *Summa Theologica,* pt. 1, question 16, article 5, "Whether God Is Truth?" An analogy to Aquinas's idea of God as *prima veritas* can also be seen in the Jewish tradition. Cf. Gershom Gerhard Scholem, on the Kabbalists' interpretation of the nature of Torah: "What is it that God can actually reveal, and of what does the so-called word of God consist that is given to the recipients of revelation? The answer is: God reveals nothing but Himself as He becomes speech and voice. The expression through which the divine power presents itself to man in manifestation, no matter how concealed and how inward, is the name of God. It is this that is expressed and given voice in Scripture and revelation, no matter how hieroglyphically. It is encoded in every so-called communication that revelation makes to man" (*The Messianic Idea in Judaism and Other Essays on Jewish Spirituality,* 293).

30. Aquinas, *Summa Theologica,* II-II, question 4, article 1.

That in turn might also seem only a pious formula, especially if the idea of "making the intellect assent to what is not apparent" is interpreted, the way the idea of a "leap of faith" so often is, as illogically assenting to a proposition when one has no rational reason to do so. But as we saw above in the discussion of "formed" in comparison with "unformed" faith, the issue Aquinas is concerned with is not mere propositional assent. Even founded on the best of rational reasons, such assent in itself would pertain only to unformed or "dead" faith; it would not be the beginning of participation in "eternal life," that is, in the life of God himself. *Fides formata,* living faith, is animated by *caritas,* God's own transcendent love, which is his own true being and life. It is the inward presence of this vitalizing, subjective "form" *(caritas)* that makes faith the beginning of "eternal life . . . in us," and it is the knowing from within of that eternal life (the divine love) by the "innermost knowledge" *(intima cognitio),* which is a "reading inwardly" of the experiential mystery of that love, that constitutes what Aquinas means here by the intellect's "assent to what is not apparent."

This, then, points to a further dimension in the idea of dialogical truth. Not only is that truth known in the dialogue of a community of authentic inquirers, and not only is it an endlessly open process of dynamic equilibrium, an infinite approximation process in search of ever more relatively adequate interpretations of objective reality, but it can also be understood from a theological point of view—following out the implications of Aquinas's idea of God as *prima veritas,* "first truth"—as actual present participation in the true goal of the quest, which is to share in the life of divine love. Interpretation is an effort of articulation and objectification; participation is at least the beginning of present experiential involvement in an actuality that can never be adequately articulated and objectified, because it is by its very nature inherently subjective. This actuality is not an object one can stand apart from and contemplate from without; it is a life one can only be immersed in, that one is involved in and depends on for one's very being. The dialogical community of interpreters moved by the radical love of truth may seek objective knowledge of objects proportionate to objective knowing, but at the same time those who participate in that community also live in and experience an unarticulated, irreducible *intima cognitio,* a knowing from within, of the love that draws them forward into all truth and that they reach for implicitly in all their striving. The energy underlying this process is a spiritual dynamism that reaches toward the point at which ultimate being, truth, and love will be found to coincide—if the existence we participate in as human beings actually does have the ultimate dimension of depth that religious faith, in various traditions, sometimes believes in.

Whether that is actually the case is inherently uncertain, of course. From the previous discussion, I hope it is clear that this fact of uncertainty must remain just as evident from the point of view of any believer who understands what cognition is as it would be from that of a nonbeliever. The deep difference between the two, I think, has nothing to do with the validity or invalidity of logical arguments and logical conclusions; it has to do with what one loves and is willing to wager the meaning of one's own life and of all existence on.

The idea of dialogical truth as an incipient but nevertheless real participation in the ultimate "first truth" that is the luminous actuality of divine love indicates, therefore, a further and deeper implication of what it might mean to speak of a radically self-transcending "self," or of what kind of "subject" begins to emerge in the quest for dialogical truth. Not only would this be the comprehensive subjectivity of a community of authentic inquiry, but it would also be a "self" that comes into the fullness of its true life by reaching in love beyond itself toward others and toward all of being, both objective and subjective. This self-transcending subjectivity would be best understood not as an entity but as a continuous, lifelong process of dying to the "self" of mechanistic, reflexive egoism in the hope of rising into the new life of what in Chapter 6 we saw Lawrence Kohlberg call "cosmic" consciousness.[31] From the point of view of a person living this process as a faithful commitment, self-transcending love would be both the way and the goal: one begins in the way of love by sharing with others in the path of dialogical truth, and to do so is to live already in the goal, which is to dwell lovingly in love. The "subject" that emerges in this process could be called a "transcendent self" both in the sense that it transcends the boundaries of selves as individualistically conceived and unites their dialogical community in a shared subjective life and in the sense that it is the incipient personal presence of the transcendent source itself—a self-transcending selfhood that might be said to touch on and begin to participate in the luminosity and love of the "first truth." Or at least that is one way it could be interpreted, if looked at from a panentheistic theological point of view.

Sigmund Freud would probably be surprised to find his dictum, "Where 'it' was, there should be 'I,'" interpreted in the context of such theological ideas, but then genuinely open inquiry must seek to explore every possible interpretation. So even if he rejected such an interpretation himself, Freud

31. See Chapter 6, note 12.

might grant the legitimacy of considering at least the possibility that when the "I" develops fully, it may involve a dimension that extends beyond the individual to participation in a universal life that all individuals are invited to share in and are even impelled to by the dynamism of their own intentional consciousness.

Whether or not this interpretation would have pleased Freud himself, I think it is clearly what Lawrence Kohlberg was trying to talk about with his idea of a "cosmic perspective" and the mystery of a "stage 7" beyond his six-stage scheme of psychological development, and the idea that the emergence of this perspective involves "a shift from figure to ground."[32] The same language could be used to talk about the emergence of transcendent subjectivity (the ground of dialogical truth) from the midst of individual selves (figures) as they unite in dialogical community. It also looks like what James Fowler was trying to talk about with his idea of a sixth stage of "universalizing faith." I think it is also implicit in Erik Erikson's idea that self-transcending "generativity" is the necessary prerequisite for individual development to culminate in fully mature "ego integrity."[33]

Faith and Radical Self-Transcendence

Something like this idea of a self-transcending self, with or without the theological connotations Kohlberg and Fowler invoke, also seems implied in Robert Kegan's conception of a progressively differentiating consciousness, with the "self" gradually becoming disembedded from both its unconscious mechanisms and its conscious meaning systems so that all of those become "object" for a reduced but intensified subjective pole of consciousness. His treatment of the differences among his third, fourth, and fifth orders of consciousness can be helpful for understanding different types of religious mentality and especially for understanding how religion might develop beyond the monological demand for a single formulation of conclusions from a single point of view toward a dialogical conception of believing as a lifelong process of interpretation.

Kegan's analysis of third-order consciousness seems a good description of the mentality of what some might call religious traditionalism, especially because it does not imply a pejorative treatment of that mentality even as it

32. See Chapter 6, note 12.

33. On Erikson's developmental stages (of which "generativity" is the penultimate and "ego integrity" the final stage), see *Childhood and Society*, 247–74.

makes clear what its limitations might be.[34] As an illustration of his third order, Kegan told the story of Peter the middle manager who loved working for a boss he respected and trusted but who felt anxious and lost when he had to create his own system and manage it as the head of an independent unit. Peter's story could easily be transposed into that of a religious person who might flourish psychologically and spiritually under a system of traditional authority but who would become disoriented if he had to consider the possibility that his institutional and scriptural sources of authority could be historically conditioned, socially constructed, and even suffer from an ideological partial blindness. We also saw how Peter was gripped by what in *The Evolving Self* Kegan had called the "interpersonal" pattern of relationship in a way that made it difficult for him to manage the needs of his relationship with his wife (feeling his parents might be lonely, he spontaneously invited them along on what had been intended to be a "second honeymoon" trip). Something like that same tendency might cause some religious traditionalists to hesitate to rock the social and religious boat by asking questions or considering new ideas, lest they upset other members of the flock or disturb group loyalties or even risk their own ostracism. It could also make them feel a need to imagine their God as a superhuman authority figure, even at the cost of having to endure the celestial finger-shaking Borg described with regard to the image of God he held at age ten. In fact, the third-order combination of interpersonal and institutional dependency Peter felt for his boss could explain why a finger-shaking God might continue to have strong appeal even for some who are well beyond ten years old.

34. I should make clear that in speaking here of "religious traditionalism" I wish to avoid any pejorative connotations because, as we saw from the discussion (in Chapter 3) of James Fowler's stages of faith, one might use the term not only to refer to the limitations of Fowler's mythic-literal and synthetic-conventional modes of faith with regard to the way they view tradition but also to refer to the more reflective and mature way of viewing tradition on the part of what he called conjunctive faith. To put it in Fowler's terms, to treat all "traditionalism" pejoratively would be to fall into the narrowness that is a pitfall of his individuative-reflective mode of faith before it has matured in the direction of the conjunctive. Kegan's use of the terms *traditional* and *modern* to refer to his third- and fourth-order types of mind might make the use of the adjectives *traditionalist* and *modernist* easy to slip into in talking about types of religious mind, but the terms have had uses in religious discourse that make that inappropriate. The Roman Catholic Church in the late nineteenth and early twentieth centuries used the term *modernist* as the name for what it considered a heresy, but the elements of that heresy did not correspond very closely to the qualities Kegan is talking about, and there are also other religious groups that use the word *traditionalist* without pejorative connotations to refer to a pattern of thinking that may be more like what Fowler called conjunctive faith (for example, there is an Eastern Orthodox Center for Traditionalist Orthodox Studies).

A third-order mind and worldview can function well as long as it is not confronted with too many challenges, and even when those do come along, it may still be able to stave off for some time the need for a new pattern of mental organization and new institutional arrangements to support it. In the history of religions there are numerous examples not only of resistance to such development but also of the sort of adaptation that can lead into Kegan's fourth-order consciousness with its self-authorizing capacity for critical reflection and judgment, deliberation, and decision and its ability to honor that capacity in others, even if it might lead them to different judgments of truth and different decisions about what to do. The surge of antimodern traditionalism in some parts of the Muslim world today that commonly goes by the names of Islamism or Islamic fundamentalism seems an example of early startled resistance to challenges that are still only beginning to be deeply felt and are probably not even yet clearly recognized on the part of many. What goes by the name of fundamentalism among Christians, on the other hand, is culturally a late holding out against intellectual challenges that many thinking Christians have been wrestling with for centuries and have already led quite a few of them to the development of fourth- or even fifth-order consciousness. Jews have been wrestling with similar issues since late antiquity, and the variety of contemporary forms that Jewish religion has taken can be understood at least in part as a panoply of possible developments in response to their challenges.

It is with Kegan's fifth order of consciousness that the idea of a radically self-transcending self comes into full view psychologically—even if his fourth order alone might serve quite well as a foundation for peaceful, respectful relations among people with different beliefs in a dialogical community. To illustrate the difference between the fourth and fifth orders, Kegan tells a further story that I did not recount in Chapter 3, about two married couples, the Ables (fourth order) and the Bakers (moving into the fifth order). Each couple has been married for twenty-five years, and each has worked out a way of dealing with difference that they find fully satisfying. In each couple the partners have quite different personalities, preferences, and systems of meaning and value, and in the early years of their marriages these could be sources of sometimes heated conflict, but they have developed ways of differing that now make them feel the differences are actually enriching.

The Ables say that what they have learned is both to be the individuals they are, with their own particular points of view, and to appreciate the integrity of the other partner and respect his or her point of view as well. (These are the hallmarks, of course, of what in *The Evolving Self* Kegan called an "interindividual" relationship.) Now when conflicts develop between them, the Ables say, "They make one or both of us come over and take a look from the other one's point of view, and we see that there's a good reason why it looks different to the other one. We are a good problem-solving team. Neither of us feels we have to do it our way all the time. We compromise. We take turns. And sometimes we even find a way to create a solution that includes a lot of both of our views. We stopped trying to get the other person to change a long time ago. We are who we are."[35]

Both of the Ables, we might say, have at least a tacit appreciation of the principles of critical realist cognitional theory, and both have sufficiently appropriated the formal operational mode of thinking in accord with those principles that they are able both to possess a critically grounded confidence in their own judgments and decisions and to respect the integrity of the process by which the other, focusing on somewhat different experiences and using different interpretive strategies, can also come reasonably to a confident affirmation of the relative adequacy of his or her interpretations. Again, this story could be transposed to describe a hypothetical fourth-order religious couple who have differing religious views but who can appreciate and respect each other's different faith commitments because they believe in each other's spiritual integrity and understand that the mental operations by which the other reaches different particular conclusions are carefully and critically enacted. This could be the case for such a couple whether they belonged to different paths within a single religion (a Protestant and a Catholic, for example, or a Sunni and a Shiite) or whether they actually followed quite different religions (say, a Christian and a Buddhist). As persons operating with fourth-order consciousnesses, they would feel confident about who they are and what they believe, because they would know exactly how they got there, what experiences and interpretations went into forming their worldviews and their selves.

Before comparing this with the story of Kegan's Bakers, let us imagine still another religious couple, in this case both with third-order consciousnesses. If we imagine them as sharing a common religion, one of the principal benefits they would probably feel they get from their marriage is that they reinforce each other's belief and encourage each other in trying to live up to their religion's precepts. Operating in the "traditional" religious mode, not only are

35. Kegan, *In over Our Heads,* 308.

they not self-authoring in the manner of the fourth order, but they would probably feel that even to try to be self-authoring would be presumptuous or even sinful. Their religious style is to trust a respected authority, either a person believed endowed with authority by a transcendent source or a text that recounts inspired messages from that source. They would probably belong to a religious community that strives for the same sort of reaffirming religious unanimity that they value in their marriage, and the combination of their community-based belief and their mutual support in their marriage for each other's faith would be a source of inner security.

A mimetic theorist like René Girard might also say that by staying close to others who profess and live the same beliefs, they put themselves in a position to be carried mimetically by those others through their own preconscious inward imitation of the feelings and attitudes they perceive in the people around them. It may also help in this if their authoritative sources of belief have some qualities of charisma or "magnetism" that give them what Girard's colleague Jean-Michel Oughourlian has called greater mimetic gravitational "mass."[36] Not only might this social support be helpful to their faith, but it might even be existentially critical, since without it their beliefs and even their identities might feel seriously threatened. Lacking a self-authoring process of interpretation, critical reflection, judgment, and decision, their beliefs may have little to hold them together but the effect of social gravitation. Or to put it another way, the members of this couple may not so much actually believe the tenets of their faith themselves as believe in the belief of others.

That is not necessarily, I should note, an inappropriate way of believing. In the days when traditional cultures were still fairly insular, it probably worked well to give the members of the culture a secure sense of a social and phenomenological "world," both secular and religious, that they could feel at home in and live fruitful lives in. Even in the ordinary course of affairs in modern society, we take a great deal on trust, since few of us are sufficiently expert in all fields of knowledge to put together all the aspects of our worldviews for ourselves. Whatever the culture, any young person beginning to ask religious questions will naturally look for well-informed adults who might offer some guidance, and to do so is a perfectly appropriate starting point for growth into religious maturity. Belief in the belief of respected others can function as a "holding environment" for someone still in preparation for developing his or

36. Oughourlian, *Puppet of Desire*, 3–4.

her own belief on the basis of careful assessing of interpretations. This can be true not only for the young, of course, but for people of any age.

In the case of the third-order religious couple we were just imagining, we could expect that as long as no very challenging questions caused either of the two to have doubts, they could continue through the years to help each other to live their faith confidently and devotedly. On the other hand, if one of them did begin to have doubts, they would probably experience that as deeply threatening, both to their beliefs and to their union. Or if we were to imagine another third-order couple who married despite serious religious differences, the success of their union would probably depend either on at least one of them developing fourth-order capacities for thinking through their differences and living with them or else on one or the other "winning the argument"—if the story did not end with both losing their faith because its psychological support fell away.

To turn now to Kegan's story of the Bakers, they sound at first almost exactly like the Ables. They have the same personality differences, and they too have learned to live with them, but then they say, "When we're at our best, though . . . we are able to stop pretending that these differences and opposites can only be found in the *other* person, or that the battles we get into are only with the other person."[37] Rather, they have found that whatever stand one or the other may take at a given time also has reasonable and even appealing alternatives; one position may be predominant at the moment, but it lives in ongoing tension with other possibilities. "It isn't easy, and it doesn't happen all the time," they say,

> but our favorite fights are the ones in which we don't try to solve the conflicts but let the conflicts "solve us," you could say. We mean by that that if a conflict doesn't go away after a while we've found it's a good bet that one of us, or both of us, has gotten drawn back into being too identified with our more comfortable position. Like the end we're holding onto so passionately is our whole story, our whole truth in the matter. When we can get out of the grip of our more familiar side then the fight doesn't feel as if the other one is trying to make us give up anything. The fight becomes a way for us to recover our own complexity, so to speak, to leave off making the other into our opposite and face up to our own oppositeness.[38]

37. Kegan, *In over Our Heads,* 309; emphasis in the original.
38. Ibid., 309–10.

As Kegan tells their stories, both the Ables and the Bakers went through an initial disillusionment with the "romantic" intimacy of a kind of merged self-hood, but the Bakers are in the midst of a further disillusionment with belief in stable, unified, individual selfhood. "Long ago, they say, they set aside the truth that the source of their closeness lay in their sharing the same identity. The truth they are now in the process of setting aside is that the source of their closeness lies in the respectful cooperation of psychologically whole and distinct selves. . . . [T]hey are suspicious of any sense of wholeness or distinction that is limited to an identification of the self with its favorite way of constructing itself."[39]

Another way to put this would be to say that both their own sense of self and their idea of selfhood as such are changing from static to dynamic, from product to process. The result is that "they experience their 'multipleness,' in which the many forms or systems that each self is are helped to emerge." What this means in terms of Kegan's subject-object analysis is that "the fifth order moves form or system from subject to object."[40] The Bakers, that is, are ceasing to be embedded in the selves they construct through self-interpretation; their consciousness becomes differentiated to the point that it is beginning to step back from "self" as such and become radically open to the ongoing flow of experience and interpretive process.

At their respective bests, both the Ables and the Bakers have found effective ways to handle conflict peacefully. The difference is that the Ables' strategy is, out of mutual love and respect, to declare a truce between opposing positions that cannot be reconciled or compromised, whereas the Bakers' can hardly even be called a strategy, since it transcends conflict by transforming it into a process of growth. As Kegan explains it, "While the Ables begin with the premise of their own completeness and see conflict as an inevitable by-product of the interaction of two psychologically whole selves, the Bakers begin with the premise of their own tendency to *pretend to* completeness (while actually being incomplete) and see conflict as the inevitable, but controvertible, by-product of the pretension to completeness."[41] When they give up that pretension, the conflict is transcended with it. Not, of course, that this is easy to do, even for the fictional Bakers, and the process of doing it could never, by its very nature as process rather than product, be final. Rather, it would be an ongoing "dying to self" of the kind that religions sometimes talk about.

39. Ibid., 311.
40. Ibid., 313, 312.
41. Ibid., 313; emphasis in the original.

Communities of Dialogical Faith

At the end of the last chapter I referred to Cardinal Newman's saying that "assent" is "an active recognition of propositions as true such as it is the duty of each individual himself to exercise at the bidding of reason, and, when reason forbids, to withhold" and to Luther's saying that "every man must do his own believing, just as every man must do his own dying," and I asked if this means that religious belief must tend toward divisiveness and conflict. By this point in the discussion it must be clear, I hope, that this is not the case, or at least not necessarily. Acts of critical judgment can be performed only by individuals, but interpretation seeks a community of interpreters in order to do its work well, and even if critical judgment affirms one interpretation as the best, what that must mean to an inquirer who is fully aware of the intrinsic nature of the cognitional process is that the interpretation judged true is the most relatively adequate given the current state of available experiential data and of ways that have been thought of to construe them. If one understands that the only truth proportionate to human cognitive operations is not finality but relative adequacy, one can be confident of one's judgments while remaining open to further disclosures and discoveries that will correct or improve them.

It is true that a thinker operating with what Kegan called a third-order consciousness, with its tendency to rely on what Kohlberg called exogenous sources of authority, might be led by such sources to hardened positions in absolute conflict with those of others. But, as I mentioned above in my story of a hypothetical third-order religious couple, that kind of exogenous belief is not so much an act of real judgment as a trusting in the judgments of others—who may or may not be thinking critically and carefully themselves. Kegan's fourth-order couple did understand, at least implicitly, what authentic rational assent is, and they did make judgments of truth that divided them. If they were a religious couple, they could well end up with strongly opposing religious views. But if that were to happen to the Ables, it is clear that they not only would be able to live with their opposing views but could even appreciate the sincerity and critical concern of each at the root of their differences. Their beliefs might divide them, but this would not be a divisiveness of a conflictual sort.

What about the way of being religious of a couple who thought in the manner of the Bakers? The answer does not leap by itself from their story as it did in the case of the Ables. It was an explicit feature of the story of the Ables that they came to definite positions of various sorts. That was not just a matter of assent to political, religious, or other positions, since it was also a matter of identity and the idea of personhood—of, as Kegan put it, knowing "who we are." But it did involve taking such positions. In the case of the Bakers, on the other hand, the emphasis was on breaking free from their identification with any final position and on the new looser and more open kind of selfhood that this was leading them into.

Kegan seems keenly aware that his fifth order may be difficult to grasp and that some might be tempted to interpret its loosening up of cognitive claims as a movement from fourth-order critical realism to simple relativism. This is probably why he devotes much of his discussion of the fifth order, as we saw in Chapter 3, to the question of "deconstructive" versus "reconstructive" postmodernism. We saw there that Kegan considers the deconstructive type dangerously antimodern. He recognizes the validity of its critique of unconsciously self-serving ideologies and of what some of the theorists he cites call modernist "absolutism," but he hopes for a reconstructive postmodernism that will preserve the value of modern modes of thinking while not treating their conclusions as absolute. "The distinction between deconstructive and reconstructive postmodernism," he says, "introduces the possibility that not every 'theory,' 'stand,' or 'way' is necessarily absolutistic or ideological. Not every 'differencing,' normatizing, or hierarchizing is necessarily a hidden and arbitrary privileging of a special interest. Not every kind of judging or prioritizing is impermissible modernist domination."[42]

But then why should anyone think it would be? I think one answer, speaking from the point of view of philosophical analysis, would be that what Kegan has called the "deconstructive" position assumes a cognitive relativism according to which there can be no legitimate judgment of truth because all positions are equally ungrounded.[43] If one adopts the relativist position (which, of course, requires not noticing that, by its own premise, it too is as ungrounded as any other), then the only basis for any position must be an arbitrary assertion of the will to dominate. Speaking from the point of view of a psychological analysis along Kegan's lines, another answer might be that Kegan's "deconstructive postmodernist" has not really completed the transition from the third order of consciousness to the fourth, or at least is reacting

42. Ibid., 329.

43. I should note, as I did in the same connection in Chapter 3, that I do not mean to imply that all of what goes by the name of "deconstructionism" is necessarily reducible to such relativism. In the present case, *deconstructive* is a technical term Kegan is putting to his own use for analyzing possible types of "postmodern" thinking.

against absolutistic assertions on the part of people who have not adequately made that transition or who do not fully understand its implications.

Kegan does not talk explicitly about cognitional theory in relation to his orders of consciousness, although his effort to defend his reconstructive postmodernism against deconstructive does begin to deal with its issues, so I am having to interpolate a bit here, but if the third order tends to be characterized by reliance on the exogenous authority of traditions whereas the fourth is, in Kegan's phrase, "self-authoring" in its construction of self and world through its own interpretations and judgments, then there are at least two ways that cognitive relativism could be expected to arise. One would be on the part of a person making the transition to self-authoring who becomes aware that self-authorized judgment could make excessive claims to finality but is not quite sure how to avoid them except by renouncing truth claims altogether. Another might be on the part of a person still fairly rooted in third-order consciousness who hears people talking about "an active recognition of propositions as true such as it is the duty of each individual himself to exercise at the bidding of reason, and, when reason forbids, to withhold" but who does not really grasp how one might do that critically and carefully and decides claims made in the name of that principle are really only an assertion of power on the part of people who want to claim authority and have others simply trust or obey them—and, of course, some of the time that might even be true.

If my own reading of Kegan's sequence of orders is correct, then people operating with fourth-order consciousness like the Ables can be expected to realize that although judgments regarding the relative adequacy of an interpretation may be definite, they will nevertheless always remain conditional. They can be definite if the conditions for determining relative adequacy have been satisfactorily fulfilled, but they remain conditional because, human cognition being what it is, there will always be possibilities of further relevant evidence or interpretations. Hence Lonergan's use of the term *virtually unconditioned* in discussing what he calls "the general form of reflective insight": "To grasp evidence as sufficient for a prospective judgment is to grasp the prospective judgment as virtually unconditioned."[44] The difference between Kegan's Ables and Bakers is not that the Ables make judgments and the Bakers do not; it is that the Bakers have a deeper realization of the conditionedness of their judgments.

44. Lonergan, *Insight*, 280. "The formally unconditioned has no conditions whatever. The virtually unconditioned has conditions indeed but they are fulfilled" (ibid.)

One might say that the Ables, having discovered how to do self-authoring interpretation and judgment, tend to emphasize the "unconditioned" in the "virtually unconditioned," whereas the emphasis for the Bakers is on the "virtually." The trick is to appreciate the relativity of all knowledge without slipping into a relativism that would deny the very possibility of knowing.

Kegan himself puts a more psychological emphasis on the difference by talking about how the Ables "identify" with their positions and the selves they construct as holding them, while the Bakers are letting go of those identifications and are becoming open to waiting expectantly to see what the flow of psychic life is leading them toward—and this is valuable for bringing out the affective and existential dimensions of the way their personhood is unfolding. But philosophical issues are implicit throughout Kegan's discussion. We saw that Piaget, on whom Kegan builds, had a great deal of cognitional theory in his developmental psychology, and we saw that Lonergan's own cognitional theory was founded not only on what he learned from philosophical and theological predecessors but also, very substantially, on what he learned from reading Piaget. The entire Piagetian tradition is in its way as much a philosophical one as a psychological one. So it does not seem inappropriate to say that Kegan himself is also something of a cognitional theorist. This becomes explicit when he talks about a theory of "theory making" in the continuation of the passage just quoted above:

> Not every kind of judging or prioritizing is impermissible modernist domination. . . . [T]he possibility of a reconstructive postmodernism suggests that one could in fact advocate identification with a theory, a stand, or a way, and that such advocacy need not necessarily be a backsliding reification of one kind of modernist authority or another. An example would be a theory that was really a theory about theory making, a theory that was mindful of the tendency of any intellectual system to reify itself, to identify internal consistency with validity, to call its fourth order subjectivity "objectivity." The expression of such a theory's "maturity" would not be the modernist capacity to defend itself against all challenges, to demonstrate how all data gathered to it can find a place within it, but to assume its incompleteness and seek out contradiction by which to nourish the ongoing process of its reconstruction.[45]

That sounds precisely like a theory of what I have been calling dialogical truth, at least in its cognitive aspect. But as I explained above, there is more to

45. Kegan, *In over Our Heads,* 329–30.

dialogical truth than only its cognitive aspect, just as there is more than a shift in mode of cognition involved in the movement from Kegan's third order to his fourth and his fifth. Viewed theologically, dialogical truth would involve participation in the life of a dialogical community and even incipient participation in the ultimate *prima veritas,* the "first truth," that is both the source and the goal of its own animating energy. For the purpose of understanding what religion can be, it helps to recognize, as I hope is now clear, that religious people, like anybody else, can make reasonable, carefully considered cognitive claims of the sort Newman talks about in his phenomenology of assent—just as, like anybody else, they can fail to understand the theoretical foundations of cognitive claims and make such claims inappropriately or absolutistically. But there is more to the life of faith than making cognitive claims, however critical and well founded. Assent is critical judgment, belief may be something more than just assent, and faith, in its full sense as *fides formata* (faith animated by love, *caritas*), is still more; what it believes its knowing is is not the beholding of an object but a knowing from within, an *intima cognitio,* of the first truth.[46]

All of this suggests another important question: if philosophy, theology, and psychology all point in the direction of some form of radical transcendence, how is one to get there? Is there a path of exploration and growth to be followed? What kind of community could support that? Speaking psychologically, Kegan says, "Multiselved parents do not mate and give birth to multiselved postmodern babies. Half a lifetime, if not more, precedes these discoveries. And good company is required every step of the way."[47] Where might such company be found, if the journey the company is needed for is not only a psychological one but also an explicitly spiritual one?

To ask this is to ask what a religious community would be if it were consciously a community of dialogical truth. Religious communities need not be that, and perhaps do not often even aspire to be that. If a religion aims at keeping its faithful committed to one particular set of interpretations, practices, and institutional arrangements, to a monological conception of the true and the good—as many have done and still do—then its ideal religious community will lean toward a sort of self-ghettoizing insulation against any alien voices

46. It was this conception of subjective knowing and its relation to faith that Kierkegaard explored in *Concluding Unscientific Postscript;* see book 2, "The Subjective Problem: The Relation of the Subject to the Truth of Christianity: The Problem of Becoming a Christian," especially part 2, chapter 2, "The Subjective Truth, Inwardness: Truth Is Subjectivity."

47. Kegan, *In over Our Heads,* 331.

either within the community or outside it. Examples abound, and I think I can safely leave them to the reader's own memory and powers of observation.

But as I explained in Chapter 7, actual religious traditions are not simply unitary and monological, even if some members of those traditions would like them to be. That aim is most easily pursued if the community is kept on a small scale, hence the numerous comparatively small sects dedicated to a particular way of thinking or way of life advocated by a particular charismatic leader. Whenever a community becomes fairly large, diversity within it is inevitable, and with it there will be pressure within the community to open up and become more dialogical even as some try to resist that trend.

One clear example of the latter sort would be the story of the Roman Catholic Church in the nineteenth and twentieth centuries. We saw in the preceding chapter how in the Galileo case the Catholic Church first responded with resistance to modern science as a threat to the authority of scripture but with the advice of both scientists[48] and theologians later reversed itself after realizing the value of scientific method and learning new ways of reading scripture like those suggested by Galileo himself. But that was just one rather limited case. The history of the first and second Vatican councils makes the nature both of the transition and of the resistance to it even clearer, because those councils were conscious efforts to deal with the full range of issues facing the Catholic Church in the modern world.

During the years leading up to Vatican I, the Roman See was increasingly challenged by all sorts of intellectual and political developments. Galileo and the world of science were clearly winning the battle of ideas, and the aristocratic political order that the papacy had previously tried to control or at least effectively influence was under threat, especially after the uprisings that swept Europe in 1848. At his election in 1846, Pius IX had been considered a potentially liberal, modernizing pope, but those uprisings turned him around completely and led him to spend the rest of his long reign trying to preserve both his ecclesiastical power and his political power as sovereign of the Papal States in Italy. In 1864, referring to the events of 1848 as "a truly awful storm excited by so many evil opinions," he issued his encyclical *Quanta cura* against such opinions with an appended "Syllabus of Errors" listing eighty of them, including, to list just a few, the beliefs that the Catholic religion should not

48. As was mentioned in the preceding chapter (note 28), Father George V. Coyne, S.J., a distinguished astronomer and director of the Vatican Observatory, was a member of the papal commission charged with reopening the Galileo case and advising the Holy See on how to deal with it.

be held as the only religion of the state to the exclusion of all other forms of worship (no. 77), and that it could be legitimate for people to adopt their own religious views on the basis of their own reasoning (no. 15), or for subjects to refuse obedience to legitimate princes and even to rebel against them (no. 63), or to think that the method and principles by which the old scholastic doctors cultivated theology are no longer suitable to the demands of our times and to the progress of the sciences (no. 13).[49] In 1870 he convoked the First Vatican Council to further his program of buttressing tradition against what was coming to be called "modernism" and to declare the dogma of papal infallibility, which it did in that year.

Part of this defensive program was an Index of Forbidden Books that continued in force until it was finally discontinued in 1966 after the Second Vatican Council. In 1907 under Pope Pius X the Sacred Congregation of the Holy Office issued a further syllabus of errors, *Lamentabili Sane,* condemning the methods and assumptions of modern biblical scholarship. This was followed two months later by the encyclical *Pascendi Dominici Gregis,* which condemned these along with "modernism" in general and commanded that no Catholic be allowed to read such literature, to publish it, or even to hold meetings to discuss it.[50] In 1908 Pius X increased the scope of the Index of Forbidden Books by ordering that the Sacred Congregation of the Index investigate not only books that had been explicitly denounced to it but also "to supervise, ex officio, books that are being published, and to pass sentence on such as deserve to be prohibited."[51]

This was probably the high point of the Papal See's effort to hold back the tide of modern critical thinking. If the Vatican had really held the political power it claimed it rightfully should, the cognitive regime it imposed would have been truly monological, stifling all voices but one official one and controlling not only all answers but even all questions. In reality, however, the Catholic Church continued to include many serious thinkers whose questions eventually had to be considered. Pius X's campaign against modernism did effectively silence Catholic biblical scholarship for several decades, but in 1943 Pius XII cautiously opened some space for it with the encyclical *Divino Af-*

49. Claudia Carlen, ed., *The Papal Encyclicals,* 1:381.

50. Encyclicals of Pius X and Pius XII can be found in ibid., vols. 3 and 4. These encyclicals can also be found on the Vatican Web site, http://www.vatican.va/offices/index.htm.

51. Acta S. Sedis, XLI, 432, quoted in "Censorship of Books," in *The Catholic Encylopedia: An International Work of Reference on the Constitution, Doctrine, Discipline, and History of the Catholic Church,* by Charles George Herbermann et al.

flante Spiritu, which acknowledged that modern developments in archaeology and textual studies needed to be taken into account in the study of the Bible.

New theological questions and perspectives in many areas continued to exert pressure to the point that in 1962 Pope John XXIII decided to convoke the Second Vatican Council to give them a hearing. In the documents produced by that council one can see signs that there was a fundamental shift not only with regard to particular theological topics but also in the conception of the foundations of thinking as such. To use Kegan's terms again, third-order loyalties were not repudiated, but the cogency of fourth-order claims regarding methods of inquiry and the integrity of scholarship were beginning to be recognized and even endorsed, if somewhat warily, as when Vatican II's "Dogmatic Constitution on Divine Revelation," *Dei Verbum,* said, "The sacred Synod encourages the sons of the Church who are Biblical scholars to continue energetically, with the work they have so well begun, with a constant renewal of vigor and with loyalty to the mind of the Church."[52]

As long as religious communities are made up of real human beings of differing ages and levels of psychological as well as educational development, it can be expected that the tug of war will continue between critically reflective (in Kegan's terms, modern or fourth-order) thinking and those who want to protect themselves and others in the flock from some of the challenges that might pose. But if we were to try to imagine an ideal religious community, well suited to provide "good company," guidance, and a holding environment for limitless possibilities of psychological, intellectual, and spiritual growth, what would be its characteristics?

If there could be a community made up entirely of people who have, in Kegan's terms, a secure grasp of the fourth order of consciousness and perhaps an initial sense of movement into the fifth, one could reasonably expect it to have little serious difficulty with friction among its members over differing ideas because everyone in it would have consciously appropriated the principles of critical realist cognitional theory and would therefore both understand the limits of cognitive claims and realize that it is possible for acts of critical assent to be simultaneously both definite and open-ended. The definiteness of a critical judgment has to do with the relative adequacy of an interpretation, which can at least in principle be revised or improved on in continuing dialogue with the other members of the community. The carefully considered

52. *Dei Verbum,* para. 23, in *Documents of Vatican II, in a New and Definitive Translation, with Commentaries and Notes by Catholic, Protestant, and Orthodox Authorities,* 126.

different positions the various members might take in the process would each be seen as a contribution to the ongoing dialogue, as long as all remained interested in pursuing ever deeper understanding. Such a community would understand itself not as a monological custodian of final truth but as a community of inquirers, and its members would not merely tolerate but actually value all its voices. They would want each member to continue to develop his or her understanding of all questions and possible answers as fully as possible, because they would understand that the fulfillment of the love of truth in each depends on the participation of as many authentic inquirers as possible. One might even say that an authentic dialogue of truth depends on a prior dialogue of love as its necessary foundation and nurturing ground.

Of course, to speak of this borders on the utopian. No such fourth- or fifth-order community could ever exist in the real world of succeeding generations, if only because, as Kegan said, people are not born with highly developed orders of consciousness but have to grow into them. So an essential question about religious possibilities is, what sort of community might be able, even before any of its members had yet developed to those orders of consciousness, to foster their development and allow them to continue once they do develop? And a closely related question would be: as such people develop among a community's members, how might the community continue to provide a "holding environment" for those of its members living in Kegan's second and third orders of consciousness that would enable them to grow further at their own pace? We saw in Chapter 3 how Kegan lamented the way "deconstructive" postmodernists, who are just beginning to have a sense of what it might mean to move beyond the fourth order of consciousness to the fifth, can slip into denying the value of the gains of the fourth. One of the challenges of any kind of development is not to interpret as terminal the point of development one has reached; the temptation to claim finality in psychological development is similar to that in the area of cognitive claims.

The challenge is therefore twofold: to allow and encourage growth to more differentiated consciousness and critical appropriation of a tradition on the basis of one's own careful thinking while providing a holding environment for those who may not yet even have much sense of what such thinking might involve. Those capable of interpreting and judging for themselves need to be able to do so, while those who are not yet ready to do that need trustworthy leaders who can help them toward it but can also help protect them from the pitfalls of its clumsy first steps. I think this is how one can understand the strains in the story of the modern Roman Catholic Church that were traced above. What makes the challenge difficult is that it is not easy to find a way to provide a holding environment that is able to nurture and appropriately protect without trying to "hold on to" those being protected.

One model worth considering for a possible solution is the tradition of rabbinic Judaism. That has conceived of itself from its earliest beginnings as a community of interpreters called to bear witness to the radical transcendence of God and to try to understand the implications of that calling. The rabbis' tradition is centered on Oral Torah, which they cherish as the living memory of their history of interpretation. Their story presents this as tracing back to Moses himself, who is said to have handed down alongside written Torah an oral tradition about how to interpret and apply it. The rabbis are people learned in that tradition who carry it forward by studying it and applying its principles to the interpretation of new issues that come up as history moves forward. The Talmud is the record of their disputations and decisions over many centuries. As I mentioned in the preceding chapter, minority positions were always recorded in the Talmud along with those that prevailed, because even if they were judged inadequate at the time, the rejected positions might contain ideas that would later prove pertinent in new cases that might arise. In this way, a dialogical pursuit of truth that could both respect judgment and remain open to future interpretation was institutionalized in the life of the Jewish people in a form that stretched from the prestigious rabbinic academies to which Jews from all over the world would send new cases down to the local schools in which Jewish boys began their intellectual and religious lives by studying the same records of ancient cases as the most learned rabbis.

To get a concrete sense of how this tradition has understood itself, it may help to consider two stories that have themselves become part of the Talmudic tradition as commentary on its nature. One is about the legitimacy of interpretation as such, even if it might come up with ideas that can be surprising: "When he ascended to Heaven, and the Holy One, blessed be He, showed him R[abbi] Akiba sitting and expounding, Moses did not understand what he was saying, but nevertheless, 'his mind was set at ease'" when he heard that, in reply to a question of his disciples: 'Master, how do you know this?' R. Akiba answered: 'It is a Halakha of Moses given at Sinai.'"[53] Those who came after

53. The word *halakha* can be translated in various ways into English, all bearing on the idea of right conduct; in this case the simplest translations might be "law" or "ethical teaching." The passage is from the Babylonian Talmud, Tractate *Menahot,* 29b, quoted in Efraim Elimelech Urbach, *The Sages, Their Concepts and Beliefs,* 1:300. For a classic modern commentary on this passage, see Scholem, *Messianic Idea in Judaism,* 283.

Moses were drawing further meanings from the same text Moses had delivered, even if they were meanings he could not have imagined himself. The moral, comments Professor Efraim Urbach, is quite clear: "The Revelation included not only the Torah and all its interpretations, but also the bestowal of the authority to interpret."[54]

The other story emphasizes that authority of the rabbis to use their own human powers of reasoning in developing their interpretations. On one occasion, the story begins, a sharp dispute arose between Rabbi Eliezer and his colleagues:

> R. Eliezer adduced every possible argument, but his colleagues remained unconvinced. He said to them: "If the law is according to my view, may this carob-tree prove it." The carob-tree moved a hundred cubits from its place, or, as some declare, four hundred cubits. They replied to him: "No proof can be brought from a carob-tree." He thereupon said to them: "If the law is according to my view, may this water-channel prove it"; and the water flowed backward. They replied to him: "No proof can be brought from a water-channel." He thereupon said to them: "If the law is according to my view, let the walls of this House of Study prove it." The walls then caved in and were on the point of falling. R. Joshua rebuked them, saying: "If students of the Torah contend with one another on a point of law, what has it to do with you?" Out of respect for R. Joshua they did not fall, and out of respect for R. Eliezer they did not become erect, but still remain aslant. He finally said to them: "If the law is according to my view, let it be proved from heaven." A *Bath Kol* [a voice from the heavens] issued forth and declared: "What have you against R. Eliezer? The legal decision is always according to his view." R. Joshua rose to his feet and exclaimed: "It is not in heaven" (Deut. xxx. 12). What does this intend? R. Jeremiah said: "The Torah having been once delivered on Mount Sinai, we pay no attention to a *Bath Kol.*"[55]

As I also touched on in the preceding chapter, the Christian tradition's tendency during much of its history has been quite the opposite. The early ecumenical councils ended their disputations with adoption of the majority position, but in doing so they went further than simply rejecting minority positions; they attempted to obliterate all memory of them—so effectively

54. Urbach, *Sages,* 1:300.

55. Tractate *Bava Metzia,* 59b, quoted in Cohen, *Everyman's Talmud,* 46–47. For additional commentary on this passage, see also Scholem's commentary on the same story in *Messianic Idea in Judaism,* 291–92.

that it is a considerable challenge now to historians of Christian thought to try to find out exactly what the disputes were really about.[56] Much of our knowledge of many of the competing positions in the early centuries of Christianity comes only from those who denounced them, since the texts of their opponents were destroyed.

This is not to say that the Christian religion has not also involved a dialogical tradition, but despite the voices of some, like the apologist Lactantius (ca. 240–ca. 320), who spoke up for freedom of inquiry as an explicitly Christian principle against those who thought faith could legitimately be coerced, from the time the Christian church began to ally itself with imperial power dialogical faith has not on the whole been considered a central value of the tradition the way it has among Jews.[57] Rather, the dialogical tradition in Christianity has survived mainly due to the inability of any one Christian group to establish absolute power over the entire Christian community. I spoke earlier of diversity of thinking among modern Roman Catholics despite efforts on the part of some leaders in the church to impose a monological regime. The same persistence of efforts to understand authentically has manifested itself throughout Christian history, hence the breakup of the medieval Western church at the time of the Reformation and the rejection by Eastern Christians of Western Christian attempts to assert authority over them.

My purpose here, however, is not to go through a catalog of religious traditions assessing how they measure up against a standard of openness or of commitment to dialogical faith. I think that closely examined, every tradition can be seen to involve a tug of war between monological and dialogical drives on the part of its members. Rather, my present purpose is simply to sketch

56. See, for example, Robert C. Gregg and Dennis E. Groh, *Early Arianism: A View of Salvation,* on the challenge of trying to determine what Arius and his early followers actually thought, which the authors argue was probably considerably different from "Arianism" as later defined.

57. Elizabeth DePalma Digeser summarizes Lactantius's argument: "The proper way to persuade a person of a religion's truth is through philosophy, eloquence, or debate; getting someone to adopt another religion 'is something that must be accomplished by words rather than by wounds, so that it may involve free will' ([*Divine Institutes*] v.19.8, 11). This is a stricture that he applies equally to both sides of the debate between traditional cult and Christian practice: 'If their system is true, it will be appropriated. We are ready to listen, if they should teach.' Although he doubts that such a disputation would be persuasive, he encourages his opponents to 'act like us, so that they may set forth an account of the whole matter; for we do not mislead, since they themselves would expose it; rather we teach, we prove, we explain' (v.19.11–12, 14)" (*The Making of a Christian Empire: Lactantius and Rome,* 109–10). Digeser says that Lactantius published the first edition of his work in 306 and that "from 310 to 313 the first Christian emperor [Constantine] was one of the *Divine Institutes*' first auditors and . . . drew upon its ideas after achieving sole rule in 324" (12–13).

how dialogical faith might be understood and operate, within any tradition, and what would be the characteristics of a religious community that could foster the growth of its members into dialogical faith as a mode of existence. Stated briefly, dialogical faith is a faithful commitment to dialogical truth, not only as a set of interpretations and judgments about their relative adequacy but also as a life lived in dialogical community in the face of a transcendent ultimacy that is understood to exceed by its very nature the power of any interpretative process to capture it with finality.

If dialogical faith can be understood in this way, then some implications for a dialogical community's structure and mode of operation follow from it. It would be a community united in a common love of something that will always elude full grasp but that the members experience as grasping them even as they reach toward it. It would understand itself as a community of inquirers centered on dialogical truth in the full sense of that phrase, reaching toward participation in the "first truth" *(prima veritas)*, the luminosity and love that is being itself, to the extent that this is possible for finite beings. This means that the community would have to cultivate not just openness in inquiry but the full flourishing of each human being as a subject capable of freely experiencing, interpreting, judging, and deliberating both individually and in community, and it would have to have an ethic and institutional form suited to ensure that.

Perhaps the best way to speak of this possibility would be to approach it as a question of the etiquette of a dialogical community, the practices that can enable genuine dialogue, or at least ensure that if, by the grace of the dynamism of questioning and the love of truth, dialogical inquiry does begin as a process of genuinely open and collaborative interpretation, it will not be stifled or discouraged. The etiquette that could ensure this would have to involve a commitment on the part of the community as a whole to give a respectful hearing to every voice, including those that express minority views. The participants would have to have the humility to recognize the relativity of all positions, realizing that the most that can be claimed for any interpretation, however carefully considered and critically tested, is *relative* adequacy. To put this theologically, the ethic of dialogical existence would rule out the possibility that any member of the community, or even the community as a whole in a given place and time, could claim the kind of absolute knowledge or finality of judgment that might be called "knowing with the mind of God." Theologically speaking, to make such a claim would not only be pridefully presumptuous but also put a close to the revelatory openness of dialogical exploration into truth. Stated as a principle of etiquette, it would be rude to try to silence one's partners in dialogue by claiming absoluteness for one's own position and declaring all others negligible or even worthless. Only by giving up the claim to such finality can one begin the endless journey into dialogical truth.

In addition to humility and mutual courtesy, the members of the dialogical community would also need courage. It takes courage and patience to live with the realization of the radical relativity of all proportionate knowledge, to realize, that is, that every judgment, even if it may come to a relative and temporary rest with "a specific sense of intellectual satisfaction and repose," is never more than a way station on an endless journey.

But that is not what would require the greatest courage. If the etiquette of dialogical faith involves commitment to giving a respectful hearing to every voice, including those that speak from unfamiliar and challenging points of view, this must imply not simply allowing them to speak but also a willingness to try actually to understand what they say and to risk allowing not just one's own views but possibly even one's very self to be changed by that hearing. This might involve only a change in interpretation within a continuing stable framework of interpretation, but it could also be much more radical, something like what the philosopher of science Thomas Kuhn called a "paradigm shift," which can feel like the destruction of one's phenomenological "world." Speaking psychologically, it might involve a change in subjectivity that would amount to the emergence of a new "self." When such change is really radical, it can be experienced not only as a cognitive crisis but also as an existential one, since the self one had been begins to dissolve while one may as yet have no clear sense of what might arise in its place. One can only hope and trust that it will lead to new life, not just the death of both world and self.

There is also a further important element that would be needed in the etiquette of a community of dialogical faith. As was mentioned above, the community would have to be concerned not only with respectful hearing of those of its members who have developed well their capacities for dialogical faith but also with the needs of those who are only beginning to develop them. This means that it would have to provide a suitable "holding environment" for all its members, one that could encourage each to function as well as possible with the interpretive capacities he or she may already have while developing further capacities in his or her own time. Those who have developed further would have to understand and empathize with those who may not yet be able to handle all the challenges of dialogical faith and may be feeling the force of the kind of psychological and existential crisis just referred to. As a matter both of courtesy and of fidelity to the inherent structure of dialogical truth, they would have to refrain from belittling the efforts of others to work with a cognitive paradigm they may themselves experience as outmoded because they have already moved beyond it.

Here I think it can be helpful to remember James Fowler's schema of stages of faith. It is not easy for those who have recently extricated themselves from Fowler's mythic-literal faith and synthetic-conventional faith to be patient with their expressions if they have just succeeded in disentangling their own subjectivity from them. We saw in Chapter 3 how Fowler's fourth stage of faith development, the individuative-reflective, tended to dismiss as naive the stages that preceded it, insisting that all meaning must be explicit and rational and that myths be demythologized. To impose that, however, on people for whom myth is still the only way they have of thinking about transcendence might deprive them of a tradition that may be naive but that may also contain depths of spiritual meaning they can draw nurturance from where they are even as it also prepares them for further growth. Speaking in terms of the contrast we saw Marcus Borg draw between the type of belief he outgrew and the one he later grew into, one might say that it would be possible to view supernatural theism and the type of deontological command-ethic that goes with that not simply as naive and misleading but also as a possible holding environment for religious growth toward a panentheistic understanding of the divine and an ethic of love that does not need to be commanded.

Another reason to avoid destroying the holding environment that mythic traditions can offer to those at earlier stages of faith is that a person still further along in faith development, at Fowler's stage of conjunctive faith or in Kegan's fifth order of consciousness, might be able to find depths of meaning in those myths that escape the narrow focus of individuative-reflective faith. Religious rationalists and modernists, too, need a holding environment as they work through what, at the individuative-reflective stage, they experience as an imperative of demythologizing they cannot yet see beyond. They may need to be patient with those who do not yet read critically, but they themselves need understanding and patient leadership from others who through conjunctive faith have learned again how to read a story as a story, not as a questionable historical document, and how to appreciate again the spiritual meaning that can continue to speak through myths to those who listen.

As I mentioned in Chapter 3, Fowler refers to the cognitive mode of conjunctive faith as "dialogical knowing" involving a willingness to engage with both people and texts in a mutual "speaking" and "hearing." Regarding the reading of scripture in this mode, he says that he learned from Saint Ignatius's *Spiritual Exercises* to supplement the critical skills he learned in seminary with something more like an I-Thou relationship with the text: "Instead of *my reading,* analyzing and extracting the meaning of a Biblical text, in Ignatian contemplative prayer I began to learn how to let the text *read me* and to let it bring my needs and the Spirit's movements within me to consciousness."[58] This too requires courage, since such reading makes one vulnerable to being changed. It is no wonder, then, that a courteous and nurturing holding environment, good companionship for the journey, is needed every step of the way. The journey into dialogical truth is like a continuous process of dying into life, even for those who have come to understand from within what it is.

If this is so, then it is worth asking again what kind of selfhood is conjunctive faith or a fifth order of consciousness ultimately headed into? What would be the selfhood of radical openness in dialogue with others, with reality, and ultimately with the source of being itself? In Chapter 7, I spoke of a way of thinking about that ultimate source as eminently personal but not a "person" in the sense in which we ordinarily use that word. Perhaps that would also be an appropriate way to speak of the mode of existence of those who, in Kegan's phrase, give up their identification with achieved and defended positions or who, as Ernest Becker phrased it, give up their "character armor."[59]

It comes naturally to us to think of a person as a thing, an entity, a product, but perhaps here we need to begin thinking of the person as a process, a flow, a current into which other currents also flow in the dialogical life. In the Buddhist tradition this way of thinking comes naturally, since the whole purpose of Buddhist practice is, through meditation and the life of dharma, to free one from identifications and open one to Buddha-mind and the flow of Buddha-nature.[60] But such thinking is not altogether unknown in the West, either. I spoke in the preceding chapter about the similarity of some of Saint Paul's sayings about living "in Christ" and with the mind of Christ to Buddhist sayings about discovering true life in Buddha-nature or breaking out of the illusion of egoistic existence to come into Buddha-mind or the mind of enlightenment. Greek patristic Christian writers also spoke in a similar man-

58. Fowler, *Stages of Faith,* 185, 186; emphasis in the original.

59. Becker, *The Denial of Death,* 56–58, 90.

60. On the naturalness with which process thinking comes to the East Asian mind, see Nisbett, "Is the World Made Up of Nouns or Verbs?" chap. 6 of *Geography of Thought.*

ner of the Spirit of God as flowing into the psychic and somatic life of humans and divinizing it, which is to say carrying it beyond itself into infinite life.[61] Dialogical truth is not a formula but a mode of existence, a process of dying into a life that one trusts may ultimately become the capacity to love with a truly self-transcending love—a goal that I think any religion would acknowledge to be by its very nature never-ending. Theologically speaking, this would mean that even at its best, religion as such can never be more than a holding environment for a faith that is embedded in the earthly beginnings of the incarnation of transcendent love.

61. See Archbishop Chrysostomos of Etna, *A Guide to Orthodox Psychotherapy: The Science, Theology, and Spiritual Practice Behind It and Its Clinical Applications,* 35–37; Thomas Hopko, *The Spirit of God,* ii, 59–99; and Russell, *Doctrine of Deification.*

CONCLUSION

The Future of Religion

Regarding the future of religion, there are many today who would ask not what future it may have but rather whether religion has a future at all or even *should* have one. Sigmund Freud once said, in a pessimistic moment in which he thought religion will probably continue, though regrettably, "The whole thing is so patently infantile, so incongruous with reality, that to one whose attitude to humanity is friendly it is painful to think that the great majority of mortals will never be able to rise above this view of life."[1] In the pages above I have made several references to Daniel Dennett's expression of a similarly negative view, and Dennett is only one of the more interesting of many contemporary critics of religion.[2] These critics believe that religion tends to be a dangerous, potentially destructive social phenomenon. Many of them also seem to believe that they can destroy it by arguments.

As for the first assertion, sympathetic as I am personally to religion, I have to acknowledge that they, like Freud, have reason to be critical; historically, religion has been responsible for some of the worst of human evil as well as the best of human good. Regarding the second assertion, however, I think such critics tend to be rather naive, as well as both presumptuous and prematurely despairing. It seems to me presumptuous to think that argument can have the

1. Freud, *Civilization and Its Discontents,* 771.

2. Sam Harris, Richard Dawkins, and Christopher Hitchens are probably the ones besides Dennett most discussed at the time of this writing, but the number is vast. For a concise survey of such literature, see Haught, *Is Nature Enough?* chap. 1. See also Haught, *God and the New Atheism: A Critical Response to Dawkins, Harris, and Hitchens.*

effect they hope, and this is not simply because religious people are insufficiently rational to feel the force of logic. Human beings will always have spiritual aspirations and will always find ways to pursue them and represent them symbolically. Just as one cannot argue a person into falling in love, it would be as naive and reductionistic to think that religious faith can be destroyed by logical arguments as to think it can be created by them.

Reductionism may, of course, have its uses. A chemist who thinks everything that has any real explanation at all can be explained by chemistry alone would be viewing the larger field of reality reductionistically, but that would not prevent him from functioning well as a chemist, and it might even help him to focus his full attention on the problems that chemistry can properly solve. The same could be true in the case of a reductionistic sociology of the sort I touched on in Chapter 6, just as in any other field that gains its special power from restricting its focus to the range of phenomena that are its special concern.

The difficulty arises when reduction of focus modulates into a refusal to acknowledge even the possibility of a larger field of vision or to allow others to consider it. This refusal can become what in Chapter 9 I described as an attempt to impose a monological cognitive regime that tries to stifle the possibility of genuinely dialogical inquiry and thereby subverts not only the objective pursuit of truth but also the development of authentic life in the inquiring subject. I was referring there to religious efforts to impose such a regime, but the same kind of lust for cognitive dictatorship is equally possible on the part of critics of religion. As we saw in Chapter 5, René Girard offers a sharp critique of the linkage among religion, violence, and scapegoating, but Girard also frequently appeals to his audiences not to make a scapegoat of religion in turn. Religions can and often do give rise to dangerously polarized worldviews, but hostile critics of religion can be subject to the same temptation, leading the two sides to face off as what Girard calls *frères ennemis*, enemy brothers. Whether it takes the form of antireligious scapegoating or reductionistic efforts to silence religion's voice, the tendency to deny any value at all to religion is, I think, a form of despair that gives up on some of the deepest hopes of humankind.

It may be true that religion can find root in the human desire to control thought and suppress questions that could arouse anxiety and doubt, but I hope that a reader who has followed my discussion this far will see that religion can also be an expression of radical openness to our deep longings for the possibility of ultimate meaning and human fulfillment. In Chapter 8 we saw Freud, in a more optimistic moment, offer the prophecy that "the abandoning of religion must take place with the fateful inexorability of a process of growth."[3] But just as we saw in Chapter 7 that even monotheistic religions can encompass ideas of God sufficiently different to amount conceptually and phenomenologically to different "Gods," so that coming to believe in one may require disbelieving in another, so also is it possible for a religious believer to sympathize with Freud's critique of the kind of religion he thought would and should be outgrown yet to hope that religion as such may not die through that process but become transformed into the very energy of growth.

Religion is not going to go away; it is too deeply rooted in the best as well as the worst of human passions to simply die out. What we may hope for, however, is that it might grow up. I have tried in this book to show what some of the obstacles to that growing up can be, either as unconscious forces within the individual or as sociological forces in groups, and also what form the avenues of growth might take as sketched by developmental psychologists in the tradition of Jean Piaget. I have also tried to show how closely this type of psychology is connected to philosophical cognitional theory and even to types of theological thinking that implicitly or explicitly, as in the case of Bernard Lonergan, draw on both of those in their analysis of the forms that faith can take. It seems to me especially significant that an examination of these issues from any of these different angles—psychological, philosophical, or theological—if one follows out their implications to the end, leads toward the same conclusion: the possibility of development toward reasonable, responsible, loving personhood through openness to the fullness of experience, to all possible questions, to all possible interpretations, and to careful critical reflection on the relative adequacy as well as the inherent limits of any symbolizations of transcendence. What this suggests, I think, is that this sort of full personhood, sketched in various ways in the imagery of diverse religious traditions, is the *natural trajectory of religious development,* because it is the natural trajectory of *human* development.

Even a reader sympathetic to this hope, however, may wonder how long that process of development is going to take and what answer it may offer for immediately pressing questions about the possibility of peace between people with radically different worldviews in a world where instant global communications force confrontations that geographic distance once mitigated. In particular, many now wonder about the prospects for peace between the modern

3. Freud, *Future of an Illusion,* 76. See Chapter 8, note 5.

West and the Muslim world. I do not have an easy answer for that question, but here are a few reflections based on the considerations presented in the preceding chapters.

To begin with, the processes of psychological and religious development can never be quick or universal in any population. These are processes that on the cultural level work themselves out over centuries and even millennia. They can do so more quickly, I think, both on the level of a culture and on that of an individual, when a culture of dialogue stimulates and facilitates them through questions and exchange of views. But the reaction to such stimuli can become defensive as well as open, and the experience of intolerable pressure can easily stimulate strong and even violent resistance. We can see this in the West as much as in Islamic and other traditional cultures. Defensive fundamentalisms can develop anywhere and in any cultural tradition, just as can spiritual and intellectual openness, and since the members of any population will inevitably vary in terms of their experience, maturity, and level of intellectual, psychological, and spiritual development, it is only to be expected that different patterns of thinking and believing will develop among them.

One hears many diagnoses of the clashes that result. I suggested in the Introduction that analyses in terms of a "new cold war" or a "clash of civilizations" may not be the best way of understanding the problem, since it casts it in the form of unitary blocs confronting each other in a quasi-military conflict. To cast it in that way can be a powerful temptation because such conflicts seem to promise a simple solution: defeat or destroy the enemy with force. There are probably still many who think the proper path is to "go to war" against "them," imagining that "they" can be easily identified as "others" different from "us."

But I think there must also be many who now realize, especially in view of some of the practical consequences of attempts to deal with the problem in that way, that such an approach is not only too simple but also ineffective and dangerous, because it slips into polarization between an imagined "us" that represents the solution and is untouched except externally by the problem and an imagined "them" that simply embodies the problem and contains no internal possibility of developing toward a solution. This dangerously heightens conflict by generating a polarized, quasi-apocalyptic worldview of simple opposition in which the "us" becomes reduced psychologically and spiritually to what René Girard calls the "mimetic double" of its opposing "them." As Girard likes to say, nothing resembles an angry dog or an angry man more than another angry dog or angry man. It is too simple because it fails to recognize not only the real issues but also the presence of the struggle over those issues both within our own society and each religious tradition as well as (as Kegan's idea of a fifth order of consciousness suggests) within each of us as individuals.

In the Introduction I suggested that a better way to understand the tension we are experiencing would be to approach it as a struggle going on all over the world and within each civilizational heritage, as people react to the pressure exerted by modern conditions on both their worldviews and their minds. I spoke of this in terms of the strain of transition from a traditional worldview, and the traditional mind that supports it and depends on it, to something new—"modernity"—with all the demands this makes for a reorganization of minds. That was a way of phrasing the issue that could introduce it simply and indicate a problem to be explored in the pages to follow. Now that we have come through that exploration and developed, I hope, a sense of both the limitations and possible deeper meaning of terms such as *traditional* and *modern* and the possible usefulness of some other terms, I would like to restate the issue in a way that I hope can further clarify the nature of the problem and also suggest a basis for hope.

The major ongoing psychological, cultural, and spiritual crisis of our age, I suggest, is the strain of developing from a relatively compact to a more differentiated consciousness. We saw in Chapter 1 how Karl Jaspers used the phrase "differentiation of consciousness" to refer to a multifaceted process of intellectual, psychological, and spiritual development that could involve in varying degrees (1) the development of self-awareness and the capacity for rational analysis, (2) the articulation in consciousness of what one had previously been aware of only implicitly and unconsciously, and (3) the distinction of psychic elements that had previously been known only compactly as a unit, especially the realization that consciousness involves both subjective and objective poles. In subsequent chapters we saw how differentiation of consciousness can involve differentiation of the operations by which both children and adults, with varying degrees of reflective awareness, construct their interpreted worlds—a differentiation in the subjective pole of consciousness that in philosophical reflection can lead eventually to a realization of the parallelism or "isomorphism" between those operations and the structure of the objective pole. We also saw, most explicitly in the thought of Robert Kegan, how the progressive emergence of reflective consciousness can lead the psychological subject through a gradual freeing up of identification from psychic contents it began as embedded in.

In an individual, this can be a difficult process under the best of circumstances, but the difficulty is compounded when the individual identifies with a cultural mind-set and system of values that sees the transition not as a process of growth but as a threat of disintegration and death both for the individual and for his or her world. This can produce a hardening of identification that closes off any possibility of opening to new possibilities, and it can stimulate a radical defensiveness that can even issue in suicidal efforts to protect one's world of meaning. Such effects are all the more likely to be the case when the surrounding world seems fundamentally hostile to a person's cherished traditions—which is probably the experience of many Muslims, and perhaps even of many other religious people, in the world today.

At the end of Chapter 7 I quoted a Muslim speaker who referred to the painful process Muslims in the West are going through right now. He also said that a devout Muslim he met in Malaysia told him, "We are waiting for Islam to come back from the West," meaning that he recognized the need for a deeper and truer understanding of Islam and that he also believed that Muslims living in the West, with all the mixture of stress and freedom that can involve, have an opportunity to contribute in a special way to developing such an understanding. I spoke in the same chapter about the consensus of interpretation that developed in the Muslim *ummah* after its first few centuries and how difficult it is to reopen questions once such a consensus has solidified. In a traditional culture there is tremendous social and inner mimetic pressure to conform to a consensus, even apart from theological interpretations about the infallibility of the community once it has reached agreement. To move from that sort of world toward the radically open-ended life of what in Chapter 9 I spoke of as dialogical faith must involve a painful wrenching away from cultural embeddedness, and, for some, to begin that process may not even be psychologically possible in the context of one's home culture. Those who have suffered the wrenching dislocation of displacement to another cultural world may be especially placed, in the pluralistic environment of their Western diaspora, to begin a new Islamic differentiation of consciousness.

If so, there is already in Islamic cultural memory a point of purchase for dialogical faith in the early experience of the Muslim *ummah* as an open community of interpreters. In the early centuries of Muslim history there was a great deal of dialogue among both Sunni and Shiite Muslims about how the Qur'an should be interpreted and its injunctions put into practice, even if that soon led to rupture between the two major parties. As I explained in Chapter 7, the fundamental principle of Sunni Islam is that all Muslims are equal before the Qur'an and that the community of Muslims is called to interpret, believe, and heed its commands. Shiites too, side by side with their belief in the authority of charismatic leaders, have had their own traditions of dialogical interpretation of the Qur'an and hadith. It is true that, due in part to Muhammad's saying that his followers would never agree on an error, the dialogical community of the early centuries eventually devolved into a community of consensus that for some centuries has tended to be a community not of active, searching interpreters but of receivers of past interpretations taken as sacrosanct and effectively final. The question for the future of Islam is whether enough religiously serious Muslims will eventually begin to feel the force of new questions about their texts and traditions to reopen the Islamic *ummah* as a dialogical community.

The news we read about the Muslim world in this time of strife probably suggests otherwise to many people, but there is also a broader picture that tends to get lost among the headlines about suicide bombers and political and military conflict. Nicholas D. Kristof, writing from Brunei in December 2006, commented in the *New York Times* that the stereotyped images of Muslims as violent and intolerant "are largely derived from the less than 20 percent of Muslims who are Arabs, with Persians and Pashtuns thrown in as well. But the great majority of the world's Muslims live not in the Middle East but here in Asia, where religion has mostly been milder," and he suggested that "there is a historic dichotomy between desert Islam—the austere fundamentalism of countries like Saudi Arabia—and riverine or coastal Islam, more outward-looking, flexible and tolerant." His own view, he said, is that "in the struggle for the soul of Islam, maritime Muslims have the edge."[4] If we add to those the diaspora Muslims in the West, there is a substantial body in which new life can emerge, and when it does begin to do so, the vast, diverse Muslim world Kristof referred to may provide fertile soil for it. It may even, as the Malaysian gentleman said, be waiting for it.

The question of the possibility of a genuinely dialogical community is not, of course, a question only for Islam. In a world as closely interconnected as the one we live in today, it is an equally urgent question for every religion, and the success of any religious community in facing its challenges is bound to benefit all. It is not just a question of how people of different faiths might be able to get along with each other without violent conflicts. It is also a question, rising from

4. Kristof, "The Muslim Stereotype," *New York Times,* December 10, 2006. Geertz, in *Islam Observed,* provides an account of how Islam was transformed in its early assimilation into Indonesia and then started becoming transformed again on encountering Middle Eastern Islam when the Dutch began offering the opportunity to make pilgrimages to Mecca.

within each faith tradition, of how really to be what it believes itself called to be—that is, it is a question of how to pursue the radical transcendence that all of the major religions of the world believe is the calling of humanity.

A pluralistic environment of the sort that modern communications impose on all of us may be stressful, but it is also a powerful stimulus to the sort of reflective intelligence that terror management theorists have shown can serve to head off polarization effects before they even begin to stir. It may also become a stimulus to the development both within and among religious traditions of what the Ghanaian American philosopher Kwame Anthony Appiah calls "rooted cosmopolitanism," by which he means a worldview and system of values that is rooted in local cultures but also makes possible a looser, more flexible cultural identification that can open their members to a worldwide culture of dialogue. Appiah ends his book *The Ethics of Identity* with the translation of a Ghanaian proverb: "In a single *polis* there is no wisdom."[5] Perhaps there may be theologians who will someday say and believe something similar about religious traditions.

So there is a basis for hope, even if the realization of that hope may take centuries. It will help, however, if we can resist demanding either of Muslims or of any other tradition of faith that it produce quick results. I spoke earlier of the fact that Jews and Christians have had since the early Middle Ages to work on the process of developing an understanding of the interpretive procedures that go into reading sacred scriptures and working out theological ideas, and that process is far from over even in the countries with the most advanced cultures of critical reflection. It would be presumptuous of non-Muslims in the West to expect the Muslim community worldwide to proceed faster through that process than the Jewish and Christian communities of the West have, especially when they have not even finished it yet themselves. But as I said, despite the complaints of those who would like religion as such simply to go away, there is no real alternative to the slow and arduous process of religious growth. Even religion's unsympathetic critics may themselves have a spiritual calling in this context—not only to refrain from contributing to a polarized atmosphere of mutual attack and defense but to try to develop understanding of the process their religious neighbors of various faiths are going through, and through that understanding to help provide a holding environment for the emergence of a worldwide culture of dialogical truth.

5. Appiah, *The Ethics of Identity*, 272. See also Appiah, "The Case for Contamination."

Bibliography

Appiah, Kwame Anthony. "The Case for Contamination." *New York Times Magazine,* January 1, 2006.

———. *The Ethics of Identity.* Princeton: Princeton University Press, 2005.

Aquinas, Thomas. *Summa Theologica.* Trans. the Fathers of the English Dominican Province. Revised by Daniel J. Sullivan. New York: Benziger Brothers, 1947–1948.

Aristotle. *The Basic Works of Aristotle.* Ed. Richard McKeon. New York: Random House, 1941.

Atran, Scott. *In Gods We Trust: The Evolutionary Landscape of Religion.* Oxford: Oxford University Press, 2002.

Augustine, Saint, Bishop of Hippo. *Confessions.* Trans. R. S. Pine-Coffin. Harmondsworth, Middlesex, England; New York: Penguin Books, 1961.

Bakhtin, Mikhail Mikhailovich. *The Dialogic Imagination: Four Essays.* Ed. Michael Holquist. Trans. Caryl Emerson and Michael Holquist. University of Texas Press Slavic Series, no. 1. Austin: University of Texas Press, 1988.

Barth, Karl. *The Word of God and the Word of Man.* 1957. Reprint, Gloucester, Mass.: Peter Smith, 1978.

Becker, Ernest. *The Denial of Death.* New York: Free Press, 1973.

———. *Escape from Evil.* New York: Free Press, 1975.

Benin, Stephen D. *The Footprints of God: Divine Accommodation in Jewish and Christian Thought.* Albany: State University of New York Press, 1993.

Berger, Peter L. *The Heretical Imperative: Contemporary Possibilities of Religious Affirmation.* Garden City, N.Y.: Anchor Press, 1979.

———. *A Rumor of Angels: Modern Society and the Rediscovery of the Supernatural.* Garden City, N.Y.: Doubleday, 1969.

———. *The Sacred Canopy: Elements of a Sociological Theory of Religion.* Garden City, N.Y.: Doubleday, 1967.

———, ed. *The Desecularization of the World: Resurgent Religion and World Politics.* Washington, D.C.: Ethics and Public Policy Center; Grand Rapids, Mich.: W. B. Eerdmans, 1999.

Berger, Peter L., and Samuel P. Huntington, eds. *Many Globalizations: Cultural Diversity in the Contemporary World.* Oxford: Oxford University Press, 2002.

Berger, Peter L., and Thomas Luckmann. *The Social Construction of Reality: A Treatise in the Sociology of Knowledge.* Garden City, N.Y.: Doubleday, 1966.

Bertonneau, Thomas F. "The Logic of the Undecidable: An Interview with René Girard." *Paroles Gelées: UCLA French Studies* 5 (1987): 1–24.

Bettelheim, Bruno. *Freud and Man's Soul.* New York: Alfred A. Knopf, 1983.

Boden, Margaret A. *Piaget.* Sussex: Harvester Press, 1979.

Borg, Marcus J. *The God We Never Knew: Beyond Dogmatic Religion to a More Authentic Contemporary Faith.* San Francisco: Harper San Francisco, 1997.

Brothers, Leslie. "A Biological Perspective on Empathy." *American Journal of Psychiatry* 146, no. 1 (January 1989): 10–19.

Brown, Peter Robert Lamont. *Augustine of Hippo: A Biography.* Berkeley and Los Angeles: University of California Press, 1967.

Bultmann, Rudolf. *Jesus Christ and Mythology.* New York: Scribner's, 1958.

Calvin, William H. *A Brain for All Seasons: Human Evolution and Abrupt Climate Change.* Chicago: University of Chicago Press, 2002.

———. *A Brief History of the Mind: From Apes to Intellect and Beyond.* New York: Oxford University Press, 2004.

Carlen, Claudia, ed. *The Papal Encyclicals.* 5 vols. Ann Arbor: Pierian Press, 1990.

Chalmers, David J. *The Conscious Mind: In Search of a Fundamental Theory.* New York: Oxford University Press, 1996.

Chrysostomos, Archbishop, of Etna. *A Guide to Orthodox Psychotherapy: The Science, Theology, and Spiritual Practice Behind It and Its Clinical Applications.* Lanham, Md.: University Press of America, 2006.

Cohen, Abraham. *Everyman's Talmud.* With an introduction to the new American edition by Boaz Cohen. New York: E. P. Dutton, 1949.

Conn, Walter E. *Christian Conversion: A Developmental Interpretation of Autonomy and Surrender.* New York: Paulist Press, 1986.

———. *Conscience: Development and Self-Transcendence.* Birmingham: Religious Education Press, 1981.

Copleston, Frederick. *A History of Philosophy.* Vol. 3, *Ockham to Suarez.* Westminster, Md.: Newman Press, 1953.

———. *A History of Philosophy.* Vol. 6, pt. 2, *Kant.* Garden City, N.Y.: Image Books, 1964.

Corbin, Henry. *Creative Imagination in the Sufism of Ibn Arabi.* Trans. Ralph Mannheim. Princeton: Princeton University Press, 1969.

Crone, Patricia. *God's Rule: Government and Islam.* New York: Columbia University Press, 2004.

Crone, Patricia, and Michael Cook. *Hagarism: The Making of the Islamic World.* New York: Cambridge University Press, 1977.

Crone, Patricia, and Martin Hinds. *God's Caliph: Religious Authority in the First Centuries of Islam.* Cambridge: Cambridge University Press, 1986.

Crossan, John Dominic, and Jonathan L. Reed. *In Search of Paul: How Jesus's Apostle Opposed Rome's Empire with God's Kingdom.* New York: Harper San Francisco, 2004.

Cullmann, Oscar. *Immortality of the Soul or Resurrection of the Dead? The Witness of the New Testament.* New York: Macmillan, 1958.

Damasio, Antonio R. *Descartes' Error: Emotion, Reason, and the Brain.* New York: Putnam, 1994.

Dapretto, Mirella, Mari S. Davies, Jennifer H. Pfeifer, Ashley A. Scott, Marian Sigman, Susan Y. Bookheimer, and Marco Iacoboni. "Understanding Emotions in Others: Mirror Neuron Dysfunction in Children with Autism Spectrum Disorders." *Nature Neuroscience* 9, no. 1 (January 2006): 28–30.

Davidson, Richard J., and Nathan A. Fox. "Patterns of Brain Electrical Activity during Facial Signs of Emotion in 10-Month-Old infants." *Developmental Psychology* 24 (1988): 230–36.

Dawkins, Richard. *The God Delusion.* Boston: Houghton Mifflin, 2006.

Dennett, Daniel C. *Breaking the Spell: Religion as a Natural Phenomenon.* New York: Viking, 2006.

Digeser, Elizabeth DePalma. *The Making of a Christian Empire: Lactantius and Rome.* Ithaca: Cornell University Press, 2000.

Documents of Vatican II, in a New and Definitive Translation, with Commentaries and Notes by Catholic, Protestant, and Orthodox Authorities. Ed. Walter M. Abbott. Introduction by Lawrence Cardinal Shehan. Translations directed by Joseph Gallagher. New York: Chapman 1966.

Doran, Robert M. *Subject and Psyche: Ricoeur, Jung, and the Search for Foundations.* Lanham, Md.: University Press of America, 1980.

Douglas, Mary. *Purity and Danger: An Analysis of Concepts of Pollution and Taboo.* New York: Praeger, 1966.

Eliade, Mircea. *The Sacred and the Profane: The Nature of Religion.* Trans. Willard R. Trask. New York: Harcourt Brace, 1959.

Epstein, Mark. *Thoughts without a Thinker: Psychotherapy from a Buddhist Perspective.* New York: Basic Books, 1995.

Epstein, Seymour. "Integration of the Cognitive and the Psychodynamic Unconscious." *American Psychologist* 49 (1994): 709–24.

Erikson, Erik. *Childhood and Society.* 2d ed. New York: W. W. Norton, 1963.

Faure, Bernard. *The Rhetoric of Immediacy: A Cultural Critique of Chan/Zen Buddhism.* Princeton: Princeton University Press, 1991.

Feldman, Noah. "Islam, Terror, and the Second Nuclear Age." *New York Times Magazine,* October 29, 2006, 50ff.

Feuerbach, Ludwig. *The Essence of Christianity.* Trans. George Eliot. Introductory essay by Karl Barth. Foreword by H. Richard Niebuhr. New York: Harper and Brothers, 1957.

Fowler, James W. *Becoming Adult, Becoming Christian: Adult Development and Christian Faith.* San Francisco: Harper and Row, 1984.

———. *Stages of Faith: The Psychology of Human Development and the Quest for Meaning.* San Francisco: Harper and Row, 1981.

Freud, Sigmund. *Civilization and Its Discontents.* Trans. Joan Riviere. In vol. 30 of *Great Books of the Western World.* Chicago: William Benton, 1952.

———. *The Future of an Illusion.* Trans. W. D. Robson-Scott. London: Hogarth Press, 1934.

———. *Leonardo da Vinci: A Psychosexual Study of an Infantile Reminiscence.* Trans. A. A. Brill. New York: Moffat, Yard, 1916.

Freud, Sigmund, and Anna Freud. *Gesammelte Werke, chronologisch geordnet.* 18 vols. London: Imago, 1940–1952.

Freud, Sigmund, James Strachey, Anna Freud, Carrie Lee Rothgeb, and Angela Richards. *The Standard Edition of the Complete Psychological Works of Sigmund Freud.* 24 vols. London: Hogarth Press, 1953–1974.

Friedman, Edwin H. *A Failure of Nerve: Leadership in the Age of the Quick Fix.* New York: Seabury, 2007.

Fromm, Erich. *The Heart of Man: Its Genius for Good and Evil.* New York: Harper and Row, 1964.

Gadamer, Hans Georg. *Truth and Method.* New York: Seabury Press, 1975.

Garrigou-Lagrange, Reginald. *Reality: A Synthesis of Thomistic Thought.* St. Louis: Herder, 1950.

Geertz, Clifford. *Islam Observed: Religious Developments in Morocco and Indonesia.* Chicago: University of Chicago Press, 1971.

Gingerich, Owen. "The Galileo Affair." *Scientific American* (August 1982): 133–43.

Girard, René. *Deceit, Desire, and the Novel: Self and Other in Literary Structure.* Trans. Yvonne Freccero. Baltimore: Johns Hopkins University Press, 1965.

———. *Job: The Victim of His People.* Trans. Yvonne Freccero. Stanford: Stanford University Press, 1987.

———. *Quand ces choses commenceront . . . : Entretiens avec Michel Treguer.* Paris: Arléa, 1994.

———. *The Scapegoat.* Trans. Yvonne Freccero. Baltimore and London: Johns Hopkins University Press, 1986.

———. *"To Double Business Bound": Essays on Literature, Mimesis, and Anthropology.* Baltimore: Johns Hopkins University Press, 1978.

———. *Violence and the Sacred.* Trans. Patrick Gregory. Baltimore: Johns Hopkins University Press, 1977.

Girard, René, with Jean-Michel Oughourlian and Guy Lefort. *Things Hidden since the Foundation of the World.* Trans. Stephen Bann and Michael Metteer. Stanford: Stanford University Press, 1987.

Goleman, Daniel. *Emotional Intelligence.* New York: Bantam Books, 1995.

Goodenough, Erwin Ransdell. *The Psychology of Religious Experiences.* New York: Basic Books, 1965.

———. *Toward a Mature Faith.* New Haven: Yale University Press, 1961.

Greenberg, Jeff, Sheldon Solomon, and Tom Pyszczynski. "Terror Management Theory of Self-Esteem and Cultural World Views: Empirical Assessments and Conceptual Refinements." In *Advances in Experimental Social Psychology,* ed. Mark P. Zanna, 29:61–139. San Diego: Academic Press, 1997.

Greenberg, Jeff, S. Solomon, T. Pyszczynski, E. Pinel, L. Simon, and K. Jordan. "Effects of Self-Esteem on Vulnerability-Denying Defensive Distortions: Further Evidence of an Anxiety-Buffering Function of Self-Esteem." *Journal of Experimental Social Psychology,* 29 (1993): 229–251.

Greenberg, Jeff, S. Solomon, T. Pyszczynski, A. Rosenblatt, J. Burling, D. Lyon, and L. Simon. "Assessing the Terror Management Analysis of Self-Esteem: Converging Evidence of an Anxiety-Buffering Function." *Journal of Personality and Social Psychology* 63 (1992): 913–22.

Greenwald, Anthony G., Sean C. Draine, and Richard L. Abrams. "Three Cognitive Markers of Unconscious Semantic Activation." *Science* 273 (September 20, 1996): 1699–1702.

Gregg, Robert C., and Dennis E. Groh. *Early Arianism: A View of Salvation.* Philadelphia: Fortress Press, 1981.

Griffiths, Bede. *The Cosmic Revelation: The Hindu Way to God.* Springfield, Ill.: Templegate, 1983.

Halm, Heinz. *Shi'ism.* Trans. Janet Watson and Marian Hill. New York: Columbia University Press, 2004.

Harris, Sam. *The End of Faith: Religion, Terror, and the Future of Reason.* New York: W. W. Norton, 2004.

Haught, John F. *God and the New Atheism: A Critical Response to Dawkins, Harris, and Hitchens.* Louisville, Ky.: Westminster John Knox Press, 2008.

———. *Is Nature Enough? Meaning and Truth in the Age of Science.* Cambridge: Cambridge University Press, 2006.

Henig, Robin Marantz. "Darwin's God." *New York Times Magazine,* March 4, 2007, 36ff.

Herbermann, Charles George, Edward A. Pace, Condé Bénoist Pallen, Thomas J. Shahan, John J. Wynne, and Andrew Alphonsus MacErlean. *The Catholic Encylopedia: An International Work of Reference on the Constitution, Doctrine, Discipline, and History of the Catholic Church.* New York: Robert Appleton, 1907.

Hitchens, Christopher. *God Is Not Great: How Religion Poisons Everything.* New York: Twelve / Warner Books, 2007.

Hodgson, Marshall G. S. *The Venture of Islam: Conscience and History in a World Civilization.* 3 vols. Chicago: University of Chicago Press, 1974.

Hopko, Thomas. *The Spirit of God.* Wilton, Conn.: Morehouse-Barlow, 1976.

Horner, Victoria, and Andrew Whiten. "Causal Knowledge and Imitation/Emulation Switching in Chimpanzees *(Pan troglodytes)* and Children *(Homo sapiens).*" *Animal Cognition* 8, no. 3 (July 2005): 164–81.

Hughes, Glenn. *Transcendence and History: The Search for Ultimacy from Ancient Societies to Postmodernity.* Eric Voegelin Institute Series in Political Philosophy. Columbia: University of Missouri Press, 2003.

Hume, David. *Treatise of Human Nature.* Ed. L. A. Selby-Bigge. Oxford: Clarendon Press, 1958.

Huntington, Samuel P. *The Clash of Civilizations and the Remaking of World Order.* New York: Simon and Schuster, 1996.

Hurlbutt, William. "Mimesis and Empathy in Human Biology." *Contagion: Journal of Violence, Mimesis, and Culture* 4 (Spring 1997): 14–25.

Iacoboni, Marco, Istvan Molnar-Szakacs, Vittorio Gallese, Giovanni Buccino, John C. Mazziotta, and Giacomo Rizzolatti. "Grasping the Intentions of Others with One's Own Mirror Neuron System." *Public Library of Science: Biology* 3, no. 3 (March 2005). Available online at http://biology.plosjournals.org.

Ilien, Albert. *Wesen und Funktion der Liebe im Denken des Thomas von Aquin.* Freiburg: Herder, 1975.

Jaspers, Karl. *Psychologie der Weltanschauungen.* 5th ed. Berlin: Springer Verlag, 1960.

Jeffers, Robinson. *The Selected Poetry of Robinson Jeffers.* New York: Random House, 1938.

John Paul II. "Discourse to the Pontifical Academy of Sciences." *Origins* 22 (November 12, 1992): 370–75. English translation. The original appeared in *Discorsi dei Papi alla Pontificia Accademia delle Scienze (1936–1993).* Vatican: Pontificia Academia Scientiarum, 1994.

Joyce, James. *A Portrait of the Artist as a Young Man.* New York: Viking Press, 1964.

Jurgensmeyer, Mark. *The New Cold War? Religious Nationalism Confronts the Secular State.* Berkeley and Los Angeles: University of California Press, 1993.

Kant, Immanuel. *Kant Selections.* Ed. Theodore Meyer Greene. New York: Scribner, 1929.

Kaufman, Gordon D. *In Face of Mystery: A Constructive Theology.* Cambridge: Harvard University Press, 1993.

Kegan, Robert. *The Evolving Self: Problem and Process in Human Development.* Cambridge: Harvard University Press, 1982.

———. *In over Our Heads: The Mental Demands of Modern Life.* Cambridge: Harvard University Press, 1994.

Kierkegaard, Søren. *Concluding Unscientific Postscript.* Trans. David F. Swenson. Princeton: Princeton University Press, 1941.

———. *Philosophical Fragments.* Trans. Howard V. Hong and Edna H. Hong. Princeton: Princeton University Press, 1985.

———. *Stages on Life's Way.* Trans. Walter Lowrie. Princeton: Princeton University Press, 1940.

Kitchener, Richard F. "Piaget's Genetic Epistemology." *International Philosophical Quarterly* 20 (1980): 377–405.

Kohlberg, Lawrence. *Essays on Moral Development.* Vol. 1, *The Philosophy of Moral Development: Moral Stages and the Idea of Justice.* San Francisco: Harper and Row, 1981.

———. *Essays on Moral Development.* Vol. 2, *The Psychology of Moral Development: The Nature and Validity of Moral Stages.* San Francisco: Harper and Row, 1984.

LaCugna, Catherine Mowry. *God for Us: The Trinity and Christian Life.* San Francisco: Harper, 1991.

Leff, Gordon. *The Dissolution of the Medieval Outlook: An Essay on Intellectual and Spiritual Change in the Fourteenth Century.* New York: New York University Press, 1976.

———. *William of Ockham: The Metamorphosis of Scholastic Discourse.* Manchester: Manchester University Press / Totowa, N.J.: Rowman and Littlefield, 1975.

Le Roy Ladurie, Emmanuel. *Montaillou: The Promised Land of Error.* New York: G. Braziller, 1978.

Lévinas, Emmanuel. *Ethics and Infinity: Conversations with Philippe Nemo.* Trans. Richard A. Cohen. Pittsburgh: Duquesne University Press, 1985.

Lieu, Samuel N. C., and Dominic Montserrat. *From Constantine to Julian: Pagan and Byzantine Views, a Source History.* London and New York: Routledge, 1996.

Lonergan, Bernard J. F. *Insight: A Study of Human Understanding.* 3d ed. New York: Philosophical Library, 1970.

———. *Method in Theology.* New York: Herder and Herder, 1972.

———. *Second Collection.* Ed. William F. Ryan, S.J., and Bernard J. Tyrell, S.J. Philadelphia: Westminster Press, 1974.

Lubac, Henri de. *The Religion of Teilhard de Chardin.* Garden City, N.Y.: Doubleday, 1968.

MacIntyre, Alasdair. *After Virtue: A Study in Moral Theory.* 2d ed. Notre Dame: Notre Dame University Press, 1984.

MacLean, Paul D. *The Triune Brain in Evolution: Role in Paleocerebral Functions.* New York and London: Plenum Press, 1990.

Marcel, Gabriel. *The Mystery of Being.* 2 vols. London: Harvill Press, 1950.

Mathews, William A. *Lonergan's Quest: A Study of Desire in the Authoring of Insight.* Toronto: University of Toronto Press, 2005.

McCracken, David. "Character in the Boundary: Bakhtin's Interdividuality in Biblical Narratives." *Semeia* 63 (1993): 29–42.

McPartland, Thomas J. *Lonergan and the Philosophy of Historical Existence.* Eric Voegelin Institute Series in Political Philosophy. Columbia: University of Missouri Press, 2001.

Meltzoff, Andrew N. "Understanding the Intentions of Others: Re-enactment of Intended Acts by 18-Month-Old Children." *Developmental Psychology* 31, no. 5 (1995): 838–50.

Meltzoff, Andrew N., and M. Keith Moore. "Early Imitation within a Functional Framework: The Importance of Person Identity, Movement, and Development." *Infant Behavior and Development* 15 (1992): 470–505.

———. "Imitation, Memory, and the Representation of Persons." *Infant Behavior and Development* 17 (1994): 83–99.

———. "Imitation in Newborn Infants: Exploring the Range of Gestures Imitated and the Underlying Mechanisms." *Developmental Psychology* 25, no. 6 (1989): 954–62.

———. "Imitation of Facial and Manual Gestures by Human Neonates." *Science* 198 (1977): 75–78.

———. "Infants' Understanding of People and Things: From Body Imitation to Folk Psychology." In *The Body and the Self*, ed. José Luis Bermúdez, Anthony Marcel, and Naomi Eilan. Cambridge: MIT Press, 1995.

———. "Newborn Infants Imitate Adult Facial Gestures." *Child Development* 54 (1983): 702–9.

———. "The Origins of Imitation in Infancy: Paradigm, Phenomena, and Theories." In *Advances in Infancy Research*, ed. L. P. Lippit, 2:265–301. Norwood, N.J.: Ablex, 1983.

Merlin, Donald. *Origins of the Modern Mind: Three Stages in the Evolution of Culture and Cognition.* Cambridge: Harvard University Press, 1991.

Mill, John Stuart. *The Collected Works of John Stuart Mill.* Ed. John M. Robson. Vols. 1–33. Toronto: University of Toronto Press, 1963–1991.

Morson, Gary Saul, and Caryl Emerson. *Mikhail Bakhtin: Creation of a Prosaics.* Stanford: Stanford Univ. Press, 1990.

Murray, John P., Mario Liotti, Paul T. Ingmundson, Helen S. Mayberg, Yonglin Pu, Frank Zamarripa, Yijun Liu, Marty G. Woldorff, Jia-Hong Gao, Peter T. Fox. "Children's Brain Activations while Viewing Televised Violence Revealed by MRI." *Media Psychology* 8, no. 1 (January 2006): 25–37.

Nahum, Menahem, of Chernobyl. *Me'or 'Enayyim.* In *Upright Practices: The Light of The Eyes.* Trans. Arthur Green. New York: Paulist Press, 1982.

Newman, John Henry. *An Essay in Aid of a Grammar of Assent.* Ed. Charles Frederick Harrold. New York: Longmans, Green, 1947.

Nicolson, Marjorie Hope. *The Breaking of the Circle: Studies in the Effect of the New Science upon Seventeenth-Century Poetry.* Rev. ed. New York: Columbia University Press, 1960.

Niebuhr, H. Richard. *Christ and Culture.* New York: Harper and Row, 1951.

———. *The Meaning of Revelation.* New York: Macmillan, 1941.

———. *Radical Monotheism and Western Civilization.* Lincoln: University of Nebraska Press, 1960.

Nisbett, Richard E. *The Geography of Thought: How Asians and Westerners Think Differently—and Why.* New York: Free Press, 2003.

Nowell, Robert. *A Passion for Truth: Hans Küng and His Theology.* New York: Crossroad, 1981.

Nygren, Anders. *Agape and Eros.* Trans. Philip S. Watson. New York: Harper and Row, 1969.

Oakley, Francis. *Omnipotence, Covenant, and Order: An Excursion in the History of Ideas from Abelard to Leibniz.* Ithaca: Cornell University Press, 1984.

Otto, Rudolf. *The Idea of the Holy: An Inquiry into the Non-rational Factor in the Idea of the Divine and Its Relation to the Rational.* Trans. John W. Harvey. 2d ed. London: Oxford University Press, 1958.

Oughourlian, Jean-Michel. *Genèse du Désir.* Paris: Carnets Nord, 2007.

———. *The Puppet of Desire: The Psychology of Hysteria, Possession, and Hypnosis.* Trans. Eugene Webb. Stanford: Stanford University Press, 1991.

Ozment, Steven E. *The Age of Reform (1250–1550): An Intellectual and Religious History of Late Medieval and Reformation Europe.* New Haven: Yale University Press, 1980.

Pegis, Anton Charles. *The Wisdom of Catholicism.* New York: Random House, 1949.

Piaget, Jean. *The Equilibration of Cognitive Structures: The Central Problem of Intellectual Development.* Trans. Terrance Brown and Kishore Julian Thampy. Chicago: University of Chicago Press, 1985.

———. *Genetic Epistemology.* New York: Columbia University Press, 1970.

———. *Logic and Psychology.* Introduction by W. Mays. New York: Basic Books, 1957.

———. *The Moral Judgment of the Child.* New York: Free Press, 1948.

———. *Psychology and Epistemology.* Trans. Arnold Rosin. New York: Grossman, 1971.

———. "Relations between Affectivity and the Mental Development of the Child." In *Sorbonne Course.* Paris: University Documentation Center, 1964.

Piaget, Jean, and Rolando Garcia. *Psychogenesis and the History of Science.* Trans. Helga Feider. New York: Columbia University Press, 1989.

Placher, William C. *The Domestication of Transcendence: How Modern Thinking about God Went Wrong.* Louisville, Ky.: Westminster John Knox Press, 1996.

Polanyi, Michael. *Personal Knowledge: Towards a Post-critical Philosophy.* Corrected ed. Chicago: University of Chicago Press, 1962.

———. *The Tacit Dimension.* 1966. Reprint, New York: Anchor Books, 1967.

Preller, Victor. *Divine Science and the Science of God: A Reformulation of Thomas Aquinas.* Princeton: Princeton University Press, 1967.

Prestige, G. L. *God in Patristic Thought.* London: SPCK, 1952.

Pyszczynski, Tom, Abdolhossein Abdollahi, Sheldon Solomon, Jeff Greenberg, Florette Cohen, and David Weise. "Mortality Salience, Martyrdom, and Military Might: The Great Satan versus the Axis of Evil." *Personality and Social Psychology Bulletin* 32 (April 2006): 525–37.

Quine, Willard Van Orman. *Word and Object.* Cambridge: MIT Press, 1960.

Rahman, Fazlur. *Islam.* Chicago: University of Chicago Press, 1979.

Rahner, Karl. *The Trinity.* New York: Crossroad, 1998.

Rice, Mabel, and Linda Woodsmall. "Lessons from Television: Children's Word Learning When Viewing." *Child Development* 59 (1988): 420–29.

Ricoeur, Paul. *Fallible Man.* Chicago: Regnery, 1965.

———. *Freedom and Nature: The Voluntary and Involuntary.* Evanston: Northwestern University Press, 1966.

———. *Gabriel Marcel et Karl Jaspers.* Paris: Éditions du Temps Present, 1948.

Ricoeur, Paul, with Mikel Dufrenne. *Karl Jaspers et la philosophie de l'existence.* Paris: Éditions du Seuil, 1947.

Robinson, John A. T. *Honest to God.* Philadelphia: Westminster Press, 1963.

Rumi, Maulana Jalal al-Din. *The Soul of Rumi: A New Collection of Ecstatic Poems.* Trans. Coleman Barks et al. San Francisco: Harper San Francisco, 2001.

Russell, Norman. *The Doctrine of Deification in the Greek Patristic Tradition.* New York: Oxford University Press, 2004.

Schimel, Jeff, Linda Simon, Jeff Greenberg, Tom Pyszczynski, Sheldon Solomon, Jeannette Waxmonsky, and Jamie Arndt. "Stereotypes and Terror Management: Evidence That Mortality Salience Enhances Stereotypic Thinking and Preferences." *Journal of Personality and Social Psychology* 77, no. 5 (November 1999): 905–26.

Scholem, Gershom Gerhard. *The Messianic Idea in Judaism, and Other Essays on Jewish Spirituality.* New York: Schocken Books, 1971.

Schüssler Fiorenza, Elisabeth. *Jesus and the Politics of Interpretation.* New York: Continuum, 2000.

Schwarz, Joel. "Subliminal Doesn't Sell." *University Week* (University of Washington), October 24, 1996, 2.

Smart, Ninian. *Worldviews: Crosscultural Explorations of Human Beliefs.* 2d ed. Englewood Cliffs, N.J.: Prentice-Hall, 1995.

Smith, Wilfred Cantwell. *Belief and History.* Charlottesville: University Press of Virginia, 1977.

———. *Faith and Belief: The Difference between Them.* 1979. Reprint, Oxford: Oneworld Publications, 1998.

Solomon, Sheldon, Jeff Greenberg, and Tom Pyszczynski. "Tales from the Crypt: On the Role of Death in Life." *Zygon* 33, no. 1 (March 1998): 9–43.

———. "Terror Management Theory of Self-Esteem." In *Handbook of Social and Clinical Psychology: The Health Perspective,* ed. C. R. Snyder and D. Forsyth, 21–40. New York: Pergamon Press, 1991.

———. "A Terror Management Theory of Social Behavior: The Psychological Functions of Self-Esteem and Cultural World Views." In *Advances in Experimental Social Psychology,* ed. Mark P. Zanna, 23:91–159. San Diego: Academic Press, 1991.

Stark, Rodney. *One True God: Historical Consequences of Monotheism.* Princeton: Princeton University Press, 2001.

———. *The Rise of Christianity: A Sociologist Reconsiders History.* Princeton: Princeton University Press, 1996.

Stark, Rodney, and Roger Finke. *Acts of Faith: Explaining the Human Side of Religion.* Berkeley and Los Angeles: University of California Press, 2000.

Suzuki, Daisetz Teitaro. *The Zen Doctrine of No-Mind: The Significance of the Sutra of Hui-neng.* Ed. Christmas Humphreys. London: Rider, 1969.

Tabler, Andrew. "Catalytic Converters." *New York Times Magazine,* April 29, 2007, 18–20.

Teilhard de Chardin, Pierre. *The Divine Milieu: An Essay on the Interior Life.* New York: Harper, 1960.

———. *The Phenomenon of Man.* New York: Harper, 1959.

Tillich, Paul. *The Courage to Be.* New Haven: Yale University Press, 1952.

———. *The Dynamics of Faith.* New York: Harper, 1958.

———. *The Protestant Era.* Trans. James Luther Adams. Chicago: University of Chicago Press, 1948.

———. *Systematic Theology.* 3 vols. Chicago: University of Chicago Press, 1951–1963.

Todorov, Tzvetan. *Mikhail Bakhtin: The Dialogical Principle.* Theory and History of Literature, vol. 13. Minneapolis: University of Minnesota Press, 1984.

Towler, Robert. *The Need for Certainty: A Sociological Study of Conventional Religion.* London: Routledge and Kegan Paul, 1984.

Tracy, David. *The Achievement of Bernard Lonergan.* New York: Herder and Herder, 1970.

Turner, Frank M. *John Henry Newman: The Challenge to Evangelical Religion.* New Haven: Yale University Press, 2002.

Turner, Mark. *The Literary Mind.* New York: Oxford University Press, 1996.

Urbach, Efraim Elimelech. *The Sages, Their Concepts, and Beliefs.* 2 vols. Trans. Israel Abrahams. Jerusalem: Magnes Press, Hebrew University, 1979.

Varela, Francisco J., Evan Thompson, and Eleanor Rosch. *The Embodied Mind: Cognitive Science and Human Experience.* Cambridge: MIT Press, 1991.

Voegelin, Eric. "The Eclipse of Reality." In *What Is History? and Other Late Unpublished Writings,* ed. Thomas A. Hollweck and Paul Caringella, 111–62. Vol. 28 of *The Collected Works of Eric Voegelin.* Columbia: University of Missouri Press, 1990.

———. *The Ecumenic Age.* Ed. Michael Franz. Vol. 4 of *Order and History.* Vol. 17 of *The Collected Works of Eric Voegelin.* Columbia: University of Missouri Press, 2000.

———. "On Debate and Existence." In *Published Essays, 1966–1985,* ed. Ellis Sandoz, 36–51. Vol. 12 of *The Collected Works of Eric Voegelin.* Columbia: University of Missouri Press, 1990.

———. "Reason: The Classic Experience." In *Published Essays, 1966–1985,* ed. Ellis Sandoz, 265–91. Vol. 12 of *The Collected Works of Eric Voegelin.* Columbia: University of Missouri Press, 1990.

Webb, Eugene. "Augustine's New Trinity: The Anxious Circle of Metaphor." In *Innovation in Religious Traditions: Essays in the Interpretation of Religious Change,* ed. Michael A. Williams, Collett Cox, and Martin S. Jaffee, 191–214. Berlin: Mouton de Gruyter, 1992. Available online at http://faculty.washington.edu/ewebb.

———. *Eric Voegelin: Philosopher of History.* Seattle: University of Washington Press, 1981.

———. "The Hermeneutic of Greek Trinitarianism: An Approach through Intentionality Analysis." In *Religion in Context,* ed. Timothy P. Fallon and Philip Boo Riley. Lanham, Md.: University Press of America, 1988. Available online at http://faculty.washington.edu/ewebb.

———. *Philosophers of Consciousness: Polanyi, Lonergan, Voegelin, Ricoeur, Girard, Kierkegaard.* Seattle: University of Washington Press, 1988.

———. *The Self Between: From Freud to the New Social Psychology of France.* Seattle: University of Washington Press, 1993.

Wills, Garry. *Papal Sin: Structures of Deceit.* New York: Doubleday, 2000.

Wilson, David Sloan. *Darwin's Cathedral: Evolution, Religion, and the Nature of Society.* Chicago: University of Chicago Press, 2002.

Winnicott, Donald Woods. *Holding and Interpretation: Fragment of an Analysis.* Ed. M. Masud R. Khan. New York: Grove Press, 1987.

———. *The Maturational Processes and the Facilitating Environment: Studies in the Theory of Emotional Development.* New York: International Universities Press, 1965.

Woodard, James W. "The Relation of Personality Structure to the Structure of Culture." *American Sociological Review* 3, no. 5 (October 1938): 637–51.

Wright, Nicholas Thomas. *The Resurrection of the Son of God.* Minneapolis: Fortress Press, 2003.

Zaehner, Robert Charles. *The Comparison of Religions.* Boston: Beacon Press, 1962.

Zilboorg, Gregory. "Fear of Death." *Psychoanalytic Quarterly* 12 (1943): 465–75.

Zimmer, Heinrich Robert. *Philosophies of India.* Ed. Joseph Campbell. Princeton: Princeton University Press, 1951.

Zizioulas, John D. *Being as Communion: Studies in Personhood and the Church.* Crestwood, N.Y.: St. Vladimir's Seminary Press, 1985.

INDEX